NATO Transformed

NATO
Transformed

The Alliance's New Roles in International Security

David S. Yost

United States Institute of Peace Press
Washington, D.C.

Cover photograph: A convoy of troop carriers and tanks in NATO's Stabilization Force enters Bosnia in 1996. Photo courtesy of AP/Wide World Photos; used by permission.

The views expressed in this book are those of the author alone. They do not necessarily reflect views of the United States Institute of Peace.

United States Institute of Peace
1200 17th Street, NW
Washington, DC 20036

First published 1998
Second printing 2000

Printed in the United States of America

The paper used in this publication meets the minimum requirements of American National Standard for Information Sciences—Permanence of Paper for Printed Library Materials, ANSI Z39.48-1984.

Library of Congress Cataloging-in-Publication Data
Yost, David S. (David Scott), 1948-
    NATO transformed : the Alliance's new roles in international security / David S. Yost.
        p. cm.
    Includes bibliographical references and index.
    ISBN 1-878379-81-X
    1. North Atlantic Treaty Organization—History. 2. North Atlantic Treaty Organization—Membership. 3. Security, International. I. Title.
    UA646.3 .Y674 1998
    355'.031091821—ddc21   98-40939
                                                                  CIP

To the memory of my father and mother
Albert Scott Yost (1921–1971)
Lois Marie Yost (1926–1969)

Contents

Foreword   ix
 by Richard H. Solomon

Preface   xv

Figure   xxi
 The European Security Architecture

Maps   xxii
 1. NATO and the Warsaw Pact, 1988
 2. Post–Cold War Eurasia, 1998

1. Introduction   1

2. NATO during the Cold War and Its Aftermath   27

3. Cooperation with Former Adversaries   91

4. Crisis Management and Peace Operations   189

5. Prospects and Challenges   269

Appendixes   303
 1. The North Atlantic Treaty
 2. Partnership for Peace Framework Document
 3. Founding Act on Mutual Relations, Cooperation, and
 Security between NATO and the Russian Federation
 4. Charter on a Distinctive Partnership between the
 North Atlantic Treaty Organization and Ukraine

Notes   333

Glossaries   395
  Key Acronyms: Concepts and Organizations in Brief
  The Evolving Membership of Major European
      Security Organizations

Index   405

Foreword

A half-century after its creation, the North Atlantic Treaty Organization wrestles with an existential crisis. Seemingly overnight, the Alliance's Cold War raison d'être vanished, as the East European communist regimes of the Warsaw Pact were swept up in the democratic revolutions of 1989–90 and the Soviet Union collapsed under the weight of its own political and economic frailties. Yet NATO still exists. Not only does it exist, but with the Soviet Union's demise, it has embarked on a grand experiment—"to create something better than the balance of power" as the new architecture of transatlantic security.

As any student of international relations knows well, such an endeavor has few successful precedents, but it is not without its formidable historical and political foundations. David Yost, professor of international relations at the Naval Postgraduate School in Monterey, California, and a senior fellow in the Jennings Randolph Program at the United States Institute of Peace during 1996–97, begins this timely and ambitious study with a masterful disquisition on how nations have sought to manage the international order over the years, from traditional balance-of-power arrangements to the more elaborate (and as yet unrealized) designs of collective security regimes—states drawn together in an obligatory pact to police themselves against any member's possible aggressive behavior.

In *NATO Transformed,* Professor Yost attempts to answer a simple, yet profound, question: Has NATO transformed itself from a strictly collective defense alliance—states drawn together to defend against an external threat—to an organization that has embraced the much broader and more demanding functions of a collective security organization? In answering this weighty question, Yost delivers what foreign policy analysts and historians may come to consider an exemplary treatment of NATO's basic difficulty in defining its rationale in the post–Cold War era.

Lord Ismay, NATO's first secretary general, once quipped that the organization's fundamental purpose was "to keep the Americans in, the Russians out, and the Germans down." Obviously, there are significant differences between then and now in this tripartite distinction, but these three powers continue to form the prism through which NATO's major security concerns can be viewed. Any change in one is bound to affect the panorama of transatlantic security. Within the past decade, all three have undergone major change.

Following the USSR's collapse, the United States began a profound reassessment of its leadership role in maintaining international security. When American foreign policy was structured around the cardinal tenet of Soviet containment, defense commitments and military spending encountered few domestic critics—and even fewer among America's allies that benefited from the stability and prosperity U.S. security guarantees provided. Today, in contrast, Washington hears a rising chorus of opinions—domestic and foreign—encouraging a more "multipolar" international order. To our allies, such multipolarity means more of a say in alliance decision making and greater scope for European autonomy in addressing security challenges. To Americans, it has come to mean that our NATO allies should shoulder more of the costs and potential casualties in future peacekeeping missions and be prepared to join with the United States in conducting operations in defense of common interests beyond Europe. Much of the early debate in the United States over NATO enlargement was revealing in this regard: Much of the concern centered not only on how enlargement would impinge on Russian sensitivities, but also on how much of the tab the U.S. would have to pick up to bring new members into the Alliance. The lack of a domestic consensus on the kind of leadership required for maintaining international security in the post–Cold War era has led Richard Haass to characterize the new U.S. role as "The Reluctant Sheriff."

Germany's reunification has rekindled anxieties in some quarters about the country's potential disproportionate influence across the continent. At the same time, Germany and France together have served as the engine of postwar European economic and political integration; and France, in particular, has stood as the voice of an "independent" (some would say "Gaullist") European security policy. Indeed, since the signing of the Maastricht Treaty in 1991, the European Union's members have endeavored to forge their own distinctly European Common Foreign and Security Policy. Yet, the fact that they have decided to pursue such a policy within NATO's Atlantacist confines speaks to just how much Europe still relies on the United States for its security. Nevertheless, there are several issues that divide the Allies, and Russia's role in the new architecture of European security is foremost among them.

Clearly, the largest and most powerful Soviet successor state does not pose the same type of military threat NATO was established to defend against, but the question of the country's potential membership in the Atlantic Alliance remains perhaps one of the more contentious issues among the NATO Allies, with the dividing line of opinion running down the middle of the Atlantic. Russia and the United States are trying to pursue additional arms reduction treaties, and Russian efforts to democratize continue, giving the Clinton administration enough reassurance to envision Russia's eventual membership in a "common security alliance."

NATO's European members are not so sanguine, some viewing Russia's commitment to democracy as tenuous at best, and waiting to see the course of the country's political development, especially in the post-Yeltsin era. The Alliance's prospective new members—countries that were part of the Soviet bloc not so many years ago—are drawn to NATO for its collective defense guarantees to counter a possible Russian neoimperialist impulse in the future. As Yost warns, Russian membership in the Alliance could very well empty NATO of its collective defense substance and lead to a renationalization of defense, as the European Allies attempt to satisfy their own security requirements against historical threats on their continent. Viewed in such a light, one must ask whether European security would be enhanced by a return to the kind of intra-European balance-of-power configurations that proved to be so unstable and so destructive in the past.

As the author of this work explains, NATO remains essentially a collective defense organization, protecting its members from external military threats or coercion. Yet evidence of the Alliance's recent preoccupation with collective security functions is manifest: NATO is expanding its scope in various ways, extending the penumbra of security to its former Cold

War adversaries through various gradations—from the three prospective new members of the Alliance, Poland, Hungary, and the Czech Republic, to the twenty-seven nations in NATO's auxiliary group, the Partnership for Peace. Collective security aspirations are also evident in NATO's recent peacekeeping missions, again with varying gradations—from its leading the Implementation Force (IFOR) and Stabilization Force (SFOR) in Bosnia as a result of the Dayton Accords, to the most recent warning actions in the skies over Serbia's province of Kosovo. NATO's expansion and enlargement—territorially as well as functionally—belies the notion that NATO remains just a collective defense organization.

If it is no longer solely a collective defense organization, can one call NATO a collective security organization? As the author of this work argues, NATO is trying to have it both ways: committed to collective defense as a hedge against Russian revanchism and other potential external threats, but also determined to pursue a new role in promoting a more secure post–Cold War Euro-Atlantic order. In fact, adapting to the new European security environment by assuming collective security functions may be the only way NATO can retain its vital collective defense role. More to the point, though, Yost also discusses the dilemmas in NATO's assuming these new functions. In trying to have it both ways, NATO risks surrendering its military effectiveness in a relatively small, close-knit collective defense pact at the expense of the inclusiveness collective security requires. NATO also risks a crisis of legitimacy by pursuing this dual purpose. When it seeks a mandate from the UN Security Council or the Organization for Security and Cooperation in Europe for its peacekeeping missions, the Alliance acknowledges the advantages of Russia's concurrence and participation—as well as the limits this implies for NATO's autonomy. Indeed, as Professor Yost concludes, collective security may come to be defined by the limits of a major-power consensus on shared interests.

If Bosnia serves as the bellwether of NATO's new collective security role, the international community must realize how constraining and frustrating those limits can be. Not only is it the venue of NATO's first "out-of-area" peacekeeping mission, but it is also the first case in which U.S. leadership in NATO peacekeeping has had to actively accommodate the interests of Russia—as a participating country in IFOR and SFOR and as a traditional ally of the same Serbian regime that has wrought so much destruction in ex-Yugoslavia. As Professor Yost concludes from his examination of the Bosnian case, the need for joint decision making and consensus among NATO Allies and Partners in collective security missions can paralyze a rapid response to an urgent situation. Surely, the Alliance's hesitation to act in the face of the brutal Serbian repression in Kosovo, and its flagging response to the chaos in Albania in early 1997, suggest that NATO may be relying on a looser—and less effective—form of collective security than its obligatory, all-embracing designs.

Yost's examination of NATO's involvement in Bosnia is perhaps the best reflection of the Institute's current work in studying the responses to contemporary conflict. Its Bosnia in the Balkans Initiative has examined ways of implementing the civilian aspects of the Dayton Accords, looking at what the region's political leaders can do to stop ethnic groups from lapsing back into conflict, including the consolidation of democratic institutions, reconstruction, and reconciliation. Through this program, the Institute has published a series of compelling reports on the ethnic and social chaos spreading across southeastern Europe and ways to resolve it, including *Dayton Implementation: The Return of Refugees; Serbia: Democratic Alternatives; Kosovo Dialogue: Too Little, Too Late; Kosovo: Escaping the Cul-de-Sac;* and *Croatia after Tudjman.*

At the other end of the spectrum, the Institute regularly convenes a panel of experts on regional politics and international security in its Working Group on the Future of Europe, devoted to exploring ways of improving cooperation among the region's states and within regional and international institutions to strengthen the foundation of the transatlantic security architecture and possibly to prevent future Bosnias. The group has also supported a number of equally compelling studies, ranging from James Goodby's book *Europe Undivided: The New Logic of Peace in U.S.-Russian Relations* (also published by the United States Institute of Peace Press) to Zbigniew Brzezinski's special report on *Managing NATO Expansion.*

As Brzezinski has acknowledged in a recent article, "The basic lesson of the last five decades is that European security is the basis for European reconciliation." The crises in the Balkans have cast a pall over the European ideal of an integrated continent that is free from irreconcilable national goals and interests. David Yost's impressive study of NATO's evolution and its current challenges will give its readers a profound insight on whether this organization can provide the requisite foundation of security to continue to pursue that ideal.

Richard H. Solomon
President
United States Institute of Peace

Preface

This book originated in my research during the 1996–97 academic year as a senior fellow in the Jennings Randolph Program for International Peace at the United States Institute of Peace. The original focus of the project was France and international security, particularly in Europe. As I investigated French views on the development of NATO's new Combined Joint Task Forces, which are intended (among other functions) to support the Atlantic Alliance's involvement in crisis management and peace operations, it became clear that it would be artificial to isolate French policies in this regard from the larger debate within the Alliance about NATO's new missions. This led to a decision to broaden the subject to the Alliance's new roles in international security.

These new roles have been accompanied by ambitious declarations about establishing a new security order for the Euro-Atlantic region, defined as Canada and the United States and all of Europe, Turkey, and the former Soviet Union, including Siberian Russia and the former Soviet republics in the Caucasus and Central Asia. Much of this rhetoric, such as the "security is indivisible" principle, and many of the concepts, such as promoting democratization and transparency in military plans and capabilities, are drawn from a tradition of thinking about international order that became known as collective security earlier in this century. Collective security aspirations have a much longer history, however, and they have inspired some famous works of political philosophy and noteworthy experiments in the organization of international order. The Introduction to this book therefore briefly discusses Immanuel Kant's famous essay on "Eternal Peace" (the wellspring of much of the collective security tradition since the Enlightenment), Woodrow Wilson's thinking about the Covenant of the League of Nations, the United Nations Charter, and other landmarks in the history of efforts to give concrete form to collective security designs.

Despite the vague aspirations voiced in some Alliance documents (and the advocacy of some commentators), this study concludes that NATO is not engaged in an effort to build a Kantian or Wilsonian system of collective security. In practice, to date the Allies have supported only what is sometimes termed the "major-power-consensus" approach to collective security—that is, interventions with the approval of a quasi-universal international organization, global or regional—and so far all the crisis management and peacekeeping operations conducted by the Alliance have been under UN Security Council mandates. Whether the Allies will someday conduct operations in support of collective security outside the framework of a quasi-universal international organization nominally dedicated to that purpose remains to be seen. The more urgent questions concern the relationship between the Alliance's long-standing (and continuing) collective defense functions and its new roles in international security. This book argues that collective defense remains the only solid foundation for Alliance cohesion and strength, an essential hedge in the event of political setbacks in Russia or elsewhere, and the most reliable basis for undertaking selected operations in support of collective security.

Not even a long book can claim to be comprehensive in dealing with such vast topics, but in this work I have attempted to illustrate the relevance of theories of international political order to the operational demands of NATO's new and traditional functions. This book does not discuss various NATO activities—for instance, the Alliance's new programs regarding topics such as environmental security, civil emergency planning, air traffic management, and science and technology. Some of these activities represent extensions of the NATO Science Program, first established in 1957, and the work of the Alliance's Committee on the Challenges of Modern Society, founded in 1969 and now redirected to involve participants from non-NATO countries, including former adversaries.

In this book, the terms "NATO" and "the Atlantic Alliance" or "the Alliance" are synonymous, unless otherwise indicated. I add this caveat because some French politicians, civil servants, military officers, and analysts like to distinguish between the Alliance, referring to the collective defense coalition established by the North Atlantic Treaty in 1949, and NATO, meaning the many institutional mechanisms the Alliance has set up over the years, including the civilian International Staff, the Defense Planning Committee, the Nuclear Planning Group, the integrated military command structure, the International Military Staff under the Military Committee, and various agencies, boards, committees, organizations, schools, and research centers. France has always been a full member of the Alliance and has thus participated fully at all times in the work of the Alliance's supreme decision-making body, the North Atlantic Council, which was established by Article 9 of the North Atlantic Treaty. Since 1966, however, to a greater extent than other member states France has pursued an à la carte approach to participation in other NATO institutions. The distinction between the Alliance and NATO, carefully preserved by some of the French, is generally not significant to people in other member states, and no effort has been made in this study to respect it. Sometimes, however, reference is made to "the Allies" to remind the reader that the Alliance is a coalition of independent sovereign states, an intergovernmental enterprise, and that it cannot do anything unless the member states agree to take action.

The United States Institute of Peace gave me a great sense of freedom and latitude, not only to conduct research on a broader topic than originally envisaged, but also to place the study in the context of theories of international political order, such as collective security and the balance of power. Richard Solomon, the Institute's president, kindly took an interest in this project, as in the projects of other fellows, and offered encouragement. Indeed, the Jennings Randolph fellowship program's administration proved to be sensible and helpful in every way imaginable. Joseph Klaits, the program director, was always welcoming and positive, and he invariably offered timely advice and support. John Crist, my program officer, was most thoughtful, understanding, and encouraging whenever questions arose—for instance, regarding the project's change in focus. Sally Blair was most congenial and supportive about the project and other professional activities and goals. Colleen Dowd and Kerry O'Donnell, members of the fellowship program staff, were always courteous and efficient.

Several other people at the Institute offered help that was sincerely appreciated, particularly Pamela Aall, Cynthia Benjamins, Sheryl Brown, Jim Cornelius, David Little, Timothy Sisk, Dave Smith, David Smock, Dan Snodderly, and Lauren Van Metre. Diana Duff Rutherford was an outstanding research assistant—not only patient and uncomplaining about my requests, but also exceptionally resourceful and effective in responding to them. Above all, Peter Pavilionis has been an extraordinary editor, astute in suggesting themes that deserved fuller development, diplomatic in raising queries about obscure passages, and tireless and meticulous in reviewing and improving various drafts.

The Institute also has my thanks for commissioning three helpful external reviews of the manuscript. While two of the reviewers remain anonymous, Richard Kugler revealed his identity, and I would like to thank him warmly for his extensive and valuable suggestions.

The year at the Institute would not have been feasible without the assistance and encouragement of my home institution, the Naval Postgraduate School. I would therefore like to express appreciation to the provost, Professor Richard Elster; the cognizant deans, Professor James Blandin and Professor Peter Purdue; and the department chairman, Captain Frank Petho, USN. The first draft of the book was extensively revised during the 1997–98 academic year, and the librarians and library staff at the Naval Postgraduate School—particularly George Goncalves, Mike Hanson, Michaele Lee Huygen, Ethel Jose, Greta Marlatt, Kate McCrave, Susan Miller, and Jeff Rothal—often furnished advice and assistance, for which I am most grateful.

This book has also benefited from the advice of expert observers in Canada, Europe, and the United States. Special thanks are owed to those who provided advice and assistance or commented on earlier drafts of this work: Donald Abenheim, Rudolf Adam, Gilles Andréani, Gérard Araud, Klaus Arnhold, Jacques Audibert, Bruce Bach, Don Bandler, Andrew Barlow, John Barrett, Klaus Becher, Fred Beauchamp, Régis de Belenet, Mark Bellamy, Paul Benkheiri, Marc Bentinck, John Berry, Manfred Bertele, Jean Bétermier, Rafael Biermann, Hens Henning Blomeyer-Bartenstein, Frank Boland, Jacques Bouchard, Richard Bowes, Yves Boyer, Frédéric Bozo, Ulrich Brandenburg, Michael Brown, Thomas Bruneau, John Bryson, Jean-François Bureau, Steve Caine, Didier Compard, Henri Conze, Tony Corn, Alain Crémieux, Hans-Joachim

Daerr, Charles Dale, Jon Day, Olivier Debouzy, François Delattre, Frank Dellermann, Jean-François Delpech, Thérèse Delpech, Charles Dick, Ed Dickens, Christopher Donnelly, Michel Drain, Michel Duclos, Jean Dufourcq, Marcel Duval, Josef Engelhardt, Roger Epp, Mark Etherton, Kevin Farrell, Alain Faupin, Brian Field, Pierre Fiorini, Adam Garfinkle, Patrick Garrity, Jean-Charles Gaudillet, Paul Gebhard, James Gentile, François Géré, Nicole Gnesotto, Philip Gordon, William Green, André Guilmain, Jean-Marie Guéhenno, Thomas Handel, John Harris, Keith Hartley, John Harvey, Pierre Hassner, François Heisbourg, Peter Herrly, Beatrice Heuser, Randy Hoag, Stanley Hoffmann, Rupert Holderness, David Honeywell, William Hopkinson, Ken Huffman, James Hurd, Bruce Ianacone, Robert Irvine, Philippe Jabaud, Clarence Juhl, William Kahn, Karl-Heinz Kamp, George Katsirdakis, Nick Kehoe, Catherine Kelleher, Craig Kelly, Jacob Kipp, Rick Kirby, Edward Kolodziej, Joachim Krause, Wolf-Dietrich Kriesel, Georges Kuttlein, Roman Laba, Yves Le Floch, Jon Lellenberg, Guido Lenzi, Donn Lewis, David Lightburn, Jean-Claude Mallet, Bruce Mann, Elie Marcuse, Andrew Marshall, Laurence Martin, Marie Masdupuy, Andrew Mathewson, Brian Mazerski, Franz-Josef Meiers, Nancy Mendrala, Winfried Mertens, Holger Mey, Edwin Micewski, Chris Miller, Michel Miraillet, Klaus Naumann, William Odom, Stephen Orosz, Francis Orsini, Guillaume Parmentier, Holger Pfeiffer, Joseph Pilat, Jean-Pierre Rabault, Michael Rampy, Norman Ray, Tjarck Roessler, John Roper, François de Rose, Michael Rühle, Diego Ruiz Palmer, Peter Ryan, Paul-Ivan de Saint-Germain, Todd Sandler, Jacques Sapir, Paul Savereux, Kurt Schiebold, Horst Schmalfeld, Gregory Schulte, Heinz Schulte, Martin Scicluna, Paul Selva, Jamie Shea, Hans-Georg Siebert, Horst Siedschlag, Robert Silano, Bernard Sitt, Daniel Sloss, Stephen Smith, Georges-Henri Soutou, Paul Stockton, Ton Strik, Carsten Svensson, Terence Taylor, Bruno Tertrais, Mikhail Tsypkin, Willem Van Eekelen, Miguel Walsh, Hans-Heinrich Weise, Thomas Welch, Bryan Wells, Samuel Wells, Nick Williams, Stephen Willmer, Pierre Wiroth, Klaus Wittmann, Sebastian Wood, Ian Woodman, Roger Wyatt, Roberto Zadra, and Salomé Zourabichvili.

In addition, parts of the manuscript were presented in forums that elicited useful comments. I am particularly grateful for the suggestions provided by the editors and reviewers for *Survival,* the journal of the International Institute for Strategic Studies. Part of the book appeared in the Summer 1998 issue of *Survival,* in an article entitled "The New NATO and Collective Security."

Those generously providing advice or assistance naturally bear no responsibility for the book's shortcomings or for the views expressed. Indeed, the views expressed are mine alone, and should not be construed as representing those of the Department of the Navy, the United States Institute of Peace, or any other U.S. government agency.

Finally, I would like to thank my wife, Catherine, for her great patience and encouragement with this project, as well as for her practical assistance in making it all possible.

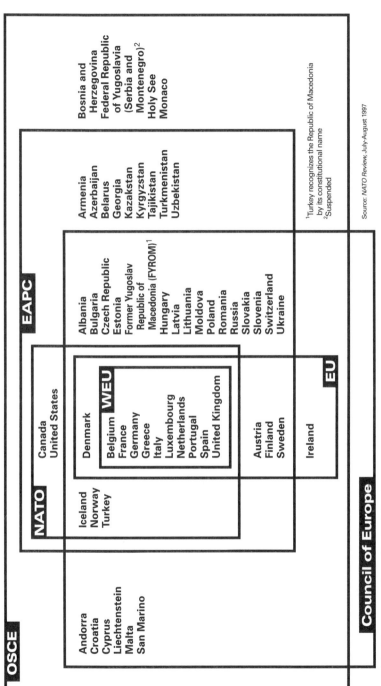

OSCE

NATO

EAPC

WEU

EU

Andorra
Croatia
Cyprus
Liechtenstein
Malta
San Marino

Iceland
Norway
Turkey

Canada
United States

Denmark

Belgium
France
Germany
Greece
Italy
Luxembourg
Netherlands
Portugal
Spain
United Kingdom

Austria
Finland
Sweden

Ireland

Albania
Bulgaria
Czech Republic
Estonia
Former Yugoslav
Republic of
Macedonia (FYROM)[1]
Hungary
Latvia
Lithuania
Moldova
Poland
Romania
Russia
Slovakia
Slovenia
Switzerland
Ukraine

Armenia
Azerbaijan
Belarus
Georgia
Kazakhstan
Kyrgyzstan
Tajikistan
Turkmenistan
Uzbekistan

Bosnia and
Herzegovina
Federal Republic
of Yugoslavia
(Serbia and
Montenegro)[2]
Holy See
Monaco

Council of Europe

The European Security Architecture

[1]Turkey recognizes the Republic of Macedonia
by its constitutional name
[2]Suspended

Source: *NATO Review*, July-August 1997

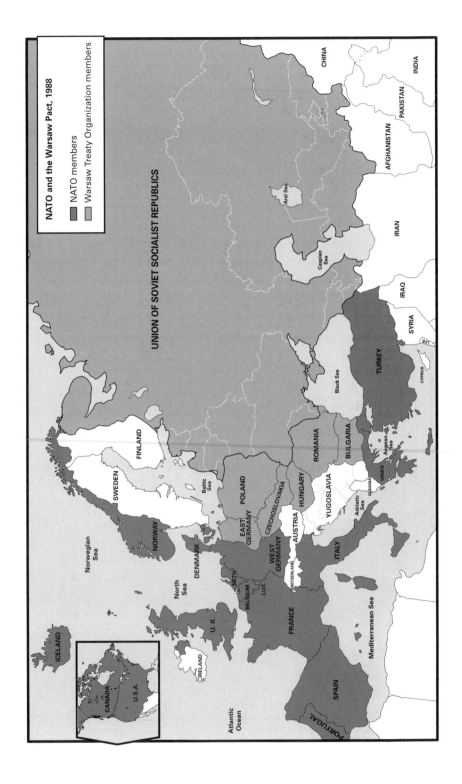

NATO and the Warsaw Pact, 1988

NATO members

Warsaw Treaty Organization members

UNION OF SOVIET SOCIALIST REPUBLICS

CHINA

INDIA

PAKISTAN

AFGHANISTAN

IRAN

IRAQ

SYRIA

LEB.

CYPRUS

TURKEY

Aral Sea

Caspian Sea

Black Sea

Aegean Sea

GREECE

ALBANIA

Adriatic Sea

BULGARIA

ROMANIA

YUGOSLAVIA

HUNGARY

AUSTRIA

ITALY

Mediterranean Sea

CZECHOSLOVAKIA

POLAND

EAST GERMANY

WEST GERMANY

SWITZERLAND

FRANCE

LUX.

BELGIUM

NETH.

SPAIN

PORTUGAL

Baltic Sea

FINLAND

SWEDEN

NORWAY

DENMARK

North Sea

Norwegian Sea

U. K.

IRELAND

ICELAND

Atlantic Ocean

CANADA

U.S.A.

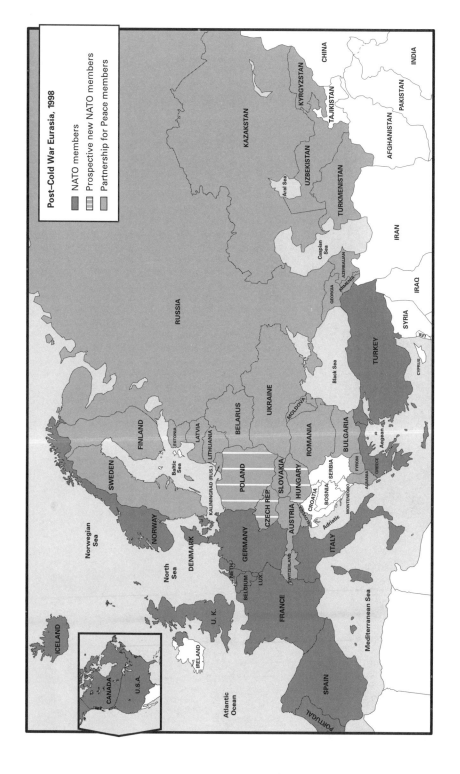

Post-Cold War Eurasia, 1998

- NATO members
- Prospective new NATO members
- Partnership for Peace members

1

Introduction

This book discusses the origins, evolution, and prospects of the North Atlantic Treaty Organization's new roles in international security. During the Cold War, from the founding of the Alliance in 1949 to the breakup of the Soviet empire in 1989–91, NATO was essentially an instrument of collective defense. That is, NATO was an alliance organized to defend its members from external coercion or aggression and, on that basis, to conduct diplomacy with its adversaries to the East and seek a peaceful resolution to East-West differences. While the Alliance has not by any means abandoned its collective defense function, since 1990–92 it has increasingly taken on roles and responsibilities that were no more than implicit in its earlier history.

Some of the new roles involve what is sometimes called "collective security," in that the Alliance is prepared to act in support of general international security interests. In June 1992, NATO foreign ministers formally declared the Alliance's willingness, on a case-by-case basis, to support peacekeeping activities under the auspices of the Conference on Security and Cooperation in Europe (CSCE). Later that year, the Alliance agreed to make troops and equipment available to CSCE and United Nations (UN) efforts to bring peace to the former Yugoslavia, initially in activities such as enforcing the arms embargo and monitoring the no-fly-zone. Since mid-1995, the Alliance's "peace operations" in the former Yugoslavia have overshadowed those of other international organizations, notably since Operation Deliberate Force, the Dayton peace talks, and the establishment in late 1995 of the multinational Implementation Force (IFOR) in Bosnia. In November and December 1996, the Allies agreed that NATO would play a major role in the post-IFOR Stabilization

Force (SFOR) in Bosnia. Since the early 1990s, it has become commonplace in the Alliance to distinguish between "Article 5" missions (to honor the mutual defense commitment in this article of the North Atlantic Treaty—see Appendix 1) and "non–Article 5" missions (to carry out tasks such as peace operations under UN auspices, even if under NATO command).

Simultaneously, the Alliance has been engaged in "outreach" to non-NATO countries in Europe, particularly former adversaries—nations that were formerly East European members of the Warsaw Pact or republics of the Soviet Union. The new institutions involved in outreach activities include the North Atlantic Cooperation Council (NACC), established in 1991 and replaced in 1997 by the Euro-Atlantic Partnership Council (EAPC); the Partnership for Peace (PfP), founded in 1994; and the NATO-Russia Permanent Joint Council (PJC) and the NATO-Ukraine Commission, both established in 1997. The fundamental purpose of all of these institutions is the promotion of positive and peaceful relations among the participating nations. In both NACC/EAPC and PfP, the major activities have included peacekeeping studies and exercises. Russia, Ukraine, and several other PfP nations (including candidates for NATO membership) have participated in IFOR and SFOR.

Since the NATO summit in January 1994, moreover, the Alliance has been engaged in a complex multidimensional process of redefining its command structure and establishing new institutional mechanisms such as Combined Joint Task Forces (CJTFs), in part because of the practical challenges of conducting peace operations. Another major incentive for establishing CJTFs has been to respond to the aspirations of European Allies to build a European Security and Defense Identity (ESDI), on the basis of the Western European Union (WEU) and other institutions, within the Alliance. CJTF and the new Alliance command structure will have multiple functions, including non–Article 5 tasks as well as collective defense. When serving with the endorsement of the Alliance as instruments for non–Article 5 tasks such as peace operations and humanitarian relief, CJTFs are expected to be available for use by NATO, the WEU, or "coalitions of the willing" composed of self-selected Allies and non-NATO countries such as Russia. The non-NATO countries making use of CJTFs could include EAPC and PfP members, as well as countries outside these institutions, as with IFOR and SFOR in Bosnia.

NATO's principal new security roles have thus been (a) pursuing dialogue and cooperation with former adversaries and other non-NATO nations in the EAPC and PfP, and (b) contributing to crisis management and "peace operations," particularly under UN auspices.

THESIS AND STRUCTURE OF THIS WORK

The history and prospects of the Alliance's two new roles—cooperation with former adversaries and other non-NATO nations in the Euro-Atlantic region, and crisis management and peace operations—are examined in this study. The new roles represent a significant transformation of the Alliance's purposes. To be sure, the Alliance originated as, and remains, a group of nations dedicated to collective defense—ensuring protection for the Allies against aggression or coercion; and the core function of collective defense (sometimes called "territorial defense") continues to be paramount for the existing Allies and for prospective new Allies such as Poland. Since 1990, however, collective security missions (that is, support for international security beyond the immediate defense of the Allies) have become increasingly prominent in the Alliance's words and deeds.

The words include NATO's offers, beginning in 1992, to support the United Nations and the CSCE (known as the Organization for Security and Cooperation in Europe, or OSCE, since 1994) in peacekeeping operations; its commitments since 1994 to security consultations with the twenty-seven non-NATO nations in PfP; and its declarations that "security is indivisible" throughout the region that since the end of the Cold War has often been called the Euro-Atlantic area, defined as the territory of all the OSCE states—that is, Canada and the United States, Europe, Turkey, and the former Soviet Union, including Siberian Russia and the former Soviet republics in the Caucasus and Central Asia.

The deeds encompass the many Partnership for Peace exercises and other activities that seek to enhance interoperability between Alliance and Partner forces in support of confidence-building and transparency, as well as humanitarian, crisis management, and peacekeeping operations; the efforts to devise CJTFs that could be used not only for collective defense but also for crisis management and peacekeeping by NATO-approved "coalitions of the willing"; and, most significantly, NATO's first military operations involving actual combat—the interventions under UN auspices in the former Yugoslavia that made possible the Dayton Accords and the NATO-led IFOR and SFOR operations.

These words and deeds, among others, confirm that even as NATO remains an instrument of collective defense, it has been transformed into a vehicle for collective security activities on an ad hoc and selective basis in the Euro-Atlantic region.

The Alliance's new collective security rhetoric and activities raise at least three fundamental questions. What are the prospects for building the peaceful Euro-Atlantic order envisaged in NATO's rhetoric? When further conflicts in and beyond the former Yugoslavia arise, what crisis management and peacekeeping operations is the Alliance likely to undertake? Given that military resources are finite, to what extent can the Alliance devise a positive synergy between its continuing collective defense functions and its new collective security activities?

One of the greatest challenges facing the Alliance today is to clarify the relationship between its long-standing core function of collective defense and its new missions in support of collective security. This challenge will have to be addressed as the Alliance reviews its Strategic Concept and prepares for its projected April 1999 summit in Washington.

To place this challenge in perspective, this book's argument is organized as follows. The rest of the Introduction is devoted to clarifying the distinction between collective defense and collective security—and, indeed, three meanings of collective security—and explaining their significance in European history. This background is essential because the Alliance's ambitions include helping to build a new international security order in the Euro-Atlantic region, and the Allies have drawn heavily on concepts of collective security.

To illustrate the magnitude of the Alliance's transformation, chapter 2 reviews the Alliance's origins and preoccupations during the Cold War, including its policies for peaceful change, and examines how and why it survived the end of the Cold War—mainly because of its internal functions, its continuing collective defense role, and its ability to meet new security requirements.

Chapter 3 examines the first of the Alliance's two new roles—cooperation with former adversaries and other non-NATO countries in the Euro-Atlantic region. Pursuing this objective has been complex and at times contentious, in part because of the tension between seeking NATO enlargement (which entails making collective defense commitments to specific new Allies) and cultivating cooperative institutions that are intended to be comprehensively inclusive, despite the prominence of the "self-differentiation" principle in PfP and the establishment of special consultative mechanisms with Russia and Ukraine. This chapter also considers dilemmas in trying to combine collective defense and collective security, including the risks in blurring the distinction between Allies and Partners, the antinomy between inclusiveness and effectiveness, and the continuing significance of major power interactions outside formal institutions.

Chapter 4 explores the Alliance's adaptations regarding crisis management and peace operations, particularly under the press of events in the former Yugoslavia. The Allies have yet to resolve sensitive issues such as the extent to which Article 5 collective defense commitments might apply during the conduct of non–Article 5 operations in support of collective security and whether the Alliance considers a mandate from the UN Security Council or the OSCE politically and legally indispensable (or simply desirable) for the conduct of such operations.

Chapter 5, the final chapter, argues that the Allies have little choice but to follow a two-track policy—pursuing collective security aspirations, to the extent that this is feasible and prudent, while maintaining their collective defense posture and orientation. Collective defense remains the only solid foundation for Alliance cohesion and strength, an essential hedge in the event of political setbacks in Russia or elsewhere, and the most reliable basis for undertaking selected operations in support of collective security.

DISTINGUISHING BETWEEN COLLECTIVE DEFENSE AND COLLECTIVE SECURITY

It is essential to clarify the distinction between the terms "collective defense" and "collective security." The distinction throws light on some of the larger issues involved in NATO's efforts to promote the establishment of a peaceful order in what since 1990 has often been called the Euro-Atlantic area—the vast region consisting of Canada and the United States, Europe, Turkey, and the former Soviet Union.

In the interests of clear thinking, a fundamental distinction must be made. Two official statements in 1990–91 illustrate how readily the concepts of collective defense and collective security can be confused. In November 1990, the NATO Allies and the members of the Warsaw Pact agreed in a Joint Declaration in Paris that they were "no longer adversaries" and that they recognized that "security is indivisible and that the security of each of their countries is inextricably linked to the security of all States participating in the Conference on Security and Co-operation in Europe."[1] A year later, in its new Strategic Concept, approved in November 1991, NATO declared, "The security of all Allies is indivisible: an attack on one is an attack on all."[2]

Despite the apparent similarity in these statements, the key distinction resides in the difference between declaring that "the security of all Allies is indivisible" and, more broadly, asserting that "security is indivisible" with regard to nations outside the Alliance but in the CSCE, a vast body including all the states in the Euro-Atlantic region. The first phrase helps to define an alliance based on a mutual defense pledge—that is, collective defense; and the latter expresses an aspiration toward collective security.

The "security is indivisible" phrase may well be an echo of the League of Nations experience with collective security. The more popular form of the phrase in the 1920s and 1930s, "peace is indivisible," is usually attributed to Soviet diplomat Maxim Litvinov.[3] The phrase in the Joint Declaration of Paris in 1990 suggests that the security of all CSCE states is endangered by any threat to the security of any member state. In December 1991, the NATO Allies and the former Warsaw Pact states, meeting in their new North Atlantic Cooperation Council, repeated the November 1990 declaration that "security is indivisible," and added, "The consolidation and preservation throughout the continent of democratic societies and their freedom from any form of coercion or intimidation therefore concern us all."[4]

These declarations imply that the security of all CSCE states would be endangered by any threat to peace, or indeed "any form of coercion or intimidation" against a CSCE state—a menace that might well involve a threat of war. It is worth recalling in this regard that Article 11 of the Covenant of the League of Nations declared that "Any war or threat of war, whether immediately affecting any of the Members of the League or not, is hereby declared a matter of concern to the whole League, and the League shall take any action that may be deemed wise and effectual to safeguard the peace of nations."[5]

What obligations for concrete action do broad declarations that "security is indivisible" imply, as opposed to the obligations inherent in a mutual defense pledge such as Article 5 of the North Atlantic Treaty? Both represent attempts to impose some order on the contingent and unpredictable threats in international politics. Both deal, in other words, with the problem of organizing relations among sovereign powers, with a view to preventing war or (if war should nonetheless break out) containing its consequences. As eminent observers such as Martin Wight, Inis Claude, Jr., and Henry Kissinger have pointed out, collective security (at least in the traditional sense of the term, exemplified in the thought and writing of Immanuel Kant and Woodrow Wilson) involves a pact against war; the threat is aggression by a currently unidentified party to the pact, which should ideally include all the states in the state system. In contrast, a collective defense pact binds together an alliance of states to deter and, if necessary, defend against one or more identifiable external threats, a state or a group of states outside the alliance.[6]

Because an alliance, or collective defense pact, is an instrument of states cooperating to seek security from the actual or prospective threats posed by others, one of its chief preoccupations is achieving a favorable, or at least acceptable, balance of power as a means of deterring war or hedging against its outbreak. The members of such an alliance are expected to honor their formal mutual defense pledges in the event of aggression against an ally, but they are not necessarily obliged to take action against acts of aggression affecting non-allies. In a Kantian or Wilsonian collective security system, however, all states in the state system would be united in a cooperative pact, and all states would be obliged to act against any aggressor, because "peace is indivisible" and every state's security interests are believed to be affected by any aggression anywhere. Traditional collective security theory holds that the general sense of security interdependence and the advance commitments to act in such a system would tend to keep the peace and result in the prompt punishment of any aggressors. As Inis Claude noted in an analysis of the premises of this theory of collective security, "The world is conceived not as a *we*-group and a *they*-group of nations, engaged in competitive power relations, but as an integral *we*-group in which danger may be posed by 'one of us' and must be met by 'all the rest of us.'"[7]

Kantian or Wilsonian collective security enterprises need not be universal in scope. While the original design of the League of Nations envisaged an organization that might ultimately be universal,[8] its membership was always limited. The aspiration to establish collective security—which is, ultimately, the idea of shared responsibility for international order and the security of others—may apply on a regional basis as well as on a global one, and the obligations assumed may be moral and political rather than legally binding.

Unfortunately, the distinction between the terms "collective defense" and "collective security" has often been deliberately blurred. The concepts of "collective security" associated with the Kantian tradition gained renewed support during World War I and became widely known and highly regarded during the 1920s and 1930s, in large part as a result of the efforts of Woodrow Wilson and other proponents of the League of Nations. "Whatever their failures," Claude has pointed out, "the Wilsonians clearly succeeded in establishing the conviction that collective security represents a brand of international morality vastly superior to that incorporated in the balance of power system." As a result, whether because of honest confusion or the "deliberate misappropriation of semantic funds," the tendency in many quarters since World War II has been to apply the term "collective security" to any alliance, particularly a pact that one approves of—including NATO.[9]

This conceptual confusion is regrettable, because "collective security," particularly in its traditional sense, was conceived as an alternative to the formation of alliances for collective defense; and distinctions between concepts of "collective security" and "collective defense" can be helpful and illuminating in understanding NATO's problems and prospects and the general challenge of organizing a peaceful international order in Europe.

To put in context the magnitude of the venture facing NATO, a brief review of the history of thinking about collective security, balance of power, and international order is necessary. This review shows that, while the ideas advanced by Kant, Wilson, and other proponents of a comprehensive system of collective security continue to command interest and to win support, at least in terms of rhetoric, in practice Alliance governments have supported only a "major power consensus" approach to collective security.

ALLIANCES AND INTERNATIONAL ORDER IN EUROPEAN HISTORY

The challenge of establishing a peaceful international order in Europe has been present since the breakdown of the medieval order and the emergence of the modern state system during the fourteenth and fifteenth centuries. Although the term "collective security" is an early twentieth century invention,[10] the central concept has been advocated—and attempts have been made to implement it—since the beginning of the modern state system in Europe. In Martin Wight's words,

> By collective security we mean a system in which any breach of the peace is declared to be of concern to all the participating states, and an attack on one is taken as an attack on all. It is amusing and at the same time sobering to reflect that this system was written into the Covenant of the League of Nations, and endlessly discussed and refined for the next 15 years, without any suspicion (so far as I know) of knowledge on the part of Woodrow Wilson, or of the League of Nations Union that it had been tried repeatedly in international history since the fifteenth century.[11]

As early examples, Wight cited the Most Holy League of Venice of 1454 ("the first system of collective security" in modern European history, in his judgment), the Treaty of London of 1518, the Association of the Hague of 1681–83, and the Quadruple Alliance of 1718.[12]

While Wight referred to the various efforts by great-power coalitions to establish a collective security system by treaty, other historians have drawn attention to the diverse yet comparable proposals by a series of statesmen and authors. The "grand design" attributed to Henry IV of France, the peace project of the Abbé de St. Pierre, Immanuel Kant's essay "Eternal Peace," and William Penn's suggestions for a European order are among the better-known predecessors of the proposals that gained widespread attention during and after World War I.[13]

The collective security tradition is rooted in an aspiration to think of interests beyond those of the nation and its allies and to consider those of international society as a whole—on a regional, if not a global, basis.

The hallmarks of the collective security tradition include a desire to avoid grouping powers into opposing camps, and a refusal to draw dividing lines that would leave anyone out. Writing on a spiritual rather than a political level, John Donne in the seventeenth century articulated one of the essential ideas of collective security, a sense of involvement in the fate of others: "No man is an Island, entire of it self; every man is a piece of the Continent, a part of the main; if a clod be washed away by the sea, Europe is the less, as well as if a promontory were, as well as if a manor of thy friends or of thine own were; any man's death diminishes me, because I am involved in Mankind; And therefore never send to know for whom the bell tolls; it tolls for thee."[14]

The ideologies of the Enlightenment popularized a tradition holding that the evils of state oppression and war resided principally in the behavior of privileged and powerful autocrats—people who might be called dictators today, except that they customarily enjoyed dynastic legitimacy and some loyalty from their subjects. Several influential Enlightenment thinkers held that the long-term solution resided in general democratization, national self-determination, and the organization of a peaceful international order by intrinsically pacific states. At the end of the eighteenth century, Immanuel Kant furnished the best-known example of such thinking. Kant held that states with "republican" constitutions would be pacific, because the citizens would "be very loath . . . to bring upon themselves all the horrors of war." Such states, Kant argued, should form a "pacific federation" that "would seek to put an end to all wars forever." This federation's members would escape from "occasions of war" by establishing "public coercive laws" applying to "an ever-growing state of nations, such as would at last embrace all the nations of the earth."[15]

Kant acknowledged that war might nonetheless occur sometimes, but held that "each commonwealth . . . may hope on real grounds that the others being constituted like itself will then come, on occasions of need, to its aid." In Kant's view, the only remedy for war and international anarchy was "a system of international right founded upon public laws conjoined with power, to which every State must submit—according to the analogy of the civil or political right of individuals in any one State."[16] Kant advanced several additional ideas associated with the collective security tradition, such as: the moral power of enlightened public opinion; the indivisibility of international security interests, in that any war or act of oppression should concern everyone; the peace-promoting effects of the "commercial spirit, which cannot exist along with war and which sooner or later controls every people";[17] the imperative need for open diplomacy and publicity regarding principles of peaceful statecraft, with no secret reservations or policies conducive to war; the imperative of disarmament, with the eventual abolition of standing armies; and the inevitability of progress in establishing a peaceful world order, despite intermittent setbacks.

Woodrow Wilson became the most prominent advocate of Kantian ideas regarding international peace and security. According to Wilson, "No peace can last, or ought to last, which does not recognize and accept the principle that governments derive all their just powers from the consent of the governed, and that no right anywhere exists to hand peoples about from sovereignty to sovereignty as if they were property."[18] As Wilson saw it, in the long-standing European system, "a small coterie of autocrats were able to determine the fortunes of their people without consulting them, were able to use their people as puppets and pawns in the game of ambition which was being played all over the stage of Europe."[19]

As these statements suggest, Kant and Wilson shared many ideas.[20] Both deplored balance-of-power arrangements as unreliable and dangerous, and both advocated replacing them with a "community of power"—a reliable predominance of strength against any malefactors that might arise within that community, which would be a comprehensive confederation of like-minded states, a veritable "League of Nations."[21] As Wilson put it, "There must be, not a balance of power, but a community of power; not organized rivalries, but an organized common peace."[22] Likewise, both recommended the rule of law in international politics, the institution of mechanisms for the peaceful resolution of conflicts, and the abolition of war as a legal means of settling disputes; war would be legitimate only as the ultimate recourse of the peaceful majority in the face of aggressors within the community of states. In Wilson's words, "What we seek is the reign of law, based upon the consent of the governed and sustained by the organized opinion of mankind."[23]

The phrase "the consent of the governed" is found in the U.S. Declaration of Independence, and points to another similarity in the thinking of Kant and Wilson—a conviction that the legitimacy of governments should be based on constitutional and democratic self-determination, rather than on the power of despots or the prescriptive right of hereditary autocrats.[24] Moreover, both believed in the political solidarity of democratically governed states, the ethical authority of enlightened public opinion, and the elimination of secret diplomacy. Indeed, the first of Wilson's Fourteen Points called for "Open covenants of peace, openly arrived at, after which there shall be no private international understandings of any kind but diplomacy shall proceed always frankly and in the public view."[25] Kant and Wilson both argued that enduring progress in international politics was feasible, and held that it should be based, whenever possible, on gradual reform rather than violence and revolution. Finally, Kant and Wilson both believed, in Kant's words, that "a powerful and enlightened people" organized as "a republic— which by its very nature must be disposed in favor of perpetual peace"—could play a special leadership role in bringing about a peaceful and law-governed international order.[26]

Yet Wilson differed from Kant in that he assigned this special leadership role to a particular nation—the United States. In asking Congress for a declaration of war in 1917, Wilson said, "the right is more precious than peace, and we shall fight for the things which we have always carried nearest our hearts—for democracy, for the right of those who submit to authority to have a voice in their own Governments, for the rights and liberties of small nations, for a universal dominion of right by such a concert of free peoples as shall bring peace and safety to all nations and make the world itself at last free."[27] In urging the public and the Senate to support ratification of the Treaty of Versailles, including the Covenant of the League of Nations, Wilson declared that America "has said to mankind at her birth: 'We have come to redeem the world by giving it liberty and justice.' Now we are called upon before the tribunal of mankind to redeem that immortal pledge."[28]

Wilson's attempt to fulfill the Enlightenment's vision of international order in a concrete League of Nations brought him into contact with practical obstacles to its realization, and these help to account for some of the differences between the eighteenth-century philosopher and the twentieth-century statesman.[29] Whereas national self-determination was an abstract principle for Kant, Wilson was confronted with the conflicting claims of real nations. Several of his Fourteen Points were concerned with the specific problems of Belgium, France, Hungary, Italy, Montenegro, Poland, Romania, Russia, Serbia, and Turkey. Partly to gain approval from France and the other victors in World War I for the League of Nations, Wilson accepted many compromises regarding boundaries and minorities. For example, various decisions gave Germans grounds to conclude that "the principle of self-determination was applied only when it worked to the disadvantage of Germans."[30] Whereas Kant called for the abolition of standing armies, Wilson supported "that moderation of armaments which makes of armies and navies a power for order merely, not an instrument of aggression or of selfish violence;"[31] and the Covenant of the League called for arms reductions "to the lowest point consistent with national safety and the enforcement by common action of international obligations."[32]

Whereas Kant offered no more than a sketchy vision of universal order, Wilson played a central role in defining the specific provisions of an actual institution.[33] Each member of the League was committed "to respect and preserve as against external aggression the territorial integrity and existing political independence of all Members of the League"; to submit all disputes to arbitration, judicial settlement, or inquiry; and to regard any state resorting to war illegally as having "committed an act of war against all other Members of the League," which would immediately impose financial and trade sanctions and, at the recommendation of the Council, contribute military forces "to protect the covenants of the League."[34]

How the military forces would be organized and commanded to enforce the League's protective commitments was vague. The Covenant stipulated that, aside from exceptions such as procedural matters, "decisions at any meeting of the Assembly or of the Council shall require the agreement of all the Members of the League represented at the meeting."[35] The apparent assumption that unanimity could be achieved readily, even in matters involving the use of force, was consistent with the Kantian postulate that an association of like-minded states could rely on the force of world public opinion. The commitments of League members were specified "so precisely that refusal to make a decision or failure to live up to the obligations of membership would be clear for all the world to see."[36] In February 1919, when Wilson presented the Covenant of the League to the delegates at the Paris Peace Conference, he said,

> . . . throughout this instrument we are depending primarily and chiefly upon one great force, and that is the moral force of the public opinion of the world—the cleansing and clarifying and compelling influences of publicity—so that . . . designs that are sinister can at any time be drawn into the open. . . . Armed force is in the background in this program, but it *is* in the background, and if the moral force of the world will not suffice, the physical force of the world shall. But that is the last resort, because this is intended as a constitution of peace, not as a league of war. . . . People that were suspicious of one another can now live as friends and comrades in a single family, and desire to do so. The miasma of distrust, of intrigue, is cleared away. Men are looking eye to eye and saying, "We are brothers and have a common purpose. We did not realize it before, but now we do realize it, and this is our covenant of fraternity and of friendship."[37]

Wilson's conviction that, if properly established, the League of Nations would be "a 99 per cent insurance against war"[38] was consistent with the general Enlightenment view that a coalition of like-minded democracies, each with its aspirations for national self-determination satisfied, would find the challenges of maintaining international order and peace quite manageable.[39] As Wight has pointed out, "The American and French Revolutions offered a new doctrine of international legitimacy. Prescription and dynastic right were replaced by democracy and national self-determination. These were expected to transform the states-system. Instead of an equilibrium of power, regulated by governments, there would be a fraternal harmony of peoples. . . . Kant and Cobden, Mazzini and the Peace Societies, assumed in their different ways that the enforcement of international order was unnecessary."[40]

The proposition that relations between democracies are inherently peaceful has featured prominently in the Kantian tradition of thinking about collective security since the Enlightenment. It should nonetheless be recalled that some of the same European autocrats whose behavior was deplored by proponents of democracy and collective security held conceptions of international order based on the balance of power that were comparable in some ways to visions of collective security. The coalition against Louis XIV's attempts to gain hegemony in Europe terminated the War of the Spanish Succession in 1713 with the Treaty of Utrecht, which held "that the peace and tranquillity of the Christian world may be ordered and stabilized in a just balance of power, which is the best and most solid foundation of mutual friendship and a lasting general concord."[41] Similarly, the coalition that defeated Napoleon's attempts to dominate Europe avowed in the Treaty of Chaumont of 1814 that their aim was "the maintenance of the balance of Europe, to secure the repose and independence of the Powers, and to prevent the invasions which for so many years have devastated the world."[42]

Indeed, in some discussions of the balance of power by eighteenth and nineteenth century observers, the obligations of states were described in terms comparable to those outlined in collective security theory. According to Emmerich de Vattel (1714–67), "The constant attention of sovereigns to all that goes on, the custom of resident ministers, the continual negotiations that take place, make of modern Europe a sort of Republic, whose members—each independent, but all bound together by a common interest—unite for the maintenance of order and the preservation of liberty."[43] According to Friedrich von Gentz (1764–1832), all states should defend any victim of aggression: "We must hear of no insulary systems, no indifference to a danger apparently foreign to their own immediate interests, no absolute neutrality."[44]

At the beginning of the nineteenth century, Lord Henry Peter Brougham (1778–1868) argued that one of the virtues of the balance of power system was "the perpetual attention to foreign affairs which it inculcates, . . . the unceasing care which it dictates of nations most remotely situated, and apparently unconnected with ourselves; the general union which it has effected of all the European powers, obeying certain laws, and actuated in general by a common principle; in fine, the right of mutual inspection, universally recognised, among civilised states." In commenting on this passage in Brougham's work, the British historian Martin Wight wrote, "Here are the germs of 'peace is indivisible,' of the idea of collective security."[45] Similarly, British prime minister William Gladstone (1809–98) argued for uniting all the powers to "neutralize and fetter and bind up the selfish aims of each" and to focus their attention on "objects connected with the common good of them all." In Wight's view, Gladstone articulated "the most elaborate theoretical formulation of the principle of concert in the

nineteenth century, and it is the foundation of the doctrine of collective security."[46]

It was this history of efforts and arguments, by statesmen as well as
commentators, that led historians such as Edward Gulick to argue that
collective security, "far from being alien to the 'age-old tradition of the
balance of power,' not only derives out of the latter, but also must be
regarded as the logical end point of the balance-of-power system, the
ideal toward which it has been moving, slowly and haltingly, for several
hundred years."[47] Quincy Wright likewise held that collective security
was "only a planned development of the natural tendency of balance of
power policies"[48]—despite the arguments of Woodrow Wilson and the
other proponents of collective security, which were based on the thesis
that collective security and balance of power are distinct approaches to
international order.

In fact, President Wilson was correct in underscoring the differences
between his conception of collective security and balance-of-power
approaches to international order. For all the similarities between the
two concepts, particularly for champions of a more coherent and institutionalized balance of power based on a high degree of international
consensus, the form of collective security that Wilson sought posited a
"community of power"—a uniting of all states behind a firm and irrev-
ocable commitment to act against any aggressor. The ideal collective
security system would allow no room for choice in any crisis; the law-
abiding states would all be obliged to punish any transgressor.

It was precisely because these obligations were well understood by
many U.S. Senators that President Wilson's design for the League of
Nations was never realized. The League represents a failed attempt to
establish an effective collective security arrangement along the lines
advocated by Kant and Wilson. The League's Covenant included some
principles essential to such an arrangement. However, the prospects for
practical implementation of these principles were hobbled by the complete absence of some powers (such as the United States), the episodic
and at times propagandistic participation of others (such as Germany
and the Soviet Union), and the lack of commitment to consistent application of the principles on the part of others (such as Britain and France).
When confronted with a critical challenge—how to deal with the Italian
aggression against Abyssinia in 1935–36—several of the small powers

showed greater resoluteness than did Britain and France, apparently because London and Paris still hoped to gain Italian support against Nazi Germany's ambitions. The failure to act in such a clear-cut case disillusioned the League's idealistic champions and the small powers that had hoped to be able to rely on it. It was therefore, in Wight's words, "a seminal failure, the generator of a whole series of other failures."[49]

The successor to the League of Nations, the United Nations, cannot be described as a collective security organization in the Kantian or Wilsonian sense, despite the fact that, as Claude notes, "The doctrine was given ideological lip service, and a scheme was contrived for making it effective in cases of relatively minor importance."[50] This result was not the one initially sought by powers such as the United States. It should be recalled that the term "United Nations" was proposed in December 1941 by U.S. president Franklin D. Roosevelt as the name for the states at war with the Axis Powers. At the October 1943 Moscow Conference, Britain, China, the USSR, and the United States agreed that the United Nations fighting the Axis Powers should establish an international organization for peace and security after the war. In describing this projected organization to the Congress, Secretary of State Cordell Hull declared that, "As the provisions of the four-power declaration are carried into effect, there will no longer be need for spheres of influence, for alliances, for balance of power, or any other of the special arrangements through which, in the unhappy past, the nations strove to safeguard their security or to promote their interests."[51]

In contrast with the League of Nations Covenant, however, the United Nations Charter affirmed at the outset that collective security principles could not be applied against a major power, and in fact could be applied only on the basis of a consensus of the major powers. This is the significance of the veto power held by the five permanent members of the UN Security Council. As a Mexican delegate said at the founding conference of the United Nations in San Francisco in 1945, this represented "a world order in which the mice could be stamped out but in which the lions would not be restrained."[52] In the absence of effective action under the auspices of the Security Council, governments are at liberty to take the self-help measures of a balance-of-power system.[53]

As a result, in practice the term "collective security" has had two prominent useful meanings since World War II.[54] The first meaning is the model of an ideal international order championed most famously, although with some differences, by Immanuel Kant and Woodrow Wilson—a pact against war made by the community of states, an arrangement for effective action against any aggressor from within that community. According to this model, all the states in the system would have formally agreed that if any one of them should become a law-breaker, a disturber of the peace, the others would have a right—and, indeed, an imperative duty—to take action to punish the aggressor and restore the peace.

The second meaning of collective security, predominant in current diplomatic practice, reflects the "lessons learned" from the League of Nations and other experiences. The fundamental collective security aspiration—to build and uphold a sense of solidarity and shared respon-sibility in matters affecting international peace and security—persists. However, action in support of collective security today usually consists of a multilateral intervention, undertaken with the implicit or explicit consensus of the major powers, directed against international aggression or internal conflict or disorder. Such intervention can take many forms, including mediation and conciliation, economic sanctions, preventive or coercive force deployments, peacekeeping and crisis management, and peace enforcement.[55] The parties initiating the action typically jus-tify their intervention—often undertaken at least partly in pursuit of their own security interests—by referring to the will of the international community, humanitarian responsibilities, or international legal princi-ples. Such actions and interventions are based on the argument that all states have an obligation to respect the principles of the UN Charter and other agreements. In recent years, states undertaking such actions and interventions have usually sought political legitimization by refer-ring to a consensus of the major powers—that is, UN Security Council authorization—or, in principle at least, to a broad regional consensus, as with the Organization for Security and Cooperation in Europe (OSCE, the successor to the CSCE).[56]

The first meaning of collective security might be characterized as the traditional "ideal" model, the Kantian or Wilsonian design. The second meaning might be called the "major-power-consensus" model, because it emphasizes the desirability of such consensus for interventions in support of collective security.

In 1955 Ernst Haas drew a similar contrast between "two basic concepts" of collective security: "the notion of 'universal moral obligations' of the League Covenant and the concert of the big powers implicit and explicit in the United Nations Charter."[57] As Haas observed, "The initial operational and ideological concept underlying the United Nations Charter was far less demanding" than that of the League Covenant, in that "collective action could take place only on issues which were not a matter of basic dispute between the permanent members."[58] Haas called for recognizing the limits of politically feasible action in support of collective security: "a theory of collective security . . . should not be based on the assumption of selfless motives," as in the Wilsonian design; instead, it should take account of the continued impact of "balancing" behavior among the "major powers" and other states, pursuing their own interests and operating within and outside international organizations, if it is to explain "the limited success of collective security principles."[59]

Some scholars have taken note of the limited prospects for the Kantian ideals embodied in the Covenant of the League of Nations—and excluded from the UN Charter with respect to the major powers, the permanent members of the Security Council—with a hint of regret. According to Martin Wight, "The British argument to justify the veto, that no enforcement action could be taken against a Great Power without a major war, and that in such circumstances the UN 'will have failed in its purpose and all members will have to act as seems best in the circumstances,' marked a retrogression from the standards of the Covenant, a recognition that the rule of law is unobtainable in international relations."[60]

As Wight pointed out, the British government's analysis in 1945 was anticipated in 1651 by Thomas Hobbes: "Lastly, when in a warre (forraign, or intestine), the enemies get a finall Victory; so as (the forces of the Common-wealth keeping the field no longer) there is no farther protection of Subjects in their loyalty; then is the Common-wealth DISSOLVED, and every man at liberty to protect himselfe by such courses as his own discretion shall suggest unto him."[61] Indeed, it could be argued that Hobbes's conclusion applies not only when the UN Security Council is unable to take an enforcement action against one of its five permanent members, but also when the Council fails to take "the measures necessary to maintain international peace and security."

In these circumstances, Article 51 provides for a state's "inherent right of individual or collective self-defense."

Wight's statement that "the rule of law is unobtainable in international relations" might nonetheless be rephrased. As the Mexican delegate's comment in 1945 suggests, the rule of law in international security affairs is imperfect and contingent, with enforcement generally inapplicable to major powers and in other cases dependent to a great extent on the configuration of relations among the major powers and their willingness to undertake, or at least condone, action against aggressors and others judged to threaten international peace and security. States may therefore appeal to principles of collective security and undertake interventions in support of collective security, but generally not in the comprehensive fashion envisaged by Kant, Wilson, and others in their tradition. Such an all-embracing system of collective security is not at hand.

In practice, actions in support of collective security—that is, interventions intended to advance general international security interests—can be taken only on the basis of a major-power consensus or outside that consensus. The prevailing pattern in the Alliance has been to seek UN Security Council or, in principle, OSCE approval for such interventions. Operations in support of collective security without such an explicit or implicit major-power consensus are nonetheless conceivable, in view of the risk that the legitimizing mechanism ostensibly representative of the international community (the Security Council or the OSCE) could become politically immobilized. Such operations in fact constitute a third type of collective security intervention, though this conception has been less prominent than the Kantian or Wilsonian model of international order or the major-power consensus model. It has probably been less conspicuous than the latter model in the post–World War II experience (despite the tendency during the Cold War for the Security Council to be paralyzed by East-West rivalry) because it implies that the intervening states would be prepared to assume additional political and strategic risks on grounds of necessity and conviction as to the rightness of their cause.

WHY CONCEPTS OF INTERNATIONAL ORDER MATTER FOR NATO

The distinction between concepts of collective defense and collective security is important for NATO because it helps to suggest which objectives may be achievable and which goals are not likely to be realized as the Alliance seeks to promote the emergence of a peaceful international order in the Euro-Atlantic region. Inis Claude has hypothesized that the interest in collective security in Western societies in the post–Cold War period may be analogous to that following the two World Wars of this century: "collective security is the ideology of a coalition that is at or near the point of winning a major war. . . . It may well be that the termination of the cold war will produce a similar peak-and-valley pattern in the graph of support for the notion of collective security. . . . Postwar-like reactions to the end of the cold war . . . include the initial exuberant expectation that this event would usher in an era of universal political and economic freedom and multilateral cooperation." According to Claude, "zeal for accepting the responsibilities of membership in a collective security system is ephemeral, . . . a passing fancy, briefly entertained by victors in coalition wars."[62]

Today, it might be argued, the victorious coalition is the Atlantic Alliance. The Alliance is not attempting to establish a full-fledged collective security system of the Kantian or Wilsonian type, but for several years it has championed ideas from the collective security tradition, particularly as that tradition has evolved since the eighteenth century. These ideas include transparency regarding military capabilities and plans, democratization (including civilian and democratic control of the military), and the proposition that "security is indivisible." The Partnership for Peace is intended to promote deepened security cooperation between the Alliance and each of its twenty-seven PfP Partners. The main operational focus of PfP exercises involves preparations to take action against any unanticipated breaches of the peace in the Euro-Atlantic region (and perhaps beyond) by dispatching crisis management and peacekeeping forces. Many PfP Partners (including Russia), moreover, have participated in IFOR and SFOR in Bosnia. On a number of occasions since the end of the Cold War, the Alliance has evinced a principled rejection of the possibility that, as a collective defense pact, it has any identifiable adversaries; and it has emphasized its new collective security missions, including crisis management and peace operations.

The collective security tradition encompasses many admirable aspirations—above all, the notion of building a comprehensive international consensus on shared responsibilities in maintaining peace and security. However, historical attempts to implement the Kantian and Wilsonian approach—to make reciprocal and comprehensive collective security commitments the principal basis of a system of order among autonomous states—have generally been unsuccessful. As Martin Wight points out, the fourth century B.C. league of the Hellenes, the Greek states, was "entirely ineffective, as every system of collective security has been."[63]

Strictly observed Wilsonian collective security commitments, experts have noted, would imply a theoretical risk of "global war"[64] or "ideological war . . . in defense of peace,"[65] because any local conflict could lead to a general war, particularly if it involved one of the major powers. In practice, however, the most serious shortcoming of such traditional collective security designs has been their naïveté about the willingness of governments to honor abstract commitments to the principle that "security is indivisible." The historical tendency, as during the League of Nations experience, has been for major powers to place little confidence in general pledges to collective security principles.

Instead, governments have relied on their own judgments, on their own military capabilities, and on alliances and understandings with specific major powers. As Inis Claude noted in a celebrated analysis,

> The men who bear the responsibility for conducting the foreign relations of states tend to regard their business as a pragmatic endeavor, requiring careful attention to cases rather than doctrinaire application of a formula. They value skill in sizing up a situation, in differentiating it from other situations, in determining the implications of alternative responses; they seek latitude and freedom of maneuver. . . . [S]tates are not prepared to do, or convinced that they should do, the things that an operative system of collective security would require them to do.[66]

The historical failures of attempts to establish comprehensive collective security arrangements of the Kantian or Wilsonian type offer grounds for caution and prudence with regard to NATO's efforts to promote collective security principles.[67] General commitments to the notion that "security is indivisible" will not be honored unless governments are convinced that doing so would be consistent with their interests. With regard to actual contingencies such as Bosnia, NATO governments have supported only the major-power consensus approach to collective security, despite their many declaratory endorsements of ideas drawn from the Kantian and Wilsonian tradition.

In early 1995, Max Jakobson, a former Finnish ambassador to the United Nations, summed up the importance of national interests in decision-making about collective security as follows:

> The initials of international organizations remain abstractions unless brought to life by the national will of the member states. . . . The reality is that, although politicians pay lip service to the idea of collective action in defense of common values or of the principle of collective security, nations will take up arms only when their own national interests are directly threatened. The Balkan crisis is not perceived to constitute such a threat.[68]

The action taken by NATO later in 1995 under U.S. leadership suggests that the Allies had finally concluded that their core interests were threatened and that action was imperative; the action was taken under UN Security Council auspices because a major-power consensus was available.

However, years of combat and bloodshed in the former Yugoslavia —and of diplomatic acrimony in the Alliance—preceded that decisive intervention in mid-1995. This experience outlines the narrow parameters for collective security in post–Cold War Europe. James Goodby, an American diplomat and scholar, has noted that the collective security aspiration "is not and never may be a condition" of international affairs.[69] Moreover, he says, "Collective action to enforce international norms will never be automatic, but instead will be highly dependent upon specific circumstances."[70] This implies that combined action in support of collective security will be undertaken selectively, and will have to "coexist with national policies aimed at maintaining a power equilibrium."[71]

As Goodby's comments suggest, in the absence of an effectively functioning collective security system of the Kantian or Wilsonian type (an arrangement that apparently has never been achieved in international history), states must depend ultimately on their own strength, usually combined with that of others in alliances for collective defense. The configuration of power relationships among alliances (and among the rare powers able to do without allies) has customarily been known as the balance of power. As has already been suggested, the balance of power may be complemented by the emergence of an explicit or implicit consensus among the major powers on collective security interventions favorable to their interests (an episodic and uncertain prospect), or an intervention by states willing to act in support of collective security outside such a major-power consensus (a potentially even more remote prospect).

The term "balance of power" may lead to confusion in at least three ways. As Wight has noted, the concept is burdened with (a) "the equivocalness and plasticity of the metaphor of 'balance'"; (b) "the overlap between the normative and the descriptive"; and (c) the "necessarily subjective" assessments of those involved in a specific balance of power. Moreover, the term has had several distinct connotations, including "an even distribution of power," "the principle that power ought to be evenly distributed," "any possible distribution of power," and "the principle that our side ought to have a margin of strength in order to avert the danger of power becoming unevenly distributed."[72]

Proponents of Kantian or Wilsonian concepts of collective security (or of an even more ambitious approach to war-prevention, world government) have deplored the intrinsic precariousness of an international order that is dependent, in the last resort, on a balance of power—despite the shared interests of states in commerce and other forms of intercourse, and despite their intermittently acknowledged moral, legal, and political obligations. Balance-of-power arrangements are precarious in that they involve a continual risk of war. Efforts to acquire a margin of security or, if possible, a preponderance of power over prospective opponents have led to arms competitions, which at times have culminated in war.[73] Anxieties about a loss of power and an increase in relative vulnerability may provoke war as well. Wars of fear, arising out of estimates of actual or prospective vulnerability, may well be more common than wars of gain or wars of doctrine in relations between major powers.[74]

For all the intellectual effort invested in analyses of "balance-of-power" politics, surprisingly little consensus has been achieved even on basic questions. For example, what explains the relative peacefulness of Europe (aside from the Crimean War, the wars of German and Italian unification, conflicts in the Balkans, and so forth) during the century from 1815 to 1914? Was the absence of any general war a result of the Concert of Europe, the consensus of an international aristocracy on the principles of a sober "balance-of-power" system? Inis Claude maintains that this "happy century . . . actually demonstrated the peace-preserving effect of the threat of a preponderantly powerful coalition. Britain, the balancer, held in its hands the possibility of turning the scales against an ambitious Continental state."[75]

In contrast, Martin Wight contends that "the pacification of Europe was due less to the working of the Concert than to there being at that time apparently limitless opportunities of independent expansion outside Europe for Britain, Russia and France, while Prussia was busy conquering Germany. When the outward expansion began to come to an end, the great powers were thrown back upon one another in Europe, and the Concert broke down in the crises that led to the First World War."[76]

Kissinger has offered yet a third interpretation: "The century of peace produced by the Congress of Vienna had been buttressed by three pillars, each of which was indispensable: a peace of conciliation with France; a balance of power; and a shared sense of legitimacy." In his view,

> it was not so much the balance of power as Europe's abdication of it that had caused the debacle of World War I. The leaders of pre–World War I Europe had neglected the historic balance of power and abandoned the periodic adjustments which had avoided final showdowns. They had substituted a bipolar world much less flexible than even the Cold War world of the future, in that it lacked the cataclysmic inhibitions of the Nuclear Age. While paying lip service to equilibrium, the leaders of Europe had catered to the most nationalistic elements of their public opinion.[77]

As Kissinger's observations suggest, many of the prerequisites for the "balance of power" managed by the sometimes idealized nineteenth-century Concert of Europe long ago disappeared, in part because of the potent political forces that some observers had expected would make it easier to achieve an effective Kantian or Wilsonian collective security system. Democratization and the rise of public opinion have constrained the freedom of action of governments, and the principle of national self-determination (at least in some cases) has hampered the definition of arrangements based on the de facto subordination of certain nationalities and/or the redrawing of state boundaries. Moreover, the shift during World War II from a European system based on a multiplicity of major powers to one dominated by two superpowers—to say nothing of changes in military technology—made many of the old assumptions obsolete.

The powers of Western Europe nonetheless turned to the most basic instrument of balance-of-power politics—an alliance for collective defense—when they felt threatened in the years immediately following World War II. Their efforts eventually led to the formation of the Atlantic Alliance. While collective defense has always been NATO's core purpose, it has long had other functions. One of the central questions at hand is to what extent NATO may successfully sustain its long-standing functions while also pursuing collective security purposes.

2

NATO during the
Cold War and
Its Aftermath

During the disintegration of the Warsaw Pact and the Soviet Union in 1989–91, prominent Soviet officials expressed confidence that NATO itself would soon fade away as well. Eduard Shevardnadze, then the Soviet foreign minister, declared in September 1990 that "in the future NATO and the Warsaw Treaty Organization will become component parts of all-European security structures and later will probably be dissolved in them."[1] Nikolai Portugalov, a well-known Soviet specialist on German affairs, wrote in October 1990—the month of Germany's reunification—that "it is logical to assume that the U.S. military and, above all, nuclear presence in West Germany will not long survive the withdrawal of our troops from the East."[2]

All the troops of the former Soviet Union were withdrawn from Germany by September 1994. The U.S. military and nuclear presence in Europe has been maintained, however, though in substantially reduced form.[3] Moreover, far from being dissolved into "all-European security structures," NATO has persisted as the central and single most effective multinational security organization in Europe.

The Soviet forecasts of NATO's demise were mistaken, partly because they were based on a false parallelism (equating NATO and the Warsaw Pact) and partly because they overlooked the solidity of NATO's foundations. The equation of NATO with the Warsaw Pact was spurious because the Warsaw Pact was a Soviet-organized body founded on coercion. It was an instrument of control for the Soviet Politburo and allied Communist dictators in the East European satellite states. It functioned as a mechanism to enforce obedience whenever local elites dared to deviate from the Soviet line (as with Czechoslovakia in 1968) and the Soviet leadership deemed the risks of intervention manageable and the dangers of tolerating democratic liberalization unacceptable—hence, the Soviet-enforced policy that became known as the Brezhnev Doctrine.[4] NATO, in contrast, was not established at the behest of a superpower leader, but emerged from a series of voluntary interactions between democratic nations in Europe and North America.

NATO's Collective Defense Origins and Preoccupations during the Cold War

The North Atlantic Treaty, it should be recalled, was not inspired by the United States, but by West European nations, particularly Britain and France. In the aftermath of the Second World War, London and Paris judged that no satisfactory equilibrium and assurance of security could be constructed without U.S. participation in an alliance that would guarantee U.S. involvement in combating aggression. After making a bilateral mutual defense pact (the Treaty of Dunkirk in 1947),[5] Britain and France in 1948 organized the Brussels Pact, which included Belgium, Luxembourg, and the Netherlands as well. This was seen as inadequate, however, in light of Soviet behavior. The Brussels Pact nations initiated talks with the United States and Canada about possible defense cooperation in July 1948, shortly after Stalin initiated a blockade of the British, French, and U.S. sectors of Berlin. Formal negotiations about the North Atlantic Treaty began in December 1948, and the treaty was signed on April 4, 1949, while the Soviet blockade of Berlin was still under way.[6]

The greatest difficulty in negotiating the North Atlantic Treaty was finding a formula that would satisfy the Europeans, who wanted a U.S. commitment that would be sufficient to deter the USSR, but that would not prevent the United States from deliberating before war. As President Truman noted in his memoirs, "The Brussels Pact nations wanted the North Atlantic pact to state that, if a member was attacked, the other members would supply all the military and other aid and assistance in their power. This, of course, implied going to war. . . . [T]his was an obligation which, in view of our Constitution, we were not prepared to assume."[7]

Thanks in part to Article 11 of the treaty, which stipulates that the treaty's provisions will be carried out in accordance with the "respective constitutional processes" of the signatories, the final formula adopted in Article 5 contains a strong commitment:

> The Parties agree that an armed attack against one or more of them in Europe or North America shall be considered an attack against them all and consequently they agree that, if such an armed attack occurs, each of them, in exercise of the right of individual or collective self-defense recognized by Article 51 of the Charter of the United Nations, will assist the Party or Parties so attacked by taking forthwith, individually and in concert with the other Parties, such action as it deems necessary, including the use of armed force, to restore and maintain the security of the North Atlantic area.

This was a revolutionary commitment by the United States, in view of its political traditions of isolationism and avoiding "entangling alliances" in peacetime.[8] At this point, however, the North Atlantic Treaty was seen as little more than a mutual defense commitment that would deter Soviet aggression and reassure Western Europe during its economic recovery. It was assumed that the West Europeans would rebuild their defense capabilities and that, after some years, they would bear the major military burdens in balancing Soviet power in Europe. To this end, the United States encouraged the countries of Western Europe to replace rivalry with cooperation and to initiate a process of political and economic integration. In a 1949 Senate hearing, Secretary of State Dean Acheson was asked, "[A]re we going to be expected to send substantial numbers of troops over there as a more or less permanent contribution to these countries' capacity to resist?" Acheson replied: "The answer to that question, Senator, is a clear and absolute 'No.'"[9]

It took the North Korean invasion of South Korea in June 1950 to "put the 'O' in NATO"—that is, to persuade the Allies to organize an integrated military command structure in peacetime and to establish the presumption of a large, long-term U.S. military presence in Europe. Many experts and officials in North America and Western Europe feared that the North Korean invasion was a Soviet stratagem. Pyongyang's attack was interpreted as evidence that the Communists (then seen as a unified monolithic bloc, including the USSR, China, North Korea, and others) were prepared to resort to armed aggression; and some hypothesized that the attack against South Korea was perhaps but a prelude or a distracting feint before a Communist attack against Western Europe. The United States and its new allies responded. In December 1950, General Dwight Eisenhower, who had served as the Supreme Commander of Allied Expeditionary Forces in Europe in 1944–45, was appointed the first Supreme Allied Commander, Europe (SACEUR). In April 1951 Allied Command Europe (ACE) became operational, with the Supreme Headquarters Allied Powers Europe (SHAPE) at Roquencourt, near Paris.[10]

The United States still hoped that the magnitude of its defense burdens in Europe could be minimized through greater West European efforts. The Federal Republic of Germany (West Germany) had been founded in 1949, but was still under an occupation regime, with no armed forces of its own, with legal responsibility to the three Western powers—Britain, France, and the United States—and with the Soviet Union continuing to assume its rights and responsibilities regarding the ultimate disposition of the German question. In September 1950 the United States proposed that West German armed forces be established, and the French promptly advanced a counterproposal for a European Defense Community (EDC).

While the French saw the strategic rationale for West German forces, given the risk of Soviet aggression in Europe, Paris nonetheless sought firm constraints on them. Defense Minister Jules Moch said that France could never "accept the creation of German divisions." German soldiers, the French suggested, should be organized in "battalion units of about 1,000 men" that would be distributed throughout the proposed European army.[11] During a harsh debate from 1950 to 1954, French proponents of the EDC presented it as the only alternative to a new Wehrmacht. EDC opponents in France argued that it would reconstitute German armed forces while subordinating the French military to a supranational European organization. U.S. and West German support for the EDC made it appear suspect in the view of many of the French as well.

When the EDC's opponents effectively defeated the project in the French National Assembly in August 1954,[12] another framework for the establishment of West German armed forces was devised. At Britain's suggestion, the 1948 Brussels Treaty furnished the basis for the London and Paris agreements of 1954. Italy and West Germany were admitted to the Western European Union (WEU), together with the original Brussels Treaty signatories—France, Britain, and the Benelux countries. West Germany renounced the production of nuclear, chemical, and biological weapons on its territory, and accepted numerous restrictions on its conventional armaments—all within the WEU framework. Britain, Canada, and the United States promised to maintain ground and air forces in Germany, subject to certain conditions. With these assurances and others, France at last agreed to the Federal Republic's entry into NATO and the establishment of West German armed forces in 1955. West Germany became the Alliance's first new member since Greece and Turkey joined in 1952.

Ostensibly as a response to these events, the Soviet Union established the Warsaw Pact in 1955, within days of West Germany's admission to NATO and the establishment of the West German armed forces. At the end of 1955, Moscow signed a treaty with the Soviet-established Communist regime in East Berlin, granting the German Democratic Republic (East Germany) some of the prerogatives of statehood, although it remained under firm Soviet control. Indeed, throughout the Cold War, the Soviet Union maintained its most potent concentration of foreign-based troops in East Germany.

In retrospect, the period from the mid-1950s to the breakdown of the Soviet empire in 1989–91 appears to have been one of political and strategic stalemate, with little change in formal political-military alignments.[13] Europe, Germany, and Berlin remained divided, and Communist rule in the Warsaw Pact was sustained, for the most part, through Soviet military power and internal security organs. Yugoslavia maintained a unique status throughout this period. Ruled by a Communist party, yet not a member of the Warsaw Pact, Yugoslavia enjoyed privileged relations with the West. Partly because of its geographic isolation, Albania succeeded in leaving the Warsaw Pact in 1968. Romania, like Albania, declined to participate in the Soviet-led suppression of democratic tendencies in Czechoslovakia by other Warsaw Pact states in 1968. Romania was reluctant to participate in the Warsaw Pact's integrative schemes and managed to achieve an exceptional degree of foreign policy autonomy, in part because it had persuaded Soviet leader Nikita Khrushchev to withdraw Soviet forces from its territory in the late 1950s.[14]

On the Western side, as part of its post-Franco "return to Europe," Spain joined NATO in 1982. Spain and Portugal were invited to accede to the WEU in 1988, and they did so in 1990; but this had little strategic significance, because the WEU at that time still adhered rigorously to the article of the Brussels Treaty (as amended in 1954) calling for the WEU members to "work in close co-operation with" the Alliance and to "rely on the appropriate military authorities of NATO for information and advice on military matters."[15]

Despite intermittent phases of détente, in which East-West tensions relaxed, the Soviet Union was a remarkably reliable stimulus for political cohesion in NATO. Soviet interventions—for instance, in East Germany in 1953, in Hungary in 1956, in Czechoslovakia in 1968, and in Afghanistan in 1979—and Soviet-provoked crises (such as the Berlin and Cuban episodes) tended to reinforce consensus in NATO on the necessity for collective defense precautions. Soviet triumphs in military technology (the world's first intercontinental ballistic missiles, for example) and periodic Soviet declarations, reaffirming profound ideological hostility, bolstered Western resolve.[16]

Although later Soviet leaders, such as Mikhail Gorbachev, spoke in more oblique terms about "the outcome of the historical competition between the two systems" (in Soviet parlance, "socialism" versus capitalist "imperialism"),[17] the essential message was the one memorably articulated by Nikita Khrushchev: "Whether you like it or not, history is on our side. We will bury you."[18] Khrushchev's declaration did not necessarily imply victory in combat: "Though the sentiment was hostile enough, the idiomatic Russian actually conveyed the notion of outlasting one's opponent, of being present at the interment of a rival."[19] According to the Marxist-Leninist ideology professed by the Soviets, their triumph was historically inevitable.[20]

NATO's collective defense preoccupations during the Cold War focused on how to deter the Soviet Union from undertaking aggression or coercion.[21] Because the protection afforded to NATO Europe by U.S. strategic nuclear commitments was seen as a decisively important element of deterrence from the earliest days of the Alliance, a primary issue throughout the Cold War was the credibility of what came to be known as U.S. "extended deterrence"—that is, the prevention of aggression or coercion against U.S. allies or security partners through threats of U.S. nuclear retaliation. Extended deterrence involves issues of credibility, command and control, and decision making that have been intrinsically more contentious and more difficult to resolve than those associated with "central deterrence"—the prevention of aggression or coercion against the United States itself. Associated issues during the Cold War concerned Allied involvement in U.S. decision making on the potential operational use of nuclear weapons, the types and roles of U.S. nuclear forces in Europe, and the utility and functions of the British and French independent nuclear forces.[22] Nuclear controversies were closely tied to European-American debates about the proper level of investment in conventional forces and burden sharing, about how to assess the NATO–Warsaw Pact conventional force balance, and about what approaches to arms control to pursue in negotiations with the Soviet Union and the Warsaw Pact as a whole.[23]

In a concerted dialogue spanning decades, the NATO Allies concluded that U.S. extended deterrence requires, among other things, U.S. nuclear forces based in Europe. A substantial consensus of officials and experts on both sides of the Atlantic holds that U.S. nuclear commitments would be less credible if they depended solely on forces at sea and in North America. Nonetheless, large-scale reductions in U.S. nuclear forces in Europe began in the late 1970s, and received a further impetus from the 1987 Intermediate-range Nuclear Forces (INF) Treaty eliminating U.S. and Soviet land-based missiles with ranges between 500 and 5,500 kilometers. U.S. and NATO decisions in September–October 1991 eliminated all U.S. ground-launched nuclear systems (including artillery, surface-to-air missiles, and surface-to-surface missiles). The only U.S. nuclear weapons remaining in Europe are a reduced number of gravity bombs for U.S. and Allied dual-capable aircraft; unconfirmed published reports put their number between 480 and approximately 700.[24]

In other words, these cutbacks spared some of the most politically visible elements of the U.S. nuclear posture then remaining in Europe—the gravity bombs for dual-capable aircraft, which give several of the Allies a direct role in nuclear risk- and responsibility-sharing. According to an unclassified NATO report in 1988, seven allies (Belgium, Germany, Greece, Italy, the Netherlands, Turkey, and the United Kingdom) have provided delivery systems and "host-nation facilities" for U.S. nuclear-capable forces.[25]

While the 1991 decisions mean that only nuclear gravity bombs associated with dual-capable aircraft remain, the central importance of their continuing presence in Europe was reaffirmed in the Alliance's 1991 Strategic Concept:

> A credible Alliance nuclear posture and the demonstration of Alliance solidarity and common commitment to war prevention continue to require widespread participation by European Allies involved in collective defence planning in nuclear roles, in peacetime basing of nuclear forces on their territory and in command, control and consultation arrangements. Nuclear forces based in Europe and committed to NATO provide an essential political and military link between the European and the North American members of the Alliance. . . . These forces need to have the necessary characteristics and appropriate flexibility and survivability, to be perceived as a credible and effective element of the Allies' strategy in preventing war. They will be maintained at the minimum level sufficient to preserve peace and stability.[26]

The document notes, moreover, that the "supreme guarantee of the security of the Allies is provided by the strategic nuclear forces of the Alliance, particularly those of the United States," and that "adequate sub-strategic forces based in Europe . . . will provide an essential link with strategic nuclear forces, reinforcing the trans-Atlantic link."[27]

Since the founding of the Nuclear Planning Group (NPG) in 1966–67, the Allies (except for France) have been able to resolve many of the consultation and decision-making issues that were so contentious during the 1950s and early 1960s. The Atlantic Alliance's nuclear arrangements include multinational risk- and responsibility-sharing and multinational decision making and policy implementation. These arrangements have promoted Alliance cohesion, increased the influence of the nonnuclear European Allies regarding U.S. nuclear policy, and reassured the Allies as to the genuineness and probable deterrent effectiveness of U.S. nuclear commitments.

While the United States is the ultimate nuclear guarantor of NATO European security, Britain and France contribute to the Alliance's overall deterrent posture.[28] Although the French have never participated in NATO's Nuclear Planning Group, France has provided an additional independent locus of nuclear decision making, which has complicated the risk calculations of any nation contemplating aggression or coercion against the Alliance. Since the early 1960s, France has insisted on the distinctness and autonomy of the French approach to nuclear strategy in relation to U.S. and NPG concepts. While France participated in the Alliance's 1990–91 Strategic Concept review and approved the 1991 document, the French are excluded from two of the key paragraphs referring to nuclear deterrence.[29] The British have committed their nuclear forces to NATO planning since 1962, though they have of course retained national command at all times. Moreover, London has reserved the possibility of national use independent of coordinated action in defense of the Alliance in cases involving "supreme national interests."[30] None of the Alliance arrangements changes the fact that any actual nuclear use decisions would depend on national choices, and would therefore ultimately reside with the U.S. president, the British prime minister, and the French president.[31]

ALLIANCE POLICIES FOR PEACEFUL CHANGE DURING THE COLD WAR

Well before the conclusion of the North Atlantic Treaty in 1949, Western leaders were dismayed not only by the scope of the Soviet Union's territorial acquisitions during World War II (the Baltic states, as well as portions of Finland, Poland, Germany, Romania, and Czechoslovakia) but also by the brutal and dictatorial policies the USSR pursued in the countries it had liberated from fascist rule. Many in the West agreed with what Winston Churchill said in his 1946 "Iron Curtain" speech: "This is certainly not the liberated Europe we fought to build up. Nor is it one which contains the essentials of permanent peace."[32]

From the outset, therefore, the Alliance defined its purposes as involving more than simply collective defense against external aggression. The Allies repeatedly declared their interest in pursuing positive political changes in Europe while avoiding war: "to live in peace with all governments and all peoples" (1949), "to seek solutions by peaceful means" (1953), and to promote "peaceful change" (1957).[33] In the 1967

Harmel Report, the two main purposes of the Atlantic Alliance were recalled in a classic formulation. The first purpose was (and remains) to maintain sufficient military strength to deter aggression and attempts at coercion, to defend the Allies in the event of aggression, and "to assure the balance of forces, thereby creating a climate of stability, security, and confidence." Fulfillment of the first purpose would create a basis for the second: "to pursue the search for progress towards a more stable relationship in which the underlying political issues can be solved."[34]

Such goals were professed from the 1950s through the 1980s. However, during the late 1950s and early 1960s, Western attitudes slowly changed with respect to two key issues: the relative importance of pursuing arms control and changes in political order in Europe, and the likely processes of change in the East. The Alliance initially held that a settlement of the German question on Western terms ("reunification of Germany through free elections,"[35] according to a 1955 communiqué) would have to precede the negotiation of arms limitations, and that the Soviets would in any case have to honor their promises at the 1945 Yalta conference for free elections in Eastern Europe before a fundamental improvement in East-West relations could take place. For several years after Stalin's death in 1953 (despite the brutal suppression of the Hungarian uprising in 1956), there was a certain sensation of fluidity, in the West at least, regarding European political order and hope that Western policies of "negotiating from strength" might somehow bring about a palpable relaxation in Soviet control over Eastern Europe and even German reunification.

Starting in the late 1950s and especially after the construction of the Berlin Wall in 1961 and the Cuban missile crisis in 1962, issues of political order in Europe began to be clearly subordinated to arms control and the pursuit of East-West détente. The Atlantic Alliance devoted increasingly less attention to issues of political order and legitimacy in the Eastern countries. While NATO communiqués in the 1950s referred to "the totalitarian menace"[36] and asserted that the peoples of Eastern Europe "have the right to choose their own governments freely, unaffected by external pressure and the use or threat of force,"[37] by 1966 the Alliance was calling for "removing barriers to freer and more friendly reciprocal exchanges between countries of different social and economic systems."[38] In the 1950s, the division of Germany was regarded as a "continuing threat to world peace."[39] During the 1960s, however, the goal of eventual German reunification was gradually transformed into simply "an essential factor for a just and lasting peaceful order in Europe,"[40] and the Alliance in 1969 applauded West Germany's proposals for a "modus vivendi between the two parts of Germany."[41]

These changes in priorities and assumptions were linked to the adoption of new views about the likely processes of change in the East. The Alliance eventually adopted the view that détente, which became shorthand for policies intended to reduce East-West tensions, could only succeed in reassuring the Soviet leadership about the Alliance's peaceful intentions and bringing about a freer circulation of people and ideas (and movement toward democratization in Eastern Europe) if many years were invested in promoting greater East-West understanding. The sensation of the 1950s as to a certain fluidity gave way to a conviction during the 1960s that change could be brought about only on the basis of a stabilization and acceptance of the existing order, which might then be transformed through a long-term process. Internal changes in the Soviet Union and East European societies, it was hoped, would lead to a gradual East-West rapprochement, thus eventually ending the military confrontation.[42]

An important element in the Cold War's East-West political competition was the CSCE, which originated in a series of proposals and counter-proposals made by NATO and the Soviet Union during the 1950s and 1960s for an all-European security conference. These proposals finally led to a conference of thirty-five participants—all the countries of Europe (except Albania), plus Canada and the United States—that took place in Helsinki during 1973–75.[43]

The concluding document of the conference, called the Final Act, was not a legally binding treaty but a political declaration covering three areas, known as "baskets." Basket I consists of a Declaration on Principles Guiding Relations between Participating States (for instance, refraining from the threat or use of force and respecting the inviolability of frontiers and the territorial integrity of states), and also confidence-building measures (for instance, prior notification of major military maneuvers). Basket II concerns cooperation in economics, science and technology, and the environment. Basket III covers cooperation in humanitarian domains, such as human rights, freedom of information, culture, and education. The CSCE process involved a series of meetings, including review conferences to discuss the implementation of the political commitments made in the 1975 Helsinki Final Act. These review conferences, in turn, commissioned specialized subconferences and meetings, such as the Stockholm conference on confidence-building measures in 1984–86.

The Helsinki Final Act commitments and the CSCE process became significant instruments in Cold War political competition for both the Soviet Union and the Atlantic Alliance. Some Western governments and political activists sought to use the Basket III commitments made by the Soviet-bloc states to call attention to the denial of human rights in these states and to demand the liberalization and movement toward democratization foreshadowed in the Basket III principles. Basket III was a yardstick and prism for assessing acts of repression by Moscow and other Warsaw Pact capitals, statements by persecuted dissidents, and struggles by workers' movements such as Solidarity in Poland.

U.S. diplomacy during the negotiation of the CSCE's 1975 Helsinki Final Act was under the direction of Henry Kissinger. Paradoxically, even though "Kissinger evidently found human rights issues largely irrelevant to superpower politics," he played an important role in insisting that the human rights provisions of the Helsinki Final Act have substantive content, in part because of what was then perceived as an increasing U.S. domestic "political need to be seen dealing toughly with the USSR."[44]

Many Americans (and many Europeans) saw the CSCE human rights pledges not only as well founded in terms of universal moral principles but also as potentially useful instruments in the political struggle with Soviet Communism. Helsinki Final Act principles such as freedom of thought and the freer and wider dissemination of information underscored the illegitimacy of one-party dictatorships in comparison with pluralistic democracies. These principles probably played a much greater role in weakening the Communist regimes of the Warsaw Pact than Kissinger and other Western officials who helped to negotiate the Helsinki Final Act had expected.[45]

For the Soviet Union, Basket I was the decisively important part of the Helsinki Final Act. The USSR claimed that it represented Western ratification of the legitimacy and permanence of the existing European order, including a certain recognition for its territorial acquisitions in

1939–45, its military presence and hegemonic position in Eastern Europe, and its "two-state" view of the German question.[46] In short, the Soviets considered the Helsinki Final Act a "super-Yalta" rather than the "anti-Yalta" accord hailed by many of its proponents in the West.[47]

Although the Soviets portrayed the Helsinki Final Act and related agreements as a recognition of the "irreversibility" of Soviet dominion in Eastern Europe, the governments of the Atlantic Alliance rejected such an interpretation. The United States, in particular, continued to refuse to recognize the Soviet incorporation of the Baltic states. Britain, France, and the United States retained their Four Power reservations regarding the ultimate disposition of the German question. West Germany repeatedly noted that the "peaceful change" of existing frontiers was not ruled out by any of its various *Ostpolitik* treaties with Warsaw Pact states or by the Helsinki Final Act, and that German reunification and national self-determination were still legally feasible.[48]

It should be acknowledged, however, that despite their declared interest in democratization in the Warsaw Pact states and a process of reconciliation ending the East-West strategic stalemate, many Westerners were reasonably satisfied with the European political order during the Cold War. Some expressed concern that an inadvertent "destabilization" of East European societies through political liberalization could result in war or, at the least, setbacks for détente as a gradual and ultimately effective process. Some even appeared willing to support repression for the sake of stability if it appeared that liberalization trends might escape control.[49] West German chancellor Helmut Schmidt said in December 1981, with respect to the imposition of martial law in Poland, "[East German leader] Honecker is as dismayed as I am, that this was necessary."[50] Some West European officials even ventured to say that the Alliance's declared political goal of ultimate German reunification should be abandoned. In September 1984, Italian foreign minister Giulio Andreotti provoked formal West German protests with the following comments: "Everybody agrees that the two Germanys should have good relations. It should be clear, however, that pan-Germanism is something that must be overcome. There are two German states and two German states must remain."[51]

Western governments also disagree_ frequently during the Cold War about how to relate the two Alliance f__ctions indicated in the Harmel

Report. For example, when would economic transactions (including technology transfers) promote favorable political change in the Warsaw Pact, and when would they serve to strengthen Soviet military power and make it harder and more costly for the West to maintain an adequate military posture? Agreements on broad principles often broke down with respect to specific cases. The U.S. approach often conflicted with the general West European view (upheld by West Germany in particular) that economic sanctions could not accomplish anything of value, and that East-West trade must be encouraged and expanded because of its political significance. Such disagreements led to difficulties in coordinating Alliance policies for change in the East.

In retrospect, it appears that the assumptions behind the Alliance's policies for peaceful change in the European political order were flawed. The vision of the gradual liberalization and democratization of the East assumed that the Soviet Union would moderate its control structure and that allied Communist regimes would accept evolutionary movement toward civil rights, pluralism, and democracy when East-West tensions had subsided and the Warsaw Pact nations had been reassured about the peaceful and nonthreatening intentions of the Atlantic Alliance. These assumptions threatened the monopoly of power maintained by the Communist regimes, however.

The Soviet bloc's Communist regimes were not established with the consent of the governed as the principle of legitimacy, but on the basis of a party elite's interpretation of an ideology of historical determinism. Although some party members were presumably faithful believers in Marxism-Leninism, the ideology was generally a tool to justify rule by what Milovan Djilas called "the new class" and to conceal its determination to hold power.[52] In a pattern that prevailed over decades, whenever popular pressures for change reached unacceptable thresholds and seemed likely to endanger a Communist regime's rule, repression to maintain power would follow. If the regime was unable to handle the pressures, allied regimes in the Warsaw Pact would offer fraternal assistance under Soviet leadership to maintain the gains of "socialism." Definite limits to Western-style liberalization appeared to apply to the Soviet Union in particular, because of its power structure and the interrelationship between its economic, military, and internal nationality problems.

The extent to which Western policies favoring gradual liberalization in the East European countries contributed to the disintegration of the Soviet empire remains unclear, and Allies differ in their general interpretations. German scholar Peter Rudolf has observed that, "In the United States, the end of the Cold War is widely perceived to be a success of containment and a hard line approach. In the prevailing view in Germany, the end of the conflict was rather a result of détente and *Ostpolitik*."[53]

In fact, the Communist regimes in Eastern Europe were not gradually liberalized so much as they were overthrown when it became evident that the Soviet Union would no longer uphold them with force. This probably would have been an infeasible proposition in any case, given that several of these regimes were disintegrating in such close succession. In some cases, leaders of the anti-communist opposition (such as Lech Walesa in Poland and Vaclav Havel in Czechoslovakia) rose to power through popular acclaim, while in other cases (such as Bulgaria and Romania) the transition to a more democratic political system has been more difficult.[54]

Such a nonviolent end to the Soviet empire—and the East-West competition—was by no means a foregone conclusion during the Cold War. In 1982, Henry Kissinger said, "The major long-term question is whether the Soviets can hold their own bloc together while waiting for the West to succumb to a long period of relaxation. Certainly our chances are as good as Brezhnev's, given the history of dissent in Eastern Europe."[55]

At that point, the East-West struggle had already lasted much longer than some architects of Western policy had thought would be necessary. The West had adopted George Kennan's 1947 recommendation of "a long-term, patient but firm and vigilant containment of Russian expansive tendencies." The outcome that Kennan had forecast came to pass, but it took decades longer than the "ten to fifteen years" he expected:

> Let us . . . suppose that the western world finds the strength and resourcefulness to contain Soviet power over a period of ten to fifteen years. What does that spell for Russia itself? . . . [T]he possibility remains (and in the opinion of this writer it is a strong one) that Soviet power, like the capitalist world of its conception, bears within it the seeds of its own decay. . . . But the United States has it in its power to increase enormously the strains under which Soviet policy must operate,

to force upon the Kremlin a far greater degree of moderation and circumspection than it has had to observe in recent years, and in this way to promote tendencies which must eventually find their outlet in either the break-up or the gradual mellowing of Soviet power.[56]

In 1983 Pierre Hassner, one of France's most distinguished scholars of international relations, wrote that "the two alliances are engaged in a process of competitive decadence. . . . [W]hile the Eastern bloc is more irreversibly sick, recent trends give the Western alliance a good boost in the race toward decay. As a comparative decayologist, however, I cannot but remember Gibbon's remark on the decline of the Roman Empire: 'This intolerable situation lasted for about three hundred years.'"[57] In the final years of the Soviet empire some Western analysts presciently identified centrifugal factors and grave sources of weakness before the USSR's impending collapse became unmistakable—for example, Zbigniew Brzezinski, Vladimir Bukovsky, Jacob Kipp, Martin Malia, Henry Rowen, and Charles Wolf, Jr.[58] No one, however, could forecast the exact moment and form of the Soviet empire's collapse.[59] Even Vladimir Bukovsky, who offered an incisive analysis of the Soviet regime's problems, suggested in 1988 that, if the Communist Party "ideologists" had their way, the "ultimate catastrophe" might come "perhaps fifteen to twenty years from now."[60]

The breakdown of the Soviet power structure—clearly the decisive element in ending the Cold War—evidently involved many factors internal to the Soviet Union: economic mismanagement and exhaustion (including disproportionate investments in military power and a neglect of public health and the environment), the rigidity of the Communist Party's "democratic centralism," the atrophy of ideological legitimacy,[61] and the rise of ethno-nationalism among the non-Russian peoples of the USSR—and even among the Russians themselves, some of whom argued that Russia itself had been victimized by Soviet Communism.

Experts have identified various critical junctures in the debacle. Myron Rush has argued that the moment was March 1985, when Mikhail Gorbachev came to power—"an aberrant figure whose course toward revolution . . . was not forced on him by an aroused society or compelling circumstances; it stemmed from his highly individual perceptions and experimental bent, his openness to the ideas of intellectuals (including close advisors like Alexander Yakovlev), and the erosion of his commitment to Marxist-Leninist ideology and the Stalinist institutions to which it had given rise." Rush sees Gorbachev as "the responsible agent," because he "brought about the abatement of fear," which had been the foundation of the Soviet regime, by allowing greater freedom of expression, and because he "caused the decisive weakening of the Party apparatus, to a point where it lost its capacity to manage the economy or defend the regime." Despite the USSR's stagnant economy and the "widespread disbelief" in the official ideology, Rush maintains, the key factor was the course pursued by Gorbachev; and "Gorbachev's coming to power was due to the working of chance contrary to the design of the succession process (which aimed to exclude 'deviationists')."[62]

Similarly, Adam Ulam concluded that "the Soviet/Communist collapse was brought about by Gorbachev's policies grounded in the conviction that he would liberalize the regime and yet preserve the dominant role of the Communist Party and the territorial integrity of the Soviet state."[63] In Ulam's view, "Had somebody other than Gorbachev been elected as the chief Communist boss in 1985, it is quite possible we would still be dealing with the Soviet Union as a superpower."[64]

According to Charles Fairbanks, "The most decisive step of all was taken in February 1990, when the CC [Central Committee] voted for Gorbachev's proposal to end its monopoly of power, agreeing in principle to a multi-party system, and to end its opposition to private property, thus abolishing the core of Leninism and the core of Marxism in one three-day meeting." From this perspective, "It is impossible to understand the collapse of Soviet communism without appreciating the role of ideas and convictions in history."[65] Although the inherent weakness of Marxist-Leninist ideology had been apparent for many years, Gorbachev's glasnost quickly exposed the Soviet regime as guilty of an immense series of crimes and blunders, and deprived it of public legitimacy.[66]

Peter Reddaway has argued that "January 1991 was . . . the decisive moment, one which showed that the USSR could no longer be held together," because Gorbachev then recognized the dangers in taking further military action to suppress self-determination in the Baltic states: "His own deeply cherished international reputation as a humane man of peace would have been destroyed, non-Baltic republics like Georgia would have seceded in protest, there would not have been enough mobilizable troops to prevent them from seceding, and even holding down a seething Baltic for the indefinite future would have been problematic."[67]

Roman Laba has described the significance of ethno-nationalist factors differently—as elements in the power struggle between Gorbachev and Yeltsin that backfired, because the Soviet elites made the mistake of believing the USSR's decades of "all-Union" propaganda and thus failed to understand the potency of aspirations to national self-determination. Because of erroneous assumptions about the cohesion of the Soviet Union, "misperceptions and miscalculations forged from Russian and Soviet imperial identity," Yeltsin and his allies intended in 1990–91 to use ethno-national appeals, notably in Ukraine and Russia, "as a way station on their road to central power in the Soviet Union. Just when they thought they had achieved central power in the Kremlin, they found instead that they had destroyed the USSR—an unexpected consequence of their actions."[68]

To be sure, another significant factor was economic. According to Anders Aslund, "Gorbachev was counseled by the best and brightest of Soviet economists, but one problem was that the communist regime had forbidden them to learn economics." The result of Gorbachev's policies—the destruction of the centrally planned command economy—was "wholly unintentional," Aslund notes, and contributed in a "truly disastrous" fashion to the USSR's downfall.[69]

To what extent did the competition with the West and with the United States in particular exacerbate Soviet economic problems? In Aslund's view, U.S. president Ronald Reagan's speeches in 1982–83 on the imminent collapse of the Soviet system were "truly prophetic." Aslund concludes that "The Soviet Union was entering its death throes, and the way both to control and speed up the process was not by compromise but through firmness and an increased show of strength. The Strategic Defense Initiative became a key challenge to the USSR, and the Soviet leaders quickly realized their impotence in the face of it."[70]

In Vladimir Kontorovich's view, "The main feature of the 1986–90 Five-Year Plan was a massive shift of investment to the high-technology sectors which in the Soviet economy were administratively subordinated to and provided the needs of the military. The objective was to preserve the country's hard-won 'strategic parity' in the face of Reagan's rearmament, renewed assertiveness (exemplified by placing intermediate-range missiles in Europe), and commitment to a technological revolution in military hardware (symbolized by SDI and smart munitions)."[71] Soviet military analysts were concerned, Jacob Kipp has pointed out, by "U.S. efforts to shift the military competition" into areas of U.S. qualitative superiority.[72] Soviet military authorities took note of the U.S. Department of Defense's interest in "competitive strategies" intended to capitalize on U.S. technological advantages and to oblige the Soviets to divert resources into costly military investments.[73]

According to some accounts, U.S. efforts to aggravate Soviet economic problems also included campaigns "to reduce dramatically Soviet hard currency earnings by driving down the price of oil with Saudi cooperation and limiting [Soviet] natural gas exports to the West" and "to reduce drastically Soviet access to Western high technology."[74] The U.S. defense buildup and program of economic sanctions against the USSR began with President Jimmy Carter's reaction to the Soviet invasion of Afghanistan in December 1979. The ensuing arms competition with the United States probably contributed to the strains on the Soviet economy that convinced Gorbachev that he would have to consider experimenting with political and economic reforms—with ruinous results for the Soviet control structure. As Ernest Gellner succinctly observed, "the Cold War was the first very major historic conflict to be decided entirely by economic means."[75]

Noneconomic factors were also involved in the Soviet collapse, however. For example, as suggested earlier, the human rights provisions in the Helsinki Final Act of the CSCE probably encouraged and facilitated the rise of unofficial social and political movements in Eastern Europe, such as Solidarity in Poland. These movements received support from Pope John Paul II, President Reagan, and various sympathizers in NATO Europe. Moreover, the United States, Pakistan, and various other countries provided assistance to the Afghans who resisted the Soviet occupation and ultimately overturned the Brezhnev Doctrine.

The dynamic interaction between the external and internal factors in the Soviet collapse must be recognized, though it is difficult to investigate the interrelationships. The factors are not entirely separable, and the causal links are not always readily identifiable, much less provable. Nor is it possible to assess the relative importance of the central elements in the collapse conclusively. In Adam Ulam's view, "The key to the drama of the late 1980s and early 1990s is to be seen in historical and psychological factors and not in the economy or the Soviet budget. Policies such as Star Wars [the U.S. Strategic Defense Initiative] did contribute to the final result, but they were far from being decisive in bringing about the last act of the drama."[76]

From this perspective, Western policies—whether aimed at encouraging democratization and pluralism, or designed to force the USSR into an unaffordable arms competition that would surely weaken it— may well have contributed to the USSR's collapse, but only in a secondary fashion. In contrast, Peter Schweizer has argued, "Had the Kremlin not faced the cumulative effects of SDI and the defense buildup, geopolitical setbacks in Poland and Afghanistan, the loss of tens of billions of dollars in hard currency earnings from energy exports, and reduced access to technology, it is reasonable to believe that it could have weathered the storm. . . . American policies could and did alter the course of Soviet history."[77]

It is difficult for contemporary observers to assess these events in a truly disinterested fashion. Some people have partisan, ideological, or professional backgrounds that may dispose them to favor specific interpretations. For instance, some former Central Intelligence Agency officials believe, on the basis of the Soviet military setbacks they observed and the significant societal effects of these losses in the USSR, that their operations in Afghanistan "helped bring about the collapse of the Soviet Union."[78] In the United States, discussions about which Soviet vulnerabilities were decisive and about the extent to which U.S. and Alliance policies contributed to the Soviet debacle often assume a partisan and contentious tone.[79] However, as John Van Oudenaren pointed out in 1991, neither the left nor the right in Western societies has an unblemished record in its Cold War diplomacy:

> The left has been quick to argue that recent events show that the Soviet military threat was always exaggerated and that the West might have been more forthcoming in arms control talks and less fearful of technology leakage. But the left clearly was wrong in arguing over the years that military competition with the USSR was futile since the Soviet people would bear any sacrifice to maintain their security, or that trying to deny the Soviet Union vital technologies was pointless,

since doing so would only encourage redoubled efforts towards self-sufficiency. External pressure on the Soviet system did contribute to change and a rethinking of the very concept of security. Indeed, it could be argued that greater pressure—and less détente—might have cracked the system earlier.

For its part, the right has been quick to criticize the left for its embarrassing intimacy with the now discredited Communist regimes and parties and for its tacit collaboration in the Communist strategy of politicizing all forms of cooperation on behalf of peace. But much of this criticism is unjustified, if only because the right itself has little to be proud of in this area. Historically, conservative governments and parties played as much if not more of a role than their Socialist and Social Democratic rivals in building up the broad network of cooperation with Communist governments and nongovernmental organizations, often with little regard for actual or potential sources of anti-Communist opposition.[80]

Some factors that helped bring down the Soviet system—including economic disorders and ethno-nationalism—remain challenges for the Alliance as it promotes the construction of cooperative security structures in the Euro-Atlantic region. Before NATO could take on this objective, however, it had to endure a phase in 1990–91 in which the rationale for its continued existence was questioned.

HOW AND WHY THE ALLIANCE SURVIVED THE END OF THE COLD WAR

During the first year after the fall of Communist regimes in Eastern Europe in late 1989, a noteworthy flirtation with collective security in the Kantian and Wilsonian tradition took place in Europe. Soviet leaders were the most prominent champions of the idea of dissolving NATO and the obviously moribund Warsaw Pact into an all-European organization for collective security. In June 1990, Mikhail Gorbachev called for going beyond "old thinking"—including the practice of building alliances "on a selective, and in fact discriminatory, basis"—in order to "move toward a world without wars."[81] A few days later the Warsaw Pact proposed "the formation of a new all-European security system and the creation of a single Europe of peace and cooperation."[82] This proposal was consistent with the terms of the Warsaw Treaty of 1955, which had called for such an arrangement.[83]

Such proposals were welcomed in various quarters in Eastern Europe—not least by Vaclav Havel, the president of Czechoslovakia. Jiri Dienstbier, the Czechoslovak foreign minister, called NATO and the Warsaw Pact "vestiges of the old confrontation," and added, "We need a new security structure, based on the CSCE, embracing everybody in Europe, and the United States."[84]

The concept of collective security based on all-European structures found noteworthy support in Social Democratic parties in both East and West Germany, but the most prominent advocate was the West German foreign minister, Hans-Dietrich Genscher.[85] In March 1990, Genscher said,

> The alliances [NATO and the Warsaw Pact] are forming new security structures in Europe, by which they are increasingly being overarched and which in the end could absorb them. . . . If in the 1967 Harmel Report we committed ourselves to establishing a lasting peaceful order in Europe, does this not necessarily include a willingness to be integrated into a permanent system of mutual collective security?. . . Power politics will be replaced by a policy of responsibility. . . . Let us build a world made up of a friendly alliance of free nations and democratic states, in which hatred and animosity are superseded by humanity and brotherhood.[86]

Such thinking was manifest in two documents marking the end of the Cold War in Europe. In November 1990, the members of NATO and the Warsaw Pact jointly declared that "security is indivisible and that the security of each of their countries is inextricably linked to the security of all States participating in the Conference on Security and Co-operation in Europe."[87] In the Charter of Paris for a New Europe, formally approved two days later, the CSCE countries made a similar "security is indivisible" statement, and called for "equal security for all our countries." The Charter of Paris also reaffirmed the principles of the 1975 Helsinki Final Act and announced decisions to establish new institutions, such as a CSCE Conflict Prevention Center in Vienna.[88]

During the course of 1991, the Soviet Union—in its final year of existence—did more than any other state to dampen enthusiasm for relying on an all-European security structure such as the CSCE. The

Soviets refused to recognize any standing for the CSCE in dealing with the status of the Baltic republics, and blocked efforts to give the CSCE Conflict Prevention Center any effective power.[89] The Soviet Union in 1991 also tried to conclude treaties with Hungary and Romania that would have prevented either country from joining any alliance that Moscow considered opposed to its interests. The CSCE's inability to take any action without the approval of all its members, including the Soviet Union, underscored its unreliability as a means of protection from Soviet pressures. In contrast, NATO had a well-developed organization and command structure, an impressive array of military capabilities, and a track record of determination in resisting Soviet threats of various types.

It was thus during 1991 that attention turned to NATO as a much more reliable security guarantor than the CSCE was likely to become. In a March 1991 speech at NATO headquarters, President Havel said that the notions "in those first weeks and months of freedom" in 1990 of dismantling the Warsaw Pact and merging NATO into "an entirely new security structure . . . within the CSCE" were an "ideal" that need not "be abandoned," because everyone could endorse the attractions of "a Europe not divided into blocs, a Europe living as a peaceloving community of democratic states and independent nations, a united Europe as a continent of safety." Havel added, however, that it had become apparent that "progress toward this vision will probably be more complicated than it originally seemed to be," in part because of various "problems and dangers"—such as "the unholy legacy" of Communism for the long-term process of building democracy and market economies; the recurrence of "nationalism, xenophobia and intolerance" throughout much of Central and Eastern Europe; and the risk of adverse "developments in the Soviet Union." As a result, Havel concluded, his nation attached "great significance . . . to its cooperation with the North Atlantic Alliance," while recognizing that it could not "become a regular member of the NATO for the time being."[90] In a comparable statement in October 1991, Hungarian prime minister Jozsef Antall said, "The point is NATO should assume responsibility for the security of the region lying between its borders and the Soviet border. The legal and organizational issues are of secondary importance."[91]

The recognition of NATO's primacy as the strongest and most reliable organizational mechanism for ensuring security in Europe was based on more than the Alliance's external functions of preparedness for collective defense and dialogue with non-NATO countries. NATO's internal functions in support of international security and the interests of the Allies also came into clearer focus as officials and experts throughout Europe and North America briefly contemplated the notion of doing without the Alliance. Although these internal functions may be categorized and defined in various ways, at least eight have been identified: maintaining U.S. engagement in European security, resolving intra–West European security dilemmas, reassuring Germany's neighbors and allies, limiting the scope of nuclear proliferation in NATO Europe, promoting a certain "denationalization" of defense planning, providing a forum for the coordination of Western security policies, supplying economic benefits to all the Allies, and encouraging and legitimizing democratic forms of government.

Maintaining U.S. engagement in European security

The first and most obvious function of NATO as an institution is that it keeps the United States effectively engaged in European security affairs, with continuous high-level interactions to define Western security policies in standing NATO institutions. Because NATO enjoys great legitimacy and high standing in the United States as a historic achievement of U.S. foreign policy and a successful mechanism for promoting international order and protecting Western security interests, the Alliance helps to sustain ongoing U.S. involvement in European security. This includes a still-substantial U.S. military and nuclear presence as well as political and strategic commitments. NATO creates a presumption of continuing U.S. engagement for the indefinite future, and this "inertia effect" is constructive and stabilizing.

Resolving intra–West European security dilemmas

The second function follows from the first. As Uwe Nerlich pointed out in 1979, the United States has served not only as "the protector" but also as "the pacifier . . . of those parts of Europe that had not fallen under Soviet dominance."[92] In a highly regarded analysis, Josef Joffe noted that, by extending protection to Western Europe against the Soviet Union, "the United States embedded still another girder into the postwar order. The lasting integration of the United States into Europe's states system dispatched the prime structural cause of conflict among its nations—the search for an autonomous defense policy. . . . [T]he United States swept aside the rules of the self-help game that had governed and regularly brought grief to Europe in centuries past. . . . Once the problem of security was dispatched, collective gain could overwhelm the zero-sum logic of rivalry and relative gain."[93]

In other words, NATO can be seen as the framework within which certain previously intractable problems of power in European international politics have been successfully addressed. As Brandeis University's Robert Art has put it, "Through its military presence, the United States helps buffer, dampen, and thereby keep within defined bounds the inevitable tensions that will continue to arise among the Western Europeans."[94] NATO has furnished the security framework of reassurance within Western Europe for political and economic integration in the institutions, beginning in 1951 with the European Coal and Steel Community, that have led to the European Union. Solving the security dilemma in West European interstate relations has facilitated the pursuit of economic and political cooperation—a process that was deliberately urged and sponsored by the United States, building on the thought and work of Jean Monnet and other European advocates of such cooperation.

Various European analysts have argued that U.S. leadership and protection have pacified and stabilized Western Europe by constraining rivalry for primacy among the leading powers in NATO Europe. Some suggest, moreover, that these effects could be extended to a broader area of Europe under U.S. leadership. According to Michael Rühle and Nick Williams, who are, respectively, German and British, "It is only the anchoring of the United States in Europe that has nurtured the hope of escaping the past patterns of insecurity for good."[95]

Some observers might consider the ability of leading officials in the Alliance to undertake mediation and crisis resolution missions in relations between Allies—for instance, the efforts by various U.S. officers serving as Supreme Allied Commander, Europe (SACEUR) to resolve Greek-Turkish disputes—as a separate Alliance function, but it may be seen as falling under the broad heading of addressing intra-Alliance security problems. Such events help to illustrate how U.S. leadership has been indispensable to the cohesion of the Alliance. According to retired British diplomat Rodric Braithwaite, "Greece and Turkey have more than once been on the verge of war. They were prevented from going over the edge not by their common membership of NATO, but by U.S. pressure unilaterally applied."[96]

Reassuring Germany's neighbors and allies

A third major security function internal to the Alliance has been to enable Germany to reassure its neighbors and allies that it is committed to forming its national defense policies in a multilateral Alliance framework, and that its power potential is balanced by that of the United States. According to a formula often attributed to NATO's first secretary general, Lord Hastings Ismay, "NATO was designed to keep the Americans in, the Russians out and the Germans down."[97] Rather than keeping the Germans "down," however, it would be more accurate to say that NATO has enabled Germany to demonstrate to its allies and to others that it is "in convoy" as a reliable and trustworthy partner.

NATO furnished, for example, part of the framework in which the French were led to accept the establishment of West German armed forces. It should be recalled that the European Defense Community (EDC) episode during 1950–54 stemmed from France's determination to place constraints on the establishment of West German armed forces through the establishment of a unified European army. After France's EDC proposal was defeated in the French National Assembly in August 1954, the solution that enabled the Federal Republic to join NATO was not limited to Bonn's commitment not to manufacture nuclear, chemical, or biological weapons and to accept constraints supervised by the Western European Union on its conventional armaments. From a French perspective, the decisive factor consisted of pledges by Britain and the United States to maintain forces on the continent. According to a history of the EDC affair, the effect of the British and U.S. pledges in September 1954 was "immediate—and profound. M. Rothschild well remembers M. René Massigli, the French Ambassador, unashamedly weeping and saying that 'for fifty years—ever since 1905—French public opinion has waited for this announcement: and at last we have it!'"[98]

NATO, the institutional mechanism for U.S. and British military commitment on the continent, provided reassurance that West Germany would move "in convoy" with the other main Western states and that its power would be balanced by that of other major Allies, particularly the United States. In a useful discussion of the "intra-Western" or "West-West" power balance within NATO, Catherine Kelleher long ago pointed out that "Germany's role within NATO . . . minimizes the political risks to Bonn of achieving continental dominance in an area of great historical sensitivity."[99]

Many Germans—and other Europeans—consider NATO crucial, partly because it provides reassurance that Germany will neither pursue an autonomous security policy nor perceive any need to seek military power commensurate with its economic strength. European analyses of prospects for security and stability on the continent typically advance the proposition that one of NATO's main purposes should be to furnish a solution to the potential problem of German power, so that Germany does not seek a special relationship with Russia or a level of military power (perhaps including nuclear weapons) that its neighbors would find threatening.[100]

In May 1989, before the great events that unfolded that fall, President Bush described the United States and the Federal Republic of Germany as "partners in leadership" and called for "self-determination for all of Germany and all of Eastern Europe."[101] Because of America's long-standing commitment to German unity, the United States did not display the reservations and hesitations manifested by France and Britain in November 1989, when the Berlin Wall was torn down and Chancellor Helmut Kohl outlined a program for German unity. Indeed, "The American reaction to Kohl's November 1989 speech was radically different from the French, British, and Soviet reactions."[102] The United States took the lead in arguing for a united Germany that would remain within NATO. From a U.S. perspective, as a high-level Department of Defense official put it in 1991, NATO "safely anchors a reunited Germany in the West and North America to the security of Europe."[103]

The United States, as a superpower balancer for German power from across the Atlantic, reassures Europeans in a way that no local power or coalition could; and NATO is the primary vehicle for U.S. engagement in European security affairs. As Josef Joffe, the foreign editor of the *Süddeutsche Zeitung,* has written, "Now, and for many years to come, only NATO plus the U.S. can mute everybody else's fears of the German colossus unlimbering its muscles."[104] According to an Italian official, "The United States is the only one among us powerful enough to counterbalance Germany."[105] In the words of Christoph Bertram, an editor of *Die Zeit* and a former director of the International Institute for Strategic Studies, "For Germany, the alliance has had, and continues to have, a special function, namely that of making German power controllable and hence acceptable to allies and political adversaries alike."[106]

British prime minister Margaret Thatcher advocated a version of the Gaullist concept known as the *Europe des Patries* ("Europe of the Fatherlands") as an alternative to proposals for a European Union becoming a multinational federal state. In a widely noted speech in 1988, shortly before the collapse of the Soviet empire, Thatcher declared, "We have not successfully rolled back the frontiers of the state in Britain only to see them reimposed at a European level with a European super-state exercising a new dominance from Brussels. Certainly, we want to see Europe more united and with a greater sense of common purpose but it must be in a way which preserves the different traditions, parliamentary powers and sense of national pride in one's own country."[107] In Thatcher's view, without such a vision of Europe's future within the Alliance, the European integration movement would lead to a German-dominated European super-state. From her perspective, NATO was essential to ensure U.S. engagement and balanced relations with Germany within the Alliance: "Only the military and political engagement of the United States in Europe and close relations between the other two strongest sovereign states in Europe—Britain and France—are sufficient to balance German power; and nothing of the sort would be possible within a European super-state."[108]

Thatcher's concerns about Germany's potential power are consistent with the observations offered by German chancellor Helmut Kohl: "No one should be under the illusion that the spectre of European nationalism has been finally laid to rest, or that this ugly apparition is confined only to the Balkans. . . . Even Western Europe is not immune to such [nationalist] temptations." Kohl then added an ominous warning: "I feel myself carried back to an ill-fated past when I hear some people stirring up public sentiment with the argument that Germany has become too large and too powerful, and therefore needs to be 'contained' by means of coalitions. It is a cruel irony that this kind of talk plays into the hands of precisely those forces, not least in Germany, which propagate old-style nationalism."[109]

Limiting the scope of nuclear proliferation in NATO Europe

A fourth major security function extends beyond Germany to other allies that are technically capable of pursuing national nuclear weapons capabilities, but that have chosen, for various reasons—including NATO protection—not to do so. The North Atlantic Treaty has been, in a sense, the West's most successful nuclear nonproliferation agreement. Only two of the NATO European Allies have independent nuclear forces.

Britain had the world's first practical nuclear weapons program, and turned to cooperation with the United States during World War II in what became the U.S.-led Manhattan Project. The British decision to follow through with a national nuclear weapons program was made in January 1947, well before the formation of the Atlantic Alliance. According to Margaret Gowing, the official historian of the British nuclear weapons program,

> The British decision to make an atomic bomb had "emerged" from a body of general assumptions. It had not been a response to an immediate military threat but rather something fundamentalist and almost instinctive—a feeling that Britain must possess so climacteric a weapon in order to deter an atomically armed enemy, a feeling that Britain as a great power must acquire all major new weapons, a feeling that atomic weapons were a manifestation of the scientific and technological superiority on which Britain's strength, so deficient if measured in sheer numbers of men, must depend. The decision was also a symbol of independence. . . . [T]here was at this time—in 1946 and 1947—no United States military commitment to come to Britain's help in war. If Britain wanted to be sure of being covered by an atomic deterrent, she had no option but to make it herself.[110]

France's nuclear weapons program was established through a complex process that included the contributions of the French scientists associated with British, Canadian, and U.S. efforts during World War II; General Charles de Gaulle's establishment of the Commissariat à l'Énergie Atomique in 1945; the series of limited decisions during the Fourth Republic (1946–58); and the wide-ranging decisions of the Fifth Republic on specific weapons designs, delivery systems, and deterrence strategies.[111] The French decision involved multiple motives in addition to reservations about relying on U.S. nuclear commitments. When de Gaulle said that "France, by acquiring nuclear arms, is performing a service for the world equilibrium,"[112] he evidently had in mind France's autonomy and international status and the political balance within the Alliance, as well as broader strategic purposes, such as enhancing deterrence by obliging Moscow to face an additional center of nuclear decision making in Europe. As previously noted, while Britain has made its nuclear forces available for Alliance planning since 1962, subject to national command, France has not participated in the Nuclear Planning Group or associated NATO bodies for consultations regarding nuclear strategy and deterrence.

U.S. nuclear commitments and NATO consultation arrangements have helped to obviate the incentives that some of the other Allies would probably feel, in their absence, to acquire nuclear weapons of their own. Depending on the political context and other factors, the withdrawal of U.S. nuclear forces might well send a message of disengagement. The perceived disavowal of U.S. nuclear commitments could lead to a renationalization of defense policies, the formation of new alliances (to compensate to some degree for the weakening or collapse of the Atlantic Alliance) and, perhaps in some cases, the pursuit of additional national nuclear weapons programs in Europe. The two most frequently cited examples of NATO Allies that might pursue the last of these courses are Germany and Turkey.[113]

In 1992, before he became under secretary of defense for policy in the Clinton administration, Walter Slocombe wrote that "A unified Germany would not readily rely indefinitely on a British or French deterrent. The practical issue, therefore, is whether there will be U.S. nuclear weapons in Europe—or German ones. So long as there is a reluctance to see German nuclear weapons, there will be a strong case for an American nuclear guarantee made manifest by the presence of nuclear weapons nearby."[114]

Slocombe's judgments are supported by a 1995 survey in which a sample of German military and civilian leaders was asked to estimate the degree of German interest in a national nuclear force under various international security scenarios. Such interest was extremely low when the security environment included NATO and an American military and nuclear presence in Europe. If the future security environment lacked

NATO and U.S. military commitments but included a European alliance, with Germany aligned with Britain and France, German interest in a national nuclear weapons program increased—in part because of "a German hesitancy to trust the commitment of French or British guarantees of nuclear protection." If the scenario included no alliances and assumed that Germany would be alone in providing for its security, a high level of interest in a national nuclear weapons program was apparent.[115]

Perhaps the most intriguing aspect of the survey was its effort to distinguish between security and nonsecurity motivations for a national nuclear weapons capability. The nonsecurity motivations include the prospect that nuclear weapons could serve as "potential symbols of a new, more assertive Germany finally taking its rightful place as a world power," and could "contribute, at least indirectly, to new feelings of German pride, prestige, and sovereignty, as well as being credible instruments for international influence." The survey found that nonsecurity motivations for seeking nuclear weapons increased when there was a rise in security motivations (the removal of credible U.S. protection, and the doubts about British and French protection). The survey's author, U.S. Air Force Major Mark Gose, concluded that "It is the American presence on the Continent that allays most of Germany's fears. It is American nuclear weapons in Germany . . . that provide her with guarantees against nuclear threats and blackmail . . . [and thus serve as] the key for diluting both security and nonsecurity motivations for Germany to become a nuclear power."[116]

Promoting a certain "denationalization" of defense planning

The fifth security function internal to the Alliance has been promoting "denationalized" defense planning, with increased attention to common interests. As John Duffield has pointed out, "To varying but usually substantial degrees, NATO countries formulate and execute their security policies as part of the alliance rather than on a purely national basis. This denationalization of security policy tempers the natural rivalry and competition for military primacy that might otherwise occur among the major European powers, and it helps to preclude any intra-European use of military posturing for political influence."[117]

If NATO is, as some historians suggest, "the first alliance formed in time of peace providing for an organized military force with a unified command,"[118] this is not solely because of the nature of modern warfare, the speed with which an enemy could mount a large-scale offensive. There are distinct advantages to NATO's integrated military structure in addition to military preparedness, such as promoting the commitment to shared defense goals and other common purposes. The first SACEUR, General Dwight Eisenhower, deliberately pursued this approach:

> The SHAPE staff system was indeed based on the principle of integration rather than the committee system of combined national representatives favored by the British and the Gaullists in France. Eisenhower decided against a nonintegrated structure on the grounds that it was militarily less efficient, would facilitate national rivalries, and would reinforce domination by the three largest allies [that is, Britain, France, and the United States] at the expense of genuine Alliance-wide participation in the mutual defense effort. As a consequence of the emphasis on the international nature of the SHAPE staff, its members and the commanders-in-chief of the principal commands were normally prevented from holding positions of authority in their national armed forces and were discouraged from asserting narrow national interests at the expense of the common effort.[119]

The Allies have achieved a level of collective military planning and cooperation unprecedented in a peacetime alliance of democratic states. Exchanges of all types of information have promoted an educated awareness of the perceptions and problems of fellow allies. Smaller and less prosperous allies have benefited from—and contributed to—the formation of a common political-military culture in the Alliance, and have gained access to advanced military technology. Through institutions such as the Nuclear Planning Group, European capitals (notably Bonn and London) have influenced the Alliance's political and strategic planning.

Indeed, to a significant degree NATO has institutionalized transparency and dialogue in defense planning. Every year the Allies participating in the collective defense planning process under the Defense Planning Committee (at present, all the Allies except France) submit detailed responses to surveys about their forces and plans, engaging in systematic and extensive information exchanges that would have been unthinkable in earlier periods of European history. The Allies work together to define planning targets, looking six or more years ahead, for their armed forces on the basis of the Alliance's Strategic Concept and ministerial guidance; and the Allies monitor each other's performance.[120]

Collective decision making regarding the acquisition and operation of certain types of capabilities and in exercises has contributed to the growth of trust among the Allies. Decades of consultations and working together have "socialized" Allies into a shared outlook on security affairs, and have given them confidence that they understand each other. This "mutual surveillance" in cooperative institutions can be seen as a form of intra-Alliance reassurance that, in the words of Stephen Flanagan, is "designed to avoid renationalization of defense policies and to take concerns about each other out of the security risk calculus of member states."[121]

NATO's cohesiveness and coherence should not be overstated, however. During the Cold War, some well-informed observers considered it a "ramshackle" structure.[122] It should be recalled that NATO is composed of distinct powers, each still interested in its own security and each with its own priorities and internal political debates and dynamics. Although NATO has achieved an unusually high level of institutionalization, one that may well be unique in history, it remains an intergovernmental organization. NATO acts only when its member governments can agree to act. The organization has no supranational authority; its international staff assists in the coordination of Alliance activities but has no directive or coercive powers. Most Alliance decisions are made through consensus on the basis of lowest-common-denominator judgments acceptable to all the member governments.

Although France has popularized a distinction between the North Atlantic Treaty (of which France has always remained a loyal signatory) and NATO's integrated military structure (from which France withdrew in 1966), the degree of "integration" achieved in NATO should not be exaggerated. Maintaining an "integrated" military structure does not mean that SACEUR commands the forces of Allies in peacetime. Most of the forces of NATO member-states are under complete national command in peacetime. Historically, aside from the headquarters staffs in the integrated military structure, only a few types of forces have been under SACEUR's command in peacetime: (a) certain communications units; (b) the Standing Naval Force Channel, a mine-countermeasure force, and the Standing Naval Force Mediterranean, composed of destroyer escorts and frigates; (c) the NATO Airborne Early Warning Force—the Alliance's largest commonly funded program—equipped with Airborne Warning and Control System (AWACS) aircraft; (d) the U.S. and Allied nuclear-capable aircraft and missiles on Quick Reaction Alert (QRA) status; and (e) parts of the integrated air defense forces in NATO Europe, with the notable exceptions of France and Spain, whose forces have participated nonetheless in the Alliance's warning and communications systems and mutually exchange air defense information with their NATO counterparts. In 1991, when U.S. and NATO decisions eliminated all of the remaining U.S. ground-launched nuclear systems in Europe, the QRA program was terminated. (As with all U.S. nuclear weapons arrangements, only the U.S. president had release authority for weapons on QRA status.) Following Spain's 1997 decision to participate fully in the new command structure, its forces are now in the process of joining that structure, and the special status of Spain's air defense units will end accordingly.

Aside from the relatively few units already placed under SACEUR's command in peacetime, no Ally's forces come under SACEUR's operational command automatically; an explicit transfer of authority from national to NATO command is required. All NATO governments retain national command authority and may withhold agreement to requests by either SACEUR or SACLANT (Supreme Allied Commander, Atlantic); these commanders are always subordinate to the Alliance's political authorities—that is, the North Atlantic Council.

Providing a forum for the coordination of Western security policies

A sixth function internal to the Alliance has been to furnish a forum for the coordination of security policies in addition to collective defense. Despite various disagreements about particular negotiations and proposals,[123] NATO governments generally cooperated closely in defining policies for arms control negotiations with adversaries to the east during the Cold War. The Alliance has remained the most effective vehicle for policy harmonization regarding the various arms control regimes that have remained in effect after the Cold War—for instance, the November 1990 Treaty on Conventional Armed Forces in Europe, known as the CFE Treaty. The CFE Treaty's requirements have been amended extensively since its conclusion, in large part because of the collapse of the Warsaw Pact and the Soviet Union. The Alliance has continued to serve as the principal mechanism for NATO governments to coordinate their policies regarding CFE Treaty modifications, however, and to share information and make decisions with respect to verification and compliance.

NATO governments were reminded of the Alliance's utility as a forum for policy coordination in matters beyond collective defense by the 1990–91 Gulf War. NATO's formal role in that conflict was limited to collective defense: preparedness to defend NATO territory in the southern region (Turkey in particular) and to defend Allied ships and aircraft in the Mediterranean Sea. Because Iraq did not attack Turkey, the Allies did not have to honor Article 5 of the North Atlantic Treaty in combat operations. Alliance procedures and logistical and communications assets were nonetheless tested in a number of unprecedented ways. NATO officials concluded that the Alliance "responded effectively to a non-Soviet threat against one of its members emanating from outside of Europe, and it prepared to deal with the possible spillover effects of violence occurring in an adjacent region."[124]

Moreover, twelve of the sixteen NATO Allies provided forces to the coalition against Iraqi aggression and thereby participated in the liberation of Kuwait. In doing so, they closely coordinated their strategies and policies, and drew heavily on forces and military infrastructure assets developed within the Alliance. General John Galvin, then commander-in-chief of the U.S. European Command (EUCOM), testified that a third of EUCOM's combat forces were redeployed to the Persian Gulf, Turkey, and Israel during the war. Galvin also called attention to the contributions by NATO Allies during the war, including the ground forces provided by Britain and France and the enormous logistical support provided by Allied installations. "Approximately 90 percent of airlift and deploying aircraft were supported as they transited through bases in Germany, France, Portugal, Spain, Italy, Cyprus, Greece, Turkey, and the U.K."[125]

The Gulf War demonstrated more than NATO's utility as a vehicle for coordinating policies and building Western consensus and cohesion with regard to a security challenge outside of Article 5 operations for collective defense. It also helped to illustrate why NATO survived the end of the Cold War: NATO works. The Alliance is a useful and adaptable asset, constructed over decades at great cost. As Robert McCalla has noted, the Allies "spent forty-five years learning how to work as a long-term coalition through a sophisticated political and military structure. . . . Developing new institutions or consultative frameworks entails start-up costs; NATO's appeal is that these costs already have been paid. . . . The wider the range of functions that an alliance fulfills beyond its core defense function, the less responsive it will be to changes in the threats it faces and the more likely it is to be transformed in purpose as its external environment changes."[126] In other words, because NATO continues to serve multiple security functions for its members (including policy coordination beyond collective defense matters), the disappearance of the specific threat that triggered the Alliance's formation—the Soviet Union—did not lead to its atrophy.

Supplying economic benefits to all the Allies

Perhaps the most fundamental economic benefit of NATO for the Allies is that it provides a framework of security and stability necessary for the pursuit of prosperity. Confidence in security has been an element in the West's economic success since 1949, when the North Atlantic Treaty was concluded. The Alliance has provided a setting of safety for the European economic integration movement, from the European Coal and Steel Community in 1951 to today's European Union. The conviction that enhanced security will bolster prospects for economic achievement constitutes one of the attractions of NATO membership for the post–Cold War applicants.

For each of the Allies, collective defense is less costly than national defense.[127] Most of the Allies have been reducing defense spending since the mid-1980s, particularly since the collapse of the Soviet empire in 1989–91, and maintaining the Alliance has reinforced the confidence of member governments regarding the prudence of their military cutbacks. The Alliance arrangements constitute an economic asset, because both NATO's current collective defense posture and the political, organizational, and material basis for an extensive reconstitution of military capabilities (should it become necessary) are retained, but at a relatively low cost. NATO's ongoing and adaptation costs are quite manageable on an incremental basis—indeed a bargain, compared with the costs posed by counterfactual challenges, such as attempting to reconstruct Alliance assets from scratch (if NATO were disbanded and then rebuilt). If NATO members could not rely on the Alliance and sought to enjoy the same level of security, all of them would have to spend more on defense than they do at present; and it is not clear that even substantially greater expenditures would provide equivalent security outside NATO.

According to Article 2 of the North Atlantic Treaty, the Allies will "seek to eliminate conflict in their international economic policies" and "encourage economic collaboration." In practice, the Allies have recognized that these aims are pursued in other international bodies dedicated primarily to economic activities, such as the European Union (EU) and the Organization for Economic Cooperation and Development (OECD). NATO accordingly "avoids unnecessary duplication of work carried out elsewhere but reinforces collaboration between its members whenever economic issues of special interest to the Alliance are involved, particularly those which have political or defense implications."[128] Thus, NATO's Economic Committee has traditionally focused on matters such as defense spending and intra-Alliance trade in military equipment.[129]

Some economists have compared the Alliance to a club, and have suggested that the economic benefits of keeping NATO as a functioning enterprise must be positive, despite complaints about "unfair" burden sharing, or else the club would have been disbanded. Instead, NATO has retained all of its original members, and other countries have sought membership over the years; by this logic, membership must offer benefits or Allies would have dropped out of the club.[130] This argument has its limits, however, because it implies that Allies might withdraw from NATO mainly on economic grounds, whatever the international circumstances. The security imperatives that drive an alliance's formation and contribute to its maintenance cannot be expressed simply in terms of economic cost-benefit analyses.

The Alliance in fact provides significant (though not readily quantifiable) economic benefits to all the Allies, even though for the most part their methods for acquiring equipment and training forces have been enormously inefficient from an economic viewpoint; additional economic gains are difficult to realize because of national autonomy. NATO is, after all, an alliance of sovereign states, a pact operated on intergovernmental principles, and it has proven its success (among other ways) by protecting the autonomy of the member states and thus their freedom to be economically inefficient. While the Alliance has pursued some significant activities with a high level of collective efficiency, most of its procurement arrangements—notably concerning armaments—have not been driven by shared economic imperatives, but by national priorities and political, industrial, and bureaucratic considerations within member states. Disputes over finances have been most visible in the interminable debate over burden sharing since the beginning of the Alliance.

Commonly funded programs may constitute the most efficient portion of the collective defense effort undertaken by the Allies. The Alliance's Security Investment Program provides for collective funding of infrastructure necessary for common defense, such as fuel pipelines and storage, air defense radars and navigation aids, communications and information systems, storage and support facilities for reinforcement, headquarters facilities, airfields, and naval bases.[131] Since the end of the Cold War, such investments have shifted away from the Alliance's traditional central region (Germany and the Benelux countries) toward Greece, Italy, and Turkey. Since 1996, such investments have also supported infrastructure facilities in support of IFOR and SFOR in Bosnia, including roads, bridges, airports, and railroads.[132] In the future, NATO will probably support infrastructure investments on the territories of new Allies.

Moreover, Allies have commonly funded not only logistics facilities, but also specialized agencies, such as the Central Europe Operating Agency, which maintains and operates the Central Europe Pipeline System; the NATO Maintenance and Supply Organization, which provides assistance with spare parts, maintenance, and repairs; and the NATO Integrated Communications and Information Systems Operating and Support Agency (NACOSA), which maintains and operates communications and information networks.[133] These assets and capabilities are acquired more cheaply, with economies of scale and other efficiencies, than would be possible if the Allies acted on a national basis and simply coordinated their efforts.

The degree of integration achieved through these Alliance activities should not be overstated. First, it should be kept in mind that all of the commonly funded NATO activities amount to about one-third of one percent of the Allies' defense spending.[134] Second, it should be recognized that NATO's financial arrangements are decentralized, with different budgets and cost-sharing agreements for particular purposes, including the approximately twenty agencies dealing with tasks such as logistics, electronic infrastructure, standardization, education, and training. All sixteen Allies contribute to the budget supporting the civilian secretariat (the International Staff at NATO headquarters) and civilian activities (including programs in scientific research, civil emergency planning, and the Partnership for Peace). Participation in the military and infrastructure budgets has varied, however, usually from a level of all sixteen Allies to fifteen (with France or Spain not participating) or fourteen (with neither France or Spain). In some cases, the number of Allies participating in a commonly funded program has been as few as twelve or even four.[135]

In general, armaments acquisition programs have not been undertaken on an Alliance-wide basis, although NATO has established a Conference of National Armaments Directors and several other institutional mechanisms to facilitate arms cooperation and standardization. As a general rule, cooperative equipment programs, including armaments, can offer economic benefits to the participants. The costs for each participant in a multinational program are typically less than if the country tried to develop and produce the equipment on its own. When France or the United States, for example, develops and manufactures equipment on its own, the total costs of the specific project in absolute terms may be less than if that project were pursued on a multinational basis; the relative costs to Paris or Washington, however, are generally higher than in a multinational program, because none of the costs are shared. Even though multinational projects involve inefficiencies and higher total costs in absolute terms, the inefficiency costs are shared and more than compensated for by the advantages of cost-sharing. In general, therefore, the relative costs for a project leader, usually a major power such as France or the United States, are lower than in a purely national program. For a smaller power, moreover, multinational programs offer access to technologies and capabilities (and employment opportunities) that would otherwise be unavailable.[136]

Nonetheless, the Allies generally have not sought maximum economic productivity and cost-effectiveness through far-reaching standardization of equipment, specialization in military roles and missions, or comprehensive and consolidated programs for the development and production of equipment. For the most part, they have not attempted to realize such efficiencies, including economies of scale. Instead, duplication of effort and suboptimal levels of coordination in procurement and training have prevailed, because of the strength of political and bureaucratic barriers to more efficient cooperation, as well as the economic ability of the Allies to afford these inefficiencies. As Keith Hartley concludes, "Retaining control over their own defense effort and independence in the operation of foreign policy, the looseness of [the Alliance] organization leaves members with an incentive to maximize private gains . . . [by] adopting weapons more likely to contribute to national welfare than to the military effectiveness of NATO. After all, domestic weapons firms and bureaucracies in the form of Defense Ministries or Departments and national armed forces are likely to pursue *their* preferences and press their own claims rather than consider the wider interests of an amorphous body such as NATO."[137]

With the exceptions of Iceland (which has no military forces) and tiny Luxembourg, each of the Allies maintains a national defense establishment with its own logistic support plans, equipment programs, education and training facilities, and (in most cases) research and development activities. Some powers manifest an unwillingness to accept dependence on foreign powers, even Allies, with regard to certain types of military capabilities and other preparations for potential contingencies. Andrew Marshall's observation in 1966 still retains considerable currency: "the national governments do not entirely want to pool their efforts. Perhaps partly because independent capabilities for defense are involved in the notion of national sovereignty. Perhaps partly because the military services of the separate countries all wish to have as much control as possible over procurement decisions with regard to major weapons systems and to have under their control national support and maintenance facilities."[138]

One of the consequences of relying mainly on national procurement and maintenance systems has been higher prices. According to Marshall, "One can only guess how much more on the average European NATO Allies pay for major equipment as compared with U.S. prices. Ten to twenty per cent might be a reasonable guess."[139] During the Cold War,

U.S. officials advocating greater standardization and closer cooperation in NATO argued that the Warsaw Pact's defense efforts were more efficient, with a higher level of "additivity" (the extent to which national militaries can be effectively combined in a multinational operation) than NATO defense efforts, partly because the Soviet Union had imposed a significant level of standardization. In 1982, U.S. secretary of defense Caspar Weinberger argued that, mostly because of various inefficiencies and duplications of effort in NATO defense preparations, the Warsaw Pact's effective output advantage in military investment was around 35 to 40 percent.[140]

In short, a long-standing result of NATO's decentralized or "permissive" approach to armaments acquisition and maintenance has been a lack of standardization and interoperability, despite many agreements, institutional arrangements, and professions of good intentions in this regard. In 1979, Robert Komer, then the adviser to the U.S. secretary of defense for NATO affairs, asked, "How can NATO commanders optimally use national forces whose radios can't use each other's frequencies, whose bombs don't fit each other's aircraft, whose artillery rounds don't fit each other's tubes, who even have trouble reading each other's map symbols?"[141] According to NATO authorities, headway in addressing such deficiencies has been "mixed, with substantially more progress having been achieved in the areas of operations and procedures . . . than in materiel."[142]

Throughout the history of the Alliance, the United States has spent a higher percentage of its gross domestic product on defense than most of the other Allies (Greece has been the only exception in recent years) and, to be sure, far more in absolute terms.[143] However, the United States has responsibilities in other regions of the world—particularly in the Western Hemisphere, the Middle East and Persian Gulf, and East Asia and the Pacific—that are, for the most part, distinct from those of Canada and the European Allies. The latter, except for Britain and France, devote almost all of their military spending to conducting and preparing for operations in or near Europe. Moreover, until recently, with the principal exception of the United Kingdom, most of the European Allies relied on conscript forces, a policy that understated the real economic cost of defense for these countries.[144] The United States and the three other Allies that account for most of the military spending

(Britain, France, and Germany) gain economic as well as political influence benefits from their leading position—a higher level of military
equipment sales and defense-related employment, including industrial
as well as military personnel.

The United States serves as the principal nuclear guarantor of the
Alliance, while most of the Allies (except for Britain and France) have
agreed to be non–nuclear-weapon states under the 1968 Nuclear Non-
Proliferation Treaty (NPT). The United States therefore assumes costs in
its nuclear weapons posture that, for the most part, are not shared by its
Allies; yet it may also derive benefits "such as prestige, enhanced security
and a greater say in planning and so on, that are unavailable to those
nations that do not possess nuclear weapons. Purely monetary measures
fail to include such factors and are therefore inherently flawed."[145]

The same point could be made about other expensive capabilities
maintained by the United States for purposes in addition to supporting
collective defense in NATO—for example, U.S. logistical capabilities,
such as sealift and airlift (including aerial refueling aircraft) and the
extensive U.S. network of satellites for intelligence, communications,
navigation, surveillance, and other purposes. NATO analysts hope that
CJTF arrangements and associated mechanisms for the release, monitoring, and recall of NATO assets will avoid duplication of effort and
enable the European Allies in particular to benefit from access to commonly funded NATO facilities and support from logistical, communications, and other national assets shared by the United States for operations endorsed by the North Atlantic Council. While this prospect
amounts to an economic advantage for the European Allies, it also represents a potential source of political and strategic influence for the
United States.

The essentially national approach to force development in the Alliance has furnished the backdrop for the burden-sharing debate, which
has been virtually continuous since NATO's founding. This debate for
the most part has consisted of the Americans asking the Europeans to
increase their level of defense effort. During the 1950s, as their postwar economic recovery proceeded, the Europeans could plead inca-
pacity. Since the 1960s, the Europeans have drawn attention to their
large purchases of U.S. arms and equipment and have stressed "output" measures instead of the "input" measures (which focus on GNP

percentages of defense spending) favored by American critics of European "free-riding." Europeans have deplored "the myth that the U.S. bears a disproportionate share of the NATO burden, especially in terms of the contribution of conventional forces. Despite continued complaints about 'free-riders,' European NATO countries provide 90 percent of the manpower, 85 percent of the tanks, 95 percent of the artillery and 85 percent of the combat airpower in the Atlantic-to-the-Urals area covered by the CFE negotiation."[146]

Since the mid-1980s, when most of the Allies (including the United States) began to make substantial reductions in their defense spending, the burden-sharing debate has become one about "burden shedding" —that is, who should be entitled to make military budget cuts and for what purposes. U.S. critics of European defense efforts have nonetheless continued to argue that the United States has been paying more than its fair share of NATO defense costs and therefore has been indirectly subsidizing wealthy economic competitors in NATO Europe. Such arguments acquired an even sharper resonance before the U.S. Senate's April 1998 vote on NATO expansion.

Burden-sharing debates have ultimately been about politics as much as economics because the economic significance of some burdens (for instance, hosting foreign troops and equipment) cannot be readily quantified, just as the economic value inherent in the options and influence that accompany the acquisition of certain military capabilities eludes precise quantification. As Klaus Knorr stated, "an ally that carries a larger economic burden than others is not necessarily subject to exploitation, for the excess in the economic load may be compensated by a larger net benefit derived from the balance in the other costs and gains."[147]

Among economists analyzing the Alliance, the tendency since the late 1960s has been to qualify heavily the argument, first introduced at that time, that the main benefit of the Alliance (security through collective defense capabilities) amounted to a "public good" and that the larger Allies (particularly the United States) would unavoidably bear a disproportionate share of the economic burdens in providing this good, with smaller Allies prone to become "free-riders" exploiting the efforts of the larger Allies.[148] Simple economic measures, such as the percentage of GNP spent on defense, have supported this argument, portraying Canada, Denmark, Iceland, Luxembourg, and others as "free-riders."

However, more complex analyses have pointed out that for specific individual Allies NATO involves benefits in addition to security through collective defense, while military spending may be devoted to purposes other than supporting collective defense in NATO. Among the other benefits are the internal functions of the Alliance discussed in this chapter, including the economic advantages of collective defense, as well as the privileges of leadership and influence. Because military spending by specific Allies (particularly Britain, France, and the United States) supports various priorities beyond defending NATO Europe, the "public-good" argument is based on a faulty premise. For this reason Todd Sandler and other economists recommend a "joint product model" that recognizes that defense spending supports purposes in addition to simply the public good of collective defense, including country-specific "private goods" as varied as gaining influence in the Alliance, maintaining public order at home, developing capabilities for national protection in wartime, conducting national (or coalition) military operations beyond the NATO area, and pursuing national research and development priorities with civilian as well as military applications. The joint product model "repeatedly appears to explain actual data better than the pure public good model."[149]

Encouraging and legitimizing democratic forms of government

The case for the eighth internal function of NATO that has sometimes been advanced—encouraging and legitimizing democratic forms of government—is rather mixed. The preamble of the North Atlantic Treaty refers to "principles of democracy, individual liberty and the rule of law." NATO is sometimes depicted as a coalition of nations determined to promote certain values or "norms"—what some would call an ideology—of principles of government (democracy) and international relations (peaceful settlement of disputes). In April 1997, U.S. secretary of state Madeleine Albright said, referring to NATO, "It brought the former fascist nations, first Italy, then Germany, then Spain, back into the family of European democracies."[150] This formulation, however, probably overstates NATO's role while giving inadequate attention to other factors that promoted the growth of democracy in these countries.

John Duffield has suggested that "the existence of NATO may provide at least as much support for the theory that ideological affinity determines alliances as it does for balance-of-power theory."[151] The difficulty with this proposition is that, while NATO has generally consisted of a coalition of democracies, there have been exceptions. When the Alliance was formed, Portugal was governed by a dictatorship little different from that in Spain; but the Azores were too important to the security of the Allies in the event of war to let Portugal's form of government pose an obstacle to membership. In other words, military necessity overcame ideological preferences. Similarly, when Greece was ruled by a military junta in 1967–74 and when Turkey was governed by the military on various occasions (1960–61, 1971–73, and 1980–83), there was never any question of refusing to conduct Alliance business with the nondemocratic regimes or of expelling these countries from the Alliance. Moreover, several European democracies (for instance, neutral states such as Ireland, Sweden, and Switzerland) chose—despite obvious ideological affinity—to refrain from seeking membership in the Alliance during the Cold War.

One can say, however, that democratic ideals were generally constructive for Alliance cohesion—and for the legitimization of the Alliance within specific member nations—during the Cold War, and that these ideals have helped to give direction for Alliance policies in post–Cold War Europe. In Duffield's view, "NATO's continued existence even after the collapse of the Soviet Union implies . . . that liberal states based on democracy, political pluralism, and the rule of law may be inclined to maintain (if not to form in the first place) alliances even in the absence of a compelling external threat, since they are much less likely to perceive one another as dangerous."[152]

Since the end of the Cold War the Allies have emphasized successful democratization as a criterion for NATO membership to give would-be Allies an incentive for good behavior. According to the Alliance's July 1997 Madrid Declaration, "NATO remains open to new members under Article 10 of the North Atlantic Treaty. . . . No European democratic country whose admission would fulfill the objectives of the Treaty will be excluded from consideration."[153] Article 10 of the Treaty, however, does not refer to democratic rule as a criterion for admission—only to being "in a position to further the principles of this Treaty and to contribute to the security of the North Atlantic area." During the Cold War, democratization was not as vital a criterion for membership as military strength or geostrategic location. Threat perceptions, however, have been drastically reduced since the collapse of the Soviet empire. Evidently, the Allies now feel freer to make democratization a requirement for membership.

NATO's Transformation since 1989

Whatever the causes of the Soviet empire's collapse, it came as a surprise to most Western officials and experts, who had generally attributed much more strength and staying power to the Soviet Union than proved to be the case. The events in 1989–91 that marked the end of the Cold War—the fall of the Berlin Wall, the collapse of Communist governments in East-Central Europe, the unification of Germany, and the disintegration of the Warsaw Pact and the Soviet Union—obliged the Allies to redefine NATO's purposes and to endow it with new roles in addition to its traditional core missions of collective defense and dialogue with adversaries.

These new roles can be defined and categorized in various ways, but the two most significant new roles are clearly cooperation with former adversaries and other non-NATO countries in new institutions such as Partnership for Peace, and crisis management and peace operations beyond the territory of NATO allies.

In conjunction with the pursuit of these two new roles, the Alliance has been engaged in a complex process of internal adaptation. This process includes the establishment of new institutions intended to promote an even closer political control over military operations such as crisis management and peacekeeping; a certain "Europeanization," with more attention to structural changes conducive to the emergence of a European Security and Defense Identity (ESDI); and a greater flexibility for the ad hoc improvisation of effective "coalitions of the willing" through Combined Joint Task Forces. Coalitions of the willing would be composed of the states volunteering to participate in specific non–Article 5 operations. For example, a coalition might include some—or all—of the Allies, selected PfP Partners, and other states. A WEU-led coalition of the willing would be consistent with ESDI aspirations. Such adaptations support the increased emphasis on the Alliance's new roles of cooperation with former adversaries and preparedness to conduct selected non–Article 5 crisis management and peace operations.

At the same time, the Alliance's collective defense function has been redefined, with much more attention than in the past to countering the proliferation of weapons of mass destruction—that is, nuclear, chemical, and biological weapons.

Cooperation with former adversaries and other non-NATO nations

At NATO's July 1990 London summit, the first after the collapse of the Communist governments in Eastern Europe in fall 1989, the Allies affirmed their determination to maintain the peace, and asserted an unprecedented confidence in the Alliance's ability to serve as an "agent of change," an instrument useful in constructing "a Europe whole and free." In the words of NATO's London Declaration, "We need to keep standing together, to extend the long peace we have enjoyed these past four decades. Yet our alliance must be even more an agent of change. It can help build the structures of a more united continent, supporting security and stability with the strength of our shared faith in democracy, the rights of the individual, and the peaceful resolution of disputes."[154]

NATO added in its London Declaration that it would "reach out to the countries of the East which were our adversaries in the Cold War, and extend to them the hand of friendship." In terms of concrete proposals, NATO suggested "military contacts" between NATO and Warsaw Pact commanders, "regular diplomatic liaison" between NATO and the states of the Warsaw Pact, and a joint declaration by the nations of NATO and the Warsaw Pact affirming that they were "no longer adversaries."[155] Such a declaration by the members of the opposing alliances was made in Paris in November 1990, less than eight months before the Warsaw Pact was formally disbanded in July 1991.

In November 1991, NATO proposed "a more institutional relationship of consultation and cooperation on political and security issues" with Bulgaria, Czechoslovakia, Estonia, Hungary, Latvia, Lithuania, Poland, Romania, and the Soviet Union.[156] (The Baltic republics regained their independence from the Soviet Union and were admitted to the United Nations in September 1991, before the collapse of the Soviet Union in December 1991.) Before its replacement by the Euro-Atlantic Partnership Council (EAPC) in May 1997, the mechanism for the "more institutional relationship" was the North Atlantic Cooperation Council

(NACC), which consisted of meetings of representatives of the invited states with NATO officials.

In their November 1991 Strategic Concept, the Allies recalled the Alliance's two classic purposes, most famously formulated in the Harmel Report, as follows: "safeguarding the security and territorial integrity of its members, and establishing a just and lasting peaceful order in Europe." The Allies added, "what is new is that, with the radical changes in the security situation, the opportunities for achieving Alliance objectives through political means are greater than ever before." As a result, "Allied security policy" would henceforth be based on "three mutually reinforcing elements . . . dialogue, co-operation, and the maintenance of a collective defense capability."[157] Michael Legge, then NATO's assistant secretary general for defense planning and policy and the chairman of the Strategy Review Group that drafted the new Strategic Concept, wrote that "the former Harmel dual approach of dialogue and defense" was expanded into "a triad of cooperation, dialogue and defense."[158]

In January 1994, NATO went well beyond declaring the addition of "cooperation" as a basic purpose. The Alliance announced its intention "to launch an immediate and practical program that will transform the relationship between NATO and participating states. This new program goes beyond dialogue and cooperation to forge a real partnership—a Partnership for Peace. We invite the other states participating in the NACC, and other CSCE countries able and willing to contribute to this program, to join with us in this Partnership."[159]

What would the Partnership for Peace (PfP) accomplish? According to the North Atlantic Council, "The Partnership will expand and intensify political and military cooperation throughout Europe, increase stability, diminish threats to peace, and build strengthened relationships by promoting the spirit of practical cooperation and commitment to democratic principles that underpin our Alliance."[160] By the end of 1996, twenty-seven non-NATO nations had joined PfP, with some much more active than others.[161]

In mid-1997, the Alliance's cooperation activities were extended with the establishment of three new institutions: the NATO-Russia Permanent Joint Council, created by the May 1997 NATO-Russia Founding

Act; the NATO-Ukraine Commission, established by the July 1997 NATO-Ukraine Charter; and the Euro-Atlantic Partnership Council, which replaced the NACC in May 1997.

The Alliance's Mediterranean Dialogue should be mentioned in this context as well. In December 1994, the North Atlantic Council declared that NATO was prepared "to establish contacts, on a case-by-case basis, between the Alliance and Mediterranean nonmember countries with a view to contributing to the strengthening of regional stability."[162] NATO has subsequently initiated a dialogue with six countries: Egypt, Israel, Jordan, Mauritania, Morocco, and Tunisia. Each dialogue has been bilateral between NATO and the specific country, although the initiative allows for multilateral meetings on a case-by-case basis. The dialogue has concerned NATO's policies, and "Mediterranean partners have been invited to participate in specific activities such as science, information, civil emergency planning and courses at NATO schools in fields such as peacekeeping, civil emergency planning, arms control, responsibility of military forces in environmental protection and European security cooperation."[163]

Crisis management and peace operations

The war in Yugoslavia did not begin until May 1991, a circumstance that helps to explain why the Alliance's July 1990 London Declaration had nothing to say about the need to be prepared for such crises. By the fall of 1991, the Alliance had adjusted its expectations. Although the European Community initially claimed responsibility for dealing with the conflict in what was soon to become known as the former Yugoslavia, the Alliance foresaw multiple risks of comparable conflicts. In the words of the November 1991 Strategic Concept,

> Risks to Allied security are less likely to result from calculated aggression against the territory of the Allies, but rather from the adverse consequences of instabilities that may arise from the serious economic, social and political difficulties, including ethnic rivalries and territorial disputes, which are faced by many countries in central and eastern Europe. The tensions . . . could . . . lead to crises inimical to European stability and even to armed conflicts, which could involve outside powers or spill over into NATO countries, having a direct effect on the security of the Alliance.[164]

The Alliance's November 1991 Rome Declaration accordingly called for capabilities "to prevent or manage crises affecting our security" in a "wide range of contingencies."[165]

In June 1992, the Allies declared their willingness "to support, on a case-by-case basis in accordance with our own procedures, peace-keeping activities under the responsibility of the CSCE, including by making available Alliance resources and expertise." This decision was made in light of the outbreaks of "violence and destruction . . . in various areas of the Euro-Atlantic region," notably in the former Yugoslavia.[166] In December 1992, the Allies extended the same principle to "peace-keeping operations under the authority of the UN Security Council." This decision formalized the various NATO activities under the Security Council's auspices under way since mid-1992. As the December 1992 communiqué noted, "For the first time in its history, the Alliance is tak-ing part in UN peacekeeping and sanctions enforcement operations."[167]

At the January 1994 summit, the Allies reaffirmed their offer to sup-port "peacekeeping and other operations" under UN or CSCE auspices, and endorsed "the concept of Combined Joint Task Forces as a means to facilitate contingency operations, including operations with partici-pating nations outside the Alliance."[168] The essential purpose of CJTFs was to facilitate the organization of effective "coalitions of the willing," particularly for non–Article 5 operations (that is, operations other than those to honor the binding commitment to collective defense in the case of external aggression against the Alliance).[169] The operations would in all likelihood be conducted by "combined" (multinational) and "joint" (multiservice) formations.

Although the formal institutionalization of the CJTF concept would take years to accomplish, a de facto CJTF was established at the end of 1995 in the form of the Implementation Force (IFOR) for Operation Joint Endeavor, the instrument for the enforcement of the military aspects of the Dayton peace agreement for Bosnia. In addition to the Allies, IFOR ultimately included eighteen non-NATO countries, fourteen of which were NACC and PfP members.[170] The follow-on force for IFOR, known as the Stabilization Force (SFOR), was activated on the day IFOR's mandate expired—December 20, 1996. All sixteen Allies con-tribute to SFOR, as do all the countries that participated in IFOR, as well as Ireland and Slovenia. NATO holds that "SFOR's mission is clear, limited and achievable: to deter renewed hostilities and to stabilize and consolidate the peace in Bosnia and Herzegovina in order to contribute to a secure environment in which civil implementation plans can be pursued."[171]

Internal adaptation: the Alliance's preparedness to support WEU-led operations and the emergence of a European Security and Defense Identity

As noted earlier, the WEU was formed in 1954 on the basis of the 1948 Brussels Treaty; Italy and West Germany then joined the original parties to the treaty—Britain, France, and the Benelux countries. During the Cold War, the WEU served primarily as a mechanism to reassure West Germany's neighbors and Alliance partners that Bonn's military capabilities would respect agreed constraints. Although the WEU's member governments made some efforts during the 1980s to give the WEU greater practical significance, it was not until the end of the Cold War that the concept of building a European Security and Defense Identity (ESDI) won a wider and more substantial consensus. The ESDI concept means a greater European capacity for autonomous military action, thanks in part to deeper political cohesion. Interest in the ESDI quickened at this point, for at least three reasons: a sense of diminished dependence on U.S. security commitments, resulting from the collapse of the Soviet empire; a determination on the part of the newly reunited Germany's European allies and partners to "embrace" Germany in a stronger common framework; and a recognition that the European NATO Allies might be wise to hedge against the risk of U.S. disengagement from European security commitments—or, at least, the possibility of U.S. nonparticipation in the management of some crises of concern to the European Allies.

The ESDI concept is not linked to a single institutional framework. Multiple organizations and efforts are involved, including bilateral enterprises (notably Franco-German and Franco-British cooperative frameworks) and trilateral endeavors (for instance, those involving French, Italian, and Spanish forces in joint exercises and training). The European Community's member governments had engaged in some foreign and security policy cooperation since the early 1970s, and by the end of the 1980s the European Community states were actively considering a more explicit engagement in defense matters, the possible utility of the

WEU in this regard, and the significance of the vaguely defined ESDI within the Alliance.

NATO's July 1990 London Declaration included only a single sentence about what was to become a major element in the Alliance's internal adaptation, being prepared to support WEU-led operations and the emergence of an ESDI: "The move within the European Community towards political union, including the development of a European identity in the domain of security, will also contribute to Atlantic solidarity and to the establishment of a just and lasting order of peace throughout the whole of Europe."[172]

By December 1990, however, the concept had become more complex and explicit: "enhancing the role of the European Allies with a view to ensuring a full and equitable sharing of leadership and responsibilities between Europe and North America. . . . A European security identity and defense role, reflected in the construction of a European pillar within the Alliance, will not only serve the interests of the European states but also help to strengthen Atlantic solidarity."[173]

This statement was made in the context of the opening that month of the European Community's Intergovernmental Conferences on Political Union and Economic and Monetary Union. These conferences led to corresponding treaties, adopted by the heads of state and government of the European Community in December 1991 at Maastricht, the Netherlands. In June 1991 the Alliance welcomed "the progress made by the countries of the European Community toward the goal of political union, including the development of a common foreign and security policy" and "a European security and defense role."[174] The Alliance's November 1991 Rome Declaration also endorsed the "enhancement of the role and responsibility of the European members" and applauded "the perspective of a reinforcement of the role of the WEU."[175]

It was not until January 1994, however, that the Alliance decided to support the emergence of an ESDI—and, more specifically, the conduct of WEU-led operations by European "coalitions of the willing"—with practical changes in its organizational structure. Although, as suggested above, one of the major purposes for devising Combined Joint Task Forces was to support non–Article 5 contingency operations conducted under NATO auspices that might involve a coalition of NATO and non-

NATO nations, another basic purpose was to facilitate the organization of such operations under WEU leadership.

The Maastricht Treaty had taken effect in November 1993, transforming the European Community into the European Union. In January 1994, the Alliance welcomed this development: "We give our full support to the development of a European Security and Defense Identity which, as called for in the Maastricht Treaty, in the longer term perspective of a common defense policy within the European Union, might in time lead to a common defense compatible with that of the Atlantic Alliance. . . . We support strengthening the European pillar of the Alliance through the Western European Union, which is being developed as the defense component of the European Union. . . . We therefore stand ready to make collective assets of the Alliance available, on the basis of consultations in the North Atlantic Council, for WEU operations undertaken by the European Allies in pursuit of their Common Foreign and Security Policy."[176]

The mechanism for making these collective Alliance assets available was to be CJTFs. It was assumed in January 1994 that reliance on Alliance assets would avoid a duplication of effort on the part of the European allies, and that it would be relatively easy to devise arrangements for "separable but not separate capabilities which could respond to European requirements and contribute to Alliance security."[177] In fact, the challenge of the Alliance's internal adaptation has proved to be politically contentious in some ways. Because the declared purposes of the ESDI include the "Petersberg tasks" approved by the WEU in 1992 (humanitarian and rescue operations; peacekeeping; and crisis management, including "peacemaking"), the internal adaptation issues associated with the ESDI constitute a key challenge for the Alliance in preparing for (and conducting) crisis management and peace operations.

Redefining collective defense: the new emphasis on countering the proliferation of weapons of mass destruction

It was not until after the outbreak of the Gulf War (August 1990–February 1991)—the Iraqi occupation of Kuwait and the operations under the authority of the UN Security Council to expel the Iraqi forces—that the Alliance began to identify countering the spread of weapons of mass destruction (WMD) as one of the main challenges in the post–Cold War world. The subject was not even mentioned in the Alliance's July 1990 London Declaration. In December 1990, however, the North Atlantic Council noted that "The proliferation of weapons of mass destruction and the spread of destabilizing military technology have implications for Allies' security and illustrate that in an ever more interdependent world, we face new security risks and challenges of a global nature. . . . Where they pose a threat to our common interests we will consider what individual or joint action may be most appropriate under the circumstances."[178]

By June 1991, the UN Special Commission and the International Atomic Energy Agency and other organizations had made a number of unanticipated discoveries about the magnitude and progress of Iraqi programs to build chemical, biological, and nuclear weapons. The Allies noted the dangers of WMD proliferation demonstrated by the Gulf War, but saw no need at that time for Alliance action. Instead, the Allies restated their "commitment to the earliest possible achievement of advances in the international forums dealing with specific proliferation issues," such as efforts to conclude a Chemical Weapons Convention and strengthen the Biological Weapons Convention.[179] Similarly, the November 1991 Rome Declaration did not call for any specific Alliance initiative, and it repeated support for international arms control regimes.[180] In contrast, the November 1991 Strategic Concept referred specifically to the need for "missile defenses" in light of "the proliferation of ballistic missiles and weapons of mass destruction" and for "precautions of a purely defensive nature" against chemical weapons, "even after implementation of a global ban."[181]

Nonetheless, it was not until the January 1994 summit that the Alliance "decided to intensify and expand NATO's political and defence efforts against proliferation, taking into account the work already underway in other international fora and institutions." The Allies directed "that work begin immediately . . . to develop an overall policy framework to consider how to reinforce ongoing prevention efforts and how to reduce the proliferation threat and protect against it."[182] The Alliance established a Joint Committee on Proliferation, composed of a Senior Political-Military Group on Proliferation and a Senior Defense Group on Proliferation (DGP). The Joint Committee on Proliferation has been noteworthy, among other reasons, because France has participated fully. The DGP is co-chaired by the United States and, on a rotating basis, a European ally; France served as the first European co-chair. In June 1996 the North Atlantic Council endorsed recommendations by the DGP "to improve Alliance military capabilities to address the risks posed by NBC [nuclear, biological, and chemical weapons] proliferation."[183]

The continuing collective defense role

The new emphasis on countering WMD proliferation has not entailed an abandonment of the Alliance's traditional collective defense role. While the Soviet Union constituted the main focus of the Alliance's collective defense planning during the Cold War, the North Atlantic Treaty makes no reference to the Soviet Union or any other specific potential adversary, and the Article 5 obligations of the Allies were never limited exclusively to contingencies involving the USSR. By the same token, since the end of the Cold War, uncertainties about Russia's future have not provided the sole rationale for maintaining the Alliance's collective defense posture. During the 1990–91 Gulf War, for example, it was feared that Iraq might attack Turkey, and the Allies took precautionary steps to hedge against that possibility. Since the end of the Cold War, some Allies have explicitly made a distinction between different types of Article 5 contingencies. In the 1996 British defense white paper, for instance, two of the seven types of missions for British forces embrace the mutual-defense pledge: "A limited regional conflict involving a NATO Ally who calls for assistance under Article 5 of the Washington Treaty" and "General War—a large scale attack against NATO."[184]

Such distinctions implicitly acknowledge both significant changes in international circumstances—the greater potential for limited regional contingencies—and persisting concerns about Russia's future. According to the 1991 Strategic Concept, the Alliance's "fundamental security tasks" continue to include the following: to "deter and defend against any threat of aggression against the territory of any NATO member state" and to "preserve the strategic balance within Europe."[185] Because the Strategic Concept was approved in November 1991, a month before the collapse of the Soviet Union, it uses the word "Soviet" in discussing what must be considered in defining the strategic balance in Europe:

"Even in a non-adversarial and co-operative relationship, Soviet military capability and build-up potential, including its nuclear dimension, still constitute the most significant factor of which the Alliance has to take account in maintaining the strategic balance in Europe."[186]

In political terms, as the Allies have multiplied their efforts to cultivate cooperative relations with Moscow, it has become increasingly awkward to refer explicitly to Russia as a potential threat to Alliance security. Nonetheless, at various points since the collapse of the Soviet Union in December 1991, U.S. officials have acknowledged—although, it seems, less frequently and more discreetly over time—that the Russian question is far from being conclusively resolved, and that it is prudent to hedge against reversals in Russian politics and policies. In January 1992, Secretary of Defense Dick Cheney suggested that the United States would need to maintain a deterrence posture vis-à-vis Russia until it had "unambiguous evidence of a fundamental reorientation of the Russian government: institutionalization of democracy, positive ties to the West, compliance with existing arms reduction agreements, possession of a nuclear force that is non-threatening to the West (with low numbers of weapons, non-MIRVed, and not on high alert status), and possession of conventional capabilities nonthreatening to neighbors."[187]

Cheney's successor as defense secretary, Les Aspin, said in March 1993 that while the United States and other Western countries obviously hoped that democracy and reform would prevail in Russia, two other possible outcomes had to be considered. Reversals could lead to "an ultranationalistic, hostile and authoritarian form of government," or "there could be a breakdown of authority, and nobody would be in charge."[188] In October 1993, Aspin mentioned the possibility that "anti-Western elements [could] take control of the Russian government." This might have been the situation Aspin had in mind when he referred to the option of reconstituting U.S. nuclear forces and other capabilities if the United States faced "a threatening reversal of events."[189]

In a rare and significant reference to NATO's continuing collective defense function vis-à-vis Russian military power, U.S. under secretary of defense Walter Slocombe said in June 1996, "The course that we are seeking for Russia foresees an optimistic outcome, and maintains an optimistic outlook. But we are not naive about Russia, and we are acutely conscious of the dangers, of the hard lessons of history. Should

Russia turn away from its new path, we can re-evaluate our approach and indeed we would have to do so. An integral part of our pragmatic partnership policy for Russia is that we continue to remain strong, so that we have a military hedge against whatever might come."[190]

Similarly, in an unusually explicit allusion to potential "direct threats against the soil of NATO members that a collective defense pact is designed to meet," in October 1997 Secretary of State Madeleine Albright referred to "questions about the future of Russia. We have an interest in seeing Russian democracy endure. We are doing all we can with our Russian partners to see that it does. And we have many reasons to be optimistic. At the same time, one should not dismiss the possibility that Russia could return to the patterns of its past."[191]

As these statements suggest, concerns about Russia as a potential threat to the Alliance are rooted mainly in uncertainties about the country's long-term political future. Why Western officials and experts have concerns about Russia's prospects for successful democratization is no mystery. Historians and other scholars of the country's political culture report that the precedents for stable democracy are minimal to nonexistent in Russia. Moreover, Russia has virtually no tradition of peaceful political successions. In 1988, before the Soviet empire's collapse, and before he became the special adviser for Central and East European affairs to NATO's secretary general, Christopher Donnelly called attention to the fact that Russia's political history has repeatedly featured a "pendulum effect" of relatively liberalizing efforts terminated by war, revolt, or revolution, and the reimposition of dictatorial rule: "a change of ruler in Russia and the USSR has rarely been natural and graceful, but often accompanied by assassination, disgrace, war, or a combination of these factors."[192]

The situation in Russia since the Soviet collapse has been one of continuing social and economic upheaval, with ambivalent relations toward the West. The regime is nominally democratic but falls far short of Western standards and pursues rather erratic and inconsistent policies, in part because of power struggles within the Russian government and, more broadly, within Russia as a whole. According to Vladimir Shlapentokh, a prominent sociologist and specialist in Russian affairs, "in the next few years, and possibly even longer, . . . Russia will continue to be a country with a stagnant economy, extremely high social polarization of the population, and permanent internal political conflicts."[193]

The internal political conflicts have led at times to violent and deadly confrontations—for instance, in October 1993, when Yeltsin called upon the military to attack his parliamentary adversaries. Given the magnitude of the economic and social crisis in Russia, some Western experts fear that the country's post-Yeltsin future could include an authoritarian regime led by someone like Gennadi Zuganov, the Communist Party leader, or Vladimir Zhirinovsky, the head of the so-called Liberal Democratic Party.[194] In 1995, Andrei Kozyrev, then the Russian foreign minister, warned that while the "collapse of the totalitarian system has opened up unprecedented vistas for political and economic freedom in Russia," it has also "triggered the kind of decay and inertia that can bury everything: the Russian economy, its statehood, law and order, and eventually freedom itself." In his view, Russia's problems have "created a feeding ground for political forces that openly strive to establish a nationalist dictatorship of a fascist nature rather than merely a revival of the previous system."[195]

Some of the contending political camps in Russia may succeed in their efforts to rally support and build national unity on the basis of radical populist ideologies, including militant Russian nationalism and antagonism toward the West. Sergey Rogov, the director of Russia's Institute of the USA and Canada, has compared today's Russia with Germany's Weimar Republic, adding that there are "strong internal forces pushing Russia into 'self-isolation' as a disgruntled nation seeking to undermine the international order . . . with a 'more assertive' stance toward protecting what are seen as Russia's national interests."[196]

Western concerns about Russia's potential to threaten the Alliance's security interests are not rooted in the country's current conventional military might. As Alexei Arbatov, deputy chairman of the Russian parliament's Defense Committee, acknowledged, "As recently as 1988, the Soviet Union and its Warsaw Pact allies held a quantitative edge over NATO of about 3–1 in main weapons of conventional ground and air forces. But as a consequence of the collapse of the Warsaw Pact, the disintegration of the Soviet Union, and as a result of reductions in compliance with the CFE Treaty, today Russia is quantitatively inferior to NATO forces by a ratio of from 1–2 to 1–3."[197] The state of the Russian military is probably far worse than these numbers suggest, because it has an array of grave problems: shortages of able-bodied personnel, brought on by desertion, draft evasion, malnutrition, and illness; inadequate and unpaid salaries; deficiencies in food, clothing, and housing, even for officers; underfunded and insufficient training and maintenance; and, above all, a dramatic decline in status, morale, cohesion, and discipline, with growing evidence of pervasive crime and corruption.[198]

The deterioration of the military's morale stems in part from the fact that other armed forces in Russia—various internal security forces, including the Presidential Security Service, special units of the Counter Intelligence Service, Border Troops, and the troops of the Ministry of Internal Affairs—have been growing and receiving normal salaries and perquisites not accorded to the regular armed forces. While Yeltsin's distrust for the regular military services may have deepened as a result of the army's hesitation about supporting him against the parliament in 1993, a general determination to prepare for further domestic turbulence probably also accounts for the expansion of the internal security forces.[199]

If the regular armed forces had the funds to redress their shortcomings, British analyst Charles Dick has argued, the likely result would be "a rebuilding of the old Soviet Army, writ smaller, with all that implies for the growth of nationalist, anti-Western and authoritarian sentiment."[200] Russian military officers are probably divided in many ways, however, and some studies question the extent to which these officers would be willing to use force against separatists or domestic political rivals. According to Deborah Ball, "If the central government continues to insist that the military become embroiled in internal domestic disputes, then the Russian military may go the way of the Soviet Union—complete disintegration."[201]

The likelihood of Moscow's engaging in confrontational or aggressive behavior toward the Alliance under the current government may be rated as low, for various reasons beyond the substantially weakened state of Russia's conventional armed forces. To begin with, the country's governing political and business elites probably recognize that such behavior would not be in Russia's economic interests. Rather than direct aggression or coercion against the Alliance as a whole or a specific Ally, which seems implausible in current circumstances, the greater risk is that of Russian military intervention in other former Soviet republics. Such interventions have already taken place in the Caucasus, Moldova, and Central Asia. Alliance interests could be engaged if an intervention spilled over into conflict involving an Ally such as Turkey or countries with which several Allies have cultivated close relations, such as the Baltic states. According to a recent analysis, while "there is no credible Russian military threat" to Central Europe today, "[t]he armed forces of Estonia, Latvia, and Lithuania are so small, weak, and geographically exposed that the Russian Army, even in its present condition, is generally viewed as capable of rolling over the Baltic States at will."[202]

Collective defense contingencies could also arise involving Russia and Turkey, because of disputes regarding other former Soviet republics. For example, some Russian officials have discerned Turkish designs on former Soviet holdings in the Caucasus and Central Asia. In fact, Turkish efforts to gain influence in Islamic areas of the former Soviet Union alarmed Russia enough for it to take countermeasures in 1992–93: "Russia began to amass forces and leverage to become the sole and decisive arbiter of the Nagorno-Karabakh war and to defeat Turkey's grand design. . . . Moscow aided insurgents against an anti-Moscow Azeri government, supported the Armenian forces fighting Azerbaidzhan, and deterred, by nuclear threats, any Turkish plans to act on behalf of Baku."[203]

Such reports of vague nuclear threats against Turkey by Russian military officers or civilian officials have gained little public attention in the West. Some Russian analysts have nonetheless argued that Russia's conventional military weakness could lead to the operational employment of nuclear weapons. According to Paul Felgengauer, a prominent Russian military analyst, "The Russian Army could easily suffer defeat in a local conflict in the Caucasus or in Central Asia. The political and military consequences of such a defeat could prove wholly unacceptable to Russia, and a direct threat to use nuclear weapons or even a limited 'demonstration' nuclear strike could for this reason suddenly become the last realistic possibility of winning or evening up a war that has been lost, although no one in Moscow is seriously planning such actions at this time, of course."[204] The risk of such use of nuclear weapons may be higher than is generally suspected, in view of reports about the primitive character of some Russian technical security measures.[205]

Russian officials and commentators have increasingly underscored the central importance of nuclear capabilities in guaranteeing the country's security. Although concerns continue to be raised about biological weapons programs in Russia, despite the government's denials, Russian nuclear forces command the Alliance's attention far more than any other "unconventional" assets.[206] NATO governments generally agree that the Alliance still requires an effective military posture to ensure stability in its relations with Russia, to furnish a solid foundation for dialogue and cooperation, and to provide a hedge against potential political upheavals in Russia. Furthermore, Allied officials and experts judge that the nuclear dimension of the Alliance's military posture may have a distinctively important stabilizing effect.

British officials in particular have described the continuing Russia-NATO deterrence relationship in positive terms at times. Secretary of State for Defense Malcolm Rifkind said in 1992, "Our strategy makes military recidivism by any future Russian leadership a pointless option for them. It is therefore in the interest both of the Allies and Russia as well as the other states of the former Soviet Union."[207] In 1996, David Omand, the deputy under secretary of state for policy in the Ministry of Defense, added that "we should be profoundly glad that history has bequeathed us a stable deterrence relationship maintained by both Russia and NATO."[208]

Because of the awkwardness of referring to Russia as a potential nuclear threat while trying to cultivate cooperative relations with Moscow, U.S. officials in recent years generally have been circumspect in discussing the strategic and political functions of U.S. nuclear forces vis-à-vis Russia. However, at the September 1994 press conference announcing the results of the Nuclear Posture Review that, among other decisions, confirmed the retention of U.S. nuclear forces in Europe, Deputy Secretary of Defense John Deutch said, "Let me remind you that Russia has little prospect of returning to the kind of conventional force structure that they had at the height of the Cold War due to the collapse of their economy and the change in their political situation. It is a less expensive and less demanding matter for them to return to a much more aggressive nuclear posture. If something does go wrong in Russia, it is likely that it is in the nuclear forces area that we will face the first challenge."[209]

Although the Allies have remained conscious of Russia's nuclear capabilities and overall military potential, they have seen grounds for cautious hope about prospects for continuing economic reform and further movement toward democratization. In a long-term historical perspective, the Yeltsin regime has remarkable achievements to its credit. Renowned Polish author Adam Michnik has recommended that observers discouraged by the ponderous pace (and the setbacks) in economic reform and democratization in Russia

> compare the Yeltsin regime to every known historical regime that Russia has had. . . . After all, this is the first time in its thousand-year history that Russia has had six years of freedom. It's never happened before. The whole history of freedom that Russia had known hitherto was between February and October in 1917. Of course it is true that in Russia there are corruption, nepotism, criminal mafias. That's all there. But there are also newspapers which write about it all, there are meetings where it is possible to speak about it. Put briefly, there is a realistic positive scenario available for Russia.[210]

Indeed, many Western observers would agree with Zbigniew Brzezinski's argument that a Russia interested in avoiding "dangerous geopolitical isolation . . . will have no choice other than eventually to emulate the course chosen by post-Ottoman Turkey, when it decided to shed its imperial ambitions and embarked very deliberately on the road of modernization, Europeanization, and democratization."[211]

The Allies have underscored their interest in promoting constructive trends and enhancing prospects for such a positive outcome in various ways, including bilateral national programs of cooperation with Russia, dialogue in the NATO-Russia Permanent Joint Council, and efforts in other international institutions. While the Allies hope that negative scenarios are unlikely and can be successfully averted, part of the continuing collective defense function of the Alliance resides in hedging against the unforeseen in Russia.

Reconciling traditional and new roles

The Alliance's role as an instrument of collective defense has remained central, despite a tendency to place more emphasis on non–Article 5 activities. The robustness of NATO's collective defense posture is still seen as an essential basis for relations with non-Allies, including former adversaries, and (increasingly) for constructive cooperation with them.

The challenge is to preserve the Alliance's coherence and effectiveness while reconciling the traditional role of collective defense with the new roles of cooperation with non-NATO countries in the Euro-Atlantic region, and crisis management and peace operations.

The Alliance's new roles overlap in significant ways. While the Allies consider cooperation with former adversaries and other non-NATO countries to be intrinsically valuable as a matter of principle, preparations for—and the conduct of—crisis management and peace operations have given it practical meaning.

Fourteen of the Alliance's PfP members participated in IFOR, and fifteen are contributing to SFOR. As the Allies noted in June 1996, IFOR "benefited from the experience and increased interoperability gained through PfP activities, in particular joint exercises" and the Planning and Review Process (PARP).[212] At the same time, the IFOR experience fortified PfP, as a result of a "joint Allied-Partner rolling evaluation of the lessons learned from political and military co-operation in IFOR with a view to applying such lessons to strengthening the PfP."[213] Moreover, three of the six nations in the Alliance's Mediterranean Dialogue (Egypt, Jordan, and Morocco) have contributed forces to IFOR and SFOR.

The new emphasis in collective defense on countering WMD proliferation has also enlarged options for cooperation with former adversaries and others in the Partnership for Peace. In June 1996, for example, the NATO defense ministers indicated that "The substantial progress made by the DGP [Defense Group on Proliferation] over the past two years provides a solid basis for continued co-operation among all Allies and, where appropriate, with Partners on relevant defense issues related to proliferation."[214] Consultations with Ukraine and Russia in this regard have been particularly significant.

The Alliance's work against the spread of weapons of mass destruction can be seen as an extension of its traditional collective defense function, but the Allies are well aware of the risk that WMD threats could also arise in "non–Article 5" operations.

Both of the Alliance's new roles—cooperation with former adversaries and other non-NATO nations, and crisis management and peace operations—deserve closer analysis. Significant problems of practical implementation have arisen and threaten to continue, involving dis-agreements among the NATO countries and, in some cases, participants in the Partnership for Peace. Managing these problems and disagree-ments and preserving the Alliance's ability to fulfill its traditional core mission of collective defense, as well as the new roles, will represent an enormous challenge.

3

Cooperation with Former Adversaries

The phrase "cooperation with former adversaries" understates the magnitude of the more ambitious and demanding of the Alliance's two new roles. In a series of authoritative declarations, the Allies have expressed a determination to contribute to the construction of a peaceful political order in Europe as a whole. To this end, the Alliance has established four new institutions: Partnership for Peace; the NATO-Russia Permanent Joint Council; the NATO-Ukraine Commission; and the Euro-Atlantic Partnership Council, which replaced the North Atlantic Cooperation Council in May 1997. The Allies intend to ensure that these institutions for cooperation with former adversaries (and, increasingly, other non-NATO countries) in the Euro-Atlantic region complement the Organization for Security and Cooperation in Europe. At the same time, the Allies have declared support for an open-ended process of NATO enlargement. NATO's self-assigned new role as an "agent of change" throughout Europe has raised great challenges, as well as questions about the future purposes and nature of the Alliance.

THE CHALLENGE OF DEFINING AND BUILDING A PEACEFUL POLITICAL ORDER IN EUROPE

The collapse of the Soviet empire has increasingly obliged NATO to grapple with a question that could be avoided and effectively postponed during the Cold War—how to give specific and practical content

91

to its long-standing vision of a peaceful political order in Europe. During the Cold War, the Alliance's long-term political objective was rarely expressed more precisely than in the Harmel Report: "The ultimate political purpose of the Alliance is to achieve a just and lasting peaceful order in Europe accompanied by appropriate security guarantees." The Harmel Report included no specifics as to what the "final and stable settlement in Europe" should consist of, except for the proviso that "Any such settlement must end the unnatural barriers between Eastern and Western Europe, which are most clearly and cruelly manifested in the division of Germany."[1]

Germany has been reunified since 1990, but NATO's vision of Europe's future political order has not become much more precise than reaffirmations of the more general Harmel Report goals. In the 1991 Strategic Concept, for example, NATO recalled that "the Alliance has worked since its inception for the establishment of a just and lasting peaceful order in Europe,"[2] and reaffirmed its resolve to "pursue the development of co-operative structures of security for a Europe whole and free."[3]

The Strategic Concept added that one of the Alliance's "fundamental security tasks" is "To provide one of the indispensable foundations for a stable security environment in Europe, based on the growth of democratic institutions and commitment to the peaceful resolution of disputes, in which *no* country would be able to intimidate or coerce *any* European nation or to impose hegemony through the threat or use of force."[4] In December 1996, in an extension of this vision, the North Atlantic Council advocated the construction of "cooperative European security structures which extend to countries throughout the whole of Europe without excluding anyone or creating dividing lines."[5]

In February 1997, U.S. secretary of state Madeleine Albright wrote that "Now the new NATO can do for Europe's east what the old NATO did for Europe's west: vanquish old hatreds, promote integration, create a secure environment for prosperity, and deter violence in the region where two world wars and the cold war began."[6] According to Albright, "the fundamental goal of our policy . . . is to build, for the very first time, a peaceful, democratic and undivided transatlantic community. It is to extend eastward—to central Europe and the former Soviet Union —the peace and prosperity that western Europe has enjoyed for the last fifty years."[7]

The NATO-Russia Founding Act, adopted in Paris in May 1997, offered an even more expansive vision, with goals for collective security in the Euro-Atlantic region consistent with the Kantian and Wilsonian tradition: "NATO and Russia, based on an enduring political commitment undertaken at the highest political level, will build together *a lasting and inclusive peace in the Euro-Atlantic area on the principles of democracy and cooperative security.* . . . Proceeding from the principle that *the security of all states in the Euro-Atlantic community is indivisible,* NATO and Russia will work together to contribute to the establishment in Europe of common and comprehensive security based on the allegiance to shared values, commitments and norms of behaviour in the interests of all states. . . . NATO and Russia will seek the widest possible cooperation among participating States of the OSCE with the aim of creating in Europe a common space of security and stability, without dividing lines or spheres of influence limiting the sovereignty of any state."[8]

To what extent do such visions of a harmonious and cooperative European security architecture take into account historical patterns of tension, suspicion, and rivalry? That the Allies are in fact aware of such risks, intend to hedge against them, and wish to sustain the Alliance's traditional functions while undertaking new missions has been evident. For instance, the Alliance has maintained its integrated military structure,[9] reaffirmed its core purpose of collective defense, and institutionalized its special relations with Russia and Ukraine. Moreover, the new NATO-sponsored institutions have been built in a relatively gradual step-by-step fashion. Improvisation and experimentation have at times revealed practical constraints, including resource limitations, but the general direction has been toward greater inclusiveness and an enlarged scope for more ambitious undertakings on a cooperative basis. While devising new and more comprehensive institutions, the Allies have respected the roles and competencies of other evolving organizations, such as the European Union, the OSCE, the United Nations, and the Western European Union (WEU). The OSCE, for example, has retained important responsibilities in areas such as preventive diplomacy, minority rights, and election-monitoring, and has worked in cooperation with NATO authorities in Bosnia.

To examine the development of the new institutions founded by NATO as well as the process of NATO enlargement, under discussion since the early 1990s, this chapter is organized as follows. The North Atlantic Cooperation Council and the Partnership for Peace are discussed first, because they represent the Alliance's initial efforts to institutionalize cooperative relations with former adversaries and other non-NATO countries in the Euro-Atlantic region. The focus then turns to NATO enlargement, because the Partnership for Peace has functioned as a pathway to NATO membership for some nations. NATO enlargement in turn leads to a discussion of the Alliance's relations with the most fervent opponent of enlargement—Russia—and with Ukraine. Although the Alliance has established special consultative bodies with these nations, the Allies in May 1997 also created a forum encompassing most of the nations in the region—the Euro-Atlantic Partnership Council—and decided to enhance the Partnership for Peace. After discussing these innovations, the chapter examines dilemmas and risks for the Alliance in its effort to combine collective security and collective defense functions.

THE NORTH ATLANTIC COOPERATION COUNCIL

As noted in chapter 2, the North Atlantic Cooperation Council represented NATO's first attempt to go beyond "military contacts" and "regular diplomatic liaison" with the states of the Warsaw Pact (a treaty that was formally disbanded in July 1991) and to develop—in the words of the November 1991 Rome Declaration—"a more institutional relationship of consultation and cooperation on political and security issues." The Alliance invited the foreign ministers of all the former Warsaw Pact states to meet with their NATO counterparts, and the first meeting of the North Atlantic Cooperation Council was held in December 1991. The disintegration of the Soviet Union later that month led to the expansion of the NACC to all former Soviet republics.[10]

It was agreed at the founding of the NACC in December 1991 that its members would meet annually at the foreign minister level, and every other month at the ambassadorial level, with further meetings at these levels "as circumstances warrant." The Allies and the other NACC states—which were then known as "liaison partners"—agreed to hold other meetings under the auspices of NATO committees with regard to security-related issues such as "defense planning, conceptual approaches to arms control, democratic concepts of civil-military relations, civil-military coordination of air traffic management, and the conversion of defense production to civilian purposes," and with regard to NATO's "Third Dimension" programs on science and the environment.[11]

NACC activities consisted in fact mainly of meetings—workshops, seminars, conferences, colloquiums, and so forth. For this reason, some observers called it "a gigantic talking shop where the formal opening speeches usually filled up most of the time available and the conclusions of the proceedings merely restated the questions originally posed for debate."[12] The initial agenda was repeatedly expanded in annual work plans and eventually encompassed topics such as air defense, peacekeeping, military procurement, civil emergency planning, defense budgets and economic planning, disarmament technologies, materiel and technical standardization, and communications and information systems interoperability. NATO also offered Democratic Institutions Fellowships and Science Fellowships to citizens of NACC states outside the Alliance. Beginning in 1993, a NACC Ad Hoc Group on Cooperation in Peacekeeping prepared a series of reports.

The NACC was composed of the sixteen NATO countries and twenty-two other states, all "former adversaries." This new group encompassed all the members of the Warsaw Pact, including the successor states of the Soviet Union, and Slovakia and the Czech Republic (the two states that succeeded the Czech and Slovak Federal Republic on January 1, 1993). Some observers regretted the fact that NATO limited NACC membership to its former adversaries, but it should be recognized that some other states (including Austria, Finland, Slovenia, Sweden, and Switzerland) obtained observer status in the NACC. Moreover, Ireland participated in the NACC Ad Hoc Group on Cooperation in Peacekeeping, a group that was merged with the PfP's Political-Military Steering Committee. Moreover, the NACC activities under the Military Cooperation Program were eventually subsumed under PfP as well, extending them to a larger number of participants.[13]

Because NATO is an intergovernmental organization, national views must be reconciled; and the process of reaching consensus (if indeed it can be attained) has sometimes placed national differences on display. The NACC was relatively uncontroversial within the Alliance, however. It appears that France alone was reluctant to endorse the establishment of the NACC. The French were evidently concerned about the NACC's potential impact on the CSCE as a pan-European enterprise, and wished to limit the NACC's mandate to political consultations.[14]

The French also had reservations about the meetings of NATO defense ministers with their counterparts in non-NATO NACC nations, because French defense ministers had not participated in meetings with their NATO counterparts since France's withdrawal from NATO's integrated military structure in 1966. The French had two preoccupations in this regard: resisting the tendency to give more substantial content to NACC activities, which might increasingly compete with those of the CSCE, and maintaining coherence with the Alliance participation policy they had pursued since 1966. President François Mitterrand in particular insisted that, because the French minister of defense had not participated in other meetings with NATO defense ministers, he should not meet with them in the larger framework involving NACC defense ministers. As a result, until June 1996 these meetings, which also included defense ministers from non-NACC PfP Partner states (such as Sweden and Finland) after the launching of the PfP in January 1994, were held on an informal basis without France. These meetings were sometimes called the "Group on Defense Matters"—a title that was never approved by the North Atlantic Council, because that would have required France's concurrence. In June 1996, as part of France's rapprochement with NATO institutions, a French defense minister participated for the first time since 1966 in a North Atlantic Council meeting with his counterparts, and in a meeting of NACC defense ministers.[15] Since the establishment of the EAPC in May 1997, EAPC meetings "in defense ministers session" have been convened with French participation.

NACC membership was limited from the outset to NATO and former adversaries (Warsaw Pact states and their successors) because it was conceived as a means to overcome the divisive legacy of the Cold War. However, the NACC's limits as well as its proper scope for action soon became apparent. In the beginning, NACC discussions included "problems such as the withdrawal of former Soviet troops from the Baltic states and the dispute concerning Nagorno-Karabakh." It soon became apparent to the governments that raised these issues that the other NACC participants were unwilling to do more than listen to their complaints, and that the NACC was incapable of taking any action about such matters. The focus of attention shifted to topics such as peacekeeping, scientific and environmental cooperation, arms control verification, and the conversion of defense industries. These topics were of interest to states in addition to the original NACC members, and the center of gravity shifted to an enterprise designed to be more inclusive and to encompass activities in addition to meetings—the Partnership for Peace. The NACC was replaced in May 1997 by an organization including all PfP and NACC participants—the Euro-Atlantic Partnership Council.[16]

PARTNERSHIP FOR PEACE

The Partnership for Peace was first proposed by U.S. secretary of defense Les Aspin at an informal meeting of NATO defense ministers in Travemünde, Germany, in October 1993; it was formally approved three months later, at NATO's January 1994 Brussels summit. (See Appendix 2 for the Partnership's Framework Document.) Its purposes were defined as follows: "At a pace and scope determined by the capacity and desire of the individual participating states, we will work in concrete ways towards transparency in defence budgeting, promoting democratic control of defense ministries, joint planning, joint military exercises, and creating an ability to operate with NATO forces in such fields as peacekeeping, search and rescue and humanitarian operations, and others as may be agreed."[17]

NATO has been the sponsor or "senior partner" in PfP in that the Alliance has determined the scope and purposes of PfP, including the menu of activities available for inclusion in Individual Partnership Programs (IPPs). The IPPs in turn have been approved on a "16 + 1" basis— that is, an agreement between NATO and the Partner.

The twenty-seven PfP participants (usually called "Partners") include all twenty-two non-NATO NACC participants except Tajikistan, plus Austria, Finland, Macedonia, Slovenia, Sweden, and Switzerland.[18] As NATO officials have pointed out, one could say that there are twenty-seven "Partnerships for Peace," because each Partner-state has concluded an Individual Partnership Program with NATO.

What security obligations has NATO accepted regarding PfP participants? In language that appeared to have been copied from Article 4 of the North Atlantic Treaty, the North Atlantic Council declared in January 1994 that "NATO will consult with any active participant in the

Partnership if that partner perceives a direct threat to its territorial integrity, political independence or security."[19]

Partnership for Peace was belittled at the outset by critics who replaced the word "Peace" with "Postponement" or "Procrastination" or even "Prevarication,"[20] because of an impression that PfP was simply a mechanism for stalling on the question of NATO enlargement. In fact, it has turned out to be a flexible arrangement capable of accommodating multiple functions, and PfP Partners have had various purposes. While some have seen it as a necessary "ticket to punch" to demonstrate good will with extensive PfP participation while seeking NATO membership, others (such as Switzerland) evidently have no intention or expectation of joining NATO and participate in order to promote more effective cooperation and international understanding. Still others (such as the former Soviet Central Asian republics) may "merely want to learn from it."[21]

Confounding some of the skeptics, PfP has rapidly become a pan-European security institution with greater military and political content than the OSCE. As British expert Nick Williams has noted, PfP represents "the most extensive and intensive programme of military cooperation yet conceived in Europe—quantitatively and qualitatively beyond anything achieved within the OSCE."[22]

The accomplishments of PfP include a vast array of exercises and associated exchanges, including education and training activities, and the practical application of PfP "lessons learned" in the operations in Bosnia, with Partner forces under NATO command in IFOR and (since December 1996) SFOR. These activities have promoted interoperability and transparency among the participating forces of NATO and Partner countries. PfP has also encouraged regional military cooperation, notably with regard to Poland, Ukraine, Romania, Hungary, Slovakia, the Czech Republic, and the Baltic states. Such military cooperation has contributed to the attenuation and resolution of some long-standing political differences. In December 1996, the Allies expressed support for "expanding the agreed fields of military missions within PfP to the full range of the Alliance's new missions, as appropriate, including Peace Support operations over and above previously agreed areas."[23]

In contrast with the NACC, which made no distinctions among the non-NATO participants, PfP allows for "self-differentiation." As noted above, each Partner concludes an Individual Partnership Program with NATO, selecting its choices from a menu of possible activities, exercises, and programs devised by NATO and then investing resources at a pace agreed with NATO. Moreover, in contrast with PfP, the NACC's work on peacekeeping emphasized "doctrinal rather than operational issues— developing a common approach to peacekeeping rather than establishing a real operational capability."[24]

According to Williams, the most significant differences between the NACC and PfP resided in PfP's success in introducing "a structural and procedural depth previously absent in NATO's cooperation activities." As Williams notes, PfP is given leadership by the Alliance's top political body, the North Atlantic Council, which imparts a "dynamism that is inevitably missing in NACC." Moreover, PfP has made possible permanent Partner representation at NATO's political headquarters in Brussels and at a new Partnership Coordination Cell at Mons, Belgium, near Supreme Headquarters Allied Powers Europe (SHAPE). PfP has also promoted standardization, with the transfer of more than eight hundred NATO standardization documents to Partners, regarding "military doctrine, concepts of operation and standard operating procedures." In January 1995 PfP was augmented with a Planning and Review Process (PARP) that closely parallels NATO's own defense planning system.[25] Under the enhanced Partnership for Peace program, initiated in 1997, the process of self-differentiation among Partners may go further, with some choosing a more ambitious agenda of participation in NATO-led planning and operational activities.

At the outset, PfP was intended to be virtually self-financing. That is, the Partners were expected to bear almost all the costs of their participation in the program. In practice, PfP activities have increasingly been financed by the Alliance as a whole, and specific Allies have undertaken noteworthy bilateral initiatives, either specifically as part of PfP or "in the spirit of" PfP. Secretary of Defense William Cohen in April 1997 summarized U.S. bilateral contributions as follows: "Since its inception in FY 1996, Warsaw Initiative funding has enabled partners to attend over fifty PfP exercises and other events, as well as to purchase defense articles and services, such as tactical radios, communications gear, English-language training, simulators, and search and rescue equipment. Another important aspect of our bilateral assistance is that we sponsor information exchanges with Partner MOD staffs on those crucial tools that enhance civilian control of the military to include defense planning, budgeting and recruitment/retention." While almost all of the Allies have pursued bilateral programs to assist Partners in learning about NATO military doctrines and operational procedures, Secretary Cohen discussed the contributions by Britain, Canada, Denmark, and Germany in particular detail.[26]

NATO ENLARGEMENT

NATO enlargement issues—how far enlargement should go, which countries should be invited to join (and at what point), who will pay for it, what its real purposes are, how to console those left out of the current round of enlargement, and so forth—have emerged as the most obvious signs of the magnitude of the challenge that NATO has set for itself: contributing to a new security order to prevent and contain conflict in the Euro-Atlantic region.

NATO enlargement was not a prominent issue in the years immediately following the collapse of communism in East-Central Europe in late 1989. In April 1991, Paul Wolfowitz, then U.S. under secretary of defense for policy, declared that "European security is indivisible. The United States is committed to supporting the process of democracy, as well as the independence and sovereignty of the Central-East European states." In the same speech, Wolfowitz implied that the East Europeans should not expect membership in NATO or explicit security guarantees: "Formal military alliances and guarantees are not the sole measures of national security, nor the only means of filling perceived political and security vacuums."[27]

In November 1991, when President Bush was asked about the possibility of NATO membership for the non-NATO participants in the NACC, he replied, "Let's get going now this [North Atlantic Cooperation] Council. Let's consult with them. Let's make them know that we have keen interest in their security and in their economic well-being. But I think it's premature to go beyond that."[28] Secretary of State James Baker emphasized the ambitious character of U.S. aims for the NACC. In his view, the NACC "could serve as the primary consultative body between NATO and liaison states on security and related issues" and "could play a role in controlling crises in Europe." The essential notion appears to have been to use the NACC as a vehicle to heal the division caused by the military confrontation between NATO and its former adversaries. In Baker's words, "For forty years, we stood apart from one another as two opposing blocs. Now, history has given us the opportunity to erase those blocs, to join together in a common circle built on shared universal and democratic values."[29] Although Henry Kissinger and Ronald Asmus, among others, had advocated NATO enlargement as early as 1991–92, it was never actively considered by the Bush administration.[30]

The Clinton administration's interest in NATO enlargement appears to have been encouraged by the confluence of several categories of strong advocates:

- highly respected East European leaders, such as Czech Republic president Vaclav Havel and Polish president Lech Walesa, who urged President Clinton to support their countries' applications for membership in the Alliance when they met with him in Washington at the April 1993 opening of the U.S. Holocaust Memorial Museum;
- influential leaders in Germany, particularly Defense Minister Volker Rühe, who was one of the earliest and most constant European proponents of enlargement;[31]
- groups of Americans with close ties to East-Central Europe, such as the Polish-American Congress, which championed NATO membership for ancestral lands that suffered as "captive nations" during the Cold War;
- former high-level officials, such as James Baker, Zbigniew Brzezinski, and Henry Kissinger, who argued that PfP would have to be supplemented with enlargement;[32]
- members of Congress from both parties who endorsed the argument of Senator Richard Lugar (R-Indiana) that NATO had to go "out of area or out of business," by taking in new members and assuming new tasks beyond collective defense;[33] and
- prominent foreign and security policy experts, such as Ronald D. Asmus, Richard L. Kugler, and F. Stephen Larrabee, who made a strong case for enlargement.[34]

Within the U.S. administration, the key proponents of enlargement were apparently President Clinton and officials such as Anthony Lake, his national security adviser, and Richard Holbrooke, U.S. ambassador to Germany and then an assistant secretary of state. According to interviews with administration officials, the growing support for enlargement met resistance from high-level officials in the Department of Defense, who favored making the most of Partnership for Peace, and who "feared diluting the effectiveness of NATO."[35] Reservations were also expressed initially by Strobe Talbott, then ambassador-at-large for the Newly Independent States (that is, the former Soviet republics). Talbott wrote to Secretary of State Warren Christopher in October 1993 that defining NATO enlargement criteria could be "quite provocative, and badly timed with what is going on in Russia," and recommended making PfP "the centerpiece of our NATO position."[36] After Talbott became deputy secretary of state in February 1994, however, he became more supportive of NATO enlargement.[37]

As James Goldgeier notes, "The when, who, how, and even why came only over time and not always through a formal decision-making process."[38] Supporters of enlargement within the administration hold that the decision was made between October 1993 and January 1994, whereas opponents maintain that it was during "the second half of 1994, depending on when they finally realized the president was serious."[39] The disjointed decision-making process within the U.S. government inevitably led to conflicting signals to the Allies and to an Alliance debate with uncertain premises, because it was clear that no enlargement could take place unless the United States chose to exert the required leadership. The U.S. government had conveyed the impression that pursuing PfP would buy the Alliance time for lengthy deliberations about enlargement options, but it became apparent during 1994 that the Clinton administration was determined to move forward with enlargement in the near term. As one German scholar observed, "The about-turn of the Clinton Administration induced by domestic policy factors came as a surprise for European allies, who had only just adapted to the PfP."[40]

The enlargement debate did not begin in earnest until late 1993, in the months leading up to NATO's January 1994 Brussels summit. The summit's only decision on enlargement was "to reaffirm that the Alliance, as provided for in Article 10 of the Washington Treaty, remains open to membership of other European states in a position to further the principles of the Treaty and to contribute to the security of the North Atlantic area. We expect and would welcome NATO expansion that would reach to democratic states to our East, as part of an evolutionary process, taking into account political and security developments in the whole of Europe." The Allies emphasized the launching of PfP, with the promise that "Active participation in the Partnership for Peace will play an important role in the evolutionary process of the expansion of NATO."[41]

Immediately after the January 1994 summit, President Clinton said, in response to a question, that it was "doubtful" that NATO would decline to aid an East European country subjected to aggression. Then he added, "The question is no longer whether NATO will take on new members, but when and how."[42]

NATO subsequently decided to study the questions of "how" and "why" before tackling the questions of "who" and "when." In terms of Alliance deliberations, it was at the December 1994 meeting of NATO foreign ministers that "the point of no return had been reached."[43] At that meeting, the North Atlantic Council "decided to initiate a process of examination inside the Alliance to determine how NATO will enlarge, the principles to guide this process and the implications of membership."[44]

The answers to "how" and "why" were set out in the Alliance's September 1995 *Study on NATO Enlargement*. According to this document, the seven rationales for enlargement are as follows:

- Encouraging and supporting democratic reforms, including civilian and democratic control;
- Fostering in new members of the Alliance the patterns and habits of cooperation, consultation and consensus building which characterize relations among current Allies;
- Promoting good-neighbourly relations, which would benefit all countries in the Euro-Atlantic area, both members and non-members of NATO;
- Emphasizing common defence and extending its benefits and increasing transparency in defence planning and military budgets, thereby reducing the likelihood of instability that might be engendered by an exclusively national approach to defence policies;
- Reinforcing the tendency toward integration and cooperation in Europe based on shared democratic values and thereby curbing the

countervailing tendency towards disintegration along ethnic and territorial lines;

• Strengthening the Alliance's ability to contribute to European and
international security, including through peacekeeping activities
under the responsibility of the OSCE and peacekeeping operations
under the authority of the UN Security Council as well as other new
missions; [and]

• Strengthening and broadening the Trans-Atlantic partnership.[45]

The questions of "who" and "when" were answered formally at the
NATO summit in Madrid in July 1997—at least with regard to the "first
round" of post–Cold War enlargement. The Allies invited the Czech
Republic, Hungary, and Poland to begin talks, with a view to signing
protocols of accession in December 1997 and completing the ratification
process "in time for membership to become effective by the fiftieth anniversary of the Washington Treaty in April 1999."[46]

Although the decision to address these questions at Madrid was taken
formally by the Alliance in December 1996, the United States is widely
perceived as driving the agenda and the schedule. In October 1996,
President Clinton said, "By 1999, NATO's fiftieth anniversary and ten
years after the fall of the Berlin Wall, the first group of countries we invite
to join should be full-fledged members of NATO."[47] Clinton made this
statement in Detroit during the 1996 presidential campaign: "Detroit
was regarded as a good choice for such a speech because of its population of Central and Eastern European ethnics, according to White
House aides."[48]

National debates within the Alliance

The most extensive discussions of the pros and cons of NATO enlarge-
ment within the Alliance have taken place in Germany and the United
States, while the question has received less attention in, for example,
France and Britain.

The United States. The U.S. debate may be ultimately the most significant, because the credibility of Alliance commitments hinges, in the
final analysis, on the United States above all. Accordingly, U.S. specialists in international security affairs have conducted an extensive debate
regarding NATO enlargement.[49]

In April 1997, Jeremy Rosner, special adviser to the president and the secretary of state for NATO enlargement ratification, noted that the way Senate votes regarding NATO enlargement were tallying up to that point might be misleading, because "these were 'free votes,' involving little funding and no actual security guarantees."[50] Nonetheless, the U.S. Senate in April 1998 voted 80–19 to support a resolution for ratification of the Alliance's enlargement to the Czech Republic, Hungary, and Poland; 45 Republicans and 35 Democrats endorsed the resolution, and 9 Republicans and 10 Democrats opposed it.[51]

In a valuable overview of the NATO enlargement debate in the United States in mid-1996, Rosner observed that, "Despite the lopsided 82–13 Senate vote in favor of ratification of the North Atlantic Treaty, the Truman administration faced opposition from three elements: isolationists, defense hawks, and liberal internationalists. This political triangle shows signs of forming again, possibly more potently than in 1949."[52]

As an example of a contemporary defense hawk, Rosner suggested Senator Kay Bailey Hutchison (R-Texas). The reservations expressed by former under secretary of defense Fred Iklé also focused on the potential negative impact of enlargement on NATO's military posture: "Far from solving an alleged crisis, expanding NATO now would fatally weaken it. The Atlantic Alliance must not become a chain letter—some Ponzi scheme that escapes bankruptcy only by signing up new members." Iklé deplored the fact that NATO was willing to agree, at least "in the current and foreseeable security environment," not to base "substantial combat forces" (the phrases ultimately employed in the NATO-Russia Founding Act) permanently on the territory of new Allies as a means of reassuring Russia about NATO enlargement: "[T]he advocates are willing to strip NATO of its military essence by ruling out deployment of allied forces on the territory of the new member states. The alleged political vacuum between Germany's eastern border and Russia's western border would thus be filled by a real military vacuum. . . . It would not take long for most Americans to conclude that what is good enough for the impoverished and exposed new eastern wing of NATO is good enough for rich Western Europe. The American troops would come home. This would be welcomed by those who want the North Atlantic Treaty to be no more of a deterrent to aggression than the UN Charter."[53]

In the event, Senator Hutchison supported NATO enlargement in the April 1998 vote. Some of the senators who voted against it, however, expressed "defense hawk" arguments. Senator Robert Smith (R-New Hampshire) said, "Adding three insiders creates a whole bunch of outsiders, a whole bunch of wannabes. You're going to subject NATO almost annually to the perpetual anguish of, 'Am I next? When is it my turn?'"[54] Senator James Inhofe (R-Oklahoma) said, "This is just the beginning to more and more countries. After the first three recruits, I don't see where there's an end to it."[55] Expressing a similar concern about a dilution of Alliance cohesion and effectiveness, given the number of applicants for NATO membership, Senator John Warner (R-Virginia) said, "We don't know what NATO is going to look like after we go from 16 to 28 nations. I look upon a proliferation of problems of unknown origins and unknown descriptions."[56] In an effort to slow down the "unrelenting" pressures for further enlargement that he anticipated, Senator Warner proposed amendments to delay another round of enlargement for at least three years and to require candidates for NATO to join the European Union first; both amendments were defeated.[57]

As an example of a liberal internationalist concerned about risks in NATO enlargement, Rosner referred to Senator Sam Nunn (D-Georgia), who had not yet retired from the Senate. In 1995, Nunn said, "By forcing the pace of NATO enlargement at a volatile and unpredictable moment in Russia's history, we could place ourselves in the worst of all security environments: rapidly declining defense budgets, broader responsibilities, and heightened instability."[58] In early 1997, the eminent diplomat and scholar George Kennan advanced even more dire warnings, contending that

> expanding NATO would be the most fateful error of American policy in the entire post–cold-war era. Such a decision may be expected to inflame the nationalistic, anti-Western and militaristic tendencies in Russian opinion; to have an adverse effect on the development of Russian democracy; to restore the atmosphere of the cold war to East-West relations, and to impel Russian foreign policy in directions decidedly not to our liking. And, last but not least, it might make it much more difficult, if not impossible, to secure the Russian Duma's ratification of the Start II agreement and to achieve further reductions of nuclear weaponry. . . . And it is doubly unfortunate considering the total lack of any necessity for this move. Why, with all the hopeful possibilities

engendered by the end of the cold war, should East-West relations become centered on the question of who would be allied with whom and, by implication, against whom in some fanciful, totally unforeseeable and most improbable future military conflict?[59]

Several senators who voted against NATO enlargement expressed "liberal internationalist" reasons for doing so. Senator Paul Wellstone (D-Minnesota) said, "What worries me most is that NATO expansion needlessly risks poisoning Russia's relationship with the United States, and increases the odds that Russian ultranationalists will gain power in the post-Yeltsin era."[60] Senator Daniel Patrick Moynihan (D-New York) warned that NATO enlargement could cause the United States to "stumble into the catastrophe of nuclear war with Russia."[61] Senator Robert Smith (R-New Hampshire) said,

> The most important requirement for the Poles, the Czechs and the Hungarians as far as their security is concerned is that America and Russia remain friends. . . . We are taking down tremendous numbers of [Russian nuclear] weapons that have been aimed at the United States for decades. But extending an alliance, which during the cold war the Soviet Union considered hostile, [to] the countries that she doesn't threaten is basically kicking this former giant, . . . poking them in the ribs. . . . History shows that it is unwise to treat nations like that, and it is highly dangerous for countries in the middle, because these are the countries that are going to suffer if there is a confrontation that takes place between the United States and Russia again. It is the nations in the middle in Eastern Europe that are going to get the squeeze.[62]

As an example of an isolationist, Rosner suggested Representative John Linder (R-Georgia), who argued in December 1995 that "It is time to recognize that NATO expired in August 1989. It is time for us to give it a decent burial, with full military honors."[63] Ted Galen Carpenter of the Cato Institute also offered many arguments to the effect that "the enlargement case . . . is merely one manifestation of a desperate search for new missions to justify NATO's existence in the post–Cold War world. Enlarging NATO's membership and having the alliance pursue nebulous out-of-area missions, however, is a blueprint for disaster."[64]

The extent to which any of the senators who voted against NATO enlargement can be classified as true "isolationists" is debatable. However, some of the senators who so voted expressed doubts about the rationale for NATO's continued existence or reservations about its assuming tasks other than collective defense, such as peacekeeping. Senator Tom Harkin (D-Iowa) asked, "If something is born because of the Soviet Union, what are the reasons not only for continuing it, but for expanding it? There are other means to promote democracy and economic markets. . . . Europe is powerful. Europe is wealthy. There is no Soviet Union. There is no external threat."[65] Senator Larry Craig (R-Idaho) said, "The new NATO will signal an end of NATO as a defense alliance and the beginning of its new role as a regional peacekeeping organization."[66] Senator John Ashcroft (R-Missouri) warned, "It would be perilous indeed if we were to change the nature of NATO to make it a global police operation instead of the defender of territory that it was designed to be."[67]

It should be noted that Senator Smith expressed both "defense hawk" and "liberal internationalist" arguments against NATO enlargement—as did some others. Senator Warner, for example, employed "liberal internationalist" reasoning when he asked, "will the Senator allow me to observe that the American taxpayers, since 1992, have contributed $2.6 billion in the spirit of that [Russian-American] friendship to help Russia dismantle its weapons systems? And here this [NATO enlargement] comes along and takes a red-hot poker and jams it right in their ribs."[68] These examples suggest that, however useful categories may be for classifying arguments, legislators find merits in more than one school of thought.

The arguments in support of NATO enlargement in the U.S. debate have not been simply echoes of the rationales advanced by the Clinton administration. While administration officials rarely mention risks of Russian neo-imperialism, coercion, or aggression or the need to curtail potential power competitions in Central Europe, some American proponents of enlargement have done so. According to Peter Rodman, for example, "The only potential great-power security problem in Central Europe is the lengthening shadow of Russian strength, and NATO still has the job of counter-balancing it."[69] Some senators who voted for NATO enlargement, such as Senator Jesse Helms (R-North Carolina), deplored the Clinton administration's insistence that it was not directed against Russia: "A central strategic rationale for expanding NATO must be to hedge against the possible return of a nationalist or imperialist

Russia, with 20,000 nuclear missiles and ambitions of restoring its lost empire."[70]

Retired U.S. Army General William Odom, a former director of the National Security Agency, has dismissed the Russian-threat case for enlargement: "The new military threat is an extremely weak argument, unlikely to persuade anyone who is familiar with the state of the Russian military and its industrial base. Although a new Russian imperialism is already evident in Central Asia and the Transcaucasus, the burden of that empire will impede a serious Russian military modernization that could actually pose a threat to Central Europe."[71]

Odom endorses the arguments favored by the administration regarding NATO's ability to provide a reliable framework for democratization, free-market prosperity, and constructive solutions to border and minority questions. However, he underscores an argument rarely heard over the administration's emphasis on trans-European understanding and the putative consensus on "security is indivisible" principles—the need to forestall the emergence of competitive diplomacy in Central Europe involving powers such as Russia, Germany, France, and Britain. "Central Europe will again become the scene of some, if not all, of the perverse dynamics of the interwar period unless NATO enlarges to preempt them."[72] Central Europe's citizens are, of course, sensitive to such dynamics. As Czech Republic president Vaclav Havel observed, "A security vacuum in Central Europe exists today and could arouse unnecessary temptation among nationalists and those we suspect of nostalgia for power blocs and regional dominance."[73]

Among Clinton administration officials, Holbrooke was exceptionally explicit in publicly advancing the argument that NATO enlargement is necessary for geopolitical or balance-of-power reasons—to preserve stability and prevent German-Russian rivalries in Central Europe. According to Holbrooke, "for Germany and Russia, the two large nations on the flanks of central Europe, insecurity has historically been a major contributor to aggressive behavior. . . . The West must expand to central Europe as fast as possible in fact as well as in spirit. . . . Stability in central Europe is essential to general European security, and it is still far from assured."[74] Rather than referring plainly to Germany and Russia, officials such as Secretary of State Albright spoke in more general terms about the risk that the Alliance's failure to enlarge "could cause confidence to crumble in central Europe, leading to a search for security by other means, including costly arms buildups and competition among neighbors."[75]

Germany. The arguments in German discussions for the most part have paralleled those in the United States. In Germany, the arguments for near-term enlargement include "projecting stability" eastward; not allowing Russia a veto over NATO's security arrangements; honoring the West's moral responsibility to foster democracy in Europe; and providing a framework for the long-term consolidation of democratization and free-market economic reform, as well as more effective resolution of minority and border disputes, among the nations of East-Central Europe. The arguments against early enlargement include the risks that such enlargement could provoke nationalist reactions in Russia, paralyze Alliance decision making, import new instabilities into NATO in the form of minority and border disputes, and draw new East-West dividing lines that could "create a self-fulfilling prophecy of future confrontation."[76]

In NATO Europe, Germany has been seen as the strongest proponent of enlargement, with Defense Minister Volker Rühe considered the first and most consistent advocate, ever since his widely noted March 1993 lecture in London.[77] Rühe's firm advocacy of enlargement and his tendency to take distinct positions about timing and candidates—for example, declaring publicly in August 1995 that the Baltic states cannot expect near-term membership—has put him at odds at times with colleagues in the Foreign Ministry and the Chancellor's Office who preferred to postpone specifying candidates as long as possible, in view of sensitivities in Russia and Eastern Europe.[78]

At least three aspects of German discussions about NATO enlargement issues have been distinctive. First, Germany's economic and cultural influence in Central and Eastern Europe has been greater than that of other NATO allies. Second, the sense of moral and political responsibility for the fate of these countries appears to be greater in Germany than in other Allied countries, as a result of the 1939 Molotov-Ribbentrop Pact defining Nazi and Soviet spheres of influence in Eastern Europe and the widespread destruction wrought by Nazi Germany. Third, Germany has naturally had a sharper sense than most other Allies of geographic exposure to potential trouble in the former Soviet empire. As recently as April 1996, Rühe argued: "The opening of the

Alliance to the East is a vital German interest. One does not have to be a strategic genius to understand this. You only have to look at the map. A situation in which Germany's eastern border is the border between stability and instability in Europe is not sustainable in the long run. Germany's eastern border cannot be the eastern border of the European Union and NATO. Either we export stability or we import instability."[79] Arguments for moving the Alliance's defensive border eastward so that Germany would not be on NATO's front line were subsequently dropped from public policy statements, because they were inconsistent with the official Alliance rhetoric asserting that there will be "no dividing lines" in the new Europe.[80]

Geopolitical calculations, particularly with regard to relations with Poland and other neighbors, have nonetheless continued to appear in German reflections on NATO enlargement. In December 1997, Karsten Voigt, a Social Democratic member of the Bundestag, said that enlargement would be constructive because it would "bind Germany into a structure which practically obliges Germany to take the interests of its neighbors into consideration."[81] Another structural advantage of an enlarged Alliance is that it would enable Germany's neighbors to forgo autonomous policies and more limited coalitions:

> Leaders in Bonn understood earlier than those in Paris or London that the security void which had been created in the heart of the continent would ultimately have to be filled by someone. . . . Bereft of any serious institutional affiliation, the countries of the region would begin to construct their own security arrangements. What would these arrangements have looked like? Very much like the ones which had already plunged Europe into two world wars this century: Poland and Romania (the two biggest countries in the region) against Russia, Slovakia and Romania against Hungary, and the Czechs with the Poles in order to deflect Germany's influence. Had that happened, Germany would have then been faced with the option of either participating in central Europe's local alliances or reaching a deal with Moscow in order to keep the region under control—precisely the choices which previous generations of German politicians faced, with such disastrous consequences. For Bonn, therefore, the only solution was to work for the integration of these countries into both NATO and the European Union, not only in order to ensure security in the heart of Europe, but also in order to spare the Germans themselves any new historic choices between East and West.[82]

Despite the reservations expressed by some German experts in security affairs, NATO enlargement has been uncontroversial in Germany.[83] It is widely agreed that "NATO enlargement serves Germany's political, strategic, and moral interests."[84] The Bundestag approved resolutions shortly before the July 1997 Madrid summit favorable to including Romania and/or Slovenia in addition to the Czech Republic, Hungary, and Poland; the government, however, chose not to advocate further candidates actively and, to some extent, mediated among the Allies on the scope of enlargement. "Kohl's role as a mediator at the NATO summit, and his insistence on having other potential candidates, including the Baltic countries, explicitly named in the final communiqué, took off the heat in the ensuing debate."[85]

The Bundestag approved enlargement to the Czech Republic, Hungary, and Poland in March 1998 by a huge majority—a vote of 554 in favor, 37 against, and 30 abstaining. Foreign Minister Klaus Kinkel emphasized Germany's "historic and moral duty" to welcome its eastern neighbors to the Alliance and criticized opponents for taking an "immoral" position, while Defense Minister Rühe said that to refuse the candidates would be "a historic and moral scandal." The majority of Green members of the Bundestag nonetheless abstained or voted against enlargement, on the grounds that it would damage relations with Russia and endanger stability in Europe. Bundestag members from the Party of Democratic Socialism (the former East German Communists) said that the OSCE, not NATO, should be the basis for building an all-European security order, and that enlarging NATO would divide Europe along a line further to the east.[86]

France. In contrast to the relatively extensive discussions of NATO enlargement in Germany and the United States, little public debate has taken place in France. Furthermore, whereas some high-level officials in Germany and the United States began advocating NATO enlargement in 1993, some of them publicly (with varying degrees of explicitness), several official French statements in late 1993 in anticipation of the January 1994 Alliance summit expressed reservations about enlargement. Alain Juppé, then the foreign minister, said that enlargement might dilute the Alliance, create new dividing lines, and cause fears in Russia, offering Moscow a pretext to transform the Commonwealth of Independent States into a competing organization.[87] In January 1994, just before the summit, François Léotard, then defense minister, said, "To knock at NATO's door is to knock at America's door and ask for the American guarantee. That is understandable, but it is not our conception. We want the request for security to be directed to the countries of Europe. Hence our proposal for association with the WEU."[88]

After the January 1994 Alliance summit approved the principle of enlargement, the official French line shifted to expressing concern lest enlargement take place too rapidly, in a "premature" fashion that might "weaken the Alliance" and "give the impression of encircling those who would have been excluded."[89] It was only after Jacques Chirac became president in May 1995 that the French stopped expressing doubts publicly and declared, in the words of the new foreign minister, Hervé de Charette, that they regarded enlargement "in a very positive spirit" and would in particular support Romania's candidacy.[90]

In mid- to late 1996, de Charette and Defense Minister Charles Millon hinted that France might block enlargement if it did not gain satisfaction on its proposals regarding the internal adaptation of the Alliance. This maneuver lacked credibility, however, for two reasons. First, in late 1996 and early 1997 President Chirac had publicly and emphatically promised the Poles, the Czechs, the Hungarians, and the Romanians to support their applications. Second, as Pascal Boniface observed, "It would be difficult to explain to the candidate countries seeking entry into NATO that France refused to admit them because it had not obtained the concessions it expected from the United States regarding the structures of the southern command."[91] The French therefore concentrated on a more credible threat—to stop the process of France's rapprochement with NATO institutions. France's refusal to go further with "reintegration," pending satisfaction of its proposals regarding the Alliance's internal adaptation, has been its official position since June 1997.

French discussions of enlargement have been exceptional in at least three ways. First, in part because of a widespread sense of detachment about NATO matters that has been cultivated in the more than thirty years since France left the Alliance's integrated military structure in 1966, many of the French see NATO as the vehicle through which the United States extends security protection to Europeans. NATO guarantees are seen as essentially a U.S. responsibility, and NATO enlargement signifies, in the words of Paul-Marie de la Gorce, "an extension of the zone that it [America] wanted to protect and ensure control over," an expression of "the hegemonic will of the United States over the Old Continent."[92] President François Mitterrand evidently interpreted U.S. interest in enlargement as an attempt by the United States "to extend its influence in Eastern Europe, at low cost and to the detriment of the countries of Western Europe, which, moreover, are bearing the burden of most of the economic aid to these countries."[93]

Second, other aspects of the Alliance's future have been of much greater interest to the French—above all, Combined Joint Task Forces, the new command structure, and efforts to build a European Security and Defense Identity; these matters affect France's status in the Alliance more directly than enlargement. French discussions of enlargement place an exceptional emphasis on links to ESDI and the Alliance's internal adaptation.[94] Indeed, in the 1991–95 period, French leaders feared that a reinvigoration of the Alliance through enlargement would conflict with the pursuit of ESDI. Although French officials rarely expressed this concern publicly, it was always a factor in their thinking on enlargement. One of the French responses was to organize meetings between the foreign ministers of the WEU countries and those of selected East European countries.[95]

Third, the French in 1997 championed a larger "first round" of post–Cold War enlargement than did Britain, the United States, and some other Allies, and organized support for Romania in particular. According to a British scholar, "Supporting Romania was Chirac's way of showing that France will rejoin NATO [institutions] on its own terms, and was actively influencing European security arrangements. . . . Chirac also calculated that an explicit bid for Romania could never harm the French: if Romania was ultimately rebuffed, it would not be France which would suffer a loss of face, but if Romania did manage to get into the alliance, it would be France which would bask in the glory."[96]

The French, however, gave several substantive reasons for including Romania: that it would be unwise to separate Hungary and Romania, in view of the large ethnic Hungarian minority in Romania and the prospect of Hungary entering the European Union before Romania; that it would help to stabilize the Balkan/Danubian region, an area of greater insecurity than Central Europe; that it would provide a "north/south balance" in enlargement; that Romania had made progress in meeting democratization and marketization criteria and in resolving border and minority questions with Hungary; and that its rejection might provoke nationalism and border and minority problems with its neighbors. Some French observers mentioned three additional considerations: that Romania could serve as a counterweight to "Anglo-Saxon and Germanic influence and methods" and to the predominant use of English in the Alliance; that Romania might be an ally beholden to France to compensate for the "satellites" that Germany may gain with Czech, Polish, and Hungarian membership in NATO; and that Paris and Bucharest have traditionally had a close political and economic relationship. It was noted that Bucharest may be an important market for French goods, especially armaments; and that during the Cold War, Romania was the only Warsaw Pact state to purchase any military equipment from the West—helicopters from France.[97]

In France's public discussions of NATO enlargement, the few commentaries that have appeared have been quite critical. Former prime minister Michel Rocard asked,

> Is it urgent, is it intelligent to confirm to the Russian people and to their leaders, who still possess around ten thousand nuclear warheads, that we distrust them, that we are consolidating their encirclement, and that we are putting ourselves in a position to be able to rapidly deploy strategic weapons all around them? Could we not explain to the Poles, the Hungarians, the Czechs, the Slovaks and the Romanians . . . that their true security depends on agreement between the West and Russia? A serious and binding security treaty between the Atlantic Alliance and Russia must precede any enlargement of NATO. To fail to understand that is to put peace at risk. It is time to reconsider and to slow down a process that was recklessly initiated, and to ensure properly the security of half the world.[98]

In another article, Rocard warned that NATO enlargement could result in Russian decisions to abandon nuclear arms control and to undertake rearmament programs, as well as bolstering nationalist currents in Russian politics. According to Rocard, "Like a bulldozer running without a driver, Western diplomacy is lumbering towards NATO enlargement without thought, coordination, or debate. . . . This would be assuredly the greatest diplomatic blunder of the West in half a century."[99] Other prominent public figures—including former president

Valéry Giscard d'Estaing and Gaullist leader Philippe Séguin—also expressed concerns about the potential impact of enlargement on relations with Russia.[100]

It is perhaps not surprising that French commentators have been among the most vocal in expressing the view that the enlargement agenda has been driven by U.S. domestic political imperatives, and that U.S. management of the enlargement process could lead to one of France's nightmares during the Cold War—a Washington-Moscow partnership settling Europe's affairs over the heads of the Europeans. Hubert Védrine, who was President Mitterrand's diplomatic adviser for fourteen years (1981–95), wrote in April 1997 that Russia

> is supposed to be consoled by a partnership that is to be invented with NATO, at the risk of reconstituting—to crown it all—a situation of [U.S.-Russian] condominium that would wind up depriving a European defense of any latitude. Is this but a drawback, or is it the very purpose? In private, many European officials consider this an absurd decision-making process, in which no one may ask whether enlargement is truly in Europe's interest, whether one could not deal with the question of Central Europe in another way, and whether it should not rather be Europe [that is, the European Union] proposing a treaty to Russia.[101]

Since Védrine became France's foreign minister in June 1997, his views have assumed greater weight.

The French Senate approved ratification of the protocols for Alliance membership for Poland, Hungary, and the Czech Republic in May 1998, and the National Assembly gave its endorsement the following month. The National Assembly debate was consistent with previous French discussions of enlargement in that questions concerning U.S. influence in NATO, the construction of a European Security and Defense Identity, and France's own status in the Alliance figured prominently. Representatives of all party groups supported the enlargement protocols, except for the Communist spokesman, Jean-Claude Lefort, who contended that NATO enlargement would create new divisions in Europe; he argued that developing the OSCE as an instrument of "common security" would better serve the interests of the three prospective new Allies and all other European nations. The National Assembly endorsed the protocols with a show of hands and no recorded votes.[102]

Other NATO nations. As the German and French examples suggest, distinctive arguments and considerations of interest and influence are present in every NATO nation. Italy supported France's case for Romania, and suggested that its neighbor Slovenia also be admitted in the first post–Cold War round of enlargement. According to Jonathan Eyal, "The British, who accepted NATO's enlargement as inevitable rather than desirable, always wanted it to be as small as possible."[103] Some observers consider Turkey the least predictable ally with regard to the ratification of NATO enlargement. Turkish officials have indicated that Ankara's price for supporting NATO enlargement may be a definite prospect of their country's membership in the European Union. Absent such a commitment, the Turks may demand compensation in some other form from either the European Union or the United States.[104] Indeed, the main issues in European-American relations regarding NATO enlargement may well include cost-sharing, the responsibilities to be assumed by the EU, and the linkage to continuing political-military stabilization requirements in Bosnia.[105]

Key issues in NATO enlargement

Interviews with well-informed observers in several NATO nations suggest that four reservations about NATO enlargement are particularly salient: its potential impact on Alliance cohesion; the implications for the "also-rans," the unsuccessful applicants in the first wave of post–Cold War enlargement; the risk of an unnecessary confrontation with Russia; and the gravity of accepting new collective defense obligations.

The potential impact on Alliance cohesion. Of the twelve current applicants for NATO membership, only three were invited to begin accession negotiations in July 1997. Some critics are nonetheless concerned that the addition of any more nations could complicate Alliance decision making, which is already ponderous and intermittently prone to stalemate or expedients such as the recurrent "Danish footnotes" during the nuclear controversies of the early to mid-1980s.[106]

Some Western critics of NATO enlargement maintain that Russia's anxieties about enlargement leading to a more powerful Alliance are misplaced, contending that the addition of new members will contribute to the erosion of the Alliance's cohesion. In their view, although the

Alliance will be larger and closer to Russian soil, it will be increasingly less capable of undertaking effective collective defense operations, to say nothing of its inability to undertake the aggression that some Russians profess to fear. Such a result will follow, they argue, from the immense challenge of trying to "socialize" the political-military establishments of the new Allies. Despite the progress made under PfP auspices, much remains to be done in this regard, and the process of "NATO-ization" across East-Central Europe could be protracted and disruptive. Internal political upheavals in one or more of the new Allies, some suggest, could be more disruptive to the Alliance as a whole and harder to contain than the military takeovers in Greece and Turkey during the Cold War.

The risk of disputes among the prospective new Allies of East-Central Europe and their neighbors seems so substantial to some European NATO observers that they have wondered whether the Alliance might have to develop formal conflict-mediation institutions more elaborate than the ad hoc mechanisms applied at times to the Greek-Turkish case, or perhaps even expulsion procedures.

Implications for the "also-rans." One of the most complex questions raised by enlargement is the fate of the disappointed suitors, the nations not accepted for membership in the first round of post–Cold War NATO enlargement.

The number of formal applicants for NATO membership, it should be noted, has fluctuated. In June 1996, the North Atlantic Council indicated that the Alliance was engaged in an "individual, intensified dialogue with, so far, fifteen interested countries."[107] The number had fallen to twelve by April 1997.[108] The twelve current applicants are Albania, Bulgaria, the Czech Republic, Estonia, the Former Yugoslav Republic of Macedonia (FYROM), Hungary, Latvia, Lithuania, Poland, Romania, Slovakia, and Slovenia. The three countries that pursued an "intensified dialogue" on membership for a while but have decided for the present to hold off on a formal application are Azerbaijan, Finland, and Ukraine.

To offer reassurance to the applicants that will be left out of the first round of post–Cold War enlargement, Secretary of State Albright said, "NATO's area of concern has always been wider than its area of membership and it always will be."[109] Moreover, U.S. officials have continued to reaffirm Warren Christopher's "open door" policy: "When the first new members pass through NATO's open door, it will stay open for all those who demonstrate that they are willing and able to shoulder the responsibilities of membership."[110] According to Secretary of Defense William Cohen, "Central and East European states not included in the first round of new members will not be isolated and will be able to continue to prepare for membership if they wish to. The first new members will not be the last. No aspirant nation will be excluded from continuing to work towards membership."[111]

Perhaps the clearest statement of the rationale for this approach has been offered by Under Secretary of Defense for Policy Walter Slocombe:

> NATO must avoid the risk that taking in some countries will imply the permanent exclusion of others, thereby either inviting a new division of the Continent or undercutting those who are working for reform in places like Russia, Ukraine, and elsewhere. The first new members will not be the last, and security for all, not just NATO members, must be preserved. Therefore, NATO enlargement must not only be inclusive, rather than exclusive, . . . it will necessarily be a steady, deliberate, and gradual process. . . . Enlargement will be a long process whose scope cannot be determined in advance.[112]

In other words, to avoid implying the "permanent exclusion" of some countries, NATO enlargement must be an "inclusive" process of indefinite scope and duration. It appears that an open-ended process is seen as the necessary complement to taking in only a few new Allies. Various arguments favored making the first round of post–Cold War enlargement a small one. For instance, it might then be easier to contain near-term Russian annoyance, to limit the financial costs, to reassure the disappointed by contending that further rounds of enlargement could take place at a later time, and to minimize whatever negative effects enlargement might have on Alliance cohesion. The "also-rans" or "have-nots" would receive compensation and consolation in the form of an enhanced PfP (as discussed later in this chapter).[113]

The counterarguments to starting out with a small group of new Allies are nonetheless worth pondering. Those left out of the first round may see themselves (and be seen by Moscow) as consigned to a "gray area" of lesser protection or even a Russian sphere of influence, despite NATO's assurances about an "open door" for further enlargement. These perceptions regarding the implications for those excluded from the initial wave of enlargement could create instabilities and inse-curities in the "also-ran" countries not included in the first group of new Allies. An open-ended enlargement process may create what some have called a "festering sore" of long-frustrated aspirants to membership, with resentments comparable to those of many Turks with regard to Ankara's indefinitely postponed membership in the European Union.

Furthermore, some argue, an open-ended process could cause more irritation in Moscow than a specific timetable for enlargement. Further rounds of enlargement could amount to "ticking clocks" in Moscow—imperatives for timely action in the rhetoric of Russian nationalists who see (or at least portray) enlargement as threatening. Thus the scene might be set for further discord and confrontation between NATO and Russia.

During the weeks before the July 1997 NATO summit in Madrid, the Allies debated whether to invite Romania and Slovenia—in addition to the Czech Republic, Hungary, and Poland—to begin accession talks with NATO. In the event, these unsuccessful applicants received special mention in the Madrid Declaration: "With regard to the aspiring mem-bers, we recognize with great interest and take account of the positive developments towards democracy and the rule of law in a number of southeastern European countries, especially Romania and Slovenia." The only other aspirants who received specific mention were the Baltic republics: "At the same time, we recognize the progress achieved towards greater stability and cooperation by the states in the Baltic region which are also aspiring members." All aspirants were "strongly encouraged" to participate in PfP and the EAPC, to "further deepen their political and military involvement in the work of the Alliance."[114]

The scope of enlargement beyond the three countries invited in July 1997 depends on many factors. Some official U.S. statements have implied that NATO could embrace the "other half" of Europe. In Octo-ber 1997, for example, Secretary of State Albright said,

[F]or centuries virtually every European nation treated virtually every other as a military threat. That pattern was broken only when NATO was born and only in the half of Europe NATO covered. With NATO, Europe's armies prepared to fight beside their neighbors, not against them; each member's security came to depend on cooperation with others, not competition. That is one reason . . . why we need a larger NATO, so that the other half of Europe is finally embedded in the same cooperative structure of military planning and preparation. . . . We have an interest not only in the lands west of the Oder river, but in the fate of the 200 million people who live in the nations between the Baltic and Black Seas.[115]

The fears some experts have expressed of a swift and uncontrollable process of further enlargement eroding NATO's cohesion and effectiveness may be misplaced, however. Indeed, some question whether another round of enlargement will be endorsed promptly if the Czech Republic, Hungary, and Poland accede to the Alliance in 1999. British analyst Jonathan Eyal asks, "Does anyone seriously suggest that, having won this battle, Western governments will start another round of negotiations immediately thereafter?. . . Germany had a legitimate interest in including its neighbouring states within the alliance as soon as possible. But what conceivable interest does it have to continue the process? And do governments really suggest that the best way of dealing with Russia is to pick a fight about another NATO enlargement every couple of years?"[116] In other words, the "clocks ticking in Moscow" argument may also work against further rounds of enlargement.

German scholars Karl-Heinz Kamp and Peter Weilemann have suggested that "some kind of pause . . . seems likely" for four reasons: first, the invitation to the Czech Republic, Hungary, and Poland means "a demanding agenda that includes accession negotiations, ratification debates, and specific decisions for making membership work"; second, "pressing issues" such as the new command structure and CJTF "have proven especially difficult to resolve"; third, because of the "sometimes harsh NATO debate" on the current round of enlargement, "opening another debate on additional new members will be resisted"; and, "finally, Russia remains firmly opposed to the expansion of NATO to the former Soviet republics, especially the Baltic states."[117] The possibility that further rounds of enlargement may not take place in the near future underscores the importance of enhancing PfP and other programs for Alliance cooperation with the aspirants to NATO membership not chosen for the current round.

Risk of unnecessary confrontation with Russia. From a West European perspective, the impetus to enlarge the Alliance—particularly since the fall of 1994—seems to have stemmed in large part from presidential and congressional campaign politics in the United States, especially the rivalry for voters with family backgrounds in Eastern and Central Europe. Some West European circles of opinion deplore this distinctly American political factor in the debate over NATO's future, because it ignores larger questions about the potential negative impact of enlargement on European security, specifically the possibility that the enlargement process may antagonize the Russians and increase the risk of confrontation and conflict with Moscow.

As in other Alliance statements, the NATO defense ministers asserted in December 1996 that "The accession of new members will . . . help to consolidate the security and stability of the entire Euro-Atlantic area."[118] Some observers in NATO countries are nonetheless concerned that, particularly if it is not handled adroitly, the enlargement of the Alliance could instead lead to confrontation and polarization. They warn that the Russians might conclude they are being threatened and humiliated and try to reassert control over some former Soviet republics or take other retaliatory measures.

An apparent contradiction in NATO's drive for enlargement has been the tendency of the United States and other Allied governments to argue that Russia's irritation regarding NATO enlargement can be "compensated for" with a "special relationship" of security cooperation between NATO and Russia, even though the main goal of applicants for NATO membership is protection against Russia. In view of this apparent contradiction, some observers are uncertain about how to interpret official declarations that NATO enlargement is not based on any fear of actual or potential threats from Russia: "Russia must understand that NATO will enlarge on its own terms, on a schedule now broadly agreed within the Alliance. But to say that is not to imply that NATO enlargement threatens—or sees a threat in—Russia, or is insensitive to Russia's interests or concerns."[119]

A number of East European countries clearly are seeking NATO membership precisely because they see Russia as a potential threat to their security. They fear that a future Russian government might try to rebuild an empire approximating tsarist or Soviet spheres of influence. As one of Germany's leading experts on the former Soviet empire has written,

> Against the background of Central Europe's historical experience, NATO offers the best possible hope for this traditionally unstable region to stabilize on a permanent basis. The Western alliance has

done away with the very factors which had been the sources of Central European instability during the interwar years: the region's geographic separation from the West, the existence of an imperially-minded German state seeking to dominate the region and Western weakness as had resulted from Britain's and particularly North America's standing apart. . . . The fact that Belarus seems to be dominated by Russia again and that Ukraine may conceivably share the same fate, reinforces the Central European countries' drive for NATO membership.[120]

It is clear that the prospective new Allies continue to see Russia as a threat, and are interested in balancing Russia's power potential and gaining protection against Russia. For example, in April 1997, Polish foreign minister Dariusz Rosati predicted, on the basis of Russian declarations, that Russia will use "all possible means to delay the process" of NATO enlargement. In Warsaw's view, the dictatorial behavior of the leadership in Minsk and the recent union agreement between Russia and Belarus could allow Moscow to bring Russian tanks hundreds of kilometers further west. It is in this context, a French journalist reports, that Rosati supports Ukraine's efforts to build a closer relationship with NATO, referring to Ukraine's "important geopolitical situation."[121] It appears that one of Ukraine's motives in supporting NATO enlargement is indeed to improve its geostrategic position vis-à-vis Russia. "An alliance bordering on Ukraine—as it will do when Poland and Hungary join—is the best proof Ukraine has that its survival as an independent state is now of crucial importance to the rest of Europe."[122]

To what extent, then, can the process of NATO enlargement be reconciled with the Alliance's aims of promoting a wider process of security cooperation in Europe? In June 1996, the North Atlantic Council declared, "We reaffirm our determination that the process of opening the Alliance to new members should not create dividing lines in Europe or isolate any country. . . . The enlargement of the Alliance is consistent with a wider process of cooperation and integration already underway in today's Europe."[123] This process, however, is not entirely under NATO's control. Many Russian leaders have made their hostility to NATO enlargement clear, and the Russians have declined to participate actively in the Partnership for Peace.

Henry Kissinger, among others, has taken issue with the official rhetoric from the Alliance and its member governments about pursuing enlargement without creating any "dividing lines" in Europe: "[A]n alliance depends on drawing lines around a specified territory that the members undertake to defend. Any meaningful enlargement of NATO inevitably brings about a new dividing line—this is why the historical nations of Central Europe aspire to NATO membership. They want to join the old, not the new, NATO."[124]

The gravity of accepting new collective defense obligations. Some European critics of the drive for NATO enlargement deplore what they see as a lack of seriousness regarding the organization's new collective defense obligations. NATO's internal security functions, such as its tendency to moderate potential intra-Alliance disputes (discussed in chapter 2), are advanced as rationales for enlargement more often than the need to enhance NATO's collective defense potential.

In the Alliance's own *Study on NATO Enlargement* the reasons for "why" enlargement should be undertaken are remarkable in that not one of the seven cited earlier refers explicitly to the collective defense mission of protecting the Allies against aggression or coercion from external threats. The declared rationales for enlargement all refer to "collective security" purposes such as peacekeeping, or to the internal functions of NATO such as fostering "habits of cooperation, consultation and consensus building."

Not surprisingly, U.S. officials have taken the same approach.[125] The purpose of enlargement is consistently described as "projecting stability" to the countries of Central and Eastern Europe.[126] Some official statements on the rationales for NATO enlargement even discount "military and geopolitical considerations" and instead highlight "nonmilitary" goals. According to U.S. deputy secretary of state Strobe Talbott, the Alliance has "made respect for democracy and international norms of behavior explicit preconditions for membership, so that enlargement of NATO would be a force for the rule of law both within Europe's new democracies and among them." Such conditionality, Talbott reports, is a post–Cold War opportunity: "During the cold war, military and geopolitical considerations mainly determined NATO's decisions. Promoting democracy within NATO states and good relations among them was only complementary—desirable but not the primary motive for bringing in new members. But today, with the end of the cold war, other, nonmilitary, goals can and should help shape the new NATO."[127]

Some elaborate statements of purpose seem deliberately to avoid any reference to collective defense and instead focus on the security functions internal to the Alliance. In April 1997, Secretary of Defense Cohen testified as follows:

> Enlargement is part of the transformation of the European security architecture, and is necessary to:
>
> - Provide stability for the new democracies of Europe;
> - Further a European integration committed to Western values;
> - Promote a multilateral (not a nationalistic) defense concept;
> - Solidify democratic and economic reforms in a transatlantic institution; and
> - Associate new members in NATO's efforts, throughout Europe and even beyond, to meet tomorrow's security challenges.[128]

Secretary Cohen's final point appears to refer to peacekeeping and crisis management contingencies, rather than collective defense. Similarly, one of Secretary of State Albright's most widely distributed discussions of the purposes of NATO enlargement conspicuously omitted collective defense: "At the same time, we will gain new allies who are eager and increasingly able to contribute to our common agenda for security, from fighting terrorism and weapons proliferation to ensuring stability in trouble spots like the former Yugoslavia."[129]

It is probably for reasons of diplomatic discretion vis-à-vis Russia that references to the Alliance's continuing collective defense mission are scarce, particularly in discussions of enlargement. In her prepared testimony to the Senate Armed Services Committee in April 1997, Albright said that "NATO will continue to evolve, but its core function of collective defense will be maintained and enhanced." She did not indicate any potential source of a threat requiring collective defense, but said, "NATO poses no danger to Russia, just as Russia poses no danger to NATO. We do no favor to Russia's democrats to pretend otherwise."[130] She added, "The bottom line is, our future allies will bear the cost of defending freedom, because they know the price of losing freedom."[131] She did not, however, at any point in her statement, allude more specifically to a potential challenger to NATO's security. At the same hearing, Secretary of Defense Cohen said, "The reduced threat gives us the ability to bring new members along without breaking the backs of their fledgling market economies."[132] He did not, however, specify the source of the threat that has been reduced.

Cohen's testimony was nonetheless unusual because of its explicit discussion of collective defense requirements for the prospective new Allies: "Of course, NATO's core function will remain the defense of its members' territory. . . . While our current NATO doctrine means we do not, under current or expected circumstances, need to permanently station substantial combat forces on new members' territories, we do intend to include new members fully in NATO command arrangements, to foster reform of their military forces, and to modernize their reception and reinforcement capability through a combination of new member and NATO common funding. NATO will not accept any limits on its infrastructure."[133] He did not identify the threat that NATO reinforcements would be expected to meet on the territory of new Allies.

However, as was noted in chapter 2, in June 1996 U.S. under secretary of defense Walter Slocombe made an exceptional and noteworthy reference to NATO's continuing collective defense function vis-à-vis Russian military power, a reference consistent with the discussion of the need to "preserve the strategic balance within Europe" in the Alliance's 1991 Strategic Concept.[134] Slocombe said, "The course that we are seeking for Russia foresees an optimistic outcome, and maintains an optimistic outlook. But we are not naive about Russia, and we are acutely conscious of the dangers, of the hard lessons of history. Should Russia turn away from its new path, we can re-evaluate our approach and indeed we would have to do so. An integral part of our pragmatic partnership policy for Russia is that we continue to remain strong, so that we have a military hedge against whatever might come."[135]

In October 1997, moreover, Slocombe related the risks of reversals in Russia to NATO enlargement, noting that

a fundamentally different—and far more demanding—set of defense requirements would arise if trends in Russia or elsewhere developed in such a way as to renew a direct territorial threat to NATO members. Such a threat does not exist, nor is there an expectation that it will reemerge. Moreover, the United States and its allies would have years of warning and preparation time in the very unlikely event such a dramatic change in the European security environment were to occur. . . . [T]here can be no question that the cost of responding to such a threat would be substantial. Just ten years ago, for example, the United States and most of its allies were spending nearly twice as much of GDP on defense as today. There can, however, be no question that, if we had to meet such a threat, we could do so more effectively and less expensively in an expanded alliance than in a Europe still divided along Cold War lines. In such circumstances, the added manpower, military capability, political support and strategic depth afforded by NATO enlargement would amply justify whatever additional cost there were in having additional members in the Alliance.[136]

Although public acknowledgments of the Alliance's continuing collective defense purpose can occasionally be sighted, some critics of NATO enlargement maintain that not enough attention has been devoted to the responsibilities involved in admitting new Allies. In their view, enlargement entails the acceptance of additional collective defense responsibilities on the part of the existing Allies, while the security benefits of gaining further Allies are not of an obviously equal magnitude.

In December 1996, the NATO defense ministers announced their decision to ask NATO military authorities "to carry out . . . analyses of the military factors associated with the accession of potential new members" and "the committees responsible for financial matters to assess the resource implications."[137] In view of the fact that the Alliance had announced its basic decision in favor of enlargement almost three years before, at the January 1994 NATO summit, it seemed extraordinary to some that the Alliance had not already conducted these assessments. Indeed, some critical observers wondered, should they not have preceded the decision to announce an intention to welcome new members into the Alliance? Some of the arguments advanced in the debate about whether to invite three, four, or five countries to join the Alliance in the weeks and days before the July 1997 Madrid summit implied that collective defense considerations were not central elements in the decision.

It should be recalled that France was not alone in advocating Romania's admission to the Alliance. Belgium, Canada, Greece, Italy, Portugal, Spain, and Turkey also supported Romania's application. In Jonathan Eyal's judgment,

> Nobody was actually persuaded by Romania's entire case, or by the publicity campaign which the country launched; but Romania became a symbol for all the deficiencies of the enlargement process as con-

ceived during 1996. The alliance has long argued that Europe's security problems were on the continent's peripheries: in the Balkans and the Baltics in particular. And yet, where was NATO proposing to begin the enlargement? In central Europe, precisely the area where everyone agreed no immediate security risk existed. The more a country needed security, the less likely that country was to be accepted into NATO.[138]

Some critics of NATO enlargement maintain that it is being pursued with inappropriate criteria. In their view, it is a mistake to take a "beauty contest" and "social engineering" approach to NATO membership— that is, stressing criteria such as demonstrated commitment to democratic principles and civilian control of the armed forces—when the top criterion should be the country's ability to make a net contribution to NATO's defense, after the additional risks and obligations of accepting the candidate as an Ally have been assessed. Moreover, the practical aspects of actually defending the new Allies, if necessary, should have been given greater consideration. From this perspective, Hungary should not have been invited without Austria, Slovakia, or Slovenia to provide geographic contiguity and to avoid leaving Hungary in an isolated position.

This criticism is often joined to contentions that the enlargement agenda has been driven by political and emotional considerations instead of strategic analysis, especially in the United States. Anthony Lake, President Clinton's national security adviser during 1993–96, reported that the president was "deeply impressed" by the appeals made by "men like Vaclav Havel of the Czech Republic and Lech Walesa of Poland" just before the "moving ceremony" at the opening of the U.S. Holocaust Memorial Museum in Washington, D.C., in April 1993: "Could they look to the West in confidence, or must they look to the East in fear?"[139] According to Stephen S. Rosenfeld, "the quotient of guilt and emotion in NATO enlargement is high. . . . Twice in this century, at Munich on the eve of World War II and at Yalta as the war closed, the Western powers flinched and in effect consigned a broad swath of historical Europe to terror and totalitarian rule."[140] Secretary of State Albright visited Prague and referred to the 1938 Munich agreement in declaring that "an injustice has been undone" by NATO's July 1997 decision to invite the Czech Republic to join the Alliance.[141] James Hoagland has suggested that "Guilt and emotion rather than strategy" help to explain support for enlargement in Germany as well. German chancellor Helmut Kohl has reportedly said that for him NATO enlargement concerns "one country: Poland. Admitting Poland expiates German guilt."[142]

From the perspective of many critics, the U.S. government has also been strongly influenced by moral, emotional, and political appeals made by constituencies in the United States with East European ethnic backgrounds. Both major parties, it is noted, have competed for such constituencies. According to a German scholar's analysis of the NATO enlargement debate in the United States, "the Republicans are vying for support in those sixteen states in which 6 to 18 percent of the population are of eastern Central European and Eastern European origin."[143] James Goldgeier points out that, "even if ethnic pressures did not drive the decision, Clinton would have alienated these vocal and powerful domestic constituencies had he decided against expanding NATO; Republicans thus would have gained another issue to use in congressional elections later that year [1994]. If domestic politics did not drive the decision, they gave it more resonance for the White House."[144]

Some observers have highlighted the fact that the Clinton administration appeared to attach greater urgency to NATO enlargement beginning in the fall of 1994, and that NATO enlargement was a prominent theme in the "Contract with America" platform that may have contributed to Republican victories in that season's congressional elections.[145] In the 1996 presidential election, President Clinton took the position that new Allies should enter NATO no later than 1999, while Republican nominee Bob Dole accused the president of "foot-dragging" and argued that 1998 would be a better date.[146] In July 1997, in remarks to the Belgian prime minister that were not intended for publication, Canadian prime minister Jean Chretien said that President Clinton's motives in promoting NATO enlargement were rooted in U.S. domestic politics: "It's not for reasons of state. It's all done for short-term political reasons. . . . Take the quarrel over whether to admit the Baltic states. That has nothing to do with world security. It's because in Chicago, Mayor [Richard] Daley controls lots of votes for the [Democratic] nomination."[147]

Critics who deplore the limited amount of attention given to collective defense in NATO enlargement also regret the way in which the political dynamic of commitments, once they have been made, tends to dampen further analysis.[148] The decisions announced at the July 1997 Alliance summit mean that so much political capital and prestige has been invested in enlargement that a failure to follow through with at least the first post–Cold War round might send a signal of weakness to the Russians, and could be damaging to the Alliance's credibility and to the political and economic stability of the prospective new Allies.

Finally, some European observers have raised probing questions in off-the-record discussions on NATO enlargement: How credible would Article 5 collective defense guarantees be in an expanded Alliance? Would the current sixteen Allies answer *"oui,"* if the question *"mourir pour Danzig?"* were asked again?[149] Are the West Europeans prepared to make Article 5 commitments only because the putative Russian threat is now minimal, and because the United States is seen in both Eastern and Western Europe as the ultimate guarantor of the Alliance's collective defense pledges? Would new Allies honor their Article 5 commitments if they felt exposed to Russian pressure?

Such concerns about the collective defense implications of enlargement appear to be exceptional. The preponderant view is that collective defense is not a particularly urgent priority for the Alliance, in view of Russia's conventional military weakness and continuing hopes for its progress toward democratization. While anxieties about Russia's future have clearly constituted a significant motive for some NATO membership applicants, the Allies do not appear to have sponsored a process of enlargement mainly because of such anxieties. Rather, they appear confident in their ability to honor new Article 5 commitments, and they specified in the May 1997 NATO-Russia Founding Act that their intention is to carry out "collective defence and other missions by ensuring the necessary interoperability, integration, and capability for reinforcement rather than by additional permanent stationing of substantial combat forces."[150]

Collective security concepts have been championed for various reasons, including the diplomatic advantages for relations with states offended by—or not likely to be included in—NATO's continuing collective defense mission. Evidently, collective defense is rarely discussed in public as a purpose in enlargement because it would sound antagonistic to Russia (raising the question, Collective defense against whom?) and might dishearten the applicants for membership left out of the current round (confirming that they are not guaranteed such protection). More-over, NATO governments may see advantages vis-à-vis their electorates in not placing great emphasis on the fact that the Alliance is assuming additional defense responsibilities while gaining new members. Alliance governments have emphasized an "open door" to further rounds of enlargement, general rationales such as promoting democratization, and the prospect of including almost every state in the Euro-Atlantic region in NATO-sponsored institutions.[151]

RUSSIA AND NATO

No issue is more central to the Alliance's goal of building a peaceful political order in Europe than relations with Russia. This complex issue is examined here from six angles: what U.S. officials maintain that Russians should think about NATO enlargement; what Russians profess to think about NATO enlargement; Russian participation in the Partnership for Peace; Russian views on the possible accession of former Soviet republics to NATO membership; Russian-NATO deliberations about terms for future relations; and the possibility of Russian membership in NATO.

What U.S. officials maintain Russians should think about NATO enlargement

High-level U.S. officials have argued that Russian interests are served by NATO enlargement because it will prolong U.S. engagement in Euro-pean security, promote stability in East-Central Europe, and ensure that Germany in particular remains "part of an integrated security structure," rather than pursuing "independent national security policies."[152] As Sec-retary of State Albright has noted, "Russia, no less than the rest of us, needs stability and prosperity in the centre of Europe."[153] Furthermore, Albright has argued that the Russians should learn to move beyond an adversarial worldview: "The truth is, the quest for freedom and security in Europe is not a zero-sum game, in which Russia must lose if central Europe gains, and central Europe must lose if Russia gains. Such think-ing has brought untold tragedy to Europe and America, and we have a responsibility as well as an opportunity to transcend it."[154] In her view, "Russian opposition to NATO enlargement is . . . a product of old misperceptions about NATO and old ways of thinking about its former satellites in central Europe. Instead of changing our policies to accommodate Russia's outdated fears, we need to encourage Russia's more modern aspirations."[155]

In a Europe to be endowed with cooperative security structures and composed of democratic states, it is argued, Russia should not persist with outmoded conceptions such as "buffer zones." As Albright said, "After all, if Russia wishes to be part of an undivided Europe, then it cannot look at countries like Poland or Estonia or Ukraine as a buffer zone that *separates* Russia from Europe."[156] Moreover, she added, "we cannot build a Europe whole and free until a democratic Russia is wholly part of Europe." As a democratic country, Russia should "play an important role in Europe—as a great power, and no longer as an imperial power."[157] Similarly, in arguing that the Alliance should avoid a "threat-based" and "anti-Russian" approach to NATO enlargement, Deputy Secretary of State Strobe Talbott has called attention to "the other equally valid, less provocative reasons for enlargement, which Russia should accept and even support: the promotion of democracy, free markets, and regional stability."[158]

At any rate, U.S. officials have argued that the Alliance cannot allow its enlargement to be postponed or blocked by Russian objections. "It would not be in our interest to delay or derail enlargement in response to the claims of some Russians that this constitutes an offensive act. Doing so would only encourage the worst political tendencies in Moscow. It would send a message that confrontation with the West pays off."[159]

What Russians profess to think about NATO enlargement

It appears that one of the incentives leading Clinton administration officials to downplay NATO's collective defense function is a wish to emphasize NATO's transformation into an entity that devotes increasing attention to pan-European "collective security" purposes. U.S. officials at times have even held out the possibility of Russian membership in NATO, in conjunction with attempts to persuade Russians that NATO enlargement is not threatening to Russia. This effort seems to have been less than entirely successful, because many Russian politicians, officials, and commentators continue to describe NATO enlargement as contrary to Russian security interests, even if not a near-term military threat.[160]

Rather than seeing NATO enlargement as a benign process of "exporting stability" that is in the general interest of all nations in the Euro-Atlantic area, including Russia, many Russian officials and experts profess to view the NATO enlargement process as an expansion of the Alliance's sphere of influence. From the perspective of these Russians, NATO's rhetoric is contradictory: If NATO wants to build a relationship of partnership and cooperation with Russia, why are NATO governments extending collective defense commitments to nations that have expressed distrust and antagonism toward Russia? The standard Russian prescription calls for "expanding the role of the OSCE as the basis for a new pan-European security system" and "the transformation of NATO from a military alliance into a peacekeeping/making organization" that would function as a "tool at the disposal of the OSCE."[161]

Some Russian analysts reportedly consider NATO enlargement and the Dayton settlement in Bosnia evidence of U.S. assertiveness and muscle-flexing. That is, the United States is seen to be taking advantage of Russia's weakness to impose an American-designed European security order. In this perspective, Russia's participation in IFOR and SFOR under de facto U.S. command is deemed a humiliating and degrading subordination of the Russian military, which is forced to watch while the United States favors the Muslim Bosniaks over the Serbs. NATO enlargement is also portrayed as an expansion of a U.S.-directed sphere of influence, in violation of Western commitments supposedly made in 1990, when the reunited Germany remained in NATO.

Many Russians have asserted that there was an agreement with the Western powers that, in the words of Vladimir Lukin, chairman of the International Affairs Committee of the State Duma, "the unification of Germany was conditional on the nonexpansion of NATO to the east."[162] In September 1993, Russian president Boris Yeltsin noted that the September 1990 treaty on German reunification includes "stipulations banning the deployment of foreign troops in the eastern federal Laender of the Federal Republic of Germany," and argued that "The spirit of these stipulations rules out any possibility of a NATO expansion eastwards."[163] Russians usually cite Mikhail Gorbachev as their authority in claiming that Moscow made an unwritten "gentlemen's agreement" with the United States in February 1990 that NATO would not enlarge beyond the admission of the territory of the former East Germany into the united Germany.[164]

Russians who are convinced that such a bargain was made consider NATO enlargement a betrayal and an exploitation of Russia's current weakness. Some speculate that it could someday assume a mythic status comparable to how Weimar Germany viewed the Treaty of Versailles. The Russian impressions may derive from vague assurances offered by Germany and the United States as to not exploiting Russia's position of weakness. In the words of a British scholar, "Helmut Kohl did not formally promise anything about NATO's future intentions. But at the same time there is no doubt that the main thrust of the German-Soviet discussions—and, indeed, the discussions between the United States and the Soviet Union at the time—was precisely in the direction of reassuring Moscow that its 'loss' in central Europe would not be translated into a Western 'gain.'"[165]

According to Condoleezza Rice and Philip Zelikow, American scholars with access to official records who prepared an authoritative study of German unification, the possibility of ruling out NATO enlargement beyond the territory of the former East Germany was indeed discussed with the Soviets in February 1990 by U.S. secretary of state James Baker, at the suggestion of West German foreign minister Hans-Dietrich Genscher. Before Baker left Moscow, however, the White House instructed him to limit his concessions to the Soviets to the principle that only German forces could be stationed on the territory of the former East Germany. Baker has confirmed this account of events.[166] European observers have pointed out that the insistence of many Russians that such an arrangement was in fact concluded, albeit on an informal basis, implies that these Russians in fact support "great power" sphere-of-influence arrangements, rather than national self-determination and the rights of states freely to choose whether to seek membership in specific alliances or other security arrangements.

Do any Russians accept Western analyses that conclude that the U.S. military and nuclear presence in Europe—as part of the entire NATO framework of mutual defense commitments and consultations—actually serves Russian security interests by underpinning deterrence; reducing the risk of war; bolstering political stability; and discouraging renationalization, nuclear proliferation, and the formation of new competitive coalitions in Europe? In all likelihood, some Russian politicians and analysts understand and appreciate the merits of this argument, and can even see its applicability to an enlarged Alliance. In the current and foreseeable dynamics of Russian politics, however, it would not be particularly popular or career-enhancing for a Russian politician (or analyst of international affairs) to acknowledge that NATO enlargement could actually play a positive role in Russian security. According to Tatiana Parkhalina, head of the West Europe department of the Russian Academy of Sciences, Russian "Westernizers," liberal democrats, and moderate nationalists who take a neutral or favorable attitude toward NATO enlargement generally "do not dare speak out openly" in this regard for fear that they will lose support to the anti-NATO nationalists attempting to exploit "the public's chauvinism and fears."[167]

The more widely articulated Russian view is that NATO enlargement reflects continuing distrust of Russia and that it contradicts the Alliance's declared interest in building all-European security structures. In the words of Vladimir Lukin,

> We want all-European security. But if we are refused room there we will have to worry about our own security. . . . Not the best option, but it is the minimum necessary if the best option proves impossible. . . . We are told: You do not have the right of veto over NATO decisions. Legally speaking this is perfectly true. Politically speaking . . . an attempt is being made to kick Russia like a puppy out of the door of a room where questions of all-European security for the strategic future are being discussed. This kind of kick can trip you up yourself.[168]

Lukin is the author of a noteworthy article advocating that Russia be welcomed into the "civilized democratic community" and suggesting that, "In predicting the advent of a democratic peace, Immanuel Kant proved to be much more prescient than those who argued that power struggles among states were something eternal, regardless of their internal political systems."[169]

Russian participation in the Partnership for Peace

Russia reacted positively to the PfP when it was launched in January 1994, apparently because the Russians saw PfP as evidence of NATO's intention to postpone decisions on enlargement, perhaps indefinitely.

In June 1994, Russia signed the PfP Framework Document, and Russia and NATO agreed to develop a more cooperative relationship within and outside PfP. However, at a December 1994 meeting of the North Atlantic Council attended by Russian foreign minister Andrei Kozyrev, Moscow declined to approve either the PfP Individual Partnership Program it had negotiated with NATO or the program for additional NATO-Russia cooperation outside PfP, ostensibly because of concerns about NATO's prospective enlargement. Russia did not approve a PfP Individual Partnership Program (IPP) agreement with NATO until May 1995. IPPs are not made public, and therefore it is difficult to make precise comparisons about levels of national participation in PfP activities. It is generally agreed, however, that Russia's participation has been minimal.

Indeed, Russia has been an exceptionally passive participant in PfP, except for the programs dealing with civil-emergency planning. Compared with that of the more vigorously engaged Partners, Russia's military involvement in PfP has been almost nonexistent. Various explanations for Russia's passivity have been suggested: above all, financial and other resource limitations; a continuing distrust of NATO and a reluctance to lend support and legitimacy to a NATO-centered and -directed network of relationships; and a wish to signal displeasure regarding NATO's projected enlargement. Russia's standoffish attitude toward most PfP activities led NATO in December 1996 to reaffirm, "We welcome Russia's participation in Partnership for Peace and encourage it to take full advantage of the opportunities which the Partnership offers."[170]

The attitude of many Russians toward PfP is aptly summarized by Vladimir Lukin: "In the final analysis it is impossible to change reality using phantoms like 'Partnership for Peace.' What is this thing? If the intention of this formula is to defer the East European countries' affiliation to NATO, 'Partnership' should be welcomed. If the intention is to anesthetize Russia for the period that its Eastern neighbors are being dragged into NATO, Russia's refusal to undergo such anesthesia should be clearly and definitely stated."[171]

The limitation of Russia's active PfP participation to civil-emergency planning may be explained in part by the fact that the nation's government today is not as monolithic as during the Soviet period. The civil-emergency work is not under the control of the Ministry of Defense, but of the Ministry for Civil Defense, Emergencies, and Elimination of Consequences of Natural Disasters (still widely known by its Soviet-era acronym, EMERCOM), headed by an unusually dynamic young minister, Sergei Shoigu. Yet EMERCOM has come under intermittent pressure from the Foreign Ministry at times to increase and at times to cut back its cooperation with NATO. Finances may be another factor, partly because cooperative civil emergency activities are less costly than military exercises. The Ministry of Defense is short of funds, while EMERCOM was able to earn some money by chartering aircraft to UNPROFOR in 1994 and 1995; those earnings, however, are being rapidly exhausted.[172]

Russian views on possible NATO membership for former Soviet republics

Russian officials have argued that if NATO enlargement is to take place, at least no former Soviet republic should be admitted to the Alliance.

Russian president Boris Yeltsin said in March 1997 that he was still seeking an agreement with the United States that no former Soviet republic can ever join the Atlantic Alliance. This proposed agreement is naturally of great concern to the Baltic states; their representatives have expressed concern that Russian nationalists could attempt to re-annex them. Ukrainian foreign minister Gennadiy Udovenko declared in March 1997 that his country's "strategic objective" is to join the Atlantic Alliance, because of concern about its "unpredictable" neighbor.[173] In May 1997, after having agreed with the Alliance on the terms of the NATO-Russia Founding Act (see Appendix 3), Yeltsin said that the agreement could be placed into question if the Alliance accepted any former Soviet republic as a member.[174] The Founding Act itself stipulates, however, that Russia and NATO will show "respect for sovereignty, independence and territorial integrity of all states and their inherent right to choose the means to ensure their own security, the inviolability of borders and peoples' right of self-determination as enshrined in the Helsinki Final Act and other OSCE documents."[175]

It would obviously be difficult for the United States (or for NATO as a whole) to agree explicitly with Russia to exclude all former Soviet republics from future Alliance membership. Aside from the fact that Article 10 of the North Atlantic Treaty states that the Allies may "invite any other European state in a position to further the principles of this

Treaty and to contribute to the security of the North Atlantic area to accede to this Treaty," such an agreement would smack of another supposed "Yalta"-type arrangement—a big-power deal determining the security options of smaller powers.[176] Moreover, such an agreement would contradict not only the comprehensiveness and inclusiveness of the "collective security" approach implicit in much of the Partnership for Peace discourse and activity, but also the attempts to reassure the "also-rans" that NATO enlargement is an open-ended process, not limited to the countries fortunate enough to be included in the first wave of post–Cold War enlargement.

Particularly in the United States and Germany, some observers foresee admitting the Baltic states to NATO and believe this could be done without a risky confrontation with Russia. Other observers contend that admitting the Baltic states would cause feelings of humiliation and outrage in Russia, become a stimulus for Russian nationalism and revanchism, and permanently sidetrack the Russian legislature's ratification of START II and future arms control accords.

Some experts in Allied nations see more risks than advantages in an open-ended process of enlargement, particularly one that leaves open the prospect of including former Soviet republics. Such an approach, in their view, could mean starting more "clocks ticking" and placing increased pressure on Russia to intervene before NATO has extended to the Baltic states or Ukraine. Some Russians have hinted that the inclusion of such states in the Alliance could constitute a casus belli for Moscow.

According to Anton Surikov, NATO enlargement represents "an attempt by Germany to resume its expansion in the eastern and southeastern directions which has been stopped twice this century. Today this aim is pursued mainly through political and economic methods under the cover of the American 'nuclear shield.'" Surikov contends that "the only possible solution lies in restraining NATO with nuclear weapons" deployments in Belarus, Kaliningrad, Crimea, Abkhazia, Georgia, and Armenia, and on ships in the Baltic, Black, and Barents Seas. In Surikov's view, while Russia could accept a neutral status for the Baltic republics analogous to that of Finland during the Cold War, NATO membership would be unacceptable; in that event, Russia would have to occupy the Baltic republics. In his words, "nobody intends to fight with Russia for the Baltic countries," in part because of Russia's nuclear forces—"one of the few convincing arguments for the West."[177]

While some might dismiss Surikov as a nationalist, more mainstream Russian politicians have articulated comparable (albeit less precise) warnings. In the words of Vladimir Lukin,

> Don't let Chechnya fool anyone: many people were similarly fooled by the war with Finland in 1939–1940. . . . Will it be better for the West to have a traumatized but still nuclear Russia again forced to withdraw into the steppes? A morally crushed but still heavily armed Russia convinced that it has little to lose? If the blind egoism of the shortsighted politicians to the west of our borders prevails we will resort to the means we still have in our hands. These are means of some kind of desperation, but effective nonetheless.[178]

From a collective defense perspective, some Western observers have argued, it might be more prudent to focus on enlargement to a small number of new Allies and to defer the question of inviting additional members, particularly former Soviet republics whose NATO membership is most sharply opposed by Russia. If the enlargement to three new Allies is successfully carried out by 1999, as has been projected, the Alliance will have its hands full with an enhanced Partnership for Peace and other activities. The passage of time without further enlargement will then play in NATO's favor, it is argued, by reassuring Moscow that NATO's enlargement objectives are in fact limited and benign, and do not threaten Russia's core security interests.

Russian-NATO deliberations about terms for future relations

Since the end of the Cold War, Moscow (under Soviet and Russian rule) has championed the dissolution of NATO or its subordination to the OSCE. The Alliance, of course, has rejected the repeated Russian proposals to this effect: "NATO decisions . . . cannot be subject to any veto or droit de regard by a non-member state, nor can the Alliance be subordinated to another European security institution."[179]

However, the Alliance has made significant efforts to secure Russian cooperation in dealing with European security problems, despite Russian objections to NATO enlargement. In October 1995, William Perry, then U.S. secretary of defense, summed up the challenge as follows:

Since the ending of the Cold War, we've had a very major objective, which is to get the dismantlement of the nuclear weapons, the ending of the balance of terror and, at the same time, dismantling some of the massive conventional weapons built up in that war. All of that action requires intense cooperation with the Russians. In parallel with that has been the bringing of the Central and Eastern European nations into the security architecture of Europe. Those two overarching security goals have at times come into conflict. In particular, because we are moving forward with plans for NATO expansion, Russia tends to back off from cooperation in those other areas.[180]

In December 1996, for example, the North Atlantic Council reiterated its "commitment to a strong, stable, and enduring security partnership between NATO and Russia. This partnership demonstrates that European security has entered a fundamentally new, more promising era."[181] As Walter Slocombe, the U.S. under secretary of defense for policy, observed with regard to Bosnia, "When we deal with the most important security problem which Europe has faced since the Cold War was over, we want to have Russia inside the circle, working with us, not outside the circle. NATO and Russia have a special relationship today in Bosnia, and Russia is demonstrating its capacity to participate in the future security architecture of Europe—as NATO is demonstrating its will to secure that cooperation."[182]

High-level Russian officials have nonetheless continued to express their reluctance to countenance NATO enlargement or to "legitimize" the organization's ambitious political and security agenda in PfP. In view of the statements emanating from Moscow, some NATO affirmations of a partnership with Russia have seemed rather one-sided, and scarcely reinforced by reciprocal expressions of commitment.

Developing such a positive relationship with Russia remains the single most important challenge for NATO's new role of promoting constructive cooperation with former adversaries. The magnitude of the challenge became apparent in December 1996, when NATO proposed "to work with Russia to establish permanent Russian military liaison missions" at NATO headquarters in Brussels; Supreme Headquarters Allied Powers Europe (SHAPE) in Mons, Belgium; and Allied Command Atlantic (ACLANT) in Norfolk, Virginia, "building on the highly successful experience of the Russian liaison mission created for IFOR, and, based on the principle of reciprocity, to establish NATO Missions at corresponding Russian institutions and headquarters."[183] Igor Rodionov, then the Russian minister of defense, reportedly rejected the proposal on the spot during a meeting with his NATO counterparts, and declared that further Russian military exchanges with NATO would depend on the NATO-Russian negotiations.[184]

U.S. officials have made clear that the Alliance remains interested in establishing such liaison missions and other forums for dialogue with Russia to serve a "larger strategic goal: to reverse the Russian perception that NATO is a threat, and to enhance transparency."[185] As Walter Slocombe points out, "Such steps are useful, not only because they facilitate NATO-Russian cooperation on military matters, but because, we believe, the more Russia and the Russian military is involved in active cooperation with NATO, the more they see of what NATO really is and really does, the more they will see that NATO is no threat to them."[186]

The negotiation of the NATO-Russia Founding Act—terms for future NATO-Russian relations in a context of an open-ended NATO enlargement process—was difficult on various grounds. In April 1997, U.S. secretary of defense William Cohen said,

> We want to minimize Russian hypernationalistic backlash to enlargement and to discourage self-imposed Russian isolation. At the same time, we will not concede to illegitimate Russian fears or claims. As our negotiations with Russia continue we will adhere closely to five principles. Russia will not be allowed to:
>
> • Delay enlargement;
> • Veto internal NATO decisions;
> • Exclude any country from membership, now or in the future;
> • Subordinate NATO to any other institution; or
> • Impose second-class membership on any new member.[187]

One of the chief concerns expressed by the Russians was that enlargement could lead to the deployment of NATO nuclear weapons on the soil of new Allies. Secretary Cohen recalled the Alliance's collective defense purposes in this regard in April 1997: "In the context of an agreed NATO-Russia Charter, NATO will reaffirm its December 1996 statement that it has 'no plan, no intention and no reason' to station nuclear weapons on the territory of new members. Of course, implicit in that statement is the fact that the Alliance reserves the right to reassess this policy if presented with a different security environment."[188]

In the end, the "three noes" about nuclear deployment on the territory of new allies were supplemented by a "fourth no" in the May 1997 NATO-Russia Founding Act. The NATO Allies added that they had no need "to change any aspect of NATO's nuclear posture or nuclear policy —and do not foresee any future need to do so. This subsumes the fact that NATO has decided that it has no intention, no plan, and no reason to establish nuclear weapon storage sites on the territory of those members, whether through the construction of new nuclear storage facilities or the adaptation of old nuclear storage facilities."[189]

Russian attempts to deny the Alliance the right to establish military infrastructure assets on the territory of new Allies were unsuccessful, but the Allies concluded that they could honor their collective defense commitments to the new members without permanently basing substantial numbers of combat troops on their territory. The Alliance ensured that the NATO-Russia Founding Act protected its collective defense options while reaffirming its intention to respect all pertinent international agreements:

> NATO reiterates that in the current and foreseeable security environment the Alliance will carry out its collective defence and other missions by ensuring the necessary interoperability, integration, and capability for reinforcement rather than by additional permanent stationing of substantial combat forces. Accordingly, it will have to rely on adequate infrastructure commensurate with the above tasks. In this context, reinforcement may take place, when necessary, in the event of defense against a threat of aggression and missions in support of peace consistent with the United Nations Charter and the OSCE governing principles, as well as for exercises consistent with the adapted CFE [Conventional Armed Forces in Europe] Treaty, the provisions of the Vienna Document 1994 and mutually agreed transparency measures.[190]

Another sensitive issue has been Russia's possible influence over the Alliance's defense decision making through various consultative bodies. In January 1997, Henry Kissinger wrote that "The panoply of proposals comes perilously close to making Russia a non-integrated member of NATO. . . . Such an enhancement of Russia's role deflects the institution from its primary mission of defense and begins the process of turning

NATO into a vague Pan-European diplomatic forum more akin to the United Nations than to a military alliance."[191]

These concerns seemed to have been vindicated at the March 1997 U.S.-Russian summit in Helsinki, when Boris Yeltsin said that the "consensus" method of decision making would be pursued in the projected NATO-Russia council: "That's how it is today, indeed, among the NATO countries. And that's how it will be once we conclude an agreement between Russia and NATO, already with the participation of Russia."[192]

Yeltsin's statement and other Russian initiatives about the scope and powers of the proposed NATO-Russia council obliged U.S. officials to issue clarifications. For example, in April 1997, Secretary Cohen declared,

the NATO-Russia Joint Council will not replace the NAC, or give Russia a voice in NATO's own decisions. . . . Russia will not participate in the NAC, the Military Committee, or subordinate NATO bodies like the Nuclear Planning Group, the Defense Planning process or in the High-Level Task Force which sets Alliance arms control policy. . . . At the same time, NATO will work with Russia, in separate bodies that will provide mechanisms for consultation and cooperation, when that is possible. . . . Russia will have a voice but not a veto or a vote. We in DOD [the Department of Defense] have carefully reviewed the proposed NATO-Russia arrangements now being worked out, to ensure that they do not compromise NATO's ability to plan effectively, prepare carefully, and act decisively in military matters, whatever position Russia takes.[193]

In May 1997, the NATO-Russia Founding Act indicated that the NATO-Russia Permanent Joint Council is to meet twice a year at the level of foreign and defense ministers and chiefs of national military staffs, and monthly at the level of military representatives and ambassadors (or permanent representatives) to the North Atlantic Council. According to the document, "Provisions of this Act do not provide NATO or Russia, in any way, with a right of veto over the actions of the other nor do they infringe upon or restrict the rights of NATO or Russia to independent decision making or action."[194]

Such stipulations did not reassure Kissinger, who argued as follows:

Since, except for the Russian representatives, the membership is identical, each country will assess the grave step of meeting without a Russian presence in terms of its overall relationship with Moscow. Thus, in practice, NATO Council sessions and Permanent Council sessions will tend to merge. . . . [T]he Permanent Joint Council will become the more prominent body. Russia is approaching de facto NATO membership. But one needs only to read statements by Russian leaders—not to speak of the legislators in the Duma—to realize that they have no interest in enhancing the vitality and relevance of the Atlantic Alliance.[195]

Whether Kissinger's fears are realized will depend on the discernment and resoluteness of the Allies. That is, it is up to them to show the judgment and political will necessary to protect collective defense and other essential NATO activities from erosion in their interactions with Russia. Some European observers are concerned that, despite its internal political fragility and its economic and military weakness, Russia has been awarded such an important role in defining the future European security order. A related fear is that the NATO-Russia Permanent Joint Council could undermine U.S. relations with NATO Europe, because it might increase Russia's influence while weakening that of the European Allies.

Indeed, Russia's participation in defining the future European security order creates a dilemma for NATO, arising in part from uncertainty about how to deal with Russian sensitivities and gain Russian cooperation. If the United States and its Allies treated Russia in accordance with its objective economic and conventional-military standing, Russia would be humiliated. The tendency in recent years has been for the United States to treat Russia as a fellow superpower (which it is, in terms of nuclear capabilities) and as a virtual equal. This implies respect, but it runs the risk of feeding delusions about Russia's power and potential, which could lead to ill-advised decisions in Moscow. Emboldened forays into the "Near Abroad" (as Moscow has dubbed the other former Soviet republics) or a rising tide of nationalist and antidemocratic sentiment that supports such actions could obviously hinder implementation of the Founding Act.

Building a cooperative relationship between NATO and Russia is an essential element in the pursuit of the Alliance's vision of a peaceful order in the Euro-Atlantic region. As Nick Williams has observed, "Without Russia in a close relationship with NATO, *after enlargement,* it would be difficult for the Alliance to sustain its claim that it wants to prevent new divisions of Europe, and that enlargement supports the objective of an undivided Europe. . . . [A]s each phase of the enlargement process unfolds, the risk of Russia withdrawing from the Partnership, and of interest waning among those who see their chances of joining NATO remaining remote, appears to grow."[196]

Kissinger's anxieties about the NATO-Russia Permanent Joint Council appear to have been disproportionate so far. The Council has convened for the meetings envisaged in the Founding Act, but little has been accomplished—partly because its procedures are quite bureaucratic, but mainly because the Russians have not been willing to exchange much information or engage in genuine dialogue, relying instead on predictable prepared positions. Thus the Russians have not been able to use the Council to influence significantly, much less interfere with, the North Atlantic Council's proceedings so far.[197] In May 1998 it was reported that the NATO-Russia Permanent Joint Council had

> made little headway because of procedural confusion and Moscow's persistent distrust of an organization that it long considered its enemy. Senior NATO diplomats say that unless the council starts to show progress, it could soon wither into insignificance and ultimately push Russia into a more isolated posture. Russia has refused to approve a security agreement to facilitate the exchange of information, backed away from establishing military liaison missions and balked at signing up for a military cooperation agenda under NATO's Partnership for Peace program that includes all other states of the former Soviet Union. At a recent meeting to exchange information on tactical nuclear weapons, the Russian delegation's presentation was "extremely fuzzy" and failed to provide any illumination on the fate of some 10,000 to 12,000 of its tactical nuclear weapons, according to NATO participants.[198]

The possibility of Russian membership in NATO

The Alliance's September 1995 enlargement study did not imply that Russia could become a member and, indeed, implicitly suggested that NATO and Russia would remain distinct entities: "NATO-Russia relations should reflect Russia's significance in European security and be based on reciprocity, mutual respect and confidence, no 'surprise' decisions by either side which could affect the interests of the other."[199]

Whether the NATO enlargement process could eventually lead to Russian membership in the Alliance has nonetheless remained an unresolved question. The concept of "uniting the whole of the Euro-Atlantic community around a common security culture" offers no warrant for excluding Russia from NATO membership, and other enlargement rationales advanced by NATO secretary-general Javier Solana could also be applied to Russia. In referring to "Central and Eastern Europe," a region that was not defined, Solana said,

> It is difficult to see how this region can develop in hope and confidence without being anchored to the stable, established democratic organizations of the West. To keep NATO as a closed shop would be to keep those countries imprisoned in their past. It would be to rob them of one of the best means of moving forward and sharing in the future peace and prosperity we in the West are aiming for. . . . We must not draw a line across Europe, dividing it into winners and losers. In the new security architecture, there will only be winners. We have made it clear that our door is and will remain open.[200]

Solana did not refer to Russia as a possible member, however, when discussing the "positive effect" of "NATO's commitment to accept new members": "With the incentive of joining the West, many have entrenched democratic reforms at home and settled long-standing bilateral disputes abroad. Hungary, Romania, Slovakia, Poland, Ukraine, the Baltic states and others have concluded or are about to conclude agreements settling the unresolved differences." Indeed, rather than referring to Russia as a possible member of NATO, Solana advocated "a strong and united NATO, working in a close and productive partnership with Russia." He expressed the judgment that "Russia will ultimately come to the conclusion that a privileged relationship with an enlarged NATO is far preferable to any other alternative."[201]

Whether the prospect of eventual Russian membership in NATO should be held open or ruled out has in fact been a public source of division in the Alliance. At a September 1994 German-American conference held shortly after the withdrawal of the last Russian occupation troops from Germany, Defense Minister Volker Rühe said that "Russia just doesn't qualify for various reasons to be integrated into the [NATO] structure, even if they [the Russians] work economic miracles. . . . Our policy must be absolutely clear, that not all countries in Central and Eastern Europe are candidates for integration. It is obvious that Poland, Hungary and the Czech and Slovak Republics are prime candidates for the European Union, as well as NATO. Russia cannot be integrated, neither into the European Union nor into NATO."[202] In Rühe's view, "If

Russia were to become a member of NATO it would blow NATO apart. . . . It would be like the United Nations of Europe—it wouldn't work."[203]

William Perry, then the U.S. secretary of defense, disagreed with Rühe, saying that the United States "is not prepared to close the door on that issue."[204] In March 1997, President Clinton restated his support for "a European Union that is expanding, and still tied . . . to the United States and Canada . . . not only economically and politically but also in terms of our security alliance, but [that] also has a special relationship with Russia, and [that] does not rule out even Russian membership in a common security alliance."[205] Despite the vagueness in the phrase "common security alliance" here and in some other official statements, U.S. openness to the principle of eventual Russian membership has been evident. Indeed, President Clinton told President Yeltsin during his September 1994 visit to Washington that "NATO was potentially open to all of Europe's new democracies, including Russia."[206]

Deputy Secretary of State Talbott reportedly was the first to champion the idea of holding open the possibility of Russian membership in NATO. "Talbott argued that the administration should not put forward any criteria on NATO membership that would automatically exclude Russia and Ukraine, and that the administration could never manage the relationship if it did not offer Russia the prospect of joining the alliance at a future date."[207] Talbott has accordingly employed formulations implying that NATO membership could be feasible for the states of the former USSR: "The prospect of being admitted to NATO provides the nations of Central Europe and the former Soviet Union with additional incentives to strengthen their democratic and legal institutions, ensure civilian command of their armed forces, liberalize their economies, and respect human rights, including the rights of national minorities."[208] With regard to Russia's NATO membership prospects, Talbott has written,

Whether a fully democratic Russia at peace with its neighbors and with itself might someday enter NATO remains an open question. Obviously for that to happen, it would be a very different Russia from the current one. It would also be a very different Europe. But the extraordinary transformations that have taken place both in Russia and throughout Europe over the past decade should make us reluctant to exclude possibilities for the future—and ambitious in pursuing them.[209]

European observers generally do not go as far as high-level U.S. officials in foreseeing the prospect of Russian membership in NATO. One German scholar has written that the Clinton administration's insistence on leaving open the "theoretical possibility" of Russian membership in NATO "can only be interpreted at present as a gesture to Moscow."[210] According to a recent assessment of the prospective post-enlargem situation by two analysts, one British and one German, some of the disappointed "also-ran" nations that were not included in the Alliance's first post–Cold War round of enlargement "may well b given the perspective of joining NATO in a 'second wave' at some indeterminate point in the future; they will need reassurance that theii .nbitions to join will ultimately be fulfilled. Finally, Russia and Ukraine are likely to have a privileged but grudging relationship with the alliance in a kind of permanent VIP lounge."[211]

NATO Europe's politicians and analysts generally appear to support Rühe's position, rather than that of U.S. political leaders who prefer to hold open the possibility of eventual Russian membership in NATO. In their view, the bedrock external security function of the Alliance remains collective defense—and that includes, in the words of the 1991 Strategic Concept, maintaining "the strategic balance within Europe" vis-à-vis Russia (a more politically palatable phrase than upholding the "balance of power").[212] From this perspective, cooperation with Russia of various kinds—political, economic, peacekeeping, and so forth—is desirable, but Russian power (particularly in the nuclear domain) must be balanced. The challenge in this regard is determining "how to manage the former Soviet Union (read: Russia) through the right mix of balancing and cooperation."[213]

In March 1997, Henry Kissinger called attention to the tendency of U.S. officials to "insist . . . resolutely on describing Russia as a partner and potential NATO member." As Kissinger noted, "No neighbor of Russia shares so benign a view of Russia's purposes. No [European] NATO country considers Russia's size, territorial extent and distant non-European frontiers compatible with NATO membership. But none dares to contradict the leader of the Alliance upon which its security ultimately depends, or wants to arouse Russia's ire by putting forward its real views."[214]

German defense minister Volker Rühe has remained an exception to Kissinger's generalization. In May 1997, Rühe said, "It goes without saying that the new strategic partnership between NATO and Russia can only be based on cooperation and not on integration. The sheer size of Russia, covering eleven time zones on the Eurasian continent, prohibits full integration into Euro-Atlantic structures. And Europe does not want to be dragged into and to be burdened by defence commitments reaching far into Asia."[215]

The European Allies generally consider U.S. rhetoric that envisages eventual Russian membership in NATO unwise. From their perspective, three arguments against Russian membership stand out:

- First, Russian membership could mean abandoning NATO's role as an instrument of collective defense and turning the Alliance into an ineffective Kantian or Wilsonian collective security regime for the Euro-Atlantic region. The harmful consequences could include the loss of the Alliance's internal security functions, such as promoting a certain "denationalization" in defense planning, which are based on its collective defense purpose, and the renationalization of defense policy within the Alliance, particularly on the part of major powers such as Germany.

- Second, Russian membership in NATO would upset existing patterns of influence in the Alliance, and might subordinate the Europeans to a U.S.-Russian dyad of power. As Hubert Védrine's comments, cited previously, suggest, some influential French observers contend that even the NATO-Russian Founding Act could lead to a U.S.-Russian condominium harmful to European defense autonomy.

- Third, if NATO retained its role as an instrument of collective defense, Russian membership would make the Alliance responsible for protecting Russia against China and other powers.[216] While some Americans might be interested in gaining Russia as an ally against China, this is generally not a high priority in Europe—and probably not in the United States either, at least at present.

The doubts about extending NATO membership to Russia are not limited to the current European Allies, of course, but are shared by the prospective new Allies as well. According to Czech Republic president Vaclav Havel, "An enlarged NATO should consider Russia not an enemy, but a partner. . . . But Russia is nonetheless a Eurasian superpower, so influential that it is hard to imagine it could become an intrinsic part of NATO without flooding the alliance with the busy agenda of Russian interests."[217]

From a European perspective, it would have been wiser not to have brought up the issue at all—to have avoided raising long-term hypothetical options or posing unanswerable questions. Some Western experts in Russian affairs have suggested that at least some prominent Russians regard U.S. statements about eventual Russian membership in NATO as patronizing and disingenuous. It is inconceivable to these Russians that the Western nations would agree either to defend Russia against China (or other powers) or to turn a functioning Alliance, a mainstay of the U.S. and Western global power position, into a vacuous collective security institution. In this Russian view, U.S. talk of future NATO membership for Russia is analogous to President Reagan's promise to share the Strategic Defense Initiative ("Star Wars") technology with the Soviet Union —a promise that probably was never taken seriously by the Soviets.

A fourth objection, advanced by some Europeans, to raising the idea of eventual Russian membership is that it could set the scene for a Russian rebuff and a political campaign against the Alliance. In such a scenario, the Russians might argue that they are not candidates for— nor are they interested in—NATO membership, and that they believe that NATO should be subordinated to the OSCE as the only comprehensive international security organ in the Euro-Atlantic region, the only body recognized as a regional arrangement according to Chapter VIII of the UN Charter. Alternatively, the Russians might actively seek NATO membership with a view to subordinating the Alliance to the OSCE. Whenever Soviet and Russian leaders raised the possibility of joining NATO—for instance, Georgi Malenkov in March 1954, Boris Yeltsin in December 1991 and September 1993, and Ivan Rybkin in October 1996 —their objective appears to have been to deprive NATO of its essential role as an instrument of collective defense.[218] Only a few European observers have noted financial or treaty-based arguments against Russian membership (for example, that while Article 10 of the North Atlantic Treaty refers to any "European" state as eligible for membership, Russia is a "Eurasian" state).[219]

The officially expressed rationales for the NATO enlargement process in the Alliance study—general aims such as promoting stabilization and democratization—offer no grounds for excluding Russia. If Russia were explicitly excluded, some defenders of official U.S. statements contend, many Russians might see NATO's purpose as ultimately one of expanding the West's zone of influence and visibly confining Russia to a much smaller sphere of influence than it has maintained for centuries, an outcome that Moscow—and most Russians—would perceive as a national humiliation. Depending in part on future political developments in Russia, this sense of alienation could lead to sharp confrontations between NATO and Russia. Ronald Steel, a visiting professor at George Washington University, has argued that Russia should be given a role "as a full and equal member" of a "wider European security network" based on the Partnership for Peace, or that "the plan for NATO expansion" should be "taken to its logical conclusion with the incorporation of Russia. To rule this out is to reinforce the belief in Moscow that NATO is being expanded as an anti-Russian alliance."[220]

Extending NATO membership to Russia, however, would mean emptying the Alliance of its collective defense substance and turning it into another OSCE, at least in the eyes of the Allies in Western Europe and of prospective new Allies such as Poland. As Henry Kissinger incisively puts it, "The proposition that NATO enlargement might eventually include Russia confuses all parties. For Russia is in, but not of, Europe; it borders Asia, Central Asia, and the Middle East, and it pursues policies along these borders that are difficult to reconcile with NATO objectives. Russian membership would dilute the Alliance to the point of irrelevance."[221]

UKRAINE AND NATO

The differences in the Alliance's public references to the cases of Russia and Ukraine have been noteworthy. NATO has been careful to pay special attention to each, with additional deference to Russia. In June 1996, for example, the North Atlantic Council called for "further strong ties of cooperation with all Partner countries, including the further enhancement of our strong relationship with Ukraine, and the development of a strong, stable and enduring partnership with Russia."[222] In December 1996, NATO expressed its interest in "expanding and strengthening cooperative relationships with all Partners, including building a strong security partnership with Russia and a distinctive relationship with Ukraine."[223]

Meeting the challenge of building positive links with Russia hinges in part on the future course of Russian-Ukrainian relations, because NATO has underscored the significance of its ties with Ukraine. In December 1996, the North Atlantic Council indicated that "Ukraine's development of a strong, enduring relationship with NATO is an important aspect of the emerging European security architecture. . . . We are committed to the development in coming months, through high-level and other consultations, of a distinctive and effective NATO-Ukraine relationship, which could be formalized, possibly by the time of the [July 1997] Summit, building on the document on enhanced NATO-Ukraine relations agreed in September 1995, and taking into account recent Ukrainian proposals."[224]

In the NATO-Ukraine Charter (see Appendix 4), concluded in July 1997, it was agreed that the North Atlantic Council will meet with Ukraine as the NATO-Ukraine Commission, "as a rule not less than twice a year."[225] In contrast with the NATO-Russia Founding Act, which includes no evaluation of NATO enlargement, the NATO-Ukraine Charter specifies that NATO and Ukraine share the view that NATO enlargement "is directed at enhancing the stability of Europe, and the security of all countries in Europe without re-creating dividing lines."[226]

Some observers speculate that the deepening of a NATO-Ukraine relationship could help persuade Moscow to pursue its own relationship with NATO, lest Russia allow itself to be isolated. In contrast with Russia, Ukraine has been an active participant in PfP exercises and other activities. Moreover, Kyiv hosts a NATO Information and Documentation Center, the first such center established by NATO in any Partner country.

The NATO-Ukraine Charter states that "the security of Ukraine" is one of the "issues of common concern" for NATO-Ukraine consultations, and specifies as topics for cooperation (among others) "armaments" and "military training, including PfP exercises on Ukrainian territory and NATO support for the Polish-Ukrainian peacekeeping battalion." According to the Charter, "NATO Allies will continue to support Ukrainian sovereignty and independence, territorial integrity, democratic development, economic prosperity and its status as a non-nuclear weapon state, and the principle of inviolability of frontiers, as key factors of stability and security in Central and Eastern Europe and in the continent as a whole." Moreover, it was agreed that "NATO and Ukraine will develop a crisis consultative mechanism to consult together whenever Ukraine perceives a direct threat to its territorial integrity, political independence, or security."[227]

How should these statements be interpreted? From a Russian viewpoint, such statements might be read as NATO's declaring an interest in discouraging a reconstitution of a Russian empire by keeping Ukraine sovereign and autonomous. What, however, would NATO—and, more specifically, the United States and other major NATO nations—do if Russia attempted to reassert control over Ukraine? It is partly to avoid having to face such questions that the Alliance is striving to make PfP and other cooperative security mechanisms successful.

The United States has become more deeply committed to the security and independence of Ukraine than any other NATO ally. As Sherman Garnett has pointed out, the United States "has never before gone so far in linking its nuclear policy to a broad-based engagement in the politics, economics and security of another state that is not an ally."[228] In a lengthy and complicated process of negotiations, the United States discovered that it would have to offer various security assurances to persuade Ukraine to transfer the Soviet nuclear weapons on its soil to Russia and become a non-nuclear party to the Nuclear Non-Proliferation Treaty (NPT). At the same time, as Garnett has observed, "Ukraine sought to change the American perception of the problem from one of nuclear disarmament and nonproliferation to one of the stability of the emerging geopolitical environment in Eurasia. . . . There is a very real chance that the two sides, not to mention Moscow, harbor different understandings of the nature of this linkage [between nuclear disarmament and security] and the obligations it imposes."[229]

The formal U.S. commitments to Ukrainian security were articulated in the January 1994 Trilateral Statement by the presidents of Russia, Ukraine, and the United States, and in the December 1994 Memorandum on Security Assurances in connection with Ukraine's accession to the NPT as a non-nuclear-weapon state. The latter document was signed by Britain's prime minister as well as the presidents of Russia, Ukraine, and the United States, and France made similar commitments to

Ukraine on a unilateral basis.[230] The December 1994 document confirms commitments to respect Ukraine's independence, sovereignty, and existing borders, in accordance with the principles of the 1975 Final Act of the Conference on Security and Cooperation in Europe; to refrain from the threat or use of force against the territorial integrity or political independence of Ukraine, and from any use of weapons against Ukraine, except in self-defense or otherwise in conformity with the United Nations Charter; and to refrain from economic coercion designed to subordinate the exercise by Ukraine of the rights inherent in its sovereignty, in accordance with the principles of the CSCE Final Act. The December 1994 document also restates the positive and negative security assurances accorded to all non-nuclear-weapon state signatories of the NPT.

In other words, Ukraine obtained reaffirmations of the commitments made to all members of the United Nations, all members of the Organization for Security and Cooperation in Europe, and all non-nuclear-weapon state signatories of the NPT. Sherman Garnett points out, however, that previously Russia had been "unwilling to repeat these concrete assertions in a bilateral context, thus implying that the special status of the CIS [Commonwealth of Independent States] undertakings on territorial integrity had precedence over CSCE undertakings." Moreover, "Ukraine in effect created a multilateral consultative mechanism around these assurances focused solely on the security problems."[231]

The December 1994 memorandum commits the parties—Britain, Russia, Ukraine, and the United States—to "consult in the event a situation arises which raises a question concerning these commitments." While this commitment fell short of an international treaty guaranteeing Ukraine's neutrality, which the former Soviet republic had initially sought as protection against possible future Russian intervention, it implies that a multilateral consultation process has displaced what Moscow would have preferred—an essentially bilateral Moscow-Kyiv relationship. The Ukrainians have also obtained significant amounts of U.S. economic and technical assistance, including programs for U.S.-Ukrainian defense cooperation.

As Garnett has noted, "These assurances are neither an alliance nor an absolute guarantee of U.S. or Western action in the face of a crisis.

Inherent in such an arrangement—as in similar diplomatic patterns of old—is the chance for misunderstanding and miscalculation."[232] Concrete tests of the meaning of these commitments could arise in future Russian-Ukrainian confrontations over issues such as Crimea, energy supplies, ethnic Russian minorities in eastern and southern Ukraine, the status of Sevastopol, and the Black Sea Fleet. Moscow's attempts to make the Commonwealth of Independent States a vehicle for Russian dominance have evoked apprehension and resistance in Ukraine. According to the controversial analysis published in October 1995 by Anton Surikov, an adviser to Russia's Defense Research Institute, "Ukraine's economy is expected to collapse in 3–5 years, the republic is likely to split, and its eastern and southern parts will obviously express a desire to reunite with Russia."[233]

What would U.S. and NATO policy be in such circumstances? It has become customary for high-level U.S. officials to affirm that "The United States has a vital national interest in the political stability, the regional peace and the consolidation of democracy in those parts of Europe, and indeed those parts of the former Soviet Union, that used to be under Communist rule."[234] However, despite Kyiv's intermittent expressions of interest in NATO membership, Ukrainian accession to the Alliance is a distant prospect, because of a general Western reluctance to confront Russia in such a sensitive area.

ENHANCING THE PARTNERSHIP FOR PEACE THROUGH THE EURO-ATLANTIC PARTNERSHIP COUNCIL AND OTHER INNOVATIONS

PfP enhancement and NATO enlargement can be viewed as essential elements in an effort to extend the pattern of pacification achieved in NATO Europe during the Cold War to a larger area.

In Walter Slocombe's words, "by creating the Partnership for Peace, NATO has done more than just building the basis for enlargement. It is in fact creating a new zone of security and stability throughout Europe. . . . We will ensure that PfP continues to provide a place in the security architecture of Europe for those nations that do not aspire to become NATO members, and that it remains a viable preparation station for those about to."[235]

According to NATO's September 1995 enlargement study, PfP will become a more significant institution for strengthening security in Europe after NATO enlargement:

> PfP is only at the beginning of its development; its full potential has not yet been achieved; and its continuing importance will not be affected by enlargement. . . . For countries that do not become members, NACC/PfP must constitute: a continuing vehicle for active cooperation with NATO; concrete evidence of NATO's continuing support and concern for their security; and their primary link to the Alliance, as a key Euro-Atlantic security institution, including for consultation with NATO in the event an active partner perceives a direct threat to its territorial integrity, political independence or security.[236]

One of the fundamental purposes of PfP enhancement is to prevent the emergence of new "dividing lines" in Europe after enlargement, by deepening close and meaningful cooperation with non-Allies. The Alliance's enlargement study declares, "NATO's enlargement must be understood as only one important element of a broad European security architecture that transcends and renders obsolete the idea of 'dividing lines' in Europe."[237] Similarly, according to a June 1996 statement by the NATO defense ministers, enhancing PfP will "serve as a means of strengthening relations with Partner countries which do not join the Alliance early or at all, thereby avoiding the creation of new dividing lines in Europe."[238]

While there will inevitably be a distinction between Allies protected by a mutual defense commitment (Article 5) and Partners that do not enjoy such protection, even in an enhanced PfP, NATO intends to give the Partnership for Peace significantly greater substance.

Specific enhancements for the Partnership for Peace

In April 1997, Secretary of Defense Cohen offered his judgments on what an enhanced PfP would consist of: "Examples of enhancements include more challenging exercises that focus on training for peace support operations, practical efforts such as including Partners in planning cells at various NATO headquarters, and expanding the scope of PfP actions beyond preparation for peacekeeping, humanitarian assistance and disaster relief to peace enforcement operations amidst calls for work on the full range of military contingencies."[239] Cohen's statement was noteworthy, because it highlighted the central question of the purposes of PfP, including the types of "military contingencies" that should be prepared for. Some experts contend that the Partnership Framework Document should be amended to "more broadly define PfP objectives and provide more political substance. At a minimum, 'peace enforcement' should be added to the list of specifiable Partnership activities."[240]

The Allies did not go that far, but in May 1997 they adopted a more general term—"peace support operations"—and announced several measures to enhance PfP. The main new elements in the enhanced PfP program include (in addition to the EAPC): an expanded range of exercises corresponding to NATO's new missions, such as peace support operations; options for Partners to provide diplomatic missions to the North Atlantic Council and military representatives to NATO's Military Committee; opportunities for Partners to provide "PfP Staff Elements" to participate in PfP-related work (including planning for NATO-led PfP exercises) at various NATO military headquarters; arrangements to make the Planning and Review Process (PARP) more like NATO defense planning; and the establishment of six international military staff positions to be filled by Partner representatives at the Partnership Coordination Cell at Mons, near SHAPE headquarters. Accordingly, the PARP will become more demanding, with tighter deadlines for meeting interoperability objectives, increased transparency among participants, and ambitious goals for the Partnership in addition to interoperability.

The purpose of these measures is to offer Partners greater involvement in PfP planning and decision making, including political guidance and oversight for future NATO-led PfP operations, and to enrich the operational content of PfP, with more demanding exercises and activities, more extensive interactions with NATO political and military bodies, and more comprehensive and exigent planning mechanisms. It was also agreed that NATO may invest more of its own funds in PfP projects.[241]

At the same time, however, a number of Allies are concerned lest collective defense be undermined through the presence on NATO staffs of officers from Partner countries not covered by Article 5 commitments and the tendency to focus more attention on PfP activities and less on collective defense.

France in particular may raise obstacles to some forms of PfP enhancement. As with France's initial reactions to the NACC, French observers have expressed concerns about the PfP's potential impact on the OSCE and its significance for France's own status in the Alliance. Because France has not participated in either NATO's Defense Planning Committee or a number of facets of the Alliance's collective planning process since it withdrew from the integrated military structure in 1966, Paris has been reluctant to see Partners more involved in Alliance-related planning activities than France itself is prepared to be. In December 1995, Paris announced that France would henceforth participate fully in the Alliance's Military Committee and some other related activities. Until (and unless) France comes more fully into the integrated military structure, however, Paris may be expected to apply the brakes on movement toward at least some enhancements of PfP activities.

Euro-Atlantic Partnership Council

The establishment of an Atlantic Partnership Council was first proposed in September 1996 by then U.S. secretary of state Warren Christopher. "Thanks to the Partnership for Peace," said Christopher,

> we can now form the first truly Europe-wide military coalitions, in which soldiers from Russia and America, Poland and Ukraine, Germany and Lithuania train side by side, ready to deploy at a moment's notice to protect our security. To this end, we should expand the Partnership's mandate beyond its current missions. We should involve our Partners in the planning as well as the execution of NATO missions. We should give them a stronger voice by forming an Atlantic Partnership Council. In all these ways, NATO gives us a foundation to build our New Atlantic Community—one in which all of Europe and North America work together to build lasting security, one that succeeds where all past efforts have failed.[242]

Allied governments agreed that if PfP is to become an enduring element of the security architecture, the non-NATO participants must gain more influence in collective decision making, at least regarding PfP activities. In December 1996, the North Atlantic Council declared that, "With the rapid growth of our activities under both NACC and PfP, we have identified a need for greater coherence in our cooperation in a framework which will establish with Partners a more meaningful and productive cooperative and consultative process, building on the elements of NACC and PfP which we and our Partners deem most valuable.

To this end, we have agreed to work with Partners on the initiative to establish . . . a single new cooperative mechanism."[243]

Upon its establishment in May 1997, the EAPC adopted the NACC work plan as its own, with a view to replacing it with an even more extensive agenda of topics for consultations. It was nonetheless specified that "Cooperation on defense-related issues, in the military field and in the sphere of peacekeeping (including exercises), will continue as Partnership for Peace activities."[244] Moreover, "PfP in its enhanced form will be a clearly identifiable element within this flexible framework [of the EAPC]."[245]

The EAPC's founders, the NACC members and PfP Partners, declared that its establishment would be "a qualitative step forward in raising to a new level the dynamic and multifaceted political and military cooperation" already achieved in NACC and PfP, and that it would "make a strong contribution to cooperative approaches to security and form an enduring part of the European security architecture."[246]

The EAPC is to be guided by the principles of inclusiveness and self-differentiation. "It will be inclusive, in that opportunities for political consultation and practical cooperation will be open to all Allies and Partners equally. It will also maintain self-differentiation, in that Partners will be able to decide for themselves the level and areas of cooperation with NATO."[247] The EAPC is to meet monthly at the ambassadorial level in Brussels, and twice a year at the level of foreign and defense ministers. The EAPC and enhanced PfP offer options for cooperation to Partners that aspire to NATO membership but were not selected for the first post–Cold War round of enlargement. According to the July 1997 Madrid Declaration, "On the basis of the principles of inclusiveness and self-differentiation, Partner countries will thus be able to draw closer to the Alliance."[248]

Saying that the future of PfP will be developed within the "framework" of the EAPC does not throw much light on how the new forum will make decisions. The disadvantages to decision making by consensus (that is, unanimity) include the general risk of paralysis, given the number of participants, and the specific risk that Russia or others could turn such procedures into a de facto veto power. Some observers have speculated that these risks could be avoided by making the EAPC a consultative forum without votes, dependent on "coalitions of the willing" for the implementation of any decisions reached by acclamation. However, to make PfP more meaningful to Partners, especially as a vehicle for dealing with non–Article 5 contingencies, consensus decision making may be unavoidable—though consensus among forty-four would clearly be more difficult than among sixteen. (After the NATO enlargement projected to take place by 1999, consensus at forty-four would still be more difficult than among nineteen.)

Speculation about the future of the EAPC and PfP suggests that, at some future time, the PfP rather than NATO might be called upon to undertake an IFOR/SFOR type of operation in the former Soviet Union. Some observers have argued that an EAPC command, perhaps using the Alliance's CJTF assets, might be easier for the Russians to accept than a NATO command. This might imply the EAPC, rather than the North Atlantic Council, providing political guidance. In IFOR and SFOR, the North Atlantic Council has had the last word, though it has consulted extensively with non-NATO participants.

Currently, such speculation seems rather far-fetched, in view of the misgivings Russians have expressed about PfP and NATO enlargement. The Russians generally disapprove of PfP because the Alliance has been the "senior partner" in each relationship. The Alliance has determined the menu of acceptable PfP activities for each Partner to choose from. The Russians preferred the NACC, in which decision making was by consensus, over PfP; and for the same reason, they have championed the OSCE as a framework for European security deliberations. The Russians are therefore likely to favor an EAPC decision-making process resembling that of the NACC or the OSCE, although some experts would prefer to orient the EAPC toward more effective decision making. In an EAPC that functions by consensus, the Russians could effectively block any decision they did not choose to endorse—for instance, crisis management or peacekeeping operations in any former Soviet republic.

In a formal sense, the EAPC is dependent on the North Atlantic Council. In a political sense, some observers argue, NATO will feel obliged to consult and concert with the EAPC. As an exclusive forum that leaves out the Partners, it is argued, the North Atlantic Council may be devalued. The excluded might ask, Where is the legitimacy in a meeting that leaves us out? If the Partners are simply to function as NATO's unpaid consultants, what is in it for them? It seems likely that they will seek as much practical political influence as they can obtain.

The probable limits of the Euro-Atlantic Partnership Council and enhanced PfP as institutions in their own right should nonetheless be understood. That is, both the EAPC and PfP are expected to serve as frameworks for cooperation with NATO, not as multilateral organs that could compete with the OSCE or undertake peace support operations independent of NATO.

The hierarchy of NATO-sponsored Euro-Atlantic security structures has yet to be clarified. The North Atlantic Council is clearly the supreme body, but what will be the order of precedence for the NATO-Russia Permanent Joint Council, the NATO-Ukraine Commission, and the Euro-Atlantic Partnership Council? The Poles and other East Europeans fear that the Russians may try to use the NATO-Russia council to bargain about their status behind their backs. This fear is well-grounded in terms of Russian aspirations, and NATO will have to ensure that this does not happen. The Russians are likely to object to attempts to hold initial consultations in the EAPC, while the East Europeans will probably object if primacy is accorded to the NATO-Russia council. The period leading up to NATO enlargement may be especially sensitive; countries not yet admitted to NATO, such as Poland, are likely to resist being subordinated or marginalized for the sake of an Alliance accommodation with Russia.

The relationship between the OSCE and NATO's Partnership for Peace

What is NATO becoming, some critics ask, given the extensive trans-European membership of PfP, the continuous expansion of PfP activities, and the potential enhancement of Partner involvement in decision making via special arrangements for Partners involved in particular non–Article 5 contingencies and via the EAPC, which may operate in practice by an OSCE-like consensus rule? In the view of some critics, it is almost as if NATO, after having defeated attempts in 1990–91 to create an all-European collective security organization under CSCE auspices, is gradually transforming itself into an entity comparable to such a body—a mutual supervisory agency for the Euro-Atlantic region.

As NATO's secretary general pointed out in March 1997, the Alliance and its Partnership for Peace encompass "almost every country in Europe, including Russia, and reaching out as far east as Central Asia."[249] The EAPC has forty-four members. The only OSCE states not in the EAPC or PfP are Andorra, Bosnia-Herzegovina, Croatia, Cyprus, the Holy See, Ireland, Liechtenstein, Malta, Monaco, San Marino, and the Federal Republic of Yugoslavia (Serbia and Montenegro).[250]

In view of these facts, what is to be role of the OSCE, with its fifty-five participants? What is to be the relationship between the OSCE and NATO's Euro-Atlantic structures, PfP and the EAPC? Is NATO at risk of becoming an OSCE-like organization, if (as some advocate) the distinction between Article 4 and Article 5 commitments is blurred? It should be recalled that Article 5 expresses the mutual-defense commitment the Allies have made to each other, whereas Article 4 consists of a pledge to consult whenever any Ally considers that its "territorial integrity, political independence or security" is threatened. Furthermore, in the context of PfP, the EAPC, and the OSCE, the Alliance has repeatedly affirmed its devotion to "security is indivisible" principles reminiscent of previous historical experiments with collective security. At the January 1994 NATO summit, for example, the North Atlantic Council declared that "Our own security is inseparably linked to that of all other states in Europe. The consolidation and preservation throughout the continent of democratic societies and their freedom from any form of coercion or intimidation are therefore of direct and material concern to us, as they are to all other CSCE states under the commitments of the Helsinki Final Act and the Charter of Paris."[251]

PfP as an instrument of intervention and crisis management could become less usable, however, if decision making authority were shifted from NATO's North Atlantic Council to the EAPC. As noted previously, some speculate that all Partners and Allies might eventually participate in the EAPC on a basis of equality, with decision making by consensus, regarding non–Article 5 contingencies. This would probably permit effective decision making only with regard to undemanding, noncontroversial contingencies. In that case, one might imagine an EAPC-sanctioned "coalition of the willing," perhaps operating under a UN mandate. (An OSCE mandate would be unlikely if the proposed intervention involved something more intrusive than, for example, an election-monitoring team—in which case it might as well be carried out by the OSCE directly.) Such a shift in decision-making authority is contrary to the Alliance's current policy, but it is a risk that must be recognized.

DILEMMAS AND RISKS IN TRYING TO COMBINE COLLECTIVE SECURITY AND COLLECTIVE DEFENSE

A single sentence in the Alliance's 1991 Rome Declaration illustrates the magnitude of its ambitions regarding the future political order of Europe: "As an agent of change, a source of stability and the indispensable guarantor of its members' security, our Alliance will continue to play a key role in building a new, lasting order of peace in Europe: a Europe of cooperation and prosperity."[252]

To serve as "an agent of change" throughout Europe, the Alliance has established institutions such as Partnership for Peace; the NATO-Russia Permanent Joint Council; the NATO-Ukraine Commission; and the Euro-Atlantic Partnership Council. The Allies hope these institutions will function as immense "learning machines" to promote democratization, including democratic control over the military, and greater transparency and confidence in international security cooperation. Beyond serving as "the indispensable guarantor of its members' security" (the collective defense function), the Alliance has attempted "to play a key role in building a new, lasting order of peace in Europe."

With regard to all these ambitions, NATO has yet to measure fully the limits of what it can accomplish, in view of the intrinsic magnitude of the challenges and NATO's limited political and economic resources. Indeed, time and personnel constraints will no doubt affect the implementation of the EAPC, NATO-Russia, and NATO-Ukraine schedule of meetings at various levels of authority. The large increase in the number of meetings may decrease the amount of time and substantive effort invested in specific encounters.

The most serious dilemmas and risks reside in the Alliance's attempt to combine elements of collective security with collective defense. Alliance documents, of course, generally do not declare that this is the objective. The collective security spirit, however, has been unmistakable in various Alliance declarations since 1991. In December 1991, the NACC recalled that, "As stated in the Joint Declaration of Paris, *security is indivisible* and the security of each of our countries is inextricably linked to that of all States participating in the CSCE. The consolidation and preservation throughout the continent of democratic societies and their freedom from any form of coercion or intimidation therefore concern us all."[253]

According to the 1991 Strategic Concept, as noted at the beginning of this chapter, one of the Alliance's four "fundamental security tasks" is "To provide one of the indispensable foundations for a stable security environment in Europe, based on the growth of democratic institutions and commitment to the peaceful resolution of disputes, in which *no* country would be able to intimidate or coerce *any* European nation or to impose hegemony through the threat or use of force."[254] The Strategic Concept did not use the phrase "collective security," but it did underline the Alliance's determination to "pursue the development of cooperative structures of security for a Europe whole and free."[255] Similarly, rather than use the expression "collective security," Walter Slocombe lists "cooperative security" together with "collective defense" as among the Alliance's "basic principles."[256]

In the debate over NATO's new functions, some conceptual obscurity has emerged at times. As is customary, Secretary of Defense Cohen used the expression "collective defense" in his April 1997 testimony to refer to the defense of the Allies against external threats. However, he used the expression "cooperative security" to refer to efforts to support the "stability of the new democracies of Central and Eastern Europe," and at another point he alluded to "collective security": "NATO's basic principles of democracy, consensus and collective security are not a threat to Russia."[257]

Some European and American observers have complained that the Alliance (and the United States in particular) is trying to "have it both ways" by recasting NATO as if collective defense and a continuing hedge against Russian power do in fact matter, and pursuing partnership with Russia (and even allowing for potential NATO membership for Russia) as if collective defense does not matter, because Russia will become a colleague in a vague Euro-Atlantic "cooperative security" enterprise dedicated to the proposition that "security is indivisible."

The aspirations of the Baltic states illustrate this apparent inconsistency, or ambivalence, about NATO's purposes. According to Simon Lunn, the acting secretary general of the North Atlantic Assembly, a body composed of parliamentarians from NATO countries, "The problem is that the Balts want to join the old NATO when we are talking about building a new NATO. . . . The risk for them, and us, is that joining NATO now would provoke the kind of security paranoia in Russia that we are trying to put to rest."[258]

Some observers have suggested that the solution to this impasse would be to transform NATO so profoundly that no Russian could fear it. Consider the observations of Paul Goble, formerly with the U.S. State Department and now at Radio Free Europe/Radio Liberty, as quoted in a *New York Times* article:

> "In some sense, while I want the Balts in NATO now, I believe that they will not enter NATO until Russia stops fearing NATO"—in other words, until NATO is so transformed that it is more of an organization of cooperative security than of collective defense. "I think that's sooner than many think," he said. "NATO is already being transformed, and I tell the Balts that the NATO they get into will not be the NATO they expect to join."[259]

Daniel Vernet, a correspondent for the French newspaper *Le Monde,* has put the matter only slightly differently:

> The countries that have the greatest reason to fear pressures, if not threats, from their big Russian neighbor, have been carefully left to the side, waiting for better times, it is said. That is to say, times when relations between NATO and Moscow will be so peaceful that the entry of the Baltic countries (for example) in the Atlantic organization will have become possible and therefore . . . useless. . . . Are the states of the former Eastern Europe not deceiving themselves about the institution they are joining? . . . [T]his Alliance is less and less interested in collective defense and is being transformed into an institution that is more political than military.[260]

To reassure Russia that the Alliance has no hostile purpose, NATO concluded the NATO-Russia Founding Act with Moscow in May 1997. This document, as noted earlier, refers to both NATO's continuing collective defense mission and the idea of NATO and Russia working to "build together a lasting and inclusive peace in the Euro-Atlantic area on the principles of democracy and cooperative security."

The limits to this process have yet to be discovered. By definition, it could break down if democratization falters in major countries such as

Russia and Ukraine, or if clashes of interests involving such states hamper cooperation and bring about a renewal of confrontation. It is not clear how to assess the probability of such events, but their significance makes it prudent for the Alliance to maintain preparedness for collective defense. Yet the level of NATO's investment in collective defense—in terms of defense budgets and military exercises, for example—has clearly declined, as more time and money have been devoted to PfP activities and peace support operations in the former Yugoslavia.

NATO enlargement underscores an implicit, or at least potential, tension between NATO's collective defense purpose and the goal of collective security throughout the Euro-Atlantic region. Political leaders in prospective new member nations such as Poland—and in other applicant states, such as the Baltics—are interested in NATO membership as a means of protection against Russia, and Russian elites are well aware of this. Russian experts and officials have generally portrayed NATO enlargement as a somewhat threatening prospect.

The dilemmas and risks in trying to combine collective security and collective defense are examined here in four conceptual areas: (a) the risks for Alliance cohesion and effectiveness in collective security; (b) in more general terms, the antinomy between inclusiveness and effectiveness; (c) some inferences from a comparable experience in international history; and (d) major power patterns of interaction outside formal institutions.

Risks for Alliance cohesion and effectiveness in collective security

If taken seriously, collective security commitments can complicate the definition of NATO's priorities. Collective security implies an expansion of commitments and obligations beyond the mutual defense pledges of an alliance, such as those expressed in Article 5 of the North Atlantic Treaty. One of the risks could therefore be an erosion of NATO's coherence as a collective defense organization during the pursuit of a diffuse collective security arrangement.

The Alliance's goal of avoiding new "dividing lines" in Europe implies dissolving distinctions between security commitments. It is worth recalling that when the debate about possibly transforming the CSCE into an all-European collective security pact was under way in 1990, Henry Kissinger drew attention to the dangers of a system that "would erode all existing psychological dividing lines. . . . For if everybody is allied with everybody, nobody has a special relationship with anybody."[261]

The emphasis in PfP and associated activities on concepts associated with collective security—the notion, for example, that there should be no dividing lines in Europe, because "security is indivisible" and all countries are concerned about any aggression or coercion anywhere in the Euro-Atlantic region—implies a dilution of collective defense, including Article 5 mutual defense pledges. The Alliance is in fact devoting less attention—and fewer resources—to collective defense capabilities, because of the focus on cultivating cooperative programs with former adversaries and the judgment that large-scale contingencies requiring collective defense are unlikely in the foreseeable future.

After the March 1997 U.S.-Russian summit in Helsinki called attention to the possibility of a NATO-Russian council, Kissinger contended that

> The Helsinki blueprint moves NATO from being an alliance toward a system of collective security. . . . Where an alliance commits itself to defend a specific territory, a system of collective security . . . defines neither the territory to be defended nor the strategy for doing it. Each member is assumed to assess threats to the peace in the same way and to be willing to take the same steps to meet those threats. . . . Theoretically, some token peace keeping forces may be created, but since neither the potential threat nor the likely theater of operations can be known in advance, these have never in the past amounted to much, either for deterrence or for strategy.[262]

Kissinger's formulation, however, overstates what is evidently envisaged by NATO and its partners in PfP. Rather than assuming that each state will "assess threats to the peace in the same way and . . . be willing to take the same steps to meet those threats," the Alliance apparently foresees a relatively feeble collective security arrangement. In contrast with more stringent Kantian or Wilsonian collective security designs (discussed in the Introduction), the Allies and Partners in PfP and the EAPC are under no particular obligation to act in specific non–Article 5 contingencies, but volunteers are at liberty to form coalitions of the willing to take action—though they may prefer to obtain a UN or OSCE mandate to do so. A UN Security Council or OSCE mandate would imply collective security operations of the "major-power-consensus" type.[263]

Concepts associated with collective security—the notion, for example, that there should be "no dividing lines" in Europe, because "security is indivisible" and all countries are concerned by any aggression or coercion anywhere in the Euro-Atlantic region—clearly fall short of the mutual defense pledge in Article 5 of the North Atlantic Treaty. Some of the proposals for the future of PfP, however, suggest that this new enterprise may be on a road to collective security that would entail a watering down—or, for some, an abolition—of distinct Article 5 commitments.

NATO enlargement holds the prospect that some of the most active Partners will become Allies. As Michael Rühle and Nick Williams conclude,

> Those remaining [in PfP] would consist of a number of countries who would be disappointed in their expectations as well as several who, for various reasons, are either unable or unwilling to move beyond a token contribution. Most importantly, among those remaining would also be a Russia which might take the enlargement of NATO as another reason to withdraw from its so far hesitant cooperation with the West. The decline of PfP into a marginal role would then be inevitable; equally inevitable would be the charge leveled at NATO of having helped bring about a new division of Europe, which it had done so much to avoid. Such an unwelcome development could be pre-empted if the military and political content of the partnership were to be enhanced—if, in other words, PfP became specifically an instrument for reducing the security differences between allies and partners substantially further.[264]

The problem with "reducing the security differences between allies and partners substantially further" is that it could dilute the value of the collective defense commitment in Article 5—the core merit of NATO membership for the current Allies, and the main attraction for the prospective new Allies. Nonetheless, faithfully reporting the "security is indivisible" spirit of a number of recent NATO communiqués and declarations, Rühle and Williams have noted that PfP could strive to promote "a sense that the security of allies and partners are inseparably linked."[265]

To do this, Rühle and Williams suggest, PfP might build on NATO's January 1994 promise of consultations "with any active participant in the Partnership if that partner perceives a direct threat to its territorial integrity, political independence or security."[266] According to Rühle and Williams,

This implies, if not the probability, at least the possibility of effective allied partner co-ordination in the face of such a threat. The challenge will lie in transforming it from a theoretical to a practical, even credible, possibility. This may not be as difficult or as vague as it sounds. The "security guarantee" enshrined in the NATO Treaty is not as solid in writing as it is credible in reality. What makes it so is the visible organization and military capability able and ready to fulfill the commitment of Article 5. In PfP terms, giving depth to the idea that allied and partner security are inseparably linked could involve the even closer association of partners in NATO activities, possibly including them in NATO's Combined Joint Task Force planning and exercising. . . . In time, PfP could also develop a force structure of its own (that is multinational divisions and corps) which involved both partner and allied units. . . . The idea that security is inseparable would gain credibility because it would be founded on firm organizational and structural arrangements. Partners would have a real sense that their security was of material concern to the alliance.[267]

Pursuing a similar line of thought, John Duffield has argued that, even without NATO membership and protection through a formal Article 5 treaty obligation, Partners will gain a genuine security commitment from the Alliance. "The more these countries interact during NATO military exercises, training for peacekeeping operations, and so on, the more they will have and will feel that they have a de facto military or security guarantee. In other words, the more that NATO is involved with them and the more they restructure their forces and decision-making processes to be compatible with NATO, the harder it will be for NATO to refuse to act if their security is endangered."[268]

This rather vague approach to obligations represents a departure from traditional mutual defense treaties and from the Alliance's own origins, when the would-be Allies argued about how specific to make the wording of Article 5 before they finally agreed on a formula that has been interpreted over time as signifying a firm commitment. This approach could be seen as involving the Allies in a web of moral and political commitments to the twenty-seven PfP Partners comparable to the obligations they would assume in a Kantian or Wilsonian collective security system for the Euro-Atlantic region. Nonetheless, some high-level U.S. officials have suggested minimizing the distinction between Allies and Partners. In 1996, Robert Hunter, then the U.S. permanent representative on the North Atlantic Council, said, "We want to make the difference between being a partner and being an ally razor thin, so that every nation, whether an ally or partner, can share in the promise of a secure future in a peaceful Europe."[269]

While Rühle and Williams acknowledge that "the blurring of the hitherto clear distinction between allies and partners" would not be without risks, they do not identify them. Such risks could include undermining the physical coherence of NATO's collective defense posture (if Allied and Partner military units were combined in a common force arrangement) and eroding the political and strategic credibility of collective defense commitments by making PfP consultation promises resemble such commitments. In other words, enhancing PfP in these ways might provide some temporary reassurance to disappointed would-be Allies, but it might also move NATO away from collective defense and toward aspirations to serve as a collective security structure of the Kantian or Wilsonian type for the Euro-Atlantic region.

Such a structure would not be likely to win credibility from the major powers. They would not rely on it for the defense of their vital interests any more than they rely on the UN or the OSCE. NATO would then be increasingly emptied of its collective defense substance, and the major powers would rely on other means to defend their vital interests. NATO's function and purpose might thus change beyond recognition, and the Alliance might enter history as another example of a failed regional collective security enterprise.

As Nick Williams pointed out in another study, "Preserving the capacity of self-defence requires a closer and more intense form of military cooperation among Allies than could ever be possible between Allies and Partners. There will always be an unbridgeable difference between collective defence as practiced within NATO and practical military cooperation as conducted *between* NATO and its Partners."[270]

Williams's observation is quite pertinent. It should be recalled that the prospective new Allies are primarily interested in Article 5 protection and see it as imperative to obtain such protection while the "window of opportunity"—created by Russia's current weakness and the widespread Western assumption that NATO enlargement is therefore a low-risk and low-cost enterprise—is still open. The "old NATO" dedicated to collective defense vis-à-vis Russia is the top priority of the prospective new allies, and participating in PfP and other "new NATO" programs with a "collective security" spirit is seen as part of the price of membership. If "new NATO" programs and activities crowded out the "old NATO" entirely, these prospective new allies would be deeply disappointed, because NATO would have become something more like the OSCE or the League of Nations and less like an alliance for collective defense. The new Allies would then, like the current Allies, be obliged to consider other arrangements to ensure the defense of their core national interests.

Some observers have nonetheless proposed that the Alliance abandon its historical essence and chief merit in the eyes of the Allies—the collective defense pledge in Article 5—and become a regional collective security organization. Charles Kupchan, a senior fellow for Europe at the Council on Foreign Relations and an associate professor at Georgetown University, has argued that "NATO enlargement would resurrect, not erase, the dividing line between Europe's east and west. . . . Russia justifiably objects to the formal enlargement of a Western military bloc from which it would be excluded." In Kupchan's view, the solution would be to abandon the collective defense commitment in Article 5 of the North Atlantic Treaty and move to a "collective security" system focused on "peacekeeping and peace enforcement; confronting external threats as well as those that might arise from within, it would coordinate multilateral operations across Europe. . . . Case-by-case decisionmaking and a broad mandate to preserve peace in the Atlantic area would be the organizing principles of a new U.S.-European security bargain and a revamped NATO. The elimination of NATO's Article 5 guarantee would weaken the alliance's deterrent power, but as long as Russia continues to pose no danger to Central or Western Europe, the tradeoff makes sense."[271]

In another work, Kupchan discussed what he deemed the "distinct advantages" of "an unrestricted expansion of NATO," with all PfP Partners eligible for eventual membership. He acknowledged the disadvantages this approach might present, notably for states not included in the initial round of enlargement, and the changes this would necessitate in the Alliance's "integrated military structure, its decisionmaking apparatus, and the meaning of its commitment to collective defense." Nonetheless, he argued that "This transformation may be unavoidable; NATO may be able to survive only if it becomes a provider of collective security rather than of collective defense." Furthermore, he made clear that he means "collective security" in the Kantian or Wilsonian sense of the term: "a collective security organization is concerned primarily with preventing conflict among its members. It is based on the principle of all against one—that members will build up military capability against an aggressor should one emerge."[272]

Despite abundant Alliance rhetoric borrowing from the broad tradition of collective security, the Allies have refrained so far from attempting to establish a system of collective security in the Kantian or Wilsonian sense. Nor have the Allies professed an interest in doing so beyond vague reaffirmations of the "security is indivisible" notion. Instead, they have in practice endorsed only the major-power-consensus form of collective security. Rather than use such a phrase, however, the Allies have generally favored the word "cooperative," as in the goal expressed in the 1991 Strategic Concept—"to pursue the development of co-operative structures of security for a Europe whole and free."[273]

However, definitions of "cooperative security" that can be considered in any way official have been scarce. The definition suggested by Rob de Wijk, head of the Defense Concepts Division of the Defense Staff at the Netherlands Ministry of Defense, is not an official statement of policy, but it may reflect thinking in at least some circles in the Alliance because de Wijk participated in the drafting of the 1991 Strategic Concept and many of the Alliance's subsequent policy statements. According to de Wijk, "NATO's new mission" is to play a role "in a system of co-operative security":

> The heart of this is mutual economic, socio-cultural and military co-operation between an ever-increasing group of countries. The object of co-operative security is to anticipate potential conflicts and prevent them breaking out, or to actively strive to suppress conflicts once they have broken out by means of joint international action within the system. Co-operative security does not mean that member states are treaty-bound to offer assistance. If that were the case it would be a question of collective, not co-operative, security. The concept of co-operative security does not assume that all crises can be controlled and that wars can always be avoided. It is intended to give direction to anticipatory actions.
>
> Besides a willingness to co-operate closely in all possible areas, the concept demands that within the system there are common norms and

standards of conduct. Within the system countries must be answerable for failing to observe these norms and standards. Third, there must be a readiness to develop instruments to allow action to be taken to prevent violation of these norms and standards, and to intervene if they should be violated. Finally, a clarity of political intentions of countries within the system is the basis for co-operation. Continuing emphasis should therefore be placed on confidence-inspiring measures such as arms control, maximum insight into each other's defense plans and proliferation control.[274]

De Wijk's formulation has the advantage of contrasting "cooperative security" as the Allies apparently intend to practice it—on a voluntary, optional basis for coalitions of the willing—with what he rightly calls "collective security," involving a treaty obligation to act, an arrangement that could be more precisely called collective security in the Kantian and Wilsonian sense. The prominence of the broader collective security tradition is evident in the support for shared norms of behavior, transparency, and confidence-building. Nonetheless, de Wijk retains—as do the Allies—a clear distinction between Article 5 collective defense obligations and the optional nature of decisions to act in contingencies involving "cooperative security." In his words, "the distinction between Article 5 and non–Article 5 [contingencies] is . . . politically and judicially relevant because it has a bearing on the degree of obligation of member states to assist each other." Furthermore, de Wijk places his formulation of "cooperative security" within the major-power-consensus variant of collective security by envisaging NATO military action in such contingencies under the OSCE's authority: "Seeing that the OSCE does not have its own military means it must obviously call upon NATO."[275]

Whether such distinctions will be sufficient to protect the Alliance from problems such as unanticipated entanglements, arising in part from misperceptions about the extent and depth of its commitments to Partners, is examined further in chapter 4.

The antinomy between inclusiveness and effectiveness

Martin Wight once advanced the proposition that "An international political organization can aim either at effectiveness, in which case it will restrict its membership to like-minded states capable of agreeing upon and pursuing a common interest, and will resemble an alliance, or at universality of membership, in which case it will include so many diverse interests that it will be incapable of political cooperation on major issues."[276]

In other words, there may well be an antinomy, or tension, between inclusiveness and effectiveness. The more selective (or exclusive) the organization, the greater the chances that its members will be able to work together constructively—for instance, as an alliance for collective defense. The more inclusive (or comprehensive) the membership of the organization, the less it will, in Wight's phrase, "resemble an alliance," and its prospects for effective cooperation may be correspondingly limited. In that event, the members may seek arrangements outside that organization and its formal institutional channels to be able to undertake effective action.

These broad theses about international organizations obviously leave out questions such as the identity of the participants in the organization, their values and interests, and the nature of the common task. If the common task concerns a nonpolitical functional arrangement (for example, an international postal union), sufficient effectiveness may well be feasible. In matters of national defense and survival, however, the propositions about the intrinsic weaknesses of comprehensively inclusive organizations may well apply. The larger and more inclusive the body, the less governments will tend to rely on it for the defense of their vital national interests—just as no state that can afford national military capabilities and that can make effective alliances would consider placing primary reliance for its security on a body such as the United Nations or the OSCE.

The "collective action" problem in economics may well be relevant to decision making beyond defense spending and burden sharing in an alliance; it may also pertain to choices about honoring commitments and accepting risks. According to Mancur Olson and other economic theorists, in endeavors with many participants, incentives to "free-ride," or at least to make minimal contributions and to benefit from the disproportionate investments of others, may arise.[277] To cite a recent analysis, "The sheer size of ideal collective security organizations thus militates against political cohesion and exacerbates the collective action problem."[278]

These propositions are relevant to NATO today because of the prevailing tendency to put forward general "security is indivisible" principles while pursuing an open-ended enlargement process, at a time when the NATO-directed Partnership for Peace already has twenty-seven members in addition to the sixteen Allies. The enlargement process and the scope of PfP have to be carefully directed, lest the Alliance lose cohesion and effectiveness as a collective defense body. In that event, whatever the merits of the transformed Alliance as an entity for dialogue and policy coordination, over time it could become an organization peripheral to the core national security interests of its members.

No grave problems for the Alliance's cohesion and effectiveness are likely to arise in an enlargement process limited to a few countries. The important long-term question in this regard is not how to provide collective defense protection for a few new Allies, but how to control the enlargement process once it is under way. It may be difficult to control this process (despite the reservations of some influential politicians), because of the U.S. insistence that the "door is open" to further rounds of enlargement and because of the Alliance's reliance on vague criteria for membership, such as progress toward democratization, that make it hard to exclude anyone on strategic grounds.

Discussions of the eventual scope of the NATO enlargement process that are confined to the twelve countries formally pursuing an "intensified dialogue" with NATO are misleading: they omit Austria, Sweden, and others that may soon join the bandwagon and that would be politically difficult for NATO to exclude. Some U.S. and European observers have suggested establishing closer links between NATO membership and membership in the EU and the WEU. This might tend to slow down the pace of NATO enlargement and to establish constructive limits. It would then be appropriate to reopen the question of possibly enlarging NATO further when additional countries join the EU.

An open-ended process of enlargement could lead, some U.S. and European observers have argued, to the "OSCE-ization" of NATO. The more rapid and more extensive the enlargement beyond the first round, the greater the risk that NATO will lose its cohesion and effectiveness in its core mission—its ability to function as a collective defense insurance policy for the existing Allies. Some European observers are apprehensive about the prospect of NATO becoming "an OSCE in uniform" or "an OSCE with teeth"—though others contend that the teeth are falling out as a result of continuing defense budget cuts in most NATO countries since the mid-1980s. The open-ended expansion of NATO would be risky, it is argued, because it would accelerate the tilt away from collective defense to collective security as the Alliance's main activity.[279]

The OSCE is sometimes called a "regional United Nations," yet it is in some ways even weaker than the United Nations. The OSCE, unlike the UN, has no Security Council to enable a coalition to take action if there is a consensus of the major powers. The OSCE is generally unable to take significant decisions without a consensus of all fifty-five members. The OSCE has no military arm, and its institutional mechanisms still require considerable development. To date, its security functions principally have been in areas such as norm setting, conflict prevention, early warning, political consultations and mediation, monitoring and fact-finding missions, protecting minority rights, the peaceful settlement of disputes, and arms control and confidence- and security-building measures. Because of its inclusiveness, the constraints on its decision-making latitude (despite the "consensus minus one" rule adopted at the January 1992 Prague meeting), and its inability to defend core security interests against coercion or aggression, the OSCE is widely considered an institution of limited effectiveness, useful mainly for certain circumscribed functions.

Nonetheless, U.S. officials have increasingly tended to adopt the inclusive rhetoric of the collective security tradition, rejecting the idea of dividing lines that would leave anyone out of the NATO-sponsored Euro-Atlantic security structures. Such rhetoric could be imprudent if it led to a weakening of NATO's collective defense. Major powers do not rely on collective security structures such as the OSCE or the UN to defend their national interests. If the pursuit of NATO-based Euro-Atlantic security structures made NATO as irrelevant to the defense of core security interests as the OSCE, the major powers in this region would probably turn to other instruments to defend their security, and many of the beneficial internal functions of the Alliance would be lost.

Some inferences from a comparable experience in international history

Some U.S. and Allied officials have at times conveyed the impression that the Alliance's efforts to help in the construction of a peaceful political order in Europe are unprecedented, and that they will make traditional concepts for the analysis of power relations in international politics obsolete. In September 1994, for example, Robert Hunter, then the U.S. permanent representative on the North Atlantic Council, said that "Both the Partnership and NATO's expansion are part of a grand experiment in European security—an experiment that has no precedent in a thousand years of searching to break a recurring cycle of conflict. The sixteen Allies are trying to create something better than the balance of power. We are doing nothing less than trying to extend the European Civil Space eastward—one cautious step after another."[280]

Ambassador Hunter's statement that NATO's current experiment "has no precedent in a thousand years of searching to break a recurring cycle of conflict" was surprising, especially in light of his comment in the same speech about "the power of democracy to help provide the conditions of peace—an idea perhaps put best by Immanuel Kant." As noted in the Introduction, the ambition to "create something better than the balance of power" by creating a "community of power" composed of like-minded states has had many precedents in international history, and—during the period since the eighteenth century Enlightenment— it has been customary for proponents of such a "collective security" approach to prefer that it be an assembly of democracies.

As Martin Wight wrote many years ago, "At the end of the First World War it was widely hoped that this [balance of power] system could be transformed or replaced by something better."[281] The best known twentieth-century advocate of the Kantian approach to international order was, of course, Woodrow Wilson, whose effort to devise "something better than the balance of power" was the League of Nations. Wilson frequently asserted that the Allied and Associated Powers ranged against the Central Powers in World War I had "fought to do away with an old order and to establish a new one, and the center and characteristic of the old order was that unstable thing which we used to call the 'balance of power.'"[282]

In March 1997, NATO secretary general Javier Solana said that NATO's enlargement should be seen as "one part of a wider package that is designed to develop closer relationships with all countries in the Euro-Atlantic area. The whole package is about uniting the whole of the Euro-Atlantic community around a common security culture. It is about consigning concepts like 'dividing lines,' 'buffer zones' and 'spheres of influence' where they belong: in the dustbin of history."[283] Solana's comments echo Cordell Hull's conviction in 1943 that, with the United Nations, "there will no longer be need for spheres of influence, for alliances, for balance of power, or any other of the special arrangements through which, in the unhappy past, the nations strove to safeguard their security or to promote their interests."[284]

Historical analogies are always less than entirely satisfactory, but there may be heuristic value in pondering some of the similarities and differences between the League of Nations and the Alliance's structures for security cooperation throughout the Euro-Atlantic region, the Partnership for Peace and the Euro-Atlantic Partnership Council.[285] Five similarities stand out, in addition to the general theme of collective security.

First, both enterprises advocate transparency in military affairs, in the interests of reducing mistrust and building confidence. The Partnership for Peace Framework Document calls for the "facilitation of transparency in national defence planning and budgeting processes,"[286] while "cooperation, transparency and trust in security affairs" are "core goals" of the Euro-Atlantic Partnership Council.[287] According to the League of Nations Covenant, "The Members of the League undertake to interchange full and frank information as to the scale of their armaments, their military, naval and air programmes and the condition of such of their industries as are adaptable to warlike purposes."[288]

Second, both recommend the settlement of conflicts without violence. The PfP Framework Document calls upon NATO Allies and Partners "to settle disputes by peaceful means"[289]—a stipulation comparable to the elaborate arbitration and enquiry procedures specified in the League of Nations Covenant for dealing peacefully with "any dispute likely to lead to a rupture."[290]

Third, both favor arms reductions in a multilateral framework. The 1990 Conventional Armed Forces in Europe (CFE) Treaty adaptations are not being negotiated under the auspices of the EAPC or PfP, but all thirty parties to the CFE Treaty are members of the EAPC. The treaty involves all the NATO countries and all the former Warsaw Pact countries, including the Soviet successor states with forces or territory in the treaty's area of application, except for the Baltic states, which chose not to participate. The process of continued treaty adaptations, including the "flanks" agreement of particular interest to Russia (which entered into force in May 1997), forms part of NATO's vision of a peaceful security order in the Euro-Atlantic region.[291] The adaptations are broadly consistent with the principles of the League Covenant: "The Members of the League recognise that the maintenance of peace requires the reduction of national armaments to the lowest point consistent with national safety and the enforcement by common action of international obligations." As with the CFE Treaty, the reductions are to take "account of the geographical situation and circumstances of each state."[292]

Fourth, both are composed primarily of small European powers. As Martin Wight noted, "the League was still a predominantly European institution, and the small powers were predominantly the satisfied and sedentary small powers of Western Europe, together with the satisfied and victorious small powers of Eastern Europe who were concerned to maintain the hard-won freedom of the Versailles settlement."[293] This observation could describe the EAPC and PfP, except that today the small powers of Eastern Europe are concerned about retaining the freedom won in the collapse of the Soviet empire.

Fifth, in each case, some of the major powers do not regard the new pan-European enterprise—the League in the interwar period, PfP and the EAPC today—as vital for their own national security. The attitude of some capitals toward PfP and the EAPC is analogous to that evinced by some powers toward the League. As Wight pointed out, "The powers at the periphery of the League system, especially the members of the British Commonwealth and the Scandinavian states, assumed that the Covenant added little or nothing to their own safety, which could be attained by more traditional means. They saw the League as a benevolent charitable institution for composing the disputes of other less fortunate and probably more cantankerous powers."[294]

At least four differences between the League and NATO's PfP and EAPC structures are significant, however.

First, the approaches to collective security are quite distinct. The security commitments undertaken in PfP and the EAPC are relatively weak and are at most "politically binding," in contrast with the treaty obligations assumed by members of the League. PfP and the EAPC lack the firm "collective security" commitment found in the League Covenant:

"The Members of the League undertake to respect and preserve as against external aggression the territorial integrity and existing political independence of all Members of the League."[295]

In the NATO-sponsored Euro-Atlantic security structures the only commitments are of two types: (1) from NATO to specific Partners, a promise to consult in crisis situations formulated in terms similar to those in Article 4 of the North Atlantic Treaty; and (2) general "security is indivisible" affirmations made by all participating states, nominally with reference to all states in the Euro-Atlantic region. In contrast with the Wilsonian design for the League of Nations as a binding system of collective security, PfP and the EAPC are simply instruments that governments may choose to apply to collective security purposes. PfP and the EAPC provide options for national decisions to participate in consultations and ad hoc coalitions of the willing for action in specific contingencies, but they create no legal obligation to take action. This is a fundamental difference in purpose: While the League was intended to provide international order and abolish war (the ultimate Kantian and Wilsonian goal), the Alliance-based structures presuppose that NATO will continue as a collective defense pact, and the other security commitments are intended to be limited—and possibly restricted to consultations alone.

A second major difference resides in the broader institutional framework. The League of Nations stood alone and (unlike the NATO-sponsored Euro-Atlantic security structures) did not benefit from the potentially complementary support of other major international institutions—the EU, the WEU, the UN, the OSCE, and the Council of Europe. The extensive cooperation within the European Union regarding various economic, political, and social matters, over a period of nearly five decades with regard to the original six founding states, is one of the factors that makes war among the EU states most improbable. (As noted in chapter 2, U.S. commitments and leadership in NATO have been essential factors in dampening the rivalries and security anxieties in Western Europe, thus furnishing a stable and trustworthy framework for the European integration movement.)

Moreover, at least in terms of prevailing policy approaches, participants in PfP and the EAPC would not be likely to undertake any collective security operation without NATO leadership and UN Security

Council or OSCE authorization. In other words, today's more complex institutional framework implies a more complicated, yet in some ways more realistic, approach to decision making. While the framers of the League Covenant simply assumed that unanimity of all members present could be achieved to enforce collective security commitments, the Alliance requires consensus only for its own policies—either to conduct an operation in support of collective security or to endorse one undertaken by a coalition of the willing. The approach currently favored by several Allies—to make NATO action dependent on Security Council or OSCE mandates—is consistent with the major-power-consensus approach to collective security, and therefore is at variance with the Kantian or Wilsonian model.

A third difference concerns the configuration of power. Unlike the unstable coalitions of the League of Nations, which were dependent on the only two major powers in the League from start to finish (Britain and France), NATO may furnish a comparatively solid and reliable foundation for the new Euro-Atlantic security architecture. While the United States never joined the League of Nations, NATO's Euro-Atlantic security structures benefit from the strong and continuing leadership of the United States. U.S. participation in meeting specific security challenges in the Euro-Atlantic region may be unpredictable and vacillating (especially with regard to demanding conflicts such as Bosnia), but the United States is committed to upholding PfP and the EAPC in general terms. The League was burdened from the outset with several dissatisfied and potentially revisionist European powers. In contrast, while there remain potent political forces in Russia that regard the end of the Soviet empire as a humiliation, the new Alliance-based security structures (and other organizations, such as the OSCE) have encouraged reconciliation processes regarding borders and minorities. The PfP, the EAPC, the NATO-Ukraine Commission, and the NATO-Russia Permanent Joint Council may provide concrete means for constructive cooperation.

Fourth, the general economic and political circumstances may be more favorable for the new Euro-Atlantic security structures than they were for the League of Nations. The League had to cope with a world depression starting in 1929, a much less favorable economic situation than that currently prevailing in the West European and North American parts of the Euro-Atlantic region. Moreover, the activities by Western governments and an array of Western institutions—the EU, the Alliance, and others—to promote democratization and free-market prosperity throughout the region are much more ambitious and purposeful than any comparable activities under the League's auspices.

These officially sponsored activities are relatively modest in comparison to the magnitude of the economic, social, and political needs throughout most of the former Soviet empire. It should be recalled, moreover, that unemployment is at exceptionally high levels in most of Western Europe, with little economic growth. Indeed, unemployment in Germany is now at its highest level since 1945.[296] In France, a significant political polarization appears to be under way, with a strengthening of parties at the extreme ends of the spectrum. Jean-Marie Le Pen may be even mightier than recent election results suggest, and he clearly favors what the French call *la politique du pire*—the worse things are, the better for him and his National Front movement. Despite these problematic circumstances, however, prospects for at least moderate prosperity and social-political peace and order in Europe remain much more hopeful than during the 1930s.

The combination of weaker and less binding commitments, a stronger institutional foundation, more extensive and more reliable participation by most (if not all) of the major powers in the Euro-Atlantic region, and a generally more favorable economic and political context makes the current experiment in collective security distinctly different from that conducted by the League of Nations. Nonetheless, NATO's Euro-Atlantic regional security project is not entirely unprecedented, and its prospects for success may depend on the participants giving more consistency and substance to the modest commitments they have assumed. Given the historical precedents, it would appear that the likelihood of their doing so is not great.

Patterns of major-power interactions outside formal institutions

It should be recalled that the major powers within and outside the League of Nations gave little attention to the League institutions when crucial questions of international security were at hand. Although this pattern was visible in the early 1920s, the most famous examples were the 1935 Hoare-Laval Pact and the 1938 Munich Conference—decisions to appease Italy and Germany, respectively.

A tendency for NATO to be governed by an informal major-power directorate has been apparent since the founding of the Alliance. At the outset, the leading powers were nominally Britain, France, and the United States, and their primacy was recognized in the Standing Group, founded in 1949 and intended to be an executive subgroup of the Military Committee, which was (and still is) composed of national military chiefs of staff or their representatives. From a French perspective, however, it seemed apparent that Britain and the United States dominated the Standing Group and Alliance decision making. After Macmillan and Eisenhower rejected de Gaulle's 1958 proposal to formalize a three-power directorate, France scaled back its participation in Alliance institutions and eventually withdrew from the integrated military structure in 1966. The Standing Group was then disbanded.

Long before 1966, however, the Alliance's most critical crisis management decisions had passed to a de facto four-power directorate. The Federal Republic of Germany had been admitted to NATO in 1955, and the Soviet-provoked Berlin crises, beginning in 1958, compelled the three Western countries with continuing Four Power rights regarding Berlin and the ultimate disposition of the German question—Britain, France, and the United States—to work closely with the Federal Republic. This pattern has persisted. Bonn, London, Paris, and Washington have routinely coordinated their views on important matters before raising them in Alliance-wide forums. During the Cold War, and before Germany's reunification, the group was known as the "Berlin Four" (or "the Quad," as they have now come to be called), with the explanation that the powers had to tend to matters relating to Berlin and the German question, or as the "Guadeloupe Four," in homage to a four-power summit that Valéry Giscard d'Estaing convened on that Caribbean island in January 1979.

The preeminence of the Quad has been annoying to other Allies, particularly Italy, which has a population and GDP comparable to those of Britain and France. Italy's defense investments for decades, however, have been significantly less than those of Britain, France, and Germany.[297] The de facto four-power leadership of the Alliance has been based on military capabilities, defense investments, and political influence, not simply on demographic and economic weight. These four powers exert preponderant influence in many fields, sometimes to the regret of other Allies. According to the Netherlands' de Wijk, for example, by late 1996 "[e]nlargement had become the domain of the United States, the United Kingdom, Germany and France. There was a tendency to ignore the views of the smaller countries."[298] Indeed, with regard to NATO enlargement, it seemed to many observers that Bonn and Washington led Alliance decision making, much as Richard Burt, a former U.S. ambassador to Germany and assistant secretary of state, had forecast in 1995: "British and French attitudes are important, but they need not and they should not drive the U.S. position. Once the United States and Germany have agreed on a course of action, the others will follow."[299]

It is noteworthy that the Bosnia Contact Group, formed in April 1994, initially consisted of the Quad plus Russia. At the outset, the Contact Group was officially composed of U.S. and Russian representatives, plus three from the International Conference on Former Yugoslavia (ICFY) who would nominally speak for the UN, the European Union, and the ICFY. As James Gow points out, "In reality, behind this official facade, as was all too readily spotted by observers and status-conscious outsiders such as Italy, the three representatives were being nominated by Germany, France and the UK. While the latter two were essential because of their involvement on the ground and their position as permanent members of the UN Security Council, Germany was considered to be important because of its major position in the EU, alongside France and the UK, and its potential influence over Croatia in particular."[300]

David Owen, who was co-chairman of the ICFY Steering Committee during 1992–95, authoritatively describes the origins of this arrangement. The Contact Group was not entirely welcomed by some EU countries, such as Italy, Spain, and the Netherlands, partly because "The Maastricht Treaty made no explicit provision for ad hoc arrangements like this." Owen defended the Contact Group as a practical necessity, adding that it "may become an important precedent for the EU as it expands from fifteen to twenty and more countries."[301] Unless their national participation was required to deal with specific issues, countries outside the Contact Group generally contributed indirectly to its proceedings through EU, UN, or ICFY channels.[302] Sometimes, however, belligerents reached beyond the Contact Group framework. In February 1995, for example, Croatia's Franjo Tudjman informed "the Contact

Group ambassadors plus China, Italy, and the Holy See" of his country's views.[303]

Italy found an opportunity to join the Contact Group during the first half of 1996. Italy held the presidency of the European Union during this period and was permitted on this basis to attend the Contact Group meetings. In August 1996, when the first meeting of the Contact Group was held after Italy's EU presidency had expired, Ireland attended as the new holder of the EU presidency, while Italy continued to participate "on an exceptional basis." Italy thus became a de facto member of the Contact Group, arguing for this status by referring to its economic and political interests in the former Yugoslavia, its geographic proximity, and the importance of its military bases. According to a French analyst, "The more the [Contact] Group is expanded, the greater the risk that it will lose its cohesion and effectiveness. The stronger the demands of the other Europeans, the more difficult it will be for the three and henceforth four 'elect' to ignore them."[304]

Some observers speculate that, outside formal institutions such as the OSCE and the new NATO-Russia Permanent Joint Council and the Euro-Atlantic Partnership Council, the major powers in Europe (the Quad plus Russia) and in the Contact Group (those powers plus Italy) may continue to find it advisable to engage in consultations on matters of common interest—much as occurred in previous eras. If such consultations take place, however, they are more likely to succeed on a discreet basis; high-level visibility can be counterproductive. French president Jacques Chirac proposed in early 1997 that the Quad and Russia meet in Paris before the July 1997 NATO summit to discuss NATO enlargement and NATO-Russia relations. Russia officially endorsed Chirac's proposal, but the United States rejected it, in part because several Allies— including Belgium, Italy, the Netherlands, and Norway—objected to the "great power directorate" flavor of the proposal.[305] In the event, the Allies gave NATO secretary general Javier Solana an enhanced political role in the negotiations that led to the May 1997 NATO-Russia Founding Act.

The impact of a small number of new Allies on the internal balance of influence within NATO may be small. The political and military weight of the three prospective new Allies would probably be too modest to change the basic parameters of the Quad pattern. It is widely assumed that the Czech Republic, Hungary, and Poland would have an "Atlanticist" orientation, and that this would strengthen U.S. influence, at least in the short term. Such an orientation might yield to other priorities over time. Prague, Budapest, and Warsaw might see incentives to demonstrate interest in ESDI projects, such as the Eurocorps, to ensure France's support for their membership in the European Union. This might be all the more likely if Russian political trends favored democratization and cooperation with the West. The Quad in all likelihood would remain preeminent, however.

The international history of major-power interactions suggests another inference. In the presence of a patently unreliable system of collective security, the major powers will seek other arrangements to protect their national security interests. In other words, if NATO pursued the path envisaged in some analyses and implicit in some high-level declarations—an open-ended process of expansion, not limited to a small number of new Allies, and not necessarily excluding even Russia; an emphasis on the "indivisibility" of security, instead of the special character of collective defense commitments; and a Partnership for Peace and Euro-Atlantic Partnership Council that would function as a mutual supervisory agency for the entire Euro-Atlantic region—the NATO-centered structure might become less and less credible as an instrument of collective defense. In that event, major nations might increasingly regard the NATO-centered structure as a forum for dialogue—a "debate club," in the more pejorative phrase that has come up in interviews on both sides of the Atlantic—comparable to the OCSE or the UN General Assembly, and not a dependable basis for the bedrock defense of national security interests.

The major powers might then seek other instruments to ensure their security with greater confidence. New collective defense coalitions might form—bilateral alliances (for instance, Germany and the United States), or small multilateral coalitions (for instance, a return to the original Brussels Pact—Britain, France, Belgium, the Netherlands, and Luxembourg—perhaps augmented by Germany and Italy). If nations lacked confidence in the reliability of these collective defense pacts and could not devise others, they might have to choose between appeasement of (and deference to) more powerful states, and the pursuit of renationalized defense capabilities, perhaps including national nuclear forces in some cases. The latter option would be more feasible for larger and more powerful states, such as Germany and Turkey, but might also be weighed by smaller states. Sweden and Switzerland gave serious consideration to national nuclear weapons programs during the 1950s and 1960s, and abandoned them—in part because they were persuaded of the stability and robustness of the security framework for Western Europe provided by NATO, even for neutral non-Allies such as themselves.[306]

The Alliance must be conscious of such risks if it is to ensure that they are kept within manageable bounds.

4

Crisis Management and Peace Operations

During the Cold War, the phrase "crisis management," in NATO circles, was applied above all to the Alliance's Article 5 mission of collective defense. It signified NATO's intention to bring any eventual violent confrontation with the Warsaw Pact to a conclusion as rapidly as possible, with a minimum of armed combat and destructive use of force. Moreover, during the Cold War, Article 6 of the North Atlantic Treaty (describing the geographical limits of the Article 5 obligations) was generally interpreted restrictively to exclude military operations "out of area"—in practice, ruling out operations other than those in defense of Allied territory and forces (including naval forces at sea) in the European area. Among other things, this served to keep the Alliance focused on security in Europe, and to avoid intra-Alliance disputes regarding the decolonization conflicts of some Allies (particularly Britain, France, and Portugal) and the non-European engagements of the United States (especially in East Asia and the Middle East).[1]

The Alliance's main preoccupation during the Cold War was defense of NATO territory against the threat of Soviet aggression or coercion; NATO operations beyond the territory of the Alliance were unthinkable. In 1983, Manfred Wörner, then the West German minister of defense, wrote that "For the Federal Republic of Germany, deployment of forces outside the NATO area is out of the question. Moreover, such operations would have no strategic meaning. Any withdrawal of forces earmarked for the defense of Europe would increase the present disadvantage of NATO in the East-West force ratio."[2]

In any case, there was no armed conflict in Europe during the Cold War comparable to those that have emerged since the disintegration of the Soviet empire and the former Yugoslavia. As noted in chapter 2, the political and strategic stalemate in Europe from the mid-1950s to 1989–91 meant that, in many ways, the situation was frozen. The Soviet interventions in East Germany, Hungary, and Czechoslovakia, and the actions of Communist regimes in Eastern Europe against domestic adversaries (such as the imposition of martial law in Poland in 1981) were in no way occasions for the Alliance to intervene. Indeed, the Alliance went out of its way to signal its restraint and its desire to avoid an East-West war during such incidents.

Since the end of the Cold War, crisis management has increasingly come to mean Alliance intervention in conflicts beyond the territory of NATO Allies. The response of the international community to Iraqi aggression against Kuwait in August 1990 was organized under the aegis of the United Nations; the only military activities that were officially NATO operations were the preparations made to defend Turkey and other Allies against Iraqi aggression, if necessary. Nonetheless, in the continuing Security Council–authorized activities relating to Iraq since Desert Storm—Operations Provide Comfort and Southern Watch —the United States, Britain, France, and Turkey have made use of NATO assets.[3]

NATO's new role in crisis management and peace operations has emerged under the press of necessity, and the agenda has been driven by events, mainly in the former Yugoslavia. The new mission has involved the definition of new policies and institutions, with particular provisions being made for coalitions of the willing that might be led by —and primarily composed of—European powers. While the aspiration to build a European Security and Defense Identity within the Alliance based on the WEU has been a major factor in shaping the Alliance's internal adaptation, other factors have also been important: requirements for close political control over the conduct of crisis management and peace operations, and the need to create structures flexible enough to accommodate the participation of non-NATO states, including countries in the Partnership for Peace.

The emergence of NATO's crisis management and peace operations role has been inseparable from the evolution of the conflicts in the former Yugoslavia. The future of this role may be heavily influenced by the course of events—and decisions by the Alliance about how to deal with them—in Bosnia. Because of the many Alliance statements affirming that "security is indivisible" in the Euro-Atlantic region, NATO's possible involvement in contingencies beyond Bosnia must also be considered. As with the Alliance's new efforts to build "cooperative security structures" encompassing former adversaries and other non-NATO countries throughout the Euro-Atlantic region, the crisis management and peace operations role could raise serious risks for the Alliance's cohesion and for its traditional core mission of collective defense.

THE ALLIANCE'S REASSESSMENTS OF SECURITY REQUIREMENTS

Former British prime minister Margaret Thatcher offered an incisive description of the post–Cold War European security environment: "The Europe that has emerged from behind the Iron Curtain has many of the features of the Europes of 1914 and 1939: ethnic strife, contested borders, political extremism, nationalist passions and economic backwardness."[4]

The Allies agreed in 1990–91 that the historical threat of a massive Soviet assault with little warning based on the USSR's conventional force superiority in Europe was increasingly implausible, and that NATO's foremost immediate preoccupations might in fact be containing the consequences of potential civil and interstate conflicts in Eastern Europe and the former Soviet Union. According to NATO's new Strategic Concept, approved in November 1991, "Risks to Allied security are less likely to result from calculated aggression against the territory of the Allies, but rather from the adverse consequences of instabilities that may arise from the serious economic, social and political difficulties, including ethnic rivalries and territorial disputes, which are faced by many countries in central and eastern Europe." The resulting tensions could "lead to crises inimical to European stability and even to armed conflicts, which could involve outside powers or spill over into NATO countries, having a direct effect on the security of the Alliance."[5]

The traditional NATO concept of forward defense of a relatively static line, primarily at West Germany's border with East Germany and

Czechoslovakia, was obviously rendered obsolete with German reunification, the collapse of the Communist regime in Prague, and the withdrawal of all Soviet forces from Czechoslovakia in 1991.[6] The new Strategic Concept called for smaller forces with "enhanced flexibility and mobility and an assured capability for augmentation when necessary," for purposes of crisis management and countering aggression against any ally.[7] Responding to threats and risks that are "multifaceted in nature and multi-directional, which makes them hard to predict and assess," the Strategic Concept recommended "immediate and rapid reaction" forces for crisis management and deterrence and defense against limited attacks, and supplemental main defense forces and reinforcements for the "unlikely" contingency of a "major conflict."[8]

The language of the Alliance's November 1991 Strategic Concept suggests that NATO did not then envisage participating in any crisis management or peacekeeping operations as they came to be understood in subsequent years; the mission remained collective defense against aggression affecting Alliance territory, not intervention beyond that territory. "The Alliance is purely defensive in purpose: none of its weapons will ever be used except in self-defense. . . . The role of the Alliance's military forces is to assure the territorial integrity and political independence of its member states, and thus contribute to peace and stability in Europe."[9]

During the Cold War, in other words, the main military mission was preparedness for deterrence and defense in the event of aggression against the Alliance. This was the Article 5 mission of collective defense. Since the end of the Cold War, a new phrase has been invented—"non–Article 5 missions"—because the Alliance is prepared to intervene in external conflicts and to support peacekeeping and other operations under the authority of the UN Security Council or the OSCE. With its intervention in the former Yugoslavia—Bosnia in particular—NATO has undertaken crisis management and peacekeeping operations in an ongoing conflict beyond the territory of the Allies.[10]

THE IMPACT OF CONFLICTS IN THE FORMER YUGOSLAVIA

The Alliance's first major statement on the civil war in Yugoslavia, in November 1991, gave no indication that the conflict would lead to

Operation Joint Endeavor, which NATO Defense Ministers in June 1996 called "the largest and most complex operation NATO has ever undertaken, a mission to help bring peace and stability to Bosnia and Herzegovina."[11] In November 1991, the heads of state and government of the NATO countries said simply that they were "deeply concerned" by the crisis, deploring "the tragic loss of life" and urging "all parties to cooperate fully with the European Community in its efforts under the mandate given to it by the CSCE, both in the implementation of cease-fire and monitoring agreements and in the negotiating process within the Conference on Yugoslavia."[12]

As this statement suggests, the conflict in what rapidly became the former Yugoslavia was not initially seen as NATO's responsibility in any way. Officials of the European Community asserted at the outset that it was a challenge for the EC to settle, and the U.S. administration agreed. Luxembourg foreign minister Jacques Poos, speaking as chairman of the EC Council of Ministers (composed of the foreign ministers of all the EC countries), said that it was "the hour of Europe," and that, "if one problem can be solved by the Europeans, it's the Yugoslav problem. This is a European country and it's not up to the Americans and not up to anybody else."[13]

It was not until mid-1992 that NATO began to assume responsibilities for aspects of peacekeeping and sanctions enforcement regarding the conflict in the former Yugoslavia.[14] This conflict was concentrated in Bosnia after that state won international recognition in April 1992. The Bosnia conflict has had at least three parties—the Serbs and the Croats, who have territorial ambitions in Bosnia and who have often worked in close liaison with their local ethnic counterparts, the Bosnian Serbs and the Bosnian Croats; and the Bosnian Muslims, more correctly termed Bosniaks,[15] who want self-determination in a multiethnic Bosnia, instead of living under Serb or Croatian rule. The Bosnian Serbs may amount to a fourth force, when and if they are genuinely pursuing policies independent of the Belgrade government.

By the end of 1992, the Alliance, in cooperation with the WEU, was enforcing the UN economic sanctions against Serbia and Montenegro and the arms embargo against the former Yugoslavia as a whole. The United Nations Protection Force (UNPROFOR), composed to a large extent of European troops (particularly from Britain and France), was using elements from NATO's Northern Army Group command for its operational headquarters, and NATO airborne early-warning aircraft were monitoring the no-fly zone over Bosnia.[16]

In the period 1992–95, the Alliance took decisions that led to naval operations, in cooperation with the WEU, to monitor and later to enforce the UN embargo and sanctions in the Adriatic. NATO air operations began with monitoring the UN no-fly zone over Bosnia and subsequently included the enforcement of the zone, close air support to UNPROFOR in Bosnia, and air strikes to break the siege of Sarajevo and other areas.

During the Cold War, East-West antagonism strained NATO's relations with the United Nations. NATO was originally organized by three of the five permanent members of the UN Security Council against the will of a fourth, the Soviet Union. During a phase of the conflict in the former Yugoslavia, it seemed as if the "interlocking institutions" foreseen in NATO communiqués had actually become "interblocking institutions" —particularly with regard to NATO-UN relations.[17]

The Bosnia conflict has had three main phases so far. During the first phase of the conflict, 1992–95, NATO had only limited roles, such as embargo and no-fly-zone enforcement and the delivery of humanitarian supplies, while the main action on the ground was carried out by UNPROFOR. The UNPROFOR operation was successful in providing some humanitarian aid and in preventing an extension of the conflict beyond the territory of the former Yugoslavia. It was a failure, however, in terms of preventing atrocities, stopping the fighting, and bringing about a settlement.

During this phase of the conflict, U.S. involvement was limited for the most part to logistical and command, control, communications, and intelligence (C3I) support and to cautiously circumscribed air and naval operations. In 1994, the commander of U.S. forces in Europe testified to Congress that U.S. personnel, including medical teams supporting UNPROFOR and "approximately 300 personnel" in the Former Yugoslav Republic of Macedonia, composed "only about 3 percent" of the peacekeeping troops in the former Yugoslavia.[18]

A turning point in NATO's involvement in the Yugoslav conflict came during this phase in February 1994, when sixty-eight people were killed and many more wounded by a Serb mortar attack on Sarajevo's central market. This attack, part of a prolonged Serbian siege of Sarajevo, convinced the Allies that they would have to enforce the UN-imposed no-fly zone over Bosnia and give the Serbs an ultimatum to withdraw their artillery from the periphery of Sarajevo. When the Bosnian Serbs again defied the no-fly zone on February 28, 1994, NATO shot down four Bosnian Serb aircraft. This was significant in NATO's history as the Alliance's first use of deadly force; with that act, in the words of one analyst, "NATO redeemed its credibility"—at least temporarily.[19] This phase of the Bosnia conflict was nonetheless one of acrimony in European-American relations. As a Dutch expert observed, the "transatlantic relationship reached an all-time low" in November 1994, with a European-American disagreement about intelligence-sharing and the enforcement of the arms embargo on the Bosnian government.[20]

The second phase of the Bosnia conflict began during the summer of 1995. While NATO imposed an end to the fighting with Operation Deliberate Force, the Dayton agreements, concluded in late 1995, called for NATO forces to assist in carrying out an elaborate plan for the construction of a single, democratic, and multiethnic Bosnia.

The third phase, since late 1995, has been one of uncertainty with regard to both NATO's staying power and the willingness of many of the belligerents to honor the commitments made at Dayton. From December 1995 to December 1996 NATO forces were present on the ground in Bosnia as part of the Implementation Force, known as IFOR. Since December 1996, IFOR has been replaced by another NATO-led force, the Stabilization Force (SFOR). Originally scheduled to last until June 1998, SFOR's mandate was officially extended indefinitely in February 1998, on the basis of North Atlantic Council decisions in December 1997.[21]

The IFOR operation, also known as Joint Endeavor, was "NATO's first-ever ground force operation, its first-ever deployment 'out of area,' and its first-ever joint operation with NATO's Partnership for Peace partners and other non-NATO countries," as a NATO press release pointed out.[22] In fact, fourteen of the twenty-seven Partners in PfP contributed forces to IFOR: Albania, Austria, Bulgaria, Czech Republic, Estonia, Finland, Hungary, Latvia, Lithuania, Poland, Romania, Russia, Sweden, and Ukraine. Four other non-NATO countries also contributed forces to IFOR: Egypt, Jordan, Malaysia, and Morocco.

As with IFOR, every NATO nation that has armed forces has contributed troops to SFOR. Iceland, the sole NATO country without military forces, has provided medical support to both IFOR and SFOR. All the non-NATO participants in IFOR are also contributing forces to SFOR. With the decisions by Ireland and Slovenia to join SFOR, the number of non-NATO participating nations (twenty) again exceeds the number of NATO nations (sixteen). The total strength of SFOR during the December 1996–June 1998 period was approximately 35,000 troops, of which 29,000 were provided by NATO countries and 6,000 by non-NATO countries.

It should be recalled that, during the period before mid-1995, when Operation Deliberate Force was undertaken as one of a series of measures to impose a peace settlement in Bosnia, the United States was quite cautious regarding any involvement of U.S. ground forces in a situation that could lead to combat fatalities. The general view during the Bush administration was that no external intervention could resolve the conflict. In September 1992, Lawrence Eagleburger, then acting secretary of state, said, "This tragedy is not something that can be settled from outside and it's about damn well time that everybody understood that. Until the Bosnians, Serbs, and Croats decide to stop killing each other, there is nothing the outside world can do about it."[23] Eagleburger has reported that President Bush and other high-level officials "believed that in the end it was almost inevitable if we were going to end this war it would take ground troops, and we were not prepared to take that step. . . . The concern was that this was the beginning of— if you will excuse the expression—a slippery slope."[24]

The initial approach of the Clinton administration, from early 1993 to mid-1995, was little different from that of the Bush administration, although UN ambassador Madeleine Albright repeatedly called for more vigorous action. When Secretary of State Warren Christopher traveled to NATO European countries to discuss the Yugoslav crisis in May 1993, he said that he was in a "listening mode" and had no plan of action.[25]

In May 1993, President Clinton said, "I don't want to see the United States get in a position where we are re-creating Northern Ireland or Lebanon or Cyprus or anything else. . . . [T]here may be some potential down the road for something to be done in connection with the peacekeeping operation, but I think it's something we have to be very skeptical about. We don't want our people in there basically in a shooting gallery."[26]

The underlying concern, according to some well-informed observers, was that a costly U.S. involvement in a Balkan "quagmire" could evolve into a conflict as socially divisive as the Vietnam War had been during the late 1960s and early 1970s. It was imperative to avoid such an outcome on several grounds, including the risk that it might jeopardize the U.S. military presence in Europe as a whole and thus the future of NATO. In mid-1994, some observers even formulated the principle as follows: "The United States must stay out of war in the Balkans in order to stay in Europe."[27]

A countervailing concern during the period from 1992 to mid-1995 was that, if the United States continued to limit its military involvement in the conflict to air and naval operations while pushing for firmer action on the ground, this could cause the Alliance to unravel. UNPROFOR was staffed in large part by ground forces from NATO allies Britain and France. These forces could have been placed at risk by either firmer action (for instance, to defend supposedly "safe areas" under UN-declared protection) or by implementation of U.S. calls to conduct air strikes against the Serbs. For the cohesion of the Alliance, it seemed in late 1994 and early 1995, the United States would have to get involved with ground forces, either to help withdraw UNPROFOR troops or to impose a peace settlement. After Operation Deliberate Force in the summer of 1995 and the conclusion of the Dayton Accords that fall, U.S. ground forces became part of IFOR. In other words, a new reasoning had displaced the previous reluctance to get involved so directly: "The United States and NATO had to place forces in Bosnia in order to impose an end to the fighting and preserve the Alliance."[28]

What factors led the United States and NATO to impose an end to combat in 1995, after years of U.S.-European (and intra-European) disagreements about what course to follow? According to an analysis at the time in *The Economist,* there were at least three key factors in the situation:

- The Serbs had placed UNPROFOR in a highly vulnerable position, with the Sarajevo airport closed, the city's utilities shut down, and aid convoys blocked.

- The Bosnian Serbs took UNPROFOR troops as hostages in May 1995, and this impelled Britain, France, and the Netherlands to form a Rapid Reaction Force to rescue them, if necessary, and to reinforce UNPROFOR.

- General Ratko Mladic, the leader of the Bosnian Serb forces, carried out massacres of Bosniaks at UN-designated "safe areas" at Srebrenica and Zepa in July 1995 and thus "had finally broken the patience of the West." NATO threatened air strikes in the event of further attacks on the UN safe areas and withdrew UNPROFOR troops to less vulnerable areas.[29]

It was in this context that the Bosnian Serbs attacked yet another Sarajevo market on August 28, 1995, killing thirty-eight people and wounding many more. NATO's Deliberate Force air operations, from August 30 to September 12, 1995, were preceded by Croatia's highly effective offensive against the Serbs in Krajina in early August—an offensive that met with no reaction from the Serbian leader, Slobodan Milosevic, in Belgrade. The Bosnian Serbs were in effect forced to accept the Dayton agreements by two factors: the determination and military strength of the NATO forces, led by the United States, and Milosevic's decision to stop supporting them. As *The Economist* noted, Milosevic's "willingness to abandon the Serbs of Krajina, Eastern Slavonia and Bosnia—and indeed, the idea of a greater Serbia—has been crucial to the success of the peace efforts."[30]

Most accounts concur with *The Economist* in emphasizing the crucial impact of the evolving military situation in mid-1995, particularly the Croatian victories over the Bosnian Serbs. Other factors—ranging from politics in the United States to long-term geostrategic assessments—are also noteworthy, however. In terms of American politics, President Clinton had incentives to take action to ensure that Bosnia would not be an issue in the 1996 elections, and to demonstrate that the White House, not Congress, was determining U.S. foreign policy. The president had vetoed legislation that would have lifted the embargo on arms sales to the Bosnian government, and it was imperative to achieve progress toward another solution to the Bosnian conflict in the summer of 1995, before Congress overrode his veto.[31]

The U.S. administration's long-term geostrategic assessments involved the fate of the Alliance; it was clearly imperative to maintain NATO's general cohesion and effectiveness. In early 1995, the United States had agreed to send as many as 20,000 troops to Bosnia to assist UNPROFOR in conducting an emergency withdrawal, if necessary. When the Bosnian Serbs began taking UNPROFOR troops as hostages in May 1995, the only choice was to conduct an emergency withdrawal or to intervene to impose a settlement, lest the United States risk the collapse of the Alliance.[32] According to an account by Richard Holbrooke, then assistant secretary of state, the critical moment of decision came in a conversation involving President Clinton, President Jacques Chirac of France, Secretary of State Warren Christopher, and Holbrooke on June 14, 1995: "The option of noninvolvement that had existed from the summer of 1991 to 1995 had disappeared. . . . We were in. . . . At that point, the [U.S.] president saw the degree to which involvement was now inevitable, and how much better it would be to have involvement built on success rather than failure."[33]

Beyond the humanitarian factors, U.S. and Allied leaders were concerned about containing the risks of a spillover of the fighting to other parts of the former Yugoslavia (such as Kosovo) and to other countries, such as Albania, Greece, Macedonia, and Turkey. Another concern was that failure to contain the conflict would undermine the credibility of the Alliance and set a dangerous precedent with regard to other ethnic antagonisms in Central and Eastern Europe.

NEW ALLIANCE INSTITUTIONS FOR CRISIS MANAGEMENT AND PEACE OPERATIONS

The two main rationales for the Alliance's "internal adaptation"—defining a new command structure and establishing new institutions—have been changing collective defense needs (with greater attention to limited, subregional contingencies) and the emergence of crisis management and peace operations as a major new mission. Of the new institutions, Combined Joint Task Forces are probably the most important. They have been the focus of a continuing, but now largely resolved, debate within the Alliance about whether distinct institutional mechanisms should be dedicated to Article 5 and non–Article 5 missions, or whether a single system should be maintained.

The CJTF concept was first suggested to the Allies by Les Aspin, then the U.S. secretary of defense, at an informal meeting of NATO defense ministers in October 1993 in Travemünde, Germany. The United States had multiple motives in suggesting CJTF. One was to respond to European aspirations for a stronger ESDI. Another was to promote "burden sharing," with the European allies accepting additional risks and responsibilities and thus lessening the political and economic costs to the United States of serving as one of the main guardians of international order. A broader motive was to make NATO's command structures and asset-utilization arrangements more flexible to allow for greater European roles and the formation of coalitions of the willing. It was assumed that all sixteen NATO Allies would be unlikely to take action together in all cases falling short of aggression against the Alliance.

Specific coalitions of the willing might consist of the United States and certain NATO European Allies, perhaps acting on occasion with non-NATO countries within or beyond Europe. If the United States chose not to participate in a specific operation, the WEU might choose to take the lead and to make use of NATO assets in doing so. These assets would thus be, in the widely used phrase, "separable but not separate." This would avoid the WEU needlessly duplicating NATO assets and perhaps thereby undermining NATO's integrated military structure. Most NATO European Allies attach a high value to this structure, partly because it keeps the United States continuously engaged in European security matters and provides a framework for commonly funded infrastructure projects. CJTF might therefore satisfy several objectives.

What are the NATO assets of interest to the European Allies in CJTF? According to one definition, NATO assets are those funded by NATO common infrastructure budgets—AWACS aircraft, headquarters elements, pipelines, radars and other air defense and air command and control systems, communications equipment, airfields, storage depots, and so forth. According to another definition, NATO assets also encompass the U.S. capabilities regularly put at the disposal of NATO: air-refueling capabilities, heavy long-distance air transport for troops and equipment (such as C-141s, C-5s, and C-17s), and satellite intelligence, communications, and navigation data. U.S. national assets clearly remain ultimately under U.S. control.

The reservations in France about CJTF since 1993 have apparently stemmed from a concern that the United States (and other NATO Allies) could use the CJTF mechanism to veto the WEU's use of specific NATO assets. Before the January 1994 summit (and subsequently), some of the French argued that the WEU's right to employ such assets should be automatic, without even an obligation to consult the other NATO partners, to avoid any "subordination" to NATO and the United States in particular.

The CJTF decision-making formula approved by the Allies in the integrated military structure (that is, at that time, all of the Allies except France and Spain) before the January 1994 NATO summit was as follows: ". . . we are committed to improving our ability to participate in a range of peacekeeping operations and to facilitate closer co-operation between NATO and the WEU in this field, including the possibility of making Alliance assets available for use in European-led operations *following consultations within the Alliance.*"[34]

The principle of "consultations within the Alliance" was retained in the January 1994 summit decision: "We therefore stand ready to make collective assets of the Alliance available, *on the basis of consultations in the North Atlantic Council,* for WEU operations undertaken by the European Allies in pursuit of their Common Foreign and Security Policy. We support the development of separable but not separate capabilities which could respond to European requirements and contribute to Alliance security."[35]

In announcing the decision to devise CJTF at the January 1994 NATO summit, the North Atlantic Council said,

> NATO must continue the adaptation of its command and force structure in line with requirements for flexible and timely responses contained in the Alliance's Strategic Concept. We also will need to strengthen the European pillar of the Alliance by facilitating the use of our military capabilities for NATO and European/WEU operations, and to assist participation of non-NATO partners in joint peacekeeping operations and other contingencies as envisaged under the Partnership for Peace. . . . As part of this process, we endorse the concept of Combined Joint Task Forces as a means to facilitate contingency operations, including operations with participating nations outside the Alliance. . . . The

Council, with the advice of the NATO Military Authorities, and in coordination with the WEU, will work on implementation in a manner that provides separable but not separate military capabilities that could be employed by NATO or the WEU.[36]

Defining CJTFs as instruments for both Article 5 and non–Article 5 functions

The January 1994 decision inaugurated a revealing debate between, on one side, the United States and most of the Allies in the integrated military structure, and, on the other side, France (supported at times by Spain and Belgium). The debate focused on the extent to which new institutions such as CJTF should be dedicated exclusively to NATO's new non–Article 5 tasks.

The French CJTF proposals in 1994 and 1995 were built, in part, on the differentiation between Article 5 missions (collective defense) and non–Article 5 missions (such as peacekeeping and crisis management). The French proposed that the integrated military structure be dedicated to Article 5 missions while CJTF would handle non–Article 5 tasks. Moreover, the French wanted to avoid any requirement for CJTF to report to the major NATO commanders, SACEUR and SACLANT, and called for establishing structures for CJTF "distinct from SHAPE."

The French motives in advancing these CJTF proposals were interpreted in terms of long-standing French policy objectives. The concept might offer a means to promote the European Security and Defense Identity despite the unwillingness (or inability) of France and its European allies to invest the resources necessary to build up military capabilities comparable to those the United States has historically made available to NATO. Furthermore, CJTF might represent a means to relegate the integrated military structure (from which France has been absent since 1966) to the least likely contingencies (Article 5 collective defense missions) and to establish new structures and procedures centered around the North Atlantic Council and the Military Committee that might maximize French influence.

Some French arguments were accepted as valid by Allies within the integrated military structure, which, as the French said, had been designed and maintained for decades to meet the Cold War threat of a massive, short-warning attack from the Soviet Union. However, the non-French observers generally deemed it possible to make adjustments in that structure while preserving its merits, such as institutionalized patterns of cooperation. In their view, SHAPE and the integrated military structure could be used for both Article 5 and non–Article 5 operations. The Allies in the integrated military structure wanted France to work more closely with them, even if the French were not yet ready to participate fully; but the French terms for CJTF seemed to be calculated to undermine the integrated military structure. Preserving the integrated military structure was a higher priority for most of the Allies than establishing CJTF and pursuing an ESDI on French terms.

Allies within the integrated military structure generally found the French CJTF proposals unpersuasive. Certain arguments advanced by the French against the integrated military structure—for example, that it is subordinate to the United States, that participation in it entails a loss of national sovereignty, and that it is excessively autonomous and inadequately controlled by the Alliance's political authorities—were seen as old French myths, dating from the 1960s and intended to justify France's special status, that were revived in a campaign to establish CJTF arrangements on French terms. Allies within the integrated military structure pointed out that the integrated headquarters are already commanded and staffed mostly by Europeans, with substantial U.S. participation and support. Most of the Europeans had invested too much in these command and planning structures to cast them aside in favor of ad hoc CJTF arrangements during a crisis.

Despite the interest manifested by the French in particular for arrangements that would imply limiting NATO's integrated military structure to Article 5 contingencies and creating new structures and Combined Joint Task Forces for non–Article 5 operations, the Allies agreed in the end on "the concept of one system capable of performing multiple functions." The new system would include "flexible arrangements capable of undertaking a variety of missions and taking into account national decisions on participation in each operation."[37]

Combined Joint Task Forces are to consist of inter-allied ("combined") and inter-service ("joint") command entities and forces. They are to provide structures and procedures for the effective "variable geometry" use of specific NATO infrastructure assets and other capabilities by specific Allies and possibly also non-NATO countries, depending on the circumstances.

Combined Joint Task Forces are intended to be capable of carrying out multiple missions in a flexible manner. A specific Combined Joint Task Force operation could be conducted under the leadership of the Western European Union; it could involve the participation of non-NATO countries from the Partnership for Peace and even countries from beyond the Euro-Atlantic region; and its objective might be to conduct a crisis management operation outside the NATO area or even beyond the Euro-Atlantic region. A WEU-led Combined Joint Task Force could draw on NATO assets, with the approval of the North Atlantic Council. According to Walter B. Slocombe, under secretary of defense for policy, "CJTFs will allow NATO assets to be used more flexibly, and especially in operations outside traditional patterns involving different mixes of contributors. CJTFs will likely provide the mechanism for the most probable NATO contingency operations."[38]

The French approved the CJTF concept on this basis, it seems, for several reasons: an impression that the Clinton administration's attitude toward the ESDI concept is more positive than was that of the Bush administration; an interest in making CJTF a practical vehicle for making NATO assets available to the WEU or other European entities; a recognition that France's European allies are unwilling to abandon the integrated military structure and its command arrangements or to pay the price of WEU capabilities duplicating those of NATO; and a judgment that CJTF arrangements could ensure that U.S. inaction would not immobilize NATO assets, which might be used by the WEU or other European entities, perhaps involving nations outside the Alliance.

Considerable resentment nonetheless persists in some French quarters regarding the role of the North Atlantic Council and other NATO bodies with respect to the CJTF mechanism, which initially appeared to some French observers as a means to gain automatic access to Alliance assets in support of ESDI. CJTFs are Alliance institutions (for both Article 5 and non–Article 5 missions) that could be made available for WEU-led operations, with the approval of the North Atlantic Council, and the Alliance is "developing arrangements for the release, monitoring and return or recall of Alliance assets and capabilities" lent to European Allies for a WEU-led operation.[39] According to Paul-Marie de la Gorce, a prominent French journalist, "When President Jacques Chirac attempted to establish this 'European system' within NATO itself, American diplomacy was able to ensure that it [the ESDI] would not be able to function without the approval, assistance, and supervision of Atlantic institutions, that is, of the United States itself."[40]

New institutions to manage and support Alliance operations

The Allies have created three new institutions, in addition to CJTF: a Capabilities Coordination Cell within the International Military Staff at NATO headquarters in Brussels to "provide staff support to the Military Committee on contingency related matters and assist the Military Committee in providing planning guidance to the Major NATO Commanders"; a Combined Joint Planning Staff at SHAPE headquarters at Mons, Belgium, to "perform centralized CJTF headquarters planning functions and co-ordination with all relevant headquarters, as well as with forces that might serve under a CJTF headquarters, and as appropriate with the WEU planning cell"; and a Policy Co-ordination Group at NATO headquarters in Brussels to "provide politico-military advice to assist the [North Atlantic] Council in managing and ensuring timely overall direction of Alliance military operations, particularly crisis management operations."[41]

These new institutions all stem in part from the desire of the Allies in the integrated military structure to satisfy French concerns about gaining enhanced political control by the North Atlantic Council over non–Article 5 missions, including crisis management and peace operations, and limiting the alleged autonomy of the major NATO commanders (SACEUR and SACLANT) and the integrated military structure.

The new institutional arrangements in NATO in fact are virtually inseparable from the new prominence of non–Article 5 missions and ESDI's development within the Alliance. The Allies agreed at the January 1994 summit that CJTF should be devised for several reasons, including a desire to avoid a financially unaffordable and politically divisive duplication of military assets, and a determination to facilitate the construction of ESDI with "separable but not separate" capabilities.[42] The new arrangements may facilitate the conduct of NATO-approved and -supported operations by the Western European Union or other coalitions of the willing. Some observers have referred to the spectrum of possibilities as "NATO-minus-plus"—that is, not all NATO Allies might participate, and non-NATO (and non-European) countries might participate, as in IFOR and SFOR.

From this perspective, one of NATO's supporting functions regarding crisis management and peace operations might become serving as a technical military authority for collective security activities—equipment interoperability, peacekeeping doctrine, symbols and terminology, standardized procedures, and so forth. Some have suggested that NATO might even be prepared to lend assets for coalitions of the willing undertaking operations beyond the Euro-Atlantic region. NATO assets could not be lent without the approval of the North Atlantic Council (NAC) as a whole, however, and NATO would retain the ability to monitor the use of such assets and to recall them.

Despite the concern provoked by speculation that PfP and the EAPC could displace the North Atlantic Council's decision-making authority, recent Alliance decisions have made clear that NATO will remain the authoritative leadership and "enabling mechanism" for PfP operations. According to the May 1997 decisions regarding enhanced PfP, "Building on the experience from IFOR/SFOR, the PCG [Policy Coordination Group] has concluded that there is scope to afford Partners joining future NATO-led PfP operations appropriate opportunities to contribute to the provision of political guidance for and oversight over such operations. Such opportunities could be afforded to contributing Partners with the understandings that *the decision to mount a NATO-led PfP operation rests with the Alliance* and that *the NAC retains the ultimate authority to direct the operation.*"[43]

Moreover, the participation of PfP Partners in NATO-led operations can take place only at NATO's invitation. As was noted at the May 1997 North Atlantic Council meeting, "Decisions to invite Partners to contribute to future NATO-led operations will be taken by the NAC, on the basis of NMAS [NATO Military Authorities] advice, taking into account both political considerations as well as the need for military effectiveness. . . . Partner involvement in future non–Article 5 operations may take many forms. As in the case of IFOR/SFOR, there will be many reasons, including both practical and political, for seeking such involvement."[44]

In short, the Allies intend to maintain their collective defense arrangements as the foundation for their non–Article 5 operations in support of collective security, with each such operation involving Partners on a case-by-case, voluntary basis, possibly making use of CJTF.

The current plans are limited, it should be noted, to achieving greater interoperability and more robust consultations with Partners. However, the North Atlantic Council would retain ultimate authority regarding the purposes and conduct of a NATO-led operation. At present, the most ambitious structural adaptation envisaged is the establishment of Partnership Staff Elements (PSEs) at various NATO commands. PSEs will include officers from Partner countries serving in international posts and working with officers from NATO countries for the collective Partnership rather than for their national governments alone. NATO officials hope that this arrangement will deepen expertise and interoperability and facilitate Partner cooperation with NATO- or WEU-led CJTFs in specific crisis management and peace support operations.[45]

Projected changes in the integrated command structure make it a new institution as well. The command structure was streamlined and simplified soon after the end of the Cold War, in part because of the changed strategic situation and the reductions in forces of all NATO Allies.[46] In December 1997, the Allies announced agreement on a much more extensive reorganization and simplification of the command structure, one that will reduce 65 headquarters to 20 when it is fully implemented. The new command structure will "take account of ESDI and CJTF requirements and, by this, enable the Alliance, based on the concept of separable but not separate capabilities, to provide European command arrangements able to prepare, support, command and conduct operations under the political control and strategic direction of the WEU."[47] Alliance institutions are thus available for WEU-led operations. This reorganization reflects the interest in ESDI that has been professed by European Allies.

EUROPEAN SECURITY AND DEFENSE IDENTITY

Since the end of the Cold War, some NATO European nations, particularly France, have revived long-standing aspirations for greater West European autonomy in security affairs, with a view to more balanced European-American relations. In recent years, this has become known as the effort to define an ESDI on the basis of the European Union and the WEU, and has included the definition of new institutional relations between NATO and the WEU. Current ESDI efforts are based on a consensus among the Allies, including France, that a "European pillar" can be built only within NATO, not outside or against it.

NATO has accordingly assumed an unprecedented instrumental role in international security: preparedness to support WEU-led operations as part of its efforts to foster the development of a strong ESDI within the Alliance.

NATO communiqués have regularly asserted that the establishment of an ESDI "will help to reinforce transatlantic solidarity."[48] Ensuring that this will be the case has taken—and will continue to require— a great deal of effort and good will on the part of the Allies.

The pursuit of an ESDI, in fact, implies striving for an "identity" distinct from, although—at least on a rhetorical basis—complementary with, Atlantic Alliance unity. The central thrust of ESDI advocacy has been to emphasize distinctness from, if not opposition to, the United States, and an undercurrent of distrust has been unmistakable in some formulations of the ESDI's purpose, particularly in France. At the end of the Cold War, many French observers expected NATO to wither away (much as the Soviets had forecast) or to remain confined to collective defense missions. Some of the French have been astonished and frustrated to observe the degree to which NATO has successfully adapted itself to post–Cold War circumstances and has become, especially since 1995, the impresario orchestrating Western activities regarding both collective defense and operations in support of collective security.

In part because of the U.S. refusal to send ground forces to Bosnia until a peace settlement was imposed in late 1995, French observers have repeatedly called attention to the possibility that the ESDI might need to call upon NATO assets for contingencies in which the United States might choose not to commit forces. U.S. officials have recently questioned whether such scenarios are plausible. In June 1996, shortly after the NATO meeting in Berlin, where a number of dispositions in support of ESDI were approved, U.S. under secretary of defense for policy Walter Slocombe said, "The U.S. will remain fully engaged in European security issues, so neither politically nor militarily is there any question of Europe needing to prepare for a U.S. withdrawal from Europe. Indeed, it is overwhelmingly likely that in any situation where involvement of military forces is justified and where NATO is prepared to authorize a military operation, the U.S. will be part of the operation."[49]

The regularly repeated insistence that the ESDI must be built in accordance with principles of "complementarity and transparency" illustrates the widespread awareness of the potential for suspicion and distrust. As early as December 1990, the North Atlantic Council emphasized "the importance of safeguarding complementarity and transparency between the two processes of the adaptation of the Alliance and of the development of European security co-operation."[50] The call for "complementarity" and/or "transparency" has been repeated in almost all subsequent Alliance statements about the ESDI, notably with regard to NATO-WEU relations.

The June 1991 North Atlantic Council communiqué was noteworthy as the first to underscore the Alliance's "strategic unity" and NATO's primacy, even in the context of an emerging ESDI: "The Alliance is the essential forum for consultation among its members and the venue for agreement on policies bearing on the security and defense commitments of Allies under the Washington Treaty."[51] In an accompanying statement, the North Atlantic Council noted that only NATO, because of its membership and capabilities, could perform all of the Alliance's core security functions, such as "to preserve the strategic balance within Europe" and "to deter and defend against any threat of aggression against the territory of any NATO member state."[52] The Alliance repeated these points in November 1991, and it has continued to reaffirm them.[53]

Beyond these core collective defense functions of the Alliance, of course, stand the more diffuse activities linked to "collective security" aspirations—above all, crisis management and peace operations. According to the June 1992 Petersberg Declaration of the WEU's Council of Ministers, in addition to the continuing collective defense obligations of the WEU members under the 1948 Brussels Treaty and the 1949 North Atlantic Treaty, "military units of WEU member States, acting under the authority of WEU, could be employed for: humanitarian and rescue tasks; peacekeeping tasks; [and] tasks of combat forces in crisis management, including peacemaking."[54]

The WEU's definition of what became known as the "Petersberg tasks" led some Europeans, particularly in France, to argue for a clear differentiation of responsibilities, one in which NATO's role would be limited to collective defense (Article 5) while the ESDI would be responsible for the more probable contingencies of crisis management and peace operations (non–Article 5 tasks) and could draw on NATO assets via CJTF arrangements. The United States and several other Allies objected that the distinction was not entirely sound: a non–Article 5 contingency could unexpectedly become an Article 5 challenge. Moreover, institutionalizing such a division of labor could be damaging to Alliance cohesion.

In June 1996, the Allies agreed to several practical arrangements in support of ESDI, but avoided dispositions that might have led to a split within the Alliance. As Walter Slocombe observed, "in the future, part of NATO's peacetime responsibilities must include preparing for such assistance, in planning, exercises, training and staffing, for WEU-led operations. All of this should be done within the Alliance and within its military command structure, not as a separate (including de facto separate), parallel structure, or by elements that are 'European only, American clean.' It is essential from the U.S. point of view not to foster a bifurcated NATO, in which, de facto if not explicitly, there are two systems, one for the U.S. and Article 5, and one for Europe and non-Article 5 operations."[55]

One of the several long-standing problems in building an ESDI within NATO was highlighted in the June 1991 communiqué: the need "to ensure that the Allies that are not currently participating in the development of a European identity in foreign and security policy and defense should be adequately involved in decisions that may affect their security."[56] This was a reference to the NATO European Allies that are not members of the European Union or the Western European Union— notably Turkey and Norway. The many NATO declarations about the importance of building the ESDI "with the participation of all European Allies"[57] and seeking agreement "in the WEU on the participation of all European allies in WEU-led operations using NATO assets and capabilities"[58] reflected the interest of Denmark, Iceland, Norway, and Turkey (the non-WEU European members of NATO) in not being excluded from decisions and operations that might be undertaken under WEU auspices.

This problem remained unresolved until May 1997, when the WEU Council of Ministers agreed that European Allies could participate in "WEU operations using NATO assets and capabilities, as well as in the planning and preparation of such operations." The council also agreed to invite "non-allied Observer States" (that is, countries that are not allies in the WEU or NATO, but that have observer status in the WEU—Austria, Finland, Ireland, and Sweden) "to make available assets and capabilities" and "to participate in WEU work related to defense planning" for non–Article 5 missions.[59]

Other challenges in building an ESDI include the following:

- the lack of European political will to spend the resources necessary to acquire the assets that would diminish dependence on American capabilities (including airlift, sealift, and space-based intelligence and communications) and enable the Europeans to avoid the reproach that the ESDI has "visibility without capability"—despite the Alliance position that the ESDI "will underline the preparedness of the Europeans to take a greater share of responsibility for their security;"[60]

- intra-European disagreements about the ultimate purpose of an ESDI, including EU decision making about its projected Common Foreign and Security Policy, the relationship between the EU and the WEU, and the problem of establishing mutual defense commitments involving neutral members of the EU such as Ireland, Sweden, Austria, and Finland;[61] and

- defining mechanisms acceptable to all the NATO Allies, notably the United States, for the use of commonly funded NATO assets in WEU-led operations.

These mechanisms have yet to be fully defined, though the general principle of North Atlantic Council consensus is clear. According to some European observers, particularly in France, de facto U.S. constraints (via the North Atlantic Council) on European access to commonly funded Alliance assets could become a point of contention in European-American relations. Simplifying access by abandoning NATO's consensus principle seems improbable, however. If this principle were abandoned, an "easy-access" arrangement for the WEU could erode Alliance cohesion and lead to potentially risky situations—for instance, European-led operations utilizing NATO assets such as some of the Alliance's AWACS aircraft, yet without the full endorsement of all the Allies. If the contingency became an Article 5 case, or simply a dangerous stalemate, the European Allies in all probability would expect U.S. support. However, if the United States is expected to be present for the "crash landings," it will understandably want to be in for the "take-offs" as well.[62]

Despite the prominence of the ESDI in NATO communiqués since 1990, NATO European military capabilities for power-projection operations are substantially inferior to those of the United States. Large-scale collective security interventions under NATO auspices are therefore likely to consist of either operations in which U.S. forces play a predominant role or actions substantially supported by U.S. military capabilities.

Because of the gap in U.S. and European investments in advanced military capabilities since the late 1970s, the United States is far ahead of its NATO European Allies in the assets needed for large-scale joint and combined operations, such as airlift, sealift, and command, control, communications, and intelligence (C3I). While this is especially true of operations beyond Europe that would require the airlift and sealift necessary for genuine "strategic mobility," it also applies to operations within Europe. Even in Bosnia, in close proximity to NATO territory, the United States had to augment existing NATO capabilities with special operations forces and unique C3 assets. According to General Klaus Naumann, the German officer serving as chairman of NATO's Military Committee, the United States furnished forty-six of the forty-eight communications satellite channels used by IFOR. In Naumann's words, "It indicates quite clearly that without American support, an operation like [IFOR in Bosnia] could not be done. . . . There is no security for Europe without the Americans."[63]

Operation Deliberate Force, the NATO air operation against the Serbs in August–September 1995, was conducted largely by the United States. Indeed, "Deliberate Force . . . illustrated that a sustained NATO combat expedition is impossible without U.S. muscle: Satellite intelligence, electronic jamming, and other technological contributions were virtually all American, and the United States flew two-thirds of all aircraft sorties."[64]

European dependence on U.S. military capabilities is distasteful to some European Allies, especially the French. Since the late 1970s, however, the European Allies have demonstrated their unwillingness to invest in military forces, notably in modernization and research and development, at levels approximating those in the United States. High-level Alliance leaders, such as Secretary General Javier Solana, Assistant Secretary General for Defense Support Admiral Norman Ray (USN, retired), and General Naumann, the chairman of the Military Committee, have warned of an emerging European-American divergence in military capabilities, with potentially far-reaching political, operational, and industrial implications.[65]

Another obstacle to building an ESDI oriented toward the relatively autonomous conduct of the "Petersberg tasks," including crisis management and peace operations, has been the lack of consensus among the major NATO European powers about how much emphasis to place on such tasks in their military investments and force structure. Of the larger powers that generally exert leadership in the Alliance (discussed in chapter 3), three—Britain, France, and the United States—are likely to continue to bear the main responsibilities in NATO-led crisis management and peace operations. Although Germany has undertaken increasing levels of responsibility and has participated in a carefully measured way in certain operations (Cambodia, Somalia, IFOR and SFOR in Bosnia), at least two factors are likely to limit German participation.

The first is capabilities. In contrast with British, French, and U.S. decisions, the German government has chosen not to emphasize investments in all-professional expeditionary forces for the protection of distant economic and security interests and the conduct of crisis management and peace operations. As recently as March 1997, German defense minister Volker Rühe told an assembly of generals, officials, and diplomats: "In the Alliance not everyone has to be able to do everything and to have everything." Rühe said that he was "disturbed by the fixation on technology in the USA" and by the tendency of the United States to "underestimate" the contribution to stability in Europe made by Germany, Norway, and other countries with conscription and, hence, an ability to mobilize large armies. Rühe's remarks and the ensuing discussion, which received a great deal of attention from defense and security experts in Europe, drew the following conclusions from General Helge Hansen, a former inspector-general of the German Army and a former commander-in-chief of Allied Forces Central Europe (CINCENT): "Without a consensus among the British, the French, and the Germans no European security policy is possible. . . . There is no security-policy agreement in Europe."[66]

According to another account of the conference, Rühe said, "I want forces as a stability factor in Europe, in which crisis reaction forces are only a complementary element. I want no professional army. I would only need that if I wanted to act worldwide, in Haiti and elsewhere." Rühe argued that a large conscript army is what Germany needs for national and Alliance defense, to promote stability in Europe, and to ensure continued U.S. engagement in Europe. In Rühe's view, Germany's "crisis reaction" forces should be limited to 50,000 troops: "An interventionary capability beyond that level we do not want."[67]

The second key factor that is likely to affect German participation in crisis management and peace operations is the nation's political and strategic culture, as it has been shaped by its post–World War II experiences.[68] It was not until July 1994 that the Constitutional Court in Karlsruhe clarified the restrictions in the Basic Law about possible German participation in military operations other than self-defense against external aggression and indicated that the federal parliament (the Bundestag) may approve German participation in internationally sanctioned "collective security" operations. In December 1996, the parliament approved the government's plans to send 2,000 ground combat troops to Bosnia, as part of SFOR—the first deployment of German combat-ready ground forces outside NATO territory since World War II. The German contribution to IFOR had consisted of "logistical, medical and engineering units."[69] German political elites and public opinion may continue to display some wariness and caution about undertaking interventions beyond the Alliance area.

The long-standing obstacles to building an ESDI have therefore persisted. These include what some observers, particularly in France, consider a West European "mentality of dependence" with regard to NATO and the United States that discourages Europeans from doing more, lest the Americans conclude that the United States could do less; national differences (including the major powers, Britain, France, and Germany) in interests and perceptions regarding international security challenges; and a general West European reluctance to pay the financial costs of greater defense autonomy, particularly in a situation of relative economic stagnation and rising welfare demands.

Nonetheless, some limited progress in the construction of an ESDI within the Alliance has been made, despite the long-standing obstacles to the concept's realization. The Allies have specified terms of reference for a European Deputy SACEUR with ESDI-related responsibilities, and the European Allies are developing European command arrangements for WEU-led operations. As the Alliance recalled in July 1997, the goal remains "the creation of militarily coherent and effective forces capable of operating under the political control and strategic direction of the WEU."[70] In June 1997, Allied defense ministers agreed that "as soon as practicable in a future exercise a CJTF operation should be led by WEU calling on Alliance assets and capabilities and employing the European command arrangements."[71]

Since mid-1996 the French government has maintained that an additional way to give greater reality to the European Security and Defense Identity that all the Allies profess to favor would be to make the command of NATO's southern region (AFSOUTH), traditionally held by a U.S. officer, a billet for a European officer. The French have argued that, because U.S. officers serve as both SACEUR and SACLANT, the two regional commands under SACEUR in the new organizational structure in Allied Command Europe—North and South—should both be filled by European officers.[72] Non-French observers from both sides of the Atlantic have noted, however, that to some extent command structures have reflected realities based on military capabilities.[73] Substantially increased European capabilities and responsibilities would lead inevitably to modified command structures, and it is unrealistic to expect such changes (notably in AFSOUTH) when most of the European Allies have been reducing their military capabilities even more than the United States.

The AFSOUTH controversy has affected intra-European relations as well as U.S.-French relations. Europeans have wondered why President Chirac did not consult with other European governments before he wrote a letter to President Clinton to propose that AFSOUTH become a billet for a European officer. When a German journalist asked Chirac, the French leader chose to answer another part of the question.[74] While some European officials supported France's AFSOUTH proposal, others did not. Guillaume Parmentier, who served as an adviser to the French defense minister in 1995–97, has written that

> Germany was divided between support in principle for the French proposals, especially those relating to the European dimension, . . . and a reluctance to put itself in an awkward position vis à vis the U.S. In the quarrel which began in the summer of 1996 between the French and the Americans over the nationality of the commander of the Southern

region, the Germans . . . supported France strongly and openly by very firm public declarations (e.g., Mr. Rühe in Oslo on 25 September 1996), probably because they felt that a visible Europeanization of NATO would reassure the Russians that NATO enlargement would not come at their expense. As a matter of fact, as soon as Russia accepted the fait accompli of NATO enlargement at the [U.S.-Russian] Helsinki summit in March 1997, the Germans retreated and came up with proposals for a division of responsibilities in the Southern region which it is fair to say were impossible for the French to accept.[75]

In September 1997 General Klaus Naumann of the German Army, the chairman of NATO's Military Committee, said that "The European nations in the region concerned do not support the French proposal. France is not speaking on behalf of Europe. The Mediterranean is NATO's most endangered region. From a NATO point of view, at this point in time, it is good to have American command in AFSOUTH."[76] While declining to accept Chirac's AFSOUTH proposal, U.S. officials have drawn attention to institutional innovations that have (in response to French suggestions) enhanced political oversight of the Alliance's military structure, and to various measures that have augmented European responsibilities in the command structure, supported the WEU, and strengthened the European Deputy SACEUR.[77]

France's June 1997 decision to remain out of the integrated military structure for the foreseeable future, in part because of the continuing controversy over command arrangements in NATO's southern region, may complicate the construction of an ESDI within NATO.[78] At the June 1996 meeting of the North Atlantic Council in Berlin, it was agreed that the Alliance's command structure would be adapted to reflect options for WEU-led operations. How this can be done if France continues to abstain from participating in this command structure remains to be seen. Part of the answer was furnished in February 1998. Alain Richard, the French defense minister, confirmed earlier indications that while France would remain outside the integrated military structure, it would participate fully in the review of the Strategic Concept and in CJTF staffs and associated operational planning bodies.[79]

With regard to ESDI, Richard said, "We must make Europe a true strategic actor. . . . The construction of Europe in defense matters seems to be marking time. However, significant steps have been taken in recent years, and first of all in the Atlantic Alliance, which is currently the only security architecture in Europe that is fully operational." The Amsterdam Treaty, concluded by the EU countries in 1997, when ratified, would provide a boost to the ESDI, Richard declared, because the WEU's 1992 Petersberg tasks are included in the treaty, because the treaty provides for closer WEU-EU cooperation and could permit a WEU-EU merger (if all the member states agreed),[80] and because "Common decision making is facilitated by the adoption of the principle of 'constructive abstention,' even if a possibility of blockage by several member states remains."[81] Moreover, Richard noted, the EU's Common Foreign and Security Policy might now receive impetus from the appointment of a High Representative (the secretary general of the EU Council of Ministers) supported by a policy planning and early warning unit.[82]

Finally, Richard referred to the accomplishments of Operation Alba, the Italian-led multinational intervention in Albania in April 1997: "After the success of Operation Alba which depended to a great extent on Italy and ourselves, some of our partners now admit that it could have been done under the auspices of the WEU."[83] The fact that no consensus among WEU countries could be found—that Britain and Germany in particular were unwilling to participate in the intervention in Albania—illustrates the obstacles to pursuing the ESDI in concrete operations. Operation Alba was not a WEU-endorsed operation, even though a WEU-recognized option for the Petersberg tasks is to rely on a "framework nation" to lead a coalition of the willing composed of WEU members and other states linked to the WEU as associate members, observers, or associate partners.

In Bosnia, although the dynamics and challenges were different from those in Albania, a European unwillingness to make the ESDI manifest in an actual operation was again apparent. In Bosnia, moreover, the French were as adamant as the rest of the European Allies in insisting that the successor to the SFOR operation scheduled for December 1996 to June 1998 would have to include U.S. ground forces. This revealed, once again, how difficult ESDI construction promises to be. As Philip Gordon has asked, "If the Yugoslav crisis on Europe's periphery—combined with a U.S. policy that was erratic, uncertain, and domineering at the same time—was not enough to motivate the EU genuinely to adopt common security policies and military integration, what will?"[84]

BOSNIA BEYOND SFOR

IFOR did not fully extinguish antagonism and conflict in Bosnia (and the rest of the former Yugoslavia) during the year from December 1995 to December 1996. During the course of 1997, U.S. and Allied observers increasingly recognized that SFOR was not likely to do so during its mandate from December 1996 to June 1998. Because the conflict in Bosnia could readily resume once external forces are withdrawn, it was finally agreed in February 1998, on the basis of North Atlantic Council decisions in December 1997, that SFOR's mandate would be extended indefinitely.

Britain, France, Germany, Russia, the United States, and other nations, within and outside NATO, continue to disagree about how to deal with a number of issues associated with the former Yugoslavia and Bosnia in particular, including the arms control regime to be established between the formerly warring factions, relations between the two armies of the Bosnian-Croat federation, and the U.S. interest in arming and training the Bosniaks. It has been easier for the Allies to agree on general aims such as "the need to avoid an arms race in the region"[85] than on how to achieve such specific aims.

In 1997 an obvious challenge for NATO—and for Europeans who aspire to building an ESDI—was to define a follow-on force for SFOR. In January 1997, U.S. secretary of defense William Cohen pledged to Congress that U.S. forces would leave Bosnia by June 1998. Cohen said that he would tell the European Allies that "it's time for them to assume responsibility [in Bosnia] and they will have to [do so]. . . . [S]etting a time line is important because it's telling our European friends that we're not going to make an unlimited commitment to that region. We are not there on a permanent or semi-permanent basis."[86] European officials, however, generally expressed reluctance to regard maintaining peace in Bosnia as entirely a European responsibility. Field Marshal Sir Peter Inge, chief of the British defense staff, said in response to Cohen's statement, "The understanding has always been, all in together, all out together."[87] In May 1997, Foreign Secretary Robin Cook repeated Britain's intention to withdraw whenever the United States does: "One out, all out."[88]

In November 1995, President Clinton announced that IFOR's goal was to support the implementation of the Dayton Accords and thereby bring about the establishment of a stable multiethnic Bosnian state. According to the president, the separation of forces and enforcement of a cease-fire by IFOR "will help to create a secure environment so that the people of Bosnia can return to their homes, vote in free elections and begin to rebuild their lives. Our Joint Chiefs of Staff have concluded that this mission should and will take about one year."[89]

Retired U.S. Army General William Odom wrote a few days after President Clinton's November 1995 speech that "The very idea of creating a stable Bosnia in one year is ludicrous." In Odom's view, U.S. and Allied state-building efforts succeeded in Germany, Italy, Japan, and South Korea because they furnished "a substitute for local government until an effective indigenous one was built and security from foreign threats. . . . In Bosnia, the task is especially complicated because success depends finally on Serbia and Croatia, and neither country is disposed to see an independent Bosnia. Thus, to succeed, the NATO operation must also bring about basic political change in both of these neighboring states, which is not a short-term undertaking." Odom argued that NATO would have to impose a cessation of fighting for a long duration, to convince the belligerents that they would have to live and work together, instead of preparing to resume fighting upon the departure of the NATO-led force. According to Odom, "A long-term NATO deployment can revitalize NATO, re-focusing it from defending against a Soviet invasion to maintaining stability in Central Europe and the former Yugoslavia. Having 40,000 European troops stationed in Bosnia for a generation is a good thing, even if it requires 20,000 American troops to keep them there. We have kept many more troops far longer in Germany, Japan and South Korea, and wisely, because not doing so would have been more costly."[90]

Even though SFOR involves a smaller deployment (35,000 during the December 1996–June 1998 deployment, of which the U.S. portion was 8,500) than IFOR, Odom's analysis looks increasingly prophetic. President Clinton's assumption that "the people of Bosnia" would be able to "return to their homes" during the one-year IFOR operation has proven to be mistaken, because the return of most refugees to their homes has yet to take place.

Similarly, Clinton's description of what happened at Dayton appears overly optimistic: "the Muslims, Croats and Serbs came to Dayton,

Ohio, in America's heartland, to negotiate a settlement. There, exhausted by war, they made a commitment to peace. They agreed to put down their guns, to preserve Bosnia as a single state, to investigate and prosecute war criminals, to protect the human rights of all citizens, to try to build a peaceful, democratic future."[91] Unfortunately, each of these propositions is doubtful, as recent events have shown.

The dilemmas associated with the future of the NATO-led SFOR operation may in fact be summarized in three points: (a) for the most part, the civil, economic, political, and judicial aspects of the Dayton Accords are not being implemented; (b) implementing these nonmilitary aspects of the Dayton Accords could endanger SFOR's current mandate, to say nothing of its longer-term sustainability; and (c) only a prolonged peace enforcement operation, lasting for decades, might succeed in bringing a durable peace, and it is unclear whether the United States and the Alliance as a whole are prepared to make such a commitment.

Nonimplementation of certain nonmilitary aspects of the Dayton Accords

The Dayton settlement was agreed to by the parties to the conflict, but under considerable pressure from the United States and other external powers. The belligerents appear likely to resume combat if NATO and its partners in SFOR withdraw, given the reluctance of many local leaders to cooperate in the reconstruction and reconciliation efforts sponsored by the EU, NATO, the OSCE, the UN, and other organizations, including nongovernmental organizations. These organizations have discovered how difficult it is to bring about a self-sustained peace, one based on sincere commitments to live and work together. The military tasks of separating the forces and preventing a renewal of hostilities were easy compared with the civil tasks (undertaken by the OSCE and the European Union, among other bodies) of economic reconstruction and building shared political institutions that are accepted as permanent and legitimate, instead of being tolerated as temporary impositions from the outside.

According to a summary of a General Accounting Office report based on in-country assessments of the Dayton Accords' implementation and interviews with NATO officials, "hardly any of the major political and economic components of Dayton have been implemented." The GAO report indicated that "many Western observers" judge that an international peace enforcement deployment will probably be necessary "for many years."[92]

In June 1997 Secretary of Defense Cohen again rejected the idea of U.S. involvement in a peace-enforcement deployment lasting beyond June 1998 (he was not to change his position on this question until November 1997), and argued that the June 1998 deadline was useful to encourage the parties to implement the Dayton commitments. "The purpose of focusing on the [June 1998] deadline is to say now let's get busy. . . . We don't have an international police task force. We haven't had the resettlement of refugees. We haven't done the war criminals."[93]

A fundamental obstacle to achieving an enduring settlement in Bosnia is that the signatories of the Dayton Accords do not agree on their proper implementation. The Bosnian Serbs continue to seek independence (or accession to Serbia) for their Republika Srpska while the Bosnian Croats pursue de facto integration with Croatia. Only the Bosniaks appear committed to the Dayton goal of a unified, democratic, multiethnic Bosnia. The Bosniaks have been the most committed to full implementation of the Dayton Accords, because they call for the pursuit of "integrationist" policies regarding Bosnian state institutions, the return of refugees to their homes, and the punishment of war criminals. These are exactly the policies opposed by the Bosnian Croats and the Bosnian Serbs, especially the latter. As a result, as Ivo Daalder has pointed out, "Rather than resolving the conflict, [the struggle over] Dayton implementation is but its continuation by other means."[94]

The question of war criminals provides an example of the difficulty in implementing the Dayton Accords. It may take generations for the local populations to overcome their resentments and grievances over the atrocities and massacres that have taken place, but part of the process of healing would be a sense that at least some justice had been done, with evidence that some of the worst malefactors had been publicly tried and punished. In July 1997, the North Atlantic Council declared, "There can be no lasting peace without justice. We call upon the leaders of the region to cooperate with the International Criminal Tribunal for the former Yugoslavia and fulfill their obligation to deliver those indicted for war crimes for trial at the International Tribunal in The Hague."[95]

In calling upon "the parties to the peace agreement to comply fully with the commitments they themselves have agreed and to implement the peace agreement without delay,"[96] the North Atlantic Council has in effect asked people indicted for war crimes to surrender themselves for trial and to abandon their political ambitions. It is unrealistic to expect the principals to do so voluntarily, when they did not sign the Dayton Accords of their own free will. As Richard Holbrooke has pointed out, "although the Bosnian Serbs (including the Bosnian Serb leader, Radovan Karadzic) signed the Dayton Agreements, they did so under duress."[97]

Nonimplementation and the sustainability of operations such as IFOR and SFOR

From the outset, the United States and other NATO governments have had incentives not to implement certain nonmilitary aspects of the Dayton Accords. Conventional wisdom holds that the political sustainability of the U.S. (and, given European policies, NATO) presence in Bosnia depends largely on avoiding fatalities among U.S. and Allied forces in hostile action. The "limited risk" principle visible in U.S. military operations relating to Bosnia in 1992–95 has been sustained, in that the United States has eschewed military operations with a high risk of large-scale fatalities. The IFOR-SFOR arrangements have been politically feasible primarily because the risk of U.S. combat fatalities has been held to a minimum.

In October 1995, it was reported that the American public's "support for peacemaking in Bosnia falls dramatically when the hypothetical casualties rise. Americans favor the mission by more than a two-to-one margin if no Americans are killed, and oppose the mission by nearly the same margin if twenty-five Americans are killed, according to a USA Today/CNN/Gallup poll. . . ."[98] In August 1997 U.S. military officials indicated that "eleven Americans have died [in Bosnia] since the Bosnian mission began in late 1995, none as a result of hostile action."[99] In December 1997 officials indicated that only one additional soldier had died. None of the twelve deaths in Bosnia had resulted from combat; most were a result of accidents or illness.[100]

Until July 1997 conventional wisdom held that any action to arrest indicted war criminals could endanger the entire SFOR operation. Trying to arrest the indicted war criminals, it was argued, could create more risks than protracting the SFOR operation without attempting such arrests. However, not pursuing the war criminals would prolong a situation of manifest injustice in the eyes of many in Bosnia, particularly the Bosniaks, and open the NATO-led force to further criticism. In March 1997, for example, Richard Holbrooke criticized the NATO-led force in Bosnia for not having done enough to support implementation of the civil and political components of the Dayton Accords. In Holbrooke's view, "its continuing refusal to even consider, let alone attempt, the arrest of Radovan Karadzic or any other indicted war criminal has been unfortunate and has given strength to the separatist cause."[101]

In July 1997 British troops undertook the first operation to capture indicted war criminals, killing one and seizing another for trial before the international tribunal in The Hague. In December 1997, Dutch forces captured two additional indicted war criminals. Analysts noted at that time that "While they have provided logistical support for both the Dutch and British operations in Bosnia, U.S. troops have yet to arrest a war crimes suspect."[102] Furthermore, it was argued, attempting to arrest notorious and influential Bosnian Serb leaders such as Radovan Karadzic and Ratko Mladic would be too risky, because it could bring about retaliation against SFOR troops, including U.S. troops, and U.S. fatalities could cause members of Congress to demand an end to U.S. participation in SFOR.

In April 1998, however, it was revealed that U.S. and Allied forces in SFOR had been closely monitoring the movements of indicted war criminals since 1996 and that they had been preparing an ambitious operation in mid-1997 to capture Karadzic and others. However, the operation was shelved when Washington learned that a French military officer had been meeting secretly with Karadzic. Paris maintained that the French officer's behavior did not compromise the operation, and that France supported efforts to apprehend the indicted. France reportedly withdrew from plans to capture Karadzic "because the American military was not willing to take part except to provide logistical and intelligence help."[103] As of April 1998, U.S. forces had captured one indicted war criminal, and the French had accepted the surrender of one. These reports suggest that operations that could provoke casualties remain highly sensitive, and that incentives to limit risks continue to guide SFOR.[104]

The fact that IFOR and SFOR troops have avoided significant casualties from hostile action to date may be attributable in part to their restraint, as well as to the limited mandate NATO accepted regarding the scope of its responsibilities in Bosnia. If the NATO-led troops had been mandated to pursue indicted war criminals and to protect refugees attempting to return to their homes in areas where "ethnic cleansing" has made them no longer welcome, they might have become the targets of retaliation by the Bosnian Serbs, the Bosnian Croats, and, in some areas, even the Bosniaks, who have the greatest stake in the success of the Dayton Accords. In short, the SFOR operation is most sustainable as long as it is safe for the troops and hence tolerable in terms of U.S. and Allied domestic politics. Ensuring this safety creates an incentive to be cautious in pursuing actual implementation of certain nonmilitary aspects of the Dayton Accords.

The presence of the NATO-led force in Bosnia since December 1995, however, has signified an investment of Alliance credibility. If an identifiable and militarily targetable group inflicted large casualties, NATO's response would probably be to stay and fight to reimpose order. Withdrawing from Bosnia, as France, the United States, and others pulled out of Somalia in 1993–94, has become implausible.

Uncertain prospects for a prolonged peace-enforcement operation

Lasting peace in Bosnia—and in the rest of the former Yugoslavia—may be feasible only when an enduring cessation of hostilities is imposed, obliging the local ethnic groups to live and work together. This was the basis for peace in the region, some observers have noted, under the Byzantine Empire, the Ottoman Empire, the Austro-Hungarian Empire, and Tito's regime. To date, it should be recalled, casualties among IFOR and SFOR troops have been almost nonexistent. If NATO governments had the political will to do so, the operation could be prolonged indefinitely at a low level of risk. This might create the conditions for a durable peace, with incremental implementation of the sensitive nonmilitary aspects of the Dayton Accords, and demonstrate NATO's ability to function as a security guarantor, at least in selected cases, in the Euro-Atlantic region, particularly in close proximity to NATO territory.

The realization of the U.S. vision of Bosnia's future—as specified in the Dayton Accords, a democratic multiethnic federation—faces long odds. It was not until December 1997 that the U.S. government publicly acknowledged that it would have even smaller chances of realization if the United States continued to suggest that its commitment (and that of the NATO-led SFOR) would terminate in June 1998, leaving the belligerents free to resume fighting.

In July 1997 Richard Solomon, president of the United States Institute of Peace, made an apt comparison of the situation in Cambodia to that in Bosnia: "You can't do these settlements quick and dirty and expect them to stick." In both Cambodia and Bosnia, Solomon notes, the problems include "a failed political order, war criminals and a local conflict that has a destabilizing influence" on the region. In each case, the challenges are formidable. In Solomon's words, "if we convey the message we don't know how to deal with them or have the political will to stick with them, there will be a serious price to pay for American leadership. . . . We have to commit enough resources to encourage others to do the same . . . [and] we shouldn't always think we can pay the minimum price and kid ourselves that we can get in and out in a year."[105]

Determination and perseverance are needed to establish the conditions for a genuine peace, as well as candor about the need to be prepared to deploy forces in Bosnia indefinitely. The local populations need confidence regarding the maintenance of order if they are to rebuild houses, schools, hospitals, roads, and all the infrastructure destroyed by war, and to undertake the more demanding task of reconstructing a civil society, with police forces and legal systems they can trust.

President Clinton's arguments in November 1995 for U.S. engagement in Bosnia for a year could be read, somewhat ironically in terms of his support at that time for a brief and limited mission, as a mandate for an open-ended commitment of indefinite duration: "If we're not there, NATO will not be there. The peace will collapse, the war will reignite, the slaughter of innocents will begin again. A conflict that already has claimed so many victims, could spread like poison throughout the region, eat away at Europe's stability, and erode our partnership with our European allies."[106]

Both the proponents and the opponents of a long-term peace-enforcement operation agree that only such an operation might succeed in creating the conditions needed for a durable peace. William Odom, who has recommended a deployment "for a generation," has argued as follows: "To produce an enduring peace, a truce must be long enough for the present leadership to pass from the scene and for economic recovery to occur."[107]

Secretary Cohen said in June 1997, "My position has been that in June of '98 the mission is over." According to Cohen, the parties to the Bosnian conflict then "can choose peace or can choose to go back to what they are doing. . . . [Y]ou cannot impose a peace unless you're willing to stay there for decades, and I don't think the American people are; I don't think the Congress is."[108]

In March 1997, Floyd Spence, chairman of the House National Security Committee, argued for ending the U.S. military presence in Bosnia on September 30, 1997, instead of June 1998. According to Spence, "Achieving a sustainable peace in Bosnia is unlikely under any realistic time frame. . . . The U.S. should begin to work immediately toward a policy that permits the orderly withdrawal of U.S. ground forces."[109]

Bosnia may be able to survive in the foreseeable future as a single state under two possible conditions: if a foreign military presence—that is, a NATO-led peacekeeping operation—continues to impose a degree of order and state unity; or, in the absence of that foreign military presence, Serbia and Croatia choose to permit Bosnia's survival as a buffer state for their mutual convenience. The latter scenario appears improbable, given past behavior by Croatia and Serbia with regard to Bosnia. As long ago as March 1991, before the breakup of Yugoslavia took place, Croatian leader Franjo Tudjman and Serbian leader Slobodan Milosevic met for secret talks during which, according to Tudjman, they discussed how to partition Bosnia-Herzegovina.[110] Tudjman, at least, has not concealed his intentions. His famous hand-drawn map of the region in the future—without an independent Bosnia—is never absent from Bosniak assessments.[111]

In late 1997 it seemed that the only choice was between establishing a follow-on force to succeed SFOR in June 1998 or accepting the failure of the Dayton Accords and the resumption of war. The main obstacle in the United States to sustaining the engagement in Bosnia has remained the widespread impression that core U.S. national security interests are not at stake. While the records of the Serbs and the Croats appear blacker than those of the other belligerents, the tendency in much of the U.S. media and in popular discussions has been to describe all the parties as guilty of atrocities,[112] and to express doubts as to whether the war's outcome (assuming that it can be confined to the territory of the former Yugoslavia) matters in any fundamental sense for U.S. and NATO security interests.

With the noteworthy exception of Secretary Cohen, who continued to argue until November 1997 that SFOR and U.S. ground force involvement in peace enforcement in Bosnia must end in June 1998, an increasingly prevalent view in the United States and other NATO governments in 1997 was that a resumption of the war and the failure of the Dayton Accords would be damaging to U.S. and NATO credibility as well as to the cohesion of the Alliance.

In March 1997 Richard Holbrooke argued that the "partition [of Bosnia] would leave the region in a perpetual state of unresolved tension, keep the international community involved longer and at greater cost, and risk igniting other boundary disputes in the region (Kosovo, Albania, and Macedonia, at a minimum, are highly explosive). . . . [I]t would be a significant setback to our overall position in Europe and within NATO if, after all that we have accomplished in Bosnia, our successes thus far were undone by a failure to finish the job. Partition, whether followed by the dismemberment of Bosnia or not, could reopen other fragile international boundary issues in southeastern Europe and the former Soviet Union, unraveling the current peace in the region."[113]

The stakes in Bosnia for the future of the Alliance are immense, because of the investment of U.S. and Allied political capital and credibility. In the words of Walter Slocombe,

> Just as the NATO-Russia relationship is being forged in Bosnia, so too is the future of NATO itself. It is in Bosnia where all sixteen members of NATO, each one making a contribution, are sending the message that NATO is the bedrock on which the future security and stability of Europe will be built. It is in Bosnia that we are demonstrating that NATO can meet new challenges. It is in Bosnia where NATO is first reaping the benefits of joint peacekeeping training with our new Peace Partners. It is in Bosnia where future NATO members are showing themselves ready and able to shoulder the burdens of membership. And it is in Bosnia where we are showing that we can work together as partners with Russian forces. It is in Bosnia that NATO is working also with neutral and other non-European states in an enterprise that affects global security.[114]

In June 1997, the House of Representatives voted 278–148 to end funding for U.S. participation in SFOR in June 1998.[115] The Senate, in a nonbinding resolution approved by voice vote, declared that all U.S. ground combat forces ought to be withdrawn from Bosnia by June 30, 1998, and that the Europeans ought to furnish any ground forces necessary thereafter. However, the Senate added that the United States could "appropriately provide support . . . including command and control, intelligence, logistics and, if necessary, a ready reserve force in the region."[116]

In a comparable effort to encourage the European Allies to put their ESDI initiative into operation, Representative Lee Hamilton (D-Indiana), the ranking Democrat on the House International Relations Committee, suggested that the post–June 1998 U.S. presence might consist of "logistical and intelligence support in Bosnia" with a "back-up, rapid-reaction force in Hungary."[117]

Secretary Cohen and General John Shalikashvili, then the chairman of the Joint Chiefs of Staff, sent a letter to Congress in July 1997 objecting that a specified withdrawal date would "constrict [the] U.S. commander's flexibility, encourage our opponents and undermine the important psychological advantage of U.S. troops." According to Cohen and Shalikashvili, the fixed withdrawal deadline could also "undercut troops' safety" and "very well undermine the cohesion of the NATO Alliance."[118]

Cognizant of the effect such debates have on the antagonists in Bosnia, the North Atlantic Council in July 1997 issued the following statement: "While SFOR's mandate comes to an end in June 1998, we have a commitment to and a long-term interest in stability in Bosnia and Herzegovina and the surrounding region. The authorities in Bosnia and Herzegovina should be in no doubt that there can be no military option for any party or ethnic group now or in the future."[119]

In late 1997 a consensus emerged on both sides of the Atlantic that SFOR would be extended, in the interests of containing the conflict at a relatively low cost and preventing a renewal of fighting that could discredit the Alliance and its member governments. Some observers speculated about the specific calculations that might take place in particular governments—for instance, the U.S. administration might decide to champion an extension of (or replacement for) SFOR, if the Europeans continued to refuse to make Bosnia a test case for a WEU-led operation, to ensure that Bosnia would not complicate the ratification of the NATO enlargement protocols or become an issue in the November 1998 U.S. congressional elections.

In July 1997, President Clinton said, "The present operation will have run its course by then [June 1998], and we'll have to discuss what, if any, involvement the United States should have there. . . . [W]e have fewer troops there now than when we started, it's been much less expensive and much less hazardous to America than a resumption of full-scale war would be."[120] White House press secretary Michael McCurry added that some sort of follow-on arrangement would be needed: "The administration has acknowledged that there will be some international presence necessary in Bosnia for some time, perhaps a considerable time, beyond the expiration of the . . . mission" in June 1998.[121]

In early November 1997, U.S. secretary of defense Cohen continued to insist that "there is no consensus as yet in terms of what form that [U.S.] interest [in Bosnia] . . . would take. It may take diplomatic engagement, financial engagement, economic engagement, or it could involve some military." Cohen added that the U.S. military contribution might be limited to communications, intelligence, and transportation support.[122] In mid-November 1997, however, administration officials and congressional leaders evidently reached a consensus on the principle of extending SFOR with U.S. ground force participation. Beyond the need to ensure stability in Bosnia, the United States wished to retain command of SFOR and press for fuller implementation of the Dayton Accords and yet diminish the force as a whole and the size of the U.S. contribution.[123]

In a December 1997 defense ministers session of the North Atlantic Council, Secretary Cohen said that there was "a need for some kind of international force. . . . It remains to be seen exactly what size, what shape, what commitment many other countries are prepared to make." Cohen added that continued U.S. troop participation might well hinge on a large European contribution, notably to an international police force.[124] The NATO defense ministers approved a communiqué that referred to "the final six months of SFOR's mission" and asked NATO military authorities, on the basis of the NAC's political-military guidance, "to develop without commitment a full range of distinct options identifying potential tasks and necessary associated forces for a future NATO-led military presence in Bosnia and Herzegovina following the end of SFOR's mandate."[125]

Later in December 1997, President Clinton announced that U.S. ground forces would remain in Bosnia beyond the original deadline of June 1998 to forestall the threats of renewed "violence" and "chaos." He said that "The people of Bosnia still need a safety net and a helping hand," and that it had been an "error" to set a specific deadline for the mission's duration.[126] The new policy, U.S. officials indicated, would be to avoid a precise "exit date" and instead to develop a set of criteria to be satisfied—"benchmarks" of accomplishment to permit force reductions and eventual disengagement.[127]

The follow-on to SFOR after June 1998 would also be called SFOR, it was decided, partly to avoid the costs of repainting trucks and printing new stationery.[128] The new SFOR would be smaller than the initial SFOR, and the U.S. contribution would decline from 8,500 to 6,900 troops. According to congressional testimony in March 1998 by U.S. under secretary of defense Slocombe, the plan is "to conduct periodic six-month reviews with the intent of making further reductions based on progress on the ground."[129] The new SFOR would include "specialized units" for certain "public security" tasks; these units would be composed of European, Latin American, and other non-U.S. paramilitary forces, sometimes called gendarmes, to relieve the burden on regular SFOR units.[130] According to U.S. officials, these units would "add a new buffer between regular military troops and any localized violence."[131]

The "benchmarks" of progress that would justify force reductions and ultimate withdrawal may be subject to protracted negotiations in the United States and other Alliance governments. In March 1998, Ambassador Robert Gelbard, the special representative of the president and the secretary of state for the implementation of the Dayton Peace Accords, testified that

> Peace in Bosnia is still fragile, and the forces of division, intolerance and ethnic hatred have not been defeated. Political pluralism and independent media must be expanded throughout Bosnia, including in the Muslim/Croat-dominated federation. Ironically, there is today more political pluralism and freedom of expression in the Republika Srpska than in the federation. . . . While we have made considerable progress in bringing indicted war criminals to justice over the last 12 months, . . . much more needs to be done. . . . With a reform government in Republika Srpska taking positive action, the Bosniaks and the Croats can no

longer hide behind Serb obstructionism. Much more needs to be done on establishment of a working and cooperative federation government and genuinely democratic institutions at the local and cantonal levels in the federation. . . . [T]he Croats [in Bosnia] must give up their separatist ambitions and cooperate on the important issues at hand such as getting an IMF [International Monetary Fund] agreement and reintegrating the Bosnian economy. At the same time, the Bosniaks must effectively share power and resist their instincts to dominate the federation. Returning Sarajevo to its pre-war status of a truly multi-ethnic city must serve as a model. . . . On return of refugees and displaced persons, we see this as at the core of returning Bosnia to its true nature of multi-ethnicity and [this] is one of the key Dayton long term success goals. We must work harder to create the conditions for the voluntary orderly return of refugees. . . . Finally, on pressure on the Federal Republic of Yugoslavia and Croatia, continued strong international pressure will be needed to ensure that both Zagreb and Belgrade play a constructive role in Bosnia. . . . Regional stability will be assured only when the Federal Republic of Yugoslavia and Croatia embrace real democratic institutions based on the rule of law.[132]

Some members of Congress have expressed frustration with such general statements of objectives. Senator John McCain (R-Arizona) has written, "Restating the political goals of the Dayton Accords as the president has done, and tying the U.S. military presence to achieving these lagging political objectives, is not sufficient or appropriate for defining a military mission. A clearly defined and achievable military mission is essential to ensuring that our forces can complete that mission and get out of Bosnia."[133]

Administration officials have faithfully followed the lead given by the president, who wrote to Congress in March 1998 as follows regarding the expected duration of U.S. participation in the new SFOR in Bosnia: "Although I do not propose a fixed end-date for this presence, it is by no means open-ended."[134] Later that month, Slocombe responded to the questions raised by Representative Hamilton:

HAMILTON: . . . [T]he patience of the Congress and the patience of the American people is not without limit. And they would want, I believe, at least a notional idea of how long the American commitment is in Bosnia. . . . I'm not asking you for a date here, but are we going to be there one year, or 10 years or is this a Cyprus situation, or [are] we going to be there 30 years? Or what can you say to us?

SLOCOMBE: I think the president has said that indefinite doesn't mean infinite. There's no way you. . .

HAMILTON: That really ties it down.

SLOCOMBE: There is no way you can say we aren't going to put a deadline on it, and then put on a deadline and then give a time. Our approach will be what in fact in practice it has been up to now, that is to as the situation develops, at regular intervals, look at the progress that's been made. And we fully expect to be able to make substantial reductions as we go forward. But I can't tell you it's going to be a year, or 10 years, although I suppose that brackets the possibilities. I can't give you a time without in effect putting on a deadline, and that's precisely what we've avoided to do.[135]

During its April 1998 deliberations on NATO enlargement, the U.S. Senate defeated an amendment by a 20–80 vote that would have required the president to allow Congress formally to endorse the Bosnia mission before U.S. ratification of the Alliance's enlargement to the Czech Republic, Hungary, and Poland. "Supporters of that amendment argued that Mr. Clinton had left Congress with only broken promises on Bosnia, from an original pledge of a one-year mission costing $1 billion, to an open-ended operation that has so far cost nearly $8 billion." According to the *New York Times*, "many" senators opposed to the amendment "agreed with the sentiment behind" it. One of those who voted against NATO enlargement, Senator Robert Smith (R-New Hampshire) said, "We must not be drawn into a posture of indefinite garrison. . . . We're still in Bosnia, with no end in sight, no plan to get out."[136]

The Clinton administration's cautious approach, favoring an incremental series of short-duration, low-risk commitments, supplemented since December 1997 with a policy of frequent reviews of an engagement of indefinite duration, responds to the demands of U.S. domestic politics. The United States remains traumatized by its experience in Vietnam. In March 1991, when U.S.-led coalition forces had succeeded in expelling Iraq's army from Kuwait, President Bush proclaimed, "It's a proud day for Americans and by God, we've kicked the Vietnam syndrome once and for all."[137] In fact, however, Desert Storm affirmed the main lessons America's political and military leaders learned in Vietnam —above all, their insistence on clear and achievable objectives and, as an April 1992 Department of Defense report put it, "overwhelming offensive capability," so that "decisive force" would ensure that the United States would "avoid getting bogged down in a long, inconclusive war."[138] As noted earlier, one of the main reasons for U.S. reluctance to employ ground forces in Bosnia in the early 1990s was the fear of a "slippery slope" leading to America's entrapment in a Vietnam-style quagmire. Such reluctance could be overcome only when the risks of casualties for these forces were reduced to a low level during the mid-1995 military operations, with the U.S. contributions made primarily by air and naval forces.

Partly as a result of the Vietnam trauma, U.S. policy currently holds that foreign military engagements must be justified by their significance for core national security interests (for example, mutual defense pledges to NATO Allies and Japan), or be manageable within finite constraints of duration, risk, or cost. In Bosnia, the risks and costs were made manageable by Operation Deliberate Force in mid-1995 and by the organization of a peace enforcement coalition far superior to the belligerents' forces; and attempts were made to impose a finite duration for the effort (a one-year deadline for IFOR, December 1995 to December 1996; and an eighteen-month deadline for SFOR, December 1996 to June 1998).

Unfortunately, not all crisis contingencies can be precisely calibrated in advance. Setting deadlines in support of "exit strategies" can be counterproductive to the success of the mission. The deadlines not only create an incentive for the local antagonists to outwait the peacekeepers, but also give them an excuse not to undertake the more challenging tasks in implementing the settlement.

In Bosnia, the deadline of June 1998 for the expiration of SFOR's mission, set in November 1996, created the risk that the United States and its Allies and coalition partners might try to catch up on the implementation of the Dayton commitments (for instance, regarding the capture of war criminals and the return of refugees) on an accelerated basis, with actions that could provoke the opponents of the Dayton Accords to retaliate against NATO troops. The dilemma was that some actions intended to save the Accords could have the contrary effect: They could threaten the sustainability of NATO's first peacekeeping operation by increasing the costs and the risks of casualties. The U.S. decision in December 1997 to support an indefinite extension of the operation improves the chances for the construction of a durable peace in Bosnia; the odds against success nonetheless remain formidable, given the immense challenges involved.[139]

An SFOR peacekeeping operation of indefinite duration may be sustainable as long as its costs are manageable and the risks of casualties are minimal. Two additional factors may also help sustain SFOR. The first is that the mission has earned a measure of U.S. public support. A March 1998 poll sponsored by the University of Maryland found that, "For the first time, . . . a clear majority supported U.S. participation in NATO's peacekeeping efforts. More than half also supported extending the NATO mission, and committing U.S. troops beyond the June [1998] deadline."[140]

The second factor is that the European Allies have demonstrated a willingness to bear a significant share of responsibility, lessening the risk of intra-Alliance friction. In December 1997, German defense minister Volker Rühe said, "As far as we are concerned, the Americans can take all of the troop reductions and still keep the key command posts. We will stick with existing troop levels as proof of our desire to shoulder more of the burden."[141] Walter Slocombe testified in March 1998 that the other participants in SFOR "provide three times as many troops as the United States does, five times as much economic assistance, nine times as many international police, and they have received ten times as many refugees."[142]

Of course, setbacks in the field could make the positive burden-sharing balance politically irrelevant in the U.S. Congress; public support for SFOR, in the United States and in other Alliance countries, might evaporate rapidly in the face of casualties. The greatest risks of such setbacks may not reside in Bosnia proper, given SFOR's presence, but in adjacent areas in the Balkans.

CONTINGENCIES BEYOND BOSNIA

Further conflicts regarding ethnic groups and national borders are quite conceivable; some are already under way in areas beyond Bosnia in the Euro-Atlantic region that NATO has declared its zone of special interest: in the Balkans; in the Caucasus, Central Asia, and elsewhere in the former Soviet Union; and in Central and Eastern Europe. Should current or latent conflicts in this region escalate, it might take the Allies even longer than it did in Bosnia to agree on the need for military action and its proper form—if, indeed, they could agree to take any such action.

The Albanian case in early to mid-1997 helped to illustrate the limits to the "security is indivisible" pledges of the Allies and the other participants in the new Euro-Atlantic security structures. No multinational intervention will be possible unless a coalition of the willing, within or outside an international organization, is prepared to undertake it. In this case, the governments willing to take action—Austria, Denmark, France, Greece, Italy, Romania, Spain, and Turkey—found that a sufficient consensus did not exist to make their intervention either a NATO- or a WEU-sponsored action.[143] The NATO Allies commended the Italian-led Multinational Protection Force and offered political support, but chose not to undertake an Alliance operation.[144]

More practical support under NATO auspices was not feasible until August 1997, when a NATO fact-finding team traveled to Albania and devised a program to assist in the restructuring of the Albanian armed forces, in cooperation with other international efforts to rebuild the police, the banking system, and other aspects of Albania's economy and government. In October 1997, the NATO-Albania Clearing House met for the first time, bringing together the sixteen NATO Allies, Albania, and the PfP Partners that wish to assist Albania. In the recent monthly meetings of the clearing house, Switzerland has participated as a permanent member, because it has an active assistance program, while Hungary, Poland, and Romania have participated with respect to specific activities they have launched in cooperation with NATO.[145]

The Albanian example is significant for additional reasons. Ethnic Albanians are numerous in both Kosovo and the Former Yugoslav Republic of Macedonia (FYROM), each of which could become a new Bosnia—that is, a new battlefield of antagonistic ethnic groups—yet with a higher potential for the conflict's spreading to neighboring states.[146] Kosovo is legally part of Serbia, and the Allies at present do not support self-determination in the sense of independence for Kosovo —only a restoration of Kosovo's previous autonomy within Serbia. While FYROM is a recognized state (though its name remains controversial), ethnic turmoil in either Kosovo or FYROM (or both) could draw in outside powers, ultimately including NATO Allies such as Greece, Turkey, and the United States.

In December 1992, it should be recalled, U.S. President George Bush wrote to Serbian President Slobodan Milosevic as follows: "In the event of conflict in Kosovo caused by Serbian action, the United States will be prepared to employ military force against the Serbians in Kosovo and in Serbia proper."[147] President Clinton repeated this warning in March 1993.[148] In March 1998, Ambassador Robert Gelbard declined to reaffirm the warning in those terms, saying that the United States would use "every possible economic sanction or other kind of tool we have diplomatically, but we're not ruling anything out." An unnamed U.S. official said, however, "the United States view remains the same as it was in December 1992—that we're not going to sit back and accept a major Serb military operation in Kosovo."[149] Secretary of State Madeleine Albright said, "We are not going to stand by and watch the Serbian authorities do in Kosovo what they can no longer get away with doing in Bosnia."[150]

Albania brought its security concerns to the Alliance's attention on March 11, 1998, when it became the first Partner to exercise its PfP emergency consultation rights. Albania's deputy defense minister, Perikli Teta, addressed the North Atlantic Council and asked whether "the deployment of a NATO peacekeeping contingent on the Albania-Yugoslav border [that is, the border with Kosovo] would contribute to stability in the region." The Allies responded that there was no "urgent requirement" to send such forces, and decided to take other measures to demonstrate, in the words of NATO secretary general Javier Solana, that "Albania has the solidarity of NATO."[151] The other measures, taken under PfP auspices, include civil emergency and humanitarian assistance (to help deal with ethnic Albanian refugees from Kosovo), military training, and aid in securing ammunition stockpiles and other military depots.[152] The Allies apparently wish to signal their concern for Albania's security without provoking or thoroughly alienating Serbian leader Slobodan Milosevic, who "remains crucial to the success of the Dayton accords and stability in Bosnia."[153]

NATO authorities may also consider an Alliance role with regard to another one of Kosovo's neighbors—FYROM. Lazar Kitanoski, FYROM's defense minister, said in March 1998 that his government and the United States were discussing a plan for stationing NATO forces in FYROM. The current mandate for the United Nations Preventive Deployment

Force (UNPREDEP) in FYROM expires in February 1999. FYROM (one of the Alliance's PfP Partners) would prefer that the follow-on force include a NATO contingent.[154] According to Kitanoski, "UNPREDEP's role is to watch and report. That's all right so long as the situation doesn't get worse. But the presence of NATO military units is very important. NATO can provide effective protection, not just for Macedonia but to avoid a bigger crisis in the Balkans."[155] However, the Alliance might choose measures other than (or in addition to) participation in a follow-on preventive deployment in FYROM, such as conducting PfP exercises or establishing a PfP training center in FYROM.[156]

As the Albanian case suggests, contingencies for Alliance action beyond Bosnia could arise because of the vague commitments made by the Allies—not only the general "security is indivisible" pledges, but also the commitments to PfP consultation. The wording in the PfP commitment—"NATO will consult with any active participant in the Partnership if that Partner perceives a direct threat to its territorial integrity, political independence, or security"[157]—is similar to that in Article 4 of the North Atlantic Treaty. The Allies have given practical meaning to the Article 5 commitment through the collective defense planning process and concrete preparations for joint and combined action. Similarly, PfP exercises and activities have created expectations and have provided a measure of credibility to the Alliance's Article 4–like commitments.

Article 4 was originally conceived during the Cold War as a sort of "trigger" or "precursor" for honoring Article 5, the mutual defense commitment. The Article 4–like pledge in PfP is now depicted as a self-standing activity—consultation, which might mean little more than NATO formally promising to listen when Partners discuss their anxieties. Implicitly, however, the consultation must be intended to consider a response to the threat. Some observers wonder if the value of the Article 4–like commitment has been compromised, or diluted, through the extension of such a pledge to each of the twenty-seven Partners. Alternatively, Partners eager to believe that NATO is committed to more than consultations might misperceive the Article 4–like pledge as a "back door" to Article 5–type commitments.

NATO membership for Poland, for example, could incur the risk that some Russians might complain about Kaliningrad's "encirclement" by NATO. The extension of NATO's integrated air defense to Poland might involve more intense air surveillance of Kaliningrad and the Baltic states, a development that some Russian officials and politicians might resent. If Russia decided to insist forcibly on rights of access to Kaliningrad (perhaps to create a pretext for action on behalf of the ethnic Russian minorities in the Baltic states), Lithuania might appeal to NATO under PfP consultation procedures. Poland and some other Allies might choose to support Lithuania. What would the Alliance as a whole do?

Even without NATO enlargement, cultivating links with the Baltic states through PfP and the EAPC (and through other bodies involving Allies, such as the Council of the Baltic Sea States) could create challenges for NATO that would not be specifically Article 5 cases. For example, what would NATO do if Russia undermined the autonomy of the Baltic states by nonmilitary means? Moscow could make more effective use of economic instruments such as trade and energy supplies, and could exploit the vulnerability of the Baltic banking systems to pose difficulties for the Baltic states and their Western partners. Rather than seize territory, Russia could reassert a sphere of influence by subtler methods. Incidents in the Baltic region could be quite significant, as a result of Russia's sensitivity over its proximity to Saint Petersburg.

A Russian attempt to reimpose influence over one or more of the Baltic states might lead to inconclusive discussions in the NATO-Russia Permanent Joint Council and in the North Atlantic Council. The result might be appeasement of Russia and a new division line, but some observers suspect that efforts to modify the status of the Baltic states could become a casus belli, given the close links that the Balts are developing with Denmark, Finland, Germany, Poland, Sweden, and the United States.[158] In January 1998, the United States signed a "Charter of Partnership" with Estonia, Latvia, and Lithuania, in which Washington promised to support eventual NATO membership for these countries and offered what was characterized as "a moral and political commitment to their independence, sovereignty and territorial integrity." Despite the statement by Latvian president Guntis Ulmanis that the charter "makes us allies" of the United States, it falls short of a treaty commitment.[159] Nonetheless, it represents part of an array of commitments by NATO and EU states to the security of the Baltic states that might be tested by Russian attempts to reassert influence through coercion. The danger of a general European war might be averted only by early action to warn Russia not to intervene, and the United States, with NATO support, would have to be the country to make such a warning. The course of such a crisis can scarcely be predicted, however; much would depend on the specific circumstances.

As the French commentator Daniel Vernet has observed, one of the enduring features of Russian diplomacy is "scorn" for the rights of small states. It is for this reason that Western efforts "to include Russia in institutions in which it would have the same status as its former satellites have failed." (That is, the Russians have shown little interest in active PfP participation.) Even more exposed, Vernet has noted, are states that were formerly parts of the Russian (and Soviet) Empire, such as the Baltic states: "The Kremlin seems to consider the possibility that they might freely choose their alliances a *casus belli*."[160] Crisis management in the collective defense sense of the term might thus become necessary, in part because of Article 4–type PfP consultation commitments to the Baltic states and other Partners.

Contingencies in the former Soviet Union

The Baltic states enjoy a unique status in Western eyes among former Soviet republics. Conflicts elsewhere on the territory of the former Soviet Union appear less likely to involve NATO-led crisis management or peace operations. It is a commonplace among specialists on the former Soviet Union that a pattern has emerged of Russian efforts to reassert influence in Georgia, Tajikistan, and other former Soviet republics.[161] It has also become apparent that no Western government would be willing to respond other than by diplomatic and economic means.

In practice, any large-scale Alliance action for crisis management or peacekeeping will probably be feasible only when a consensus can be achieved and Russian views are taken into consideration. Such Russian-NATO cooperation is most improbable on the territory of the former Soviet Union in the foreseeable future, suggesting some of the geographical and political limits to NATO involvement in crisis management and peace operations in the Euro-Atlantic region. If Russian participation or approval (preferably through the UN Security Council) cannot be obtained for an operation to deal with a non–Article 5 crisis in any of the former Soviet republics, the probability of an intervention by the Alliance would be doubtful.

The only exceptions would be cases in which the Allies were confident that Russian complaints could be tolerated and Russian action deterred, or that the risks of Russian retaliation were worth running. Such cases might be trivial, with low risks, or of such gravity—for instance, involving the Baltic states or a Russian attempt to annex parts of Ukraine or other former Soviet republics with large numbers of ethnic Russians—that they would imply the threatened state calling on the Alliance to honor its Article 4–like consultation pledge under PfP (and, in the case of Ukraine, the similar pledge in the NATO-Ukraine Charter).[162]

However implausible such extreme scenarios seem at present, honoring an Article 4–like commitment in certain circumstances could rapidly lead the Alliance into a collective defense situation, even in the absence of an Article 5 commitment to the threatened Partner. In other words, the circumstances would no longer involve collective security, but collective defense and the balance of power. If war were avoided, it would be because NATO and NATO-affiliated states enjoyed a preponderance of military power for deterrence and defense, not because collective security aspirations had succeeded in establishing a community of power.

This circumstance raises questions about the comprehensiveness of the Alliance's aims regarding "a stable security environment in Europe, based on the growth of democratic institutions and commitment to the peaceful resolution of disputes, in which *no* country would be able to intimidate or coerce *any* European nation or to impose hegemony through the threat or use of force."[163]

Since 1990, NATO governments and their counterparts throughout the Euro-Atlantic region have repeatedly endorsed inclusive "security is indivisible" rhetoric and have vaguely implied that collective security commitments in the spirit of the Kantian or Wilsonian tradition are offered. In practice, however, NATO governments are not likely in the foreseeable future—for reasons of prudence as well as domestic politics —to go beyond collective security in the major-power-consensus sense of the term. This means that the Allies will probably undertake collective security operations only when a major power endorsement can be obtained—as with the UN Security Council mandates for IFOR and SFOR in Bosnia. By definition, an intervention in support of collective security in the major-power-consensus sense cannot be undertaken against the will of an interested major power—at least, to the extent of that power's sphere of interest and influence. This approach falls far short of the Kantian or Wilsonian ideal, but it is all that can realistically be expected—unless the Allies are convinced that, given the gravity of the crisis at hand, their action is imperative and they are accordingly prepared to assume additional risks by acting outside a major-power consensus. The additional risks could include domestic political turmoil and the reactions of major powers opposed to the intervention.

Whether inside or outside the territory of the former USSR, Russia's tacit approval or actual participation in collective-security interventions is politically desirable, as with IFOR/SFOR. According to then-SACEUR General George Joulwan, IFOR involved the most significant political-military cooperation with Russia since World War II. "This joint NATO-Russian mission proves that the two former adversaries can achieve peaceful goals through military cooperation," Joulwan observed. "It has also widened mutual understanding and trust, . . . the direct result—a natural result—of a common mission. . . . This cooperation can become an enduring framework for partnership into the next century."[164]

Given this analysis, how should NATO's many "security-is-indivisible" pledges and PfP commitments be interpreted? They could be constructive if they deterred potential aggressors and established a higher standard of international conduct. They could be harmful, however, if they promoted misperceptions and encouraged countries to believe that they had acquired more protection through such vague commitments than is in fact the case. Even so, some countries are not likely to have any such illusions. According to the May 1997 NATO-Russia Founding Act, "NATO and Russia will seek the widest possible cooperation among participating States of the OSCE with the aim of creating in Europe a common space of security and stability, without dividing lines or spheres of influence limiting the sovereignty of any state."[165] Given Russian actions in the Caucasus and Central Asia, it is doubtful whether political leaders in, for example, Georgia or Azerbaijan or Tajikistan will be misled as to the true significance of such declarations.

Contingencies beyond Europe

The possibility that responses to conflicts beyond Europe will again become a source of European-American discord is obviously high, given the history of the out-of-area question. It is significant that the "Atlantic Forces" package for the U.S. military, defined during the Bush administration (and retained in a modified form by the Clinton administration), has been justified with reference to contingencies in the Middle East (specifically, in the Persian Gulf region). This conceptualization of the forces' purpose is entirely understandable, given the logistical and historical realities and the need to justify to a skeptical Congress the need for U.S. forces in Europe, despite the changes in the European political landscape since 1989–91.

The emphasis on the utility of the Atlantic Forces for contingencies beyond Europe is related to the experience of the Persian Gulf War. General John Galvin, then the commander-in-chief of the U.S. European Command (EUCOM), testified in March 1991 that a third of EUCOM's combat forces were redeployed forward to the Persian Gulf, Turkey, and Israel during the war. Galvin also called attention to the contributions by NATO Allies during the war, including the ground forces provided by Britain and France, and the enormous logistical support provided by Allied installations. "Approximately 90 percent of airlift and deploying aircraft were supported as they transited through bases in Germany, France, Portugal, Spain, Italy, Cyprus, Greece, Turkey, and the U.K."[166]

This conceptualization may eventually raise problems in European-American relations. Historically, U.S. allies in Europe have been wary of U.S. use of military bases in Europe and U.S. forces deployed in Europe for operations outside the NATO area. The Gulf War in August 1990–February 1991 was not typical of the historical pattern, and it is not clear whether comparable political-military support would be forthcoming in future cases. Indeed, U.S. officials have acknowledged that the conduct of that war was facilitated by unusual features that may not be present in future conflicts. As Paul Wolfowitz, then under secretary of defense for policy, observed in April 1991, "we were fortunate . . . over the past eight months to enjoy a very permissive environment—a dramatically reduced Soviet threat in Europe that allowed us to move U.S. forces to the Gulf, cooperative allies, extensive infrastructure in place, and a great deal of time to prepare. Some of those factors may be different next time."[167]

As long ago as 1990, some U.S. officials expressed interest in developing more cohesive U.S.-West European cooperation under NATO auspices, perhaps through the WEU, to deal with security challenges outside Europe, notably in the Middle East/Persian Gulf region. In September 1990, Robert Zoellick, then the State Department counselor, said that NATO discussions could lead to "cooperative operations" involving the United States and WEU member states, and that such arrangements "could supply a valuable mechanism for tackling regional security problems. We used this combination in the Persian Gulf in 1987 and are employing it with Iraq today."[168]

In subsequent years it has become increasingly apparent that, as a Dutch analyst recently observed, "there is a difference of opinion between the European members of the Alliance and the United States as to whether NATO is a regional or a global alliance."[169] David Gompert, Richard Kugler, Stephen Larrabee, James Thomson, and other American analysts in recent years have suggested ways in which the Alliance could serve as a mechanism for U.S.-led crisis-intervention operations far beyond Europe.[170] Moreover, prominent former U.S. officials, such as Warren Christopher and William Perry, have also endorsed "global NATO" proposals. In October 1997, Christopher and Perry argued as follows:

> Shifting the alliance's emphasis from defense of members' territory to defense of common interests is the strategic imperative. These threats include the proliferation of weapons of mass destruction, disruption of the flow of oil, terrorism, genocidal violence and wars of aggression in other regions that threaten to create great disruption. To deal with such threats, alliance members need to have a way to rapidly form military coalitions that can accomplish goals beyond NATO territory. . . . Such a "coalition of the willing" made up the Implementation Force in Bosnia under alliance command and control, and another made up the warfighting force in Desert Storm, which drew heavily on alliance training and procedures. Such coalitions will include some—but not necessarily all—NATO members, and will generally include non-members from the Partnership for Peace program. . . . For NATO to succeed, it must develop the ability to respond to today's security needs.[171]

European observers have found that such formulations raise more questions than they answer: Does "defense" really mean "pursuit"? Which interests outside the traditional NATO area can be considered truly "common," given the distinct and sometimes competing economic objectives of Allies and their differing views on how to define and react to specific cases of "genocidal violence and wars of aggression in other regions"?

The U.S. interest in the "global NATO" concept has become an official theme in policy declarations nonetheless. Secretary of State Albright told the North Atlantic Council in December 1997, "The United States and Europe will certainly face challenges beyond Europe's shores. Our nations share global interests that require us to work together with the same degree of solidarity that we have long maintained on this continent."[172] The immediate response from British foreign secretary Robin Cook echoed that of his European counterparts: "NATO has traditionally been concerned with the Euro-Atlantic area. That is where most of us see the focus for some time to come."[173]

Although some Europeans have reacted favorably to the "global NATO" concept,[174] and everyone concedes that non–Article 5 endeavors are not limited by Article 6 of the North Atlantic Treaty, the predominant reaction in NATO Europe has been negative. European observers generally find more difficulties than advantages in the "global NATO" concept. In their view, attempting to institutionalize global security functions in NATO might well prove to be counterproductive and damaging to Alliance cohesion and to the maintenance of U.S. leadership in the Alliance.

Some European Allies (including Britain, France, Germany, and the Netherlands) are acquiring more mobile and flexible capabilities that could be used in non–Article 5 operations beyond the Euro-Atlantic region on a case-by-case basis. Nonetheless, it seems likely that future Western interventions beyond Europe will follow the ad hoc pattern of the Gulf War, rather than an elaborate and formal mechanism for this purpose. Indeed, the Americans themselves might discover in practice, if an attempt were made to implement the "global NATO" concept, that placing such operations under Alliance auspices could significantly limit U.S. flexibility. It must be acknowledged, as German analyst Joachim Krause has observed, that "NATO is still a long way from defining itself as a coalition of those willing to export stability to regional theatres outside of Europe."[175]

Interventions beyond Europe probably can be done only selectively, on the basis of shared interests and consensus, by a coalition of the willing drawing on NATO assets and experience. As Michael Rühle and Nick Williams point out, "an attempt to rally the European allies into quasi-automatic action on the global stage is bound to fail. . . . [O]ne would be hard-pressed to come up with scenarios which would suggest joint military action of all 16 NATO allies outside Europe. . . . Far more likely, however, would be ad hoc coalitions by NATO and non-NATO states, whose cooperation would be aided by the use of established NATO infrastructure and procedures."[176]

In May 1997, "a senior U.S. official" was quoted as doubting "whether the alliance would find a consensus to take military action against an enemy who was blocking the Strait of Hormuz or the Suez Canal to choke off our vital oil supplies. . . . As NATO grows, it will become even more difficult to reach agreement on the gravity of any threat. That's why you are likely to see more coalitions of the willing, as in the Gulf War, rather than the one-for-all, all-for-one attitude we maintained against the Warsaw Pact."[177]

Risks posed by weapons of mass destruction in interventions beyond Europe

Interventions beyond the Euro-Atlantic region could entail an increased risk of facing adversaries armed with weapons of mass destruction (WMD)—that is, nuclear, chemical, or biological weapons. Particularly since the January 1994 NATO summit, the Alliance has established new institutions, including the Senior Defense Group on Proliferation, to examine how the Alliance can complement the efforts of other international organizations to promote nonproliferation and, if these efforts should fail, to define military capabilities to counter WMD.

Some Allies and Partners might nonetheless be deterred from participating in an intervention involving an appreciable risk of WMD use. If a NATO-sponsored coalition of the willing went forward, it might have to consider retaliating for an attack conducted with nuclear, chemical, or biological weapons against NATO Allies. However, retaliatory operations would be quite distinct from conventional military actions against WMD capabilities or production facilities undertaken at the outset of an intervention, or the possible preemptive destruction of WMD agents or facilities without overt hostile action on the part of a WMD "proliferant." The latter probably could not be undertaken by NATO. As Michael Rühle concludes, "NATO, given its democratic, multinational, and defensive nature, is incapable of any deliberately planned offensive action. . . . [I]t is simply inconceivable that NATO Allies would find the political will to launch a preventive military strike even against the facilities of a state which persisted in its development of WMD in the light of international opposition."[178]

The willingness of Germany and other possible participants in an ad hoc coalition to take action against a WMD proliferant could depend, however, on the magnitude of the risk that could emerge in the event of inaction. The most convincing argument might be the need to stop nuclear proliferation, because it would be so difficult to deal with a radical, nuclear-armed regime. A 1996 poll of German elites found that 45 percent would support the participation of the German armed forces in a preventive military strike by NATO against the development of nuclear weapons—for instance, in Libya.[179]

The general aim of helping to prevent WMD proliferation readily wins assent throughout the Alliance. However, some Allies have shown a tendency to disagree about how to deal with specific proliferants (for example, Iran and Iraq). The United States in recent years has supported a policy of "dual containment," intended to isolate Iran and Iraq, whereas some Allies—notably France and Germany—have displayed a willingness to relax the constraints imposed by the UN Security Council and the UN Special Commission on Iraq and to trade actively with Iran. This difference in approaches has long suggested some potential for discord within the Alliance.

Secretary of State Albright put some of this discord on public display at the North Atlantic Council meeting in December 1997, when she declared, with regard to the difficulties of sustaining the UN inspections effort in Iraq, that Americans believe that the United States often "takes the heat for dealing with difficult issues while others take the contracts —that our willingness to take responsibility for peace and security makes it easier for others to shirk theirs." In her view, the Allies should recognize that WMD proliferation is "the most overriding security interest of our time," one that should be seen as a "unifying threat" binding NATO together.[180] Intra-Alliance discord could become more acute in a crisis, because the Allies could well have distinct interpretations of the origins of the crisis and different views about how to deal with it, based in part on competing economic interests—to say nothing of hesitations about undertaking risky military operations.

With or without such operations, however, WMD proliferants with aircraft, long-range missiles, or ships as delivery means (or with any covert means of inserting WMD, given their portability) could pose direct threats to NATO territory and populations. As John Sopko has pointed out, future proliferants may include nonstate actors such as terrorists and religious and ethnic groups armed with chemical, biological, or radiological weapons that could be made with materials and equipment that are readily available, because of their dual-use nature—that is, the legitimate applications of these materials and equipment make them easily accessible.[181] If the obstacles to effective large-scale utilization could be surmounted, such threats could constitute Article 5 contingencies, obliging all the Allies, in principle, to participate in collective defense, assuming that the malefactors could be identified and proven to be acting on behalf of a foreign government. Nonstate actors, however, would create distinct challenges involving intelligence cooperation and coordinated action. The Alliance might well be a useful framework, among others, for such cooperation and action, which would require the Allies to think beyond traditional planning.

Within more traditional conceptions of WMD contingencies, the threat would involve a WMD-armed state threatening partners or interests in a distant region. In such cases, the obvious preference of the United States and the other Allies would be to avoid using nuclear weapons and to rely on conventional forces in dealing with aggressive WMD proliferants. At the same time, the United States and its NATO Allies have been reluctant to give up whatever deterrent value may reside in being ambiguous about a possible nuclear response to an enemy's use of WMD against U.S. or Allied forces.

According to the U.S. and British officials who recently served as the co-chairmen of NATO's Senior Defense Group on Proliferation, two of the principles that must guide the Alliance's defense response to WMD proliferation are to "complement nuclear deterrence with a mix of defensive and responsive conventional capabilities," and to "balance a mix of capabilities including nuclear forces and conventional response capabilities to devalue a proliferant's NBC [nuclear, chemical, and biological] weapons by denying the military advantages they would confer and through the prospect of an overwhelming response to their use."[182] Deciding what mix of capabilities and options the Allies—or an

Alliance-endorsed coalition of the willing—might rely on would be but one of many challenges in planning, organizing, and conducting operations against WMD-armed regional powers.[183]

PRACTICAL LIMITS AND RISKS

Despite the disappearance of the Soviet threat in East-Central Europe, the Western Allies still have enormous incentives to work together and maintain some congruence in their approach to their common security concerns—particularly in Central and Eastern Europe and the former Soviet Union. It is generally agreed throughout the Atlantic Alliance that too much is at stake, and not only in terms of security against coercion or aggression, to permit disagreements over specific crisis-management contingencies to endanger Alliance cohesion. The shared interests and values of the United States and its European allies are so important to these nations that the Atlantic Alliance will probably be maintained and successfully adapted to new requirements. However, much will depend on internal politics within each country, notably the United States, about dealing with specific crisis-management contingencies as they arise.

The process of Alliance adaptation might be facilitated if the Allies recognize the practical limits and risks associated with two widespread notions: the assertion that "security is indivisible" in the Euro-Atlantic region, and the assumption that the approval of a quasi-universal international organization is necessary to legitimize an intervention by NATO in support of international security.

The assertion that "security is indivisible" in the Euro-Atlantic region

It should be acknowledged that the frequently asserted indivisibility of security in the Euro-Atlantic region is politically unsustainable, save as a vague aspiration. Such an assertion is inconsistent with historical experience and too distant from likely circumstances and political-military requirements to be upheld in practice. Moreover, collective security pledges about the "indivisible" nature of peace and security in the Euro-Atlantic region may create unrealistic expectations and hinder clear thinking about Alliance interests and priorities. The conflicts in the former Yugoslavia, the Caucasus, and Central Asia strike many North Americans and West Europeans—to the extent that they are aware of them—as rooted in complex, intractable, age-old ethnic antipathies that are not amenable to resolution at any reasonable cost by outsiders. Clearly, NATO governments have been reluctant to intervene on an Alliance basis in most of the conflicts in the Euro-Atlantic region since the end of the Cold War. Bosnia has been the great exception, and whether additional exceptions will follow may depend principally on the fate of the Dayton Accords.

The improbable sustainability of the "security is indivisible" principle has been most evident with regard to the conflicts in and among states of the former Soviet empire. The typical reaction has been to question their relevance to U.S. and Allied security interests. In a 1992 editorial, the *New York Times* criticized Democratic presidential candidate Bill Clinton for speaking of "new threats" in the form of ethnic conflicts in the former Soviet Union "which could spill across borders." In the words of the editorial, "These ethnic turf battles are serious. But how exactly do they threaten America?"[184]

Raising such questions is not consistent with "security is indivisible" rhetoric, but they do call attention to the way in which attempts to build Kantian or Wilsonian "collective security" frameworks have broken down throughout history. In practice, governments reason and act as if security *is* divisible. As Inis Claude has pointed out, the de facto policy of the United States and other powers is one of "selective antiaggression."[185] National leaders normally make choices on a pragmatic basis and prefer to limit the obligations that could result in war. In 1991, then U.S. secretary of defense Dick Cheney commented as follows regarding the Gulf War: "I think caution is in order. . . . This happens to be one of those times when it is justified to . . . send American forces into combat to achieve important national objectives. But they are very rare. Just because we do it successfully this once, it doesn't mean we should therefore assume that it's something we ought to fall back on automatically as the easy answer to international problems in the future. We have to remember that we don't have a dog in every fight, that we don't want to get involved in every single conflict. . . ."[186]

Historical precedents suggest that Kantian or Wilsonian collective security pledges to "peace is indivisible" principles (or to binding legal instruments, such as the League of Nations Covenant) tend to break down when states consider whether their national interests are, in fact, at stake. Despite the communiqué rhetoric paying tribute to Kantian and Wilsonian ideals, the version of collective security given currency by the Allies and their Partners foresees only coalitions of the willing as an enforcement mechanism. This amounts to a rather half-hearted substitute for the universal obligation to act in a Kantian- or Wilsonian-style collective security system. Yet it has the merit of reflecting the case-by-case attitude of the Allied and Partner governments with regard to specific contingencies. The Alliance's approach to collective security is not likely in practice to go beyond certain limits, as historical experience suggests.

Crisis management and peace operations in post–Cold War Europe are comparable to nineteenth-century interventions in that it is unthinkable to consider conducting them against one of the major powers. Such operations are feasible only against small powers, generally with the actual or tacit consent of most or all of the major powers. It is noteworthy in this regard that the Contact Group on settling the Bosnia conflict has consisted of the Quad plus Russia (and since 1996, Italy). Similarly, while the Bosnia settlement (the Dayton agreement) was negotiated in the United States, specific events were scheduled in national capitals to highlight the contribution of the other Quad countries. As NATO defense ministers noted in November 1995, "We look forward to the London Peace Implementation Conference, the signing of the Dayton agreement at the Paris Conference, and the Bonn Conference on Arms Control Issues."[187]

In a long-term historical perspective, one might argue that "crisis management and peace operations" is the current formula for what would have simply been called "intervention" in the nineteenth century—intervention by a coalition of the willing undertaken with the approval of a consensus of many, if not all, of the leading powers in Europe. According to Martin Wight's analysis of the balance-of-power propositions widely observed by the nineteenth-century Concert of Europe, one of the main principles was that states "had a duty, as well as a common interest, to co-operate in averting dangers to the international order." This duty and interest encompassed "a right of intervention" in the domestic affairs of any state threatening the balance of power.[188]

Beginning in the late eighteenth century, however, support grew for what Kant and other Enlightenment philosophers deemed a more attractive approach to international order—a harmonious international community, based on principles such as representative government, self-determination, and the repudiation of balance-of-power politics. World War I appeared to be the ultimate proof of the dangers inherent in balance-of-power politics, and the League of Nations was intended as a way to establish a better system, founded on comprehensive collective security pledges of shared responsibility for the safety of other states.

The comprehensive commitments to upholding international peace and security in the League of Nations Covenant broke down, however, because states would only intervene insofar as they believed their interests were genuinely engaged. The major powers in particular did not rely on or honor general "peace is indivisible" ideals. As Martin Wight has observed, "behind the façade of the League" could be discerned "a continuation of the old system of the Concert of Europe, whereby the great powers settled matters by private bargains among themselves at the expense of small powers. . . . [T]he method throughout was the same—the great powers acting as a directorate. This is the system of power politics that the League of Nations was designed to supersede, but failed to do."[189]

The same pattern has prevailed in the involvement of the NATO Allies and other states and institutions in the Yugoslav conflict. In this case, the small states that have had to struggle and settle for what they can get (in combat and in efforts to influence the policies and commitments of the major powers) are the successor states of the former Yugoslavia.

The assumption that UN or OSCE approval is necessary before a NATO intervention

The Allies have repeatedly offered, in the words of the January 1994 summit declaration, "to support, on a case by case basis in accordance with our own procedures, peacekeeping and other operations under the authority of the UN Security Council or the responsibility of the CSCE."[190] In the foreseeable future, most (if not all) NATO governments are likely to prefer to act under an authorizing and legitimizing mandate from an organization such as the UN or the OSCE—a body that is virtually universal on a global or regional basis.

What the Allies would prefer on the basis of political desirability, however, may not be legally necessary or strategically prudent in all cases. The assumption that a UN Security Council or OSCE mandate is required to legitimize Alliance action in support of collective security raises problematic issues on two grounds: in terms of the specific character of the legitimizing body, and in terms of the risks it presents for international security.

With regard to the specific character of the legitimizing body, the issue in practice concerns only the UN Security Council. There have been no examples of armed interventions or peace enforcement operations under the OSCE's responsibility, and such examples are not likely to arise. The most severe penalty the OSCE has been able to contemplate thus far in retaliation for aggression by a member-state against another OSCE member is suspension, a penalty applied only once so far—against Yugoslavia in 1992.[191]

Although since 1992 NATO has regularly invoked the hypothetical option of an operation under a CSCE or OSCE mandate, such a mandate might well depend on UN Security Council approval. In June 1992, as noted earlier, NATO foreign ministers announced the Alliance's readiness to support peacekeeping on a case-by-case basis under CSCE responsibility. In July 1992, the CSCE heads of state or government declared that "the CSCE is a regional arrangement in the sense of Chapter VIII of the Charter of the United Nations" and that "The rights and responsibilities of the Security Council remain unaffected in their entirety."[192] According to Article 53 of the UN Charter (part of Chapter VIII), "no enforcement action shall be taken under regional arrangements or by regional agencies without the authorization of the Security Council." In these circumstances, it is not surprising that there have been no examples of an Alliance peacekeeping or crisis management intervention under OSCE auspices; it is less circuitous to work directly with the Security Council. However, in part because terms such as "enforcement action," "peacekeeping," and "peacemaking" have not yet received authoritative and generally accepted definitions and are subject to diverse interpretations, the possibility cannot be ruled out that someday the OSCE will mandate NATO to perform an operation in support of collective security (for example, monitoring a cease-fire or a border settlement) that would not involve the use of force and that would not require UN Security Council authorization.

Whether the Alliance should always depend on the OSCE and the Security Council as sources of legitimacy for intervention in support of collective security may become contentious. Some Allies, notably the United States, have pointed out that, while the Alliance has repeatedly expressed its willingness "to support, on a case by case basis in accordance with our own procedures, peacekeeping and other operations under the authority of the UN Security Council or the responsibility of the CSCE,"[193] this is not equivalent to saying that Security Council or OSCE approval is required for NATO action in support of collective security.[194] Other Allies, France in particular, contend that the Alliance's references to "its new missions of peacekeeping under the authority of the UN or the responsibility of the OSCE"[195] have established a principle that non–Article 5 interventions by the Alliance should be limited to actions mandated by the Security Council or the OSCE.

Given the views of some other Allies, it probably would be politically difficult to break with this principle, particularly in a context of deepening NATO-Russia dialogue and cooperation. (Russia has a veto in the Security Council and a virtual veto in the OSCE; and OSCE action, as noted earlier, depends in crucial cases on Security Council approval.) Depending on the circumstances of the particular contingency, an attempt to act without such a mandate might not get under way, given the strong support of Germany and other Allied countries, including Canada, for the regularly reiterated principle of seeking such a mandate.

The arguments against what some observers have termed "NATO issuing its own mandate" include the risk of alienating Russia and China as permanent members of the Security Council and thereby undermining prospects for obtaining their cooperation in other matters affecting international peace and security, and the risk of provoking political objections throughout the world and legitimizing opposition to NATO's actions (because of the Alliance's failure to obtain Security Council authorization). Some French observers have also presented a "bad example" argument—that is, acknowledging that NATO could act in support of collective security without benefit of a Security Council mandate would establish a precedent for China, India, Nigeria, Russia, and others to assert non–UN-mandated "peacekeeping" as a rationale for interventions abroad. Russia has already sought to legitimize some of its interventions in other former Soviet republics by advancing such a "peacekeeping" rationale.

The disadvantages of insisting on a Security Council or OSCE mandate may become increasingly evident, however. Relying on these bodies for a mandate could hamper the Alliance's ability to act in cases in which the gravity of the injustice and the magnitude of the threat to Allied interests demand immediate action. Both the Security Council and the OSCE are subject to political immobilization. Consensus among the five permanent members of the Security Council cannot (and should not) be taken for granted, and the Allies may not wish to be obliged to obtain Russian and Chinese permission to act. In some circumstances, therefore, the only available means of pursuing collective security might be outside the framework of a formal organization nominally dedicated to that purpose.

Traditionally, individual Allies have seen no need for Security Council or OSCE permission to undertake certain types of actions that would be called non–Article 5 missions in NATO parlance (for instance, humanitarian relief, search-and-rescue, and the evacuation of noncombatants), and why the Allies acting collectively would need it is unclear. Non–Article 5 operations such as peacekeeping are more controversial, however. While all the Allies (including the United States) would clearly prefer to undertake such operations under a Security Council or OSCE mandate, if it could be obtained, they have been unable to agree so far as to whether such a mandate is legally or politically indispensable in every case. One hypothetical possibility is a NATO-led peacekeeping operation under an agreement of all of the states involved—for instance, all of the former belligerents seeking to resolve their differences, and all of the external states providing forces to observe and support implementation of the settlement, with the operation carried out on the basis of the sovereign rights of the states in question, and without the benefit of a Security Council or OSCE mandate.[196]

If some of the Allies—such as Canada or Germany—were unwilling to act without such a mandate, other Allies might well form a coalition for action without its being an Alliance operation. As a general rule, if a government or coalition considers that its core security interests are affected, it will have only a limited amount of patience with the proposition that it must receive an explicit authorization from the "international community" to defend those interests. This will be the case even if the government or coalition in question is not the direct and immediate object of aggression and has not concluded a formal treaty of alliance with the victim of aggression. Article 51 of the UN Charter (the inherent right of individual and collective self-defense) would then take precedence over the general preference for a UN Security Council or OSCE mandate for action; an appeal to collective defense would justify action taken in support of the general collective security principle that aggression must be resisted. The rights of the NATO Allies to act under Article 51 of the UN Charter obviously are not limited to their own self-defense (the contingency specified in Article 5 of the North Atlantic Treaty), in that Allies may individually or collectively come to the aid of a threatened third party at its request, deploying forces in a preventive fashion or protecting it in combat, even in the absence of a formal mutual-defense treaty.

Some prominent observers have suggested strengthening the OSCE by endowing it with a high-level decision-making authority—an OSCE "security committee." In 1996, William Odom suggested that such a committee's members might be "Russia, Ukraine, Germany, France, Britain, and the U.S., and even perhaps Italy. The committee should have the power to act militarily to maintain peace in Europe when a consensus to do so exists among the members of this security committee."[197] One year later, Henry Kissinger suggested that a major-power grouping within the OSCE might "be composed of the five powers that negotiated German unification plus Italy and a rotating European member."[198] Neither version of the proposal has much chance of being approved by the members of the OSCE not selected for membership on the security committee. If such a body were established, it would presumably encounter difficulties similar to those in the UN Security Council, including the political use of veto power.

With regard to the Security Council, Michael Rühle has called attention to

> the danger of establishing a precedent whereby NATO could only act under a UN mandate. Such a development would make NATO's crisis management contributions hostage to the UN Security Council (UNSC), that is to the domestic evolution of Russia or China. In light of the not so low probability of a return of the UNSC to its former stalemate [that is, during the Cold War], it is essential not to foreclose the option of NATO acting independently under the UN Charter's right to assist other

states spelled out in Article 51. . . . Such an independent NATO option seems even more legitimate as there is a clear difference in quality between NATO and [the] UN as concerns [the] democratic legitimacy of the governments involved. . . . Given the tendency to establish the legal norm of "humanitarian intervention," it would seem almost grotesque if an Alliance of 16 democracies would be prevented from providing assistance to a threatened state or even an ethnic community, simply because a non-democratic member of the UNSC vetoes it.[199]

Similar views have been expressed by Willem Van Eekelen, a former secretary-general of the Western European Union. In Van Eekelen's words, "In the Kuwaiti crisis, the U.S. would have based its action on Art. 51 if it had not succeeded in obtaining an enabling resolution from the Security Council. Equally France would have invoked this article if pressed to justify its intervention in Rwanda in 1994."[200] As these judgments suggest, governments may decide to act, without having been directly attacked, in defense of national or collective interests—and sometimes in a preventive fashion. Threats do not always fall into tidy compartments. Just as a non–Article 5 case could become an Article 5 contingency, preventive collective defense could serve general collective security purposes, even in the absence of a formal Security Council blessing.

The Allies have not yet reached a consensus on how to define the parameters of their future collective actions, functionally or geographically, or with respect to the necessity (or simply the desirability) of Security Council or OSCE mandates for interventions in support of collective security. They may conclude that the most prudent course in this regard is simply to restate previous communiqué language, because it may permit some flexibility in interpretation to act on specific contingencies. After all, the North Atlantic Council as a whole, including each of the Allies, must agree for any non–Article 5 action to be a NATO operation. Another solution might be to note that all NATO operations must have an appropriate legal basis, in conformity with the principles of the UN Charter and international law. Whether the Allies would choose to act collectively for non–Article 5 purposes such as peacekeeping or peace enforcement if the major-power consensus signified by Security Council or OSCE mandates were unavailable would probably involve political and strategic judgments in particular cases as well as international legal principles. As suggested earlier, sometimes the only way to honor and uphold collective security principles might be outside an inclusive international organization, global or regional, ostensibly devoted to such principles.

According to Article 51 of the UN Charter, "Nothing in the present Charter shall impair the inherent right of individual or collective self-defense if an armed attack occurs against a Member of the United Nations, until the Security Council has taken the measures necessary to maintain international peace and security." It could therefore be argued that, in the absence of effective Security Council action, a state or a coalition of states under attack is legally entitled to take defensive action and to seek assistance from anyone willing to provide it, including NATO. The tendency in NATO European governments in recent years, however, has been to argue that crisis-management interventions and other non–Article 5 operations must be authorized by the UN Security Council, because they involve not the direct self-defense of the Allies but the security of states external to the Alliance. The prudence of this attitude is debatable, in view of the risks highlighted by Rühle, Van Eekelen, and others.

The relative ease with which the Alliance has obtained Security Council approval for the crisis management and peace operations that it has undertaken since 1992, it should be recalled, has been an aberration in comparison with the pattern that prevailed during most of the period since the founding of the United Nations in 1945. During the Cold War, it was taken for granted that the Security Council was, in Martin Wight's phrase, "a schizophrenic paralytic. Since the Security Council requires the unanimity of the great powers for action, it has scarcely ever acted."[201]

Immediately after the 1990–91 Gulf War, it was widely agreed that, as Admiral Jonathan Howe put it, "future challenges cannot be guaranteed to have such unambiguous political origins, nor are future transgressors of international standards likely to engage in such palpably repellent behavior. Therefore, a mandate for counteraction from the United Nations . . . may be less likely. This suggests that the Alliance should not make UN sanctions or endorsements necessary conditions for actions in defense of its interests."[202]

In subsequent years, however, Britain, France, and the United States—the Allies that are also permanent members of the UN Security

Council—have dealt with a Russian government that seeks to maintain reasonably positive economic and political relations with the West, and a Chinese government uninterested in exercising a veto regarding matters distant from its immediate geographical area. This situation may stem from exceptional circumstances, and it probably will not continue indefinitely. If a new Russian regime opposed crisis management and peace operations that the Alliance deemed necessary and appropriate, the current view of some Allies—that UN Security Council or OSCE approval is necessary—might yield to more imperative necessities.

The widespread assumption that the power to authorize a legitimate intervention by the Alliance resides solely with the OSCE or the UN Security Council amounts to ceding a *droit de regard* to Russia and/or China—and possibly to other governments if the number of permanent members in the UN Security Council increases—over NATO's future ability to contribute to international security. Russian or Chinese interests may conflict with those of the Alliance. Depending on Moscow and Beijing to endorse NATO-led crisis management and peace operations in support of collective security may therefore be imprudent, if not self-defeating.

The assumption that legitimizing authority resides solely with the UN Security Council or the OSCE presents risks for international security. In the collective security tradition, legitimate external intervention (as opposed to individual or collective self-defense) is undertaken by or on behalf of the international community. What happens, however, if the supposed voice of the international community—the UN Security Council or the OSCE—is politically immobilized and therefore incapable of upholding principles of collective security? Are states that witness an injustice or act of aggression threatening to international order thereby forbidden to take action?

As Inis Claude has pointed out, two principles of collective security may contradict each other in specific circumstances. "Respect for the principle of collectivism would impel a state to remain passive in the face of what it regarded as aggression, if no collective determination of the fact of aggression and authorization of counteraction were forthcoming. Adherence to the collective security maxim that anybody's aggression threatens everybody's stake in world order would impel a state to take action on the basis of its own judgment that aggression had occurred, even without benefit of collective legitimization."[203]

The principle confirming a state's right to take action against aggression and in support of collective security, even in the absence of an explicit authorization from a quasi-universal international organization, would seem to apply to the Alliance as well. In some circumstances, the only available means of pursuing collective security may be outside the framework of a formal organization nominally committed to that purpose. In Claude's words, "Wilsonian collectivism has been given expression in the function of collective legitimization assigned to the United Nations but . . . too literal and strict adherence to the idea that national policy should be constrained by the requirement of collective approbation may defeat the application of Wilson's most fundamental principle, that aggression must be opposed if world order is to be maintained."[204]

IMPLICATIONS FOR ALLIANCE COHESION AND COLLECTIVE DEFENSE

The complex relationship between collective defense and crisis management and peace operations

The new focus on non–Article 5 activities, including crisis management and peace operations in support of collective security, could have ambivalent effects on the Alliance's collective defense posture. The new focus could erode that posture in at least three ways. First, except for short-duration humanitarian actions (such as evacuating noncombatants and assisting in civil emergency disaster relief), these operations present problems of a more immediate and more politically controversial nature than maintaining a deterrence posture vis-à-vis the Soviet Union during the Cold War. As during the conflict in the former Yugoslavia, occasions for intra-Alliance discord could arise more frequently, and could undermine the cohesion necessary for the ultimately more vital purpose of collective defense.[205] According to Holger Mey, a prominent German expert in security affairs,

> It is more than questionable whether alliance solidarity can be built on ten years of joint peacekeeping experience. There are likely to be numerous quarrels within NATO about whether it is worth risking the lives of a nation's soldiers to quell century-old civil wars and ethnic conflicts in Central Asia or somewhere else. . . . To put peacekeeping missions at the very center of NATO's search for roles and missions

would not be without risks for the Alliance's cohesion. . . . Engaging in crisis management in conflicts that do not pose an existential threat and which only peripherally touch the vital interests of the alliance's members could undermine NATO's unity.[206]

Second, these operations may require capabilities, equipment, training, rules of engagement, and command structures distinct from those designed and optimized for collective defense and high-intensity combat. Troops engaged in peace operations, for example, spend less time in armored vehicles and are often "dismounted" to deal with local populations. Peace operations are not simply a "lesser included case" for forces prepared for high-intensity combat and thus for effective deterrence of aggression or coercion. Defense resources are finite, and have in fact been shrinking in most NATO countries (with the main exceptions of Greece and Turkey) since the mid-1980s.[207] Maintaining IFOR and SFOR in Bosnia, training for peace operations, and conducting exercises with PfP Partners oriented toward such operations mean that the Allies have been dedicating even fewer resources to collective defense. Some officers and experts in the Alliance have expressed concern about the extent to which combat capabilities have been eroded. NATO governments, however, have chosen to invest in PfP, in view of the value of promoting cooperation with Partners and the reduced probability of a large-scale Article 5 (collective defense) contingency.

Third, the organization of effective coalitions of the willing may become more difficult, if and when Allies judge that the crises at hand are not central enough to national security interests to justify the risks and costs involved. The promises implicit in general "security is indivisible" pledges therefore probably will not be honored in all cases with actual force commitments, as opposed to expressions of concern and regret. In some cases, a policy of nonintervention may be adopted out of myopia or indifference to the consequences. In other cases, nonintervention may be favored because of an expectation that it will lead to the triumph of specific belligerents—just as intervention is undertaken to promote a preferred outcome. As the French diplomat Talleyrand said, "non-intervention is a term of political metaphysics signifying almost the same thing as intervention."[208]

The failure to satisfy expectations and honor vague pledges could lead to recriminations and an erosion of Alliance cohesion. Collective inaction despite vague declarations of commitment could also undermine the credibility of the ultimately more important Article 5 collective defense pledges. Conversely, however improbable, comprehensive efforts to meet the obligations implicit in these pledges could cause disillusionment and frustration in major Alliance nations, such as the United States. Politicians could begin to question why such diffuse commitments to every country in the Euro-Atlantic region had been offered, and to demand even greater selectivity in agreeing to participate in specific crisis-management and peace operations. NATO enlargement, however, could create a greater penumbra of implicit responsibility for the Alliance in areas adjoining the territory of the new Allies.

Crisis-management and peace operations could nonetheless complement collective defense in some ways. In the absence of a unifying existential threat, such as the Soviet Union once presented, an exclusive focus on collective defense could lead to the Alliance's atrophy. Collective security activities—exercises and actual operations—help to keep the Alliance and its collective defense potential in place. Successful crisis management and peace operations, moreover, could lessen the chances that conflict or aggression in a limited contingency would become an Article 5 (collective defense) threat to an Ally. An intervention justified with reference to collective security responsibilities could serve national and Alliance security by upholding general principles such as the inadmissibility of aggression and by enhancing the credibility of the Alliance's declared will to undertake collective action.

Given the demands of public opinion in Western societies—notably in the United States—for avoiding casualties in military operations, particularly in "optional" crisis management and peace operations, the Alliance needs to maintain capabilities adequate to perform such operations with minimal risks. The political sustainability of non–Article 5 operations largely depends on reducing casualty risks to low levels, and this requires an ability to dominate the field in any contingencies that may arise. In other words, the practical and political factors involved in crisis management and peace operations justify the maintenance of a substantial conventional military posture even in a strategic context in which large-scale collective defense contingencies appear remote. Moreover, reinforcement from the Alliance's historical central region (that is, Germany and the Benelux countries) to support existing Allies such as Greece, Italy, Norway, Spain, and Turkey (and also prospective new allies such as Hungary, Poland, and the Czech Republic) in collective defense would require many of the same logistical capabilities needed for non–Article 5 missions beyond NATO territory.

The Alliance has upheld the principle that the same institutional mechanisms, such as CJTF and the defense planning system, are to be used for both Article 5 and non–Article 5 operations, even though participation by Allies in the latter is optional. At the same time, the Alliance has invited PfP Partners to contribute to several of these mechanisms, even though Partners are eligible to participate only in non–Article 5 operations—and even then, at the invitation of the Alliance. The practical result of these arrangements has been to bring the more active Partners into contact with some elements of the Alliance's defense planning process, notably through the Planning and Review Process (PARP). The intention is to make the capabilities, procedures, and equipment of the participating Partners more interoperable with those of the Allies and better suited to prospective NATO-led non–Article 5 operations, including crisis management.

In this fashion, some observers hypothesize, a measure of collective defense protection may be "projected outwards" to countries that are not Allies—despite the fact that NATO's formal commitment is limited to an Article 4–like consultation pledge. This could be viewed as an advantage for the Alliance to the extent that it promotes stability and lessens the threat of aggression and conflict—and as a disadvantage, in that it could mean incurring additional obligations and entanglements.

One of the Alliance's rationales for undertaking non–Article 5 tasks such as crisis management and peace operations has been to lessen the risk that Article 5 contingencies might arise: lower-risk and lower-cost collective security missions may help the Allies avoid mounting higher-risk and higher-cost collective defense operations. However, one of the reasons the Alliance has decided to retain a "single military system" for both types of operations is that the distinction between the two may be less than watertight in practice.[209] A non–Article 5 operation, for instance, could escalate into an Article 5 conflict if an external power chose to intervene in a civil war being contained by a NATO-led peacekeeping operation.

During the 1992–95 phase of the Yugoslav conflict, for example, Russia might have chosen to intervene in support of Serbia.[210] In this hypothetical case, combat might have taken place outside Alliance territory between Russian forces and those of the principal NATO Allies contributing to UNPROFOR (above all, British and French troops). If UNPROFOR troops had come under attack, would the other Allies have interpreted this as a case involving the Article 5 mutual-defense commitment? Even though the attack would have taken place within the general framework of a NATO-supported operation (including embargo and no-fly-zone enforcement), the response might not have been automatically affirmative. The Allies not participating in UNPROFOR probably would have considered various factors, including the imperative need to maintain the Alliance's cohesion and credibility, the prospects for limiting the conflict, and the larger implications of a struggle that might have become a general war. The origins and course of the conflict might have added up to an Article 5 contingency unlike the threat of Soviet-led aggression that was feared during the Cold War.

Rob de Wijk has written that "It is important that a distinction is no longer made between capabilities and structures for collective defense and those for operations outside the treaty area. Both cases involve limited regional conflicts which might possibly escalate. In today's world the distinction between Article 5 and non–Article 5 is militarily irrelevant. The distinction is politically and judicially relevant because it has a bearing on the degree of obligation of member states to assist each other."[211]

The obligation questions are complex, however. The risk that a non–Article 5 intervention could become an Article 5 challenge raises several unresolved questions. How, for example, would the Alliance and its PfP Partners respond if a crisis that was supposed to be managed by a NATO-endorsed coalition of the willing turned into an Article 5 contingency? In all likelihood, the Alliance would have continuing political responsibilities for the security of the forces provided by participating Partners and operating under the NATO umbrella, and it might well accept Partner contributions in dealing with the threat. The prevailing tendency has been to involve many of the Partners in defense planning activities while trying to maintain the distinction between Article 5 and non–Article 5 contingencies in terms of eligibility for participation in actual operations.

A crisis beyond NATO territory could rapidly and unexpectedly affect NATO territory or core defense interests, raising operational and political issues that have too often been dismissed as hypothetical. As some European observers have noted, Allies that were not members of a NATO-endorsed coalition of the willing undertaking a non–Article 5 operation might suddenly find themselves drawn into a war, depending on their interpretation of the Article 5 mutual-defense commitment, at least within the geographical zone specified by Article 6. Some French observers consider this risk an argument in favor of seeking, or even requiring, a Security Council mandate for any non–Article 5 operation involving the use of force.

Escalatory risks of this nature constitute an argument for not overstating the differences in the operational requirements placed on peacekeepers and combat troops. Disciplined and experienced combat forces are accustomed to respecting rules of engagement, and can adapt to the specific requirements of peacekeeping. In the particularly demanding case of Bosnia, in which the Alliance has had to impose and maintain peace, equipment initially acquired with a view to collective defense has proven useful. The potential long-term problem of NATO forces becoming increasingly equipped mainly for peace support operations—and, hence, ill-suited for collective defense—has been acknowledged and contained to date.

In 1996, for example, the British defense white paper underscored the need to be prepared for the risk that a non–Article 5 mission could turn into a more demanding situation calling for collective defense:

> Operations in the former Yugoslavia have shown the ability of capable, all-round forces in theatre to respond should the operation in which they are engaged change in nature, and in particular should it escalate, whether through misjudgment or deliberate intent. They have also shown the value of having ready and demonstrable access to combat capabilities for self-defense and for use, if necessary, as a demonstration of resolve and in order to deter escalation by those opposed to our presence. We do not therefore intend to create forces with only limited capabilities and training, for example for peacekeeping operations.[212]

The changing nature of collective defense

In contrast with the Cold War, when the main planning contingency was a massive Soviet-led Warsaw Pact assault against NATO as a whole, future collective defense contingencies might involve aggression by a "rogue" state, perhaps in North Africa or the Middle East, against only a single NATO Ally. A limited, subregional collective defense contingency could present problems for Alliance cohesion and decision making greater than those foreseen during the Cold War. It might be a challenge to convince some Allies that the crisis should indeed be regarded as an Article 5 case, and that their obligations under that article should be honored. The sense of a commonality of interest has declined with the disappearance of the unifying threat represented by the Soviet empire.

Since 1991, when the Alliance established the ARRC (the Allied Command Europe Rapid Reaction Corps) and articulated a new Strategic Concept, NATO's planning has recognized the increased improbability of Cold War–style contingencies, such as a Moscow-directed multi-theater offensive to be countered by in-place Alliance forces. For several years, therefore, the emphasis has been on enhanced mobility and flexibility —force attributes that also lend credibility to the reinforcement strategy for honoring collective defense commitments to new Allies in Central and Eastern Europe. Generic subregional contingencies have become the main focus for conventional force planning, rather than a "linear threat" against a particular sector, such as the kind the Warsaw Pact once posed along the inter-German border. As noted in chapter 2, the 1996 British defense white paper referred to two types of contingencies involving the Alliance mutual-defense pledge: "A limited regional conflict involving a NATO Ally who calls for assistance under Article 5 of the Washington Treaty" and "General War—a large scale attack against NATO."[213]

Limited regional contingencies may pose greater challenges for Alliance cohesion than planning for the Cold War case—a Europe-wide (and intercontinental) Soviet offensive. Some observers hypothesize that in an enlarged Alliance it may become more difficult to gain and maintain an acceptance of responsibility for the defense of others, particularly for new Allies contemplating contingencies located far from their traditional area of political-military activity and cultural identification.

For instance, some observers have asked, will the Poles feel responsible for the defense of Turkey? If Syria or Iraq attacked Turkey, would Hungarians ask, "What is that to us?" The fragmentation of the Alliance may be increasingly hard to resist in limited, subregional collective defense contingencies, to say nothing of "optional" non–Article 5 cases involving crisis management and peace operations.

Experiences during the 1990–91 Gulf War suggest that genuine Alliance cohesion problems could arise in subregional collective defense contingencies. For example, despite initial reluctance Germany sent an AlphaJet squadron to Turkey in January 1991 as part of an Allied Command Europe Mobile Force reinforcement intended to signal NATO's commitment to the defense of Turkey; German air defense units followed the next month. The German government's hesitation stemmed from concern about Soviet reactions (Moscow had yet to ratify the treaty on German unification and other accords) and, above all, domestic reactions. As Karl Kaiser and Klaus Becher have noted,

> Virtually all leaders and experts in the SPD [the Social Democratic Party], as well as some representatives of the governing coalition parties, stated that by allowing U.S. planes to operate against Iraq from Turkish bases, Turkey had provoked Iraq. Therefore a possible Iraqi attack, or "retaliation," against Turkey could not lead to the discharge of German obligations to assist in the defense of Turkey under Article 5 of the North Atlantic Treaty. In the words of opposition leader Hans-Jochen Vogel, otherwise NATO would be turned into an alliance for the support of offensive operations *(Angriffsoperationen)*. . . . Those who rejected German support in the hypothetical case of a so-called "provoked NATO obligation" *(provozierter Bündisfall),* even under conditions of a UN mandate, increasingly appeared to run away from any German political or moral obligation whatsoever, let alone political debt. In fact, Germany was only asked to grant a small fraction of the support which it had itself received over four decades and to which it owed its freedom and its prosperity, as well as its recent unification.[214]

Some observers contend that NATO governments are likely to regard definitions of concepts such as "collective defense" and "collective security" with a view to maintaining considerable political and scenario-dependent flexibility. Governments determined to act, some observers argue, will not worry about whether the action required should be defined as non–Article 5 (collective security) or Article 5 (collective defense). From this perspective, even an action to defend an interest distant from NATO territory (in the Gulf or in the Caspian Sea region) might be defined as "collective defense" by some Allies. That all the Allies would sign on for such a flexible approach to these definitions and feel bound to act as if another Gulf War were an Article 5 contingency is a doubtful proposition. Problems for Alliance cohesion and effectiveness could be raised not only by Allies determined to act and seeking an appropriate rationale to do so, but also by Allies that would prefer other forms of action or none at all.

Allies might well consider it an Article 5 case if armed attacks took place on the territory or aircraft or ships (extensions of sovereign territory) of Allies within or above the area specified by Article 6 of the North Atlantic Treaty (Allied territories and jurisdictions, including islands, in Europe, Turkey, and North America, as well as the Mediterranean Sea and the North Atlantic north of the Tropic of Cancer). However, it is less clear whether attacks on Allied forces engaged in a non–Article 5 operation beyond NATO's treaty-specified area of geographical responsibility would be interpreted as Article 5 contingencies.

Allied officials have expressed the hope and the conviction that "forward engagement"—cooperation with former adversaries and other non-NATO countries, as well as selective crisis management and peace operations—may serve as "collective defense by other means." In other words, NATO's active involvement in shaping the security environment may promote stability by reassuring PfP Partners and maintaining capabilities for timely action, whether the challenge calls for collective defense or an intervention in support of collective security. As U.S. Navy Admiral T. Joseph Lopez, commander-in-chief of Allied Forces Southern Europe (AFSOUTH), recently observed,

> NATO's great advantage is the continuing presence of effective military headquarters and forces in this volatile region. . . . The best prevention of the awful cost of war is a robust, credible military posture that is forward-deployed and forward-engaged to confront a crisis in its earliest stage at its source before it grows into generalized conflict. To prevent the Bosnias of the future, the NATO alliance conducts a strategy of cooperation and dialogue. . . . Forward-engaged military forces such as NATO's in the southern region offer political leaders the kind of flexibility and options that make it possible to deal with unstable situations early, before they mushroom.[215]

5

Prospects and Challenges

The main challenges before the Alliance include managing the ongoing process of internal adaptation in light of NATO's probable expansion and trying to grapple with the continuing political and economic turmoil and the threat of more serious episodes of armed conflict in parts of the Balkans, Central and Eastern Europe, and the former Soviet Union. Likely disagreements over specific future demands for NATO involvement in crisis management and peace operations, and the tension between sustaining the Alliance's core function of "collective defense" and its new "collective security" roles, mean that Alliance cohesion may become more difficult to maintain.

NATO originated as, and remains, a collective defense organization, but it is increasingly being used to perform collective security functions in the major-power-consensus sense of the term. What are the implications of the adjustment in focus and the assumption of new functions? What functions are politically sustainable in the long term? In short, what is NATO for in the post–Cold War era?

Collective defense means maintaining the Alliance's political cohesion and military capabilities to deter coercion and aggression and, if necessary, to conduct military operations to restore the security and integrity of the territory protected by the Alliance's commitments. Collective security concepts call upon aspirations for universally shared responsibility for peace and international order, and, as noted in the Introduction, such concepts have a long history. In December 1994, Warren

Christopher, then the U.S. secretary of state, referred to some of that history in articulating an ambition for the Alliance: "We must build a security community of all democratic nations in the Euro-Atlantic region—one that endures where the Congress of Vienna, the Concert of Europe, and Versailles ultimately failed, and one that builds on the strength of our post-war success in Western Europe."[1]

Despite Christopher's subtle allusion to the League of Nations (part of the Treaty of Versailles), the Allies to date have wisely resisted calls to move toward a Kantian or Wilsonian system of collective security. Such a system would imply obligations to deal with all cases of international aggression and injustice in the Euro-Atlantic region. In practice, despite their rather sweeping "security is indivisible" rhetoric, the Allies have pursued only collective security of the major-power-consensus type, offering to act in support of collective security under the auspices of the UN Security Council or the OSCE. The major-power-consensus approach to collective security involves less grandiose ambitions and lower expectations than a Kantian or Wilsonian design, but it is much less likely to lead to disappointment. Moreover, it has the advantage of preserving the Alliance as an effective instrument of collective defense in the foreseeable future, in conjunction with its two new roles in support of collective security.

One of the central aims of the Alliance's first new role, cooperation with former adversaries and other non-Allies, is sometimes described as "security against misperception." That is, cooperation and dialogue on a multitude of topics are expected to reduce mistrust, deepen understanding of the preoccupations of others, provide for reliable and continuous communication, and promote a sense of shared responsibility for international security. The Alliance's cooperative security role also involves purposes such as preparing some countries for Alliance membership, cultivating capabilities for joint action in crisis management and peace operations, and promoting economic reform and democratization, including civilian control of the military.

One of the key purposes of the second new role—preparing for (and conducting) crisis management and peace operations such as IFOR/SFOR in Bosnia—might ultimately be characterized as "security against an extension of war beyond manageable limits." From this perspective, an essential objective is the containment of conflicts that might otherwise lead to confrontations and possibly war between major powers in Europe or spill over into a direct (Article 5) threat to a NATO Ally. Another purpose of such operations, however, might be intervening beyond NATO territory to guard the political, strategic, and economic interests of the Alliance as a whole, or of a coalition of the willing, on the basis of international legal mandates or the approval of the major powers. (The Allies are still undecided, though, as to whether they would be willing to act in support of collective security in the absence of a UN Security Council or OSCE mandate.)

A number of observers on both sides of the Atlantic are concerned that the Alliance may be taking on too many new roles, thereby creating expectations that cannot be satisfied. They argue that NATO may suffer from a loss of focus and a dispersion of effort as it takes on all these activities, leading some to quip (and not entirely in jest) that NATO may increasingly suffer from a "multiple personalities disorder."

One of the fundamental risks is that the new roles may weaken the Alliance's cohesion and undermine its ability to carry out the core traditional mission of collective defense. Each of the new roles holds the potential for a divergence of interests among the NATO countries and NATO's new partners in the Partnership for Peace and other institutions.

Many of the PfP participants see the ultimate purpose of their cooperation as obtaining Article 5 collective-defense protection against Russia through membership in NATO. Pending actual membership, many would like more extensive participation in PfP and the EAPC, as well as NATO's Article 4–style commitments to consultation with PfP Partners, to be the functional equivalent of Article 5 protection, with the Alliance under a sense of moral and political obligation. It is assumed that Russia would be unable to rule out Alliance action to protect such states.

From a Kantian or Wilsonian perspective, however, NATO's collective-defense purpose can be seen as potentially contradicting the visions of the Alliance as the organizer of a harmonious and peaceful European order, encompassing almost all of the OSCE states in efforts to promote collective security throughout Europe. Some observers contend that the collective-defense objective implies continuing distrust of Russia and complicates the pursuit of cooperation with Russia.

The second new role—undertaking crisis management and peace operations—also promises to raise difficulties for Alliance cohesion.

The sharp and protracted disagreements during 1992–95 between the United States and its major European Allies over how to deal with the conflicts in the former Yugoslavia, Bosnia in particular, suggest how readily crisis management and peace operations can become objects of discord. Alliance cohesion was often difficult to maintain during the Cold War, notably during periods of détente with the USSR. How much more difficult will it be to maintain such cohesion when the challenge is not how to deal with a major external adversary, but how to contain and settle peripheral conflicts of far greater interest to a few allies than to the Alliance as a whole? The future of Bosnia and the rest of the former Yugoslavia is certain to be troubled, and several other ethnic conflicts are under way or brewing in the Balkans, in Central and Eastern Europe, and in the former Soviet Union.

If NATO is to remain relevant, the Alliance must squarely address four fundamental issues: the de facto downgrading of collective defense; the practical limits to NATO's assumption of collective security functions; the continuing central role of the United States; and the need for lucidity in pursuing a two-track policy encompassing NATO's new roles as well as its traditional collective defense function.

THE DE FACTO DOWNGRADING OF COLLECTIVE DEFENSE

Some observers have been concerned about the Alliance's apparent loss of focus on collective defense, or—as some have put it—the "relativization" of its importance. Investments, exercises, operations such as IFOR and SFOR, and revealing statements about NATO's priorities have illustrated a shift in emphasis away from an almost exclusive focus on collective defense toward more attention to collective security.

In June 1996, for example, U.S. under secretary of defense for policy Walter Slocombe said that the challenges facing NATO in the coming years "will be different from the traditional Cold War defense mission of meeting direct military attack on the territory of member states. Of course, NATO must retain its ability to meet that core task. But meeting the new kinds of challenge—all sixteen North American and European members together, and indeed, enlisting other European and non-European states, as we have done in Bosnia—is the task on which NATO adaptation must *chiefly* focus."[2] Similarly, in a December 1996 discussion of the Alliance's common-funded programs, the North Atlantic Council declared, "We note with appreciation progress made in moving existing resources to *the highest priority programs,* such as Partnership for Peace and the support of enhanced information activities in Moscow and Kyiv."[3]

In March 1997, NATO secretary general Javier Solana said that "The [July 1997] Summit will complete this internal transformation by deciding the form and the details of a new and smaller command structure, streamlined for crisis management and intervention."[4] In practice, the shift to such a command structure suggests that collective defense has been downgraded as an Alliance mission and that the operative function driving military planning and preparations has increasingly become crisis management and intervention beyond NATO's borders. President Clinton confirmed this adjustment in priorities in March 1997, when he described "working in Bosnia" as "the most important thing NATO is doing today."[5]

However, other high-level officials have reaffirmed the ultimate centrality of collective defense, sometimes in remarkable ways. In October 1997, for example, Secretary of State Madeleine Albright acknowledged in surprisingly candid terms that the Dayton Accords could ultimately fail to bring a durable peace, but pointed out that such a setback would not invalidate NATO's core mission of collective defense:

> We cannot know today if our mission in Bosnia will achieve all its goals, for that ultimately depends on the choices the Bosnian people will make. But we can say that whatever may happen, NATO's part in achieving the military goals of our mission has been a resounding success. Whatever may happen, our interest in a larger, stronger NATO will endure long after the last foreign soldier has left Bosnia. We can also say that NATO will remain the most powerful instrument we have for building effective military coalitions such as SFOR. At the same time, Bosnia does not by itself define the future of a larger NATO. NATO's fundamental purpose is collective defense against aggression. Its most important aim, if I can paraphrase Arthur Vandenberg, is to prevent wars before they start so it does not have to keep the peace after they stop.[6]

The Alliance has undertaken new roles distinct from collective defense to respond to the challenges at hand during a period in which large-scale collective defense contingencies—major threats of aggression or coercion against the Alliance—have increasingly seemed remote and improbable. The increased attention to limited subregional collective defense contingencies has complicated an assessment task—estimating the adequacy of the Alliance's collective defense posture—that involved many uncertainties during the Cold War, when the Soviet empire provided an obvious focus.

The Alliance's ability to deal with a collective defense contingency to the east has not necessarily been downgraded excessively, because the decline in Russian military capabilities has been substantial. From a Russian perspective, Moscow has lost most, if not all, of its historical glacis to the West—including the military forces and installations in the former Warsaw Pact countries of Eastern and Central Europe, as well as many of the military infrastructure assets, such as radars and airfields, in the non-Russian former Soviet republics. In view of Russia's social, economic, and demographic problems, Moscow's ability to rebuild a conventional military posture comparable to that of the Soviet Union as recently as the late 1980s is severely limited in the foreseeable future.

NATO's capacity to rise to the challenge—to regenerate and reconstitute necessary military capabilities—in the event of a political upheaval and a new military challenge from Russia has been weakened, however, particularly by the radical cutbacks in capabilities and installations since 1989–91. Many military facilities in NATO Europe have been closed permanently and some have been converted to other functions, while reserve capabilities—including trained personnel and industrial assets—have also been reduced. The key question is whether NATO leaders in future circumstances would have the political will to make use of warning time, if at some point an extensive reconstitution of the collective defense posture became necessary.

It can be argued that the Alliance's new roles represent, if not collective defense by another name, a form of security-building that might diminish the likelihood of any need to honor either collective defense or collective security commitments—if the new roles are pursued successfully, with a high level of consensus throughout the Alliance and the Euro-Atlantic region as a whole. However, the differences between these two types of commitments must be recognized, for they concern the Alliance's ultimate purposes—and whether such purposes can be accomplished.

Collective defense and collective security actions (even without a major-power consensus) can be pursued simultaneously. Collective defense investments ensure that military capabilities are available for selected operations in support of collective security if the Allies choose to undertake them. Such operations, however, remain constrained by the broader configuration of power relationships and by the limited obligations that governments are normally prepared to assume regarding the safety of others. More ambitious aspirations, for a collective security system in the Kantian or Wilsonian sense, would compete with a collective defense orientation, because these aspirations call for replacing balance of power arrangements and alliances, which are by definition exclusive, with an inclusive community in which peace and security would be truly "indivisible."[7]

The first of NATO's two new roles—cooperation with former adversaries and other non-NATO countries in the Euro-Atlantic region—has been pursued with a great deal of rhetoric drawing on the Kantian or Wilsonian variant of the collective security tradition. The cooperation has consisted principally of dialogue and exercises; in fact, despite the wide range of topics for dialogue, the exercises have almost exclusively involved crisis management and peace operations. The true test of the comprehensiveness and sincerity of the inclusive "security is indivisible" rhetoric of the Alliance and its partners in PfP and the EAPC has come not in risk-free cooperation, but in the concrete cases in which vague commitments to provide for the security of others must be honored or ignored.

The admittedly short historical record of such concrete cases shows that Alliance-led crisis management and peace operations have been pursued in accordance with the major-power-consensus variant of the collective security tradition. NATO could not intervene effectively to stop hostilities in Bosnia until the main Western powers, eventually led by the United States, finally agreed in 1995 to do so, initially with tacit Russian acquiescence, followed by Russian approval of a UN Security Council mandate, and, ultimately, Russian participation in IFOR and SFOR. The provisional settlement enforced by IFOR and SFOR under NATO leadership may last only as long as the major powers agree that containing this conflict through a quasi-imposed solution is worth the price. However, given the trends in Kosovo, Macedonia, and elsewhere in the Balkans, the combination of SFOR and PfP commitments may help to draw the Alliance into more extensive conflict-containment responsibilities.

The tendency to downgrade collective defense raises questions about the Alliance's long-term future, despite its new roles in international security. In 1958, Robert Osgood wrote, "The organization will be viable only so long as its members continue to feel the need of combining against the common threat that brought them together in the first place."[8] The common threat that led the Allies to combine has been gone since 1991, and yet (as argued in chapter 2) the Alliance has survived and, after the rough years regarding Bosnia policy in 1992–95, in some ways it has even thrived, with the successful accomplishment of new roles, and with a long list of countries eager to join.

Given the fluid circumstances at hand, NATO's future could be determined by a contest between centrifugal and centripetal forces. The centripetal forces reside in the benefits of the Alliance, the internal and external incentives to keep NATO going. The internal benefits, as suggested in chapter 2, are as follows: maintaining U.S. engagement in European security, resolving intra–West European security dilemmas, reassuring Germany's neighbors and allies, limiting the scope of nuclear proliferation in NATO Europe, promoting a certain "denationalization" of defense planning, providing a forum for the coordination of Western security policies, supplying economic benefits to all of the Allies, and encouraging and legitimizing democratic forms of government. The external benefits include the traditional function of collective defense, or security against threats of aggression or coercion as a basis for diplomacy, and the new function of using NATO as an instrument for activities in support of collective security. NATO has proven utility as a vehicle for coordinating action and supplying assets and experience, and the Allies have explicitly recognized and exploited this utility for operations in support of collective security since 1992.

The centrifugal forces consist of the factors that could erode NATO and make it seem irrelevant or, worse, a liability. Almost all of the Alliance's internal functions are byproducts of the need for collective defense first recognized in the late 1940s and sustained by the Soviet Union during the Cold War; logically, therefore, the internal functions can be sustained only if external functions, including collective defense, are still persuasive and compelling. Some observers on both sides of the Atlantic nonetheless maintain that the habits of working together have created so much mutual confidence among the Allies over the decades that the Alliance can be sustained in the absence of an over-bearing external threat such as the Soviet Union. There is no particular incentive to do away with the Alliance, these observers note, because it represents a low-cost insurance policy; and factors of habit, inertia, and tradition favor its maintenance. By this logic, NATO has become part of the constellation of major international institutions that generations of politicians, civil servants, military officers, and others accept and perpetuate as necessary and useful. Some U.S. and European observers even maintain that the Alliance has become "environment-independent," detached from the original external threats that brought it into being and capable of being sustained on the basis of the "self-justifying" benefits flowing from its internal functions as long as no crisis involving collective defense or collective security puts its effectiveness into question—a crucial caveat.[9]

Yet there are grounds to question whether and to what extent the Allies can sustain the centrality of collective defense in the absence of an overriding and substantial threat to Alliance security, such as the Soviet Union once posed. The uncertainties and risks presented by Russia in the foreseeable future are not equivalent to the unifying major Article 5 threat that the Soviet empire represented; the dynamic of fear of the Soviet threat that held NATO together during the Cold War has vanished. While the Allies have a continuing interest in hedging against uncertainty in Russia, in part because of Moscow's nuclear arsenal, other potential external risks for Alliance security may seem increasingly remote and subregional and of concern only to some Allies, and hence a subject of discord among Allies unwilling to commit resources to preparing for what seem to be improbable or secondary contingencies. Moreover, some Allies may be unwilling to assume risks and contribute forces if certain contingencies actually arise. For example, some Allies might question whether a conflict between Turkey and one of its neighbors in the Caucasus, the Middle East, or the Mediterranean should be interpreted as an Article 5 case.

The Alliance's new functions in support of collective security raise even greater questions about its long-term cohesion. In principle, participation in non–Article 5 contingencies is optional (in contrast with the obligatory nature of Article 5 commitments). This "coalitions-of-the-willing" method of dealing with non-unanimity may undermine Alliance cohesion, because the differences between the Allies may extend to conflicting preferences about the outcomes of conflicts outside NATO territory. While all the Allies have participated in IFOR and SFOR, such high levels of practical solidarity cannot be taken for granted in future operations. The Allies themselves have insisted on the voluntary nature of choices to participate in non–Article 5 operations. This implies that a pattern of "free-rider" behavior could emerge, with some Allies preferring to "hold the coats," as it were, of the Allies prepared to take greater risks by actually conducting interventions in support of collective security. Those taking the risks may resent such passivity, and this could constitute a centrifugal force.

In principle, ESDI could function as a centripetal force, because Europeans might successfully take on responsibilities such as those specified as the WEU's "Petersberg tasks" with an Alliance endorsement and practical support from the United States and other Allies. In practice, however, ESDI efforts might have centrifugal effects in various ways, because of European dependence on NATO assets and U.S. national assets that are customarily made available to the Alliance. A U.S.-European synchronization of analyses and interests may not be automatic in concrete contingencies, as opposed to the hypothetical cases examined in exercises. Institutions such as the Alliance can do no more than the member governments choose to make them do, and the governments are themselves composed of contending political forces with distinct agendas and interests.

The difficulties in organizing effective combined action underscore why there must be practical limits to undertaking tasks in support of collective security.

PRACTICAL LIMITS TO NATO'S ASSUMPTION OF COLLECTIVE SECURITY FUNCTIONS

According to NATO's 1991 Strategic Concept, "The security of all Allies is indivisible: an attack on one is an attack on all."[10] This collective defense pledge is more specific and binding than generalized affirmations that "security is indivisible" throughout the Euro-Atlantic region. The Allies have repeatedly made such affirmations since the end of the Cold War, notably in the context of the OSCE and NATO's trans-European cooperative structures, such as the PfP and the EAPC. Moreover, PfP participants benefit from an Alliance pledge to "consult with any active participant in the Partnership if that partner perceives a direct threat to its territorial integrity, political independence or security."[11]

The Alliance's PfP and EAPC differ from previous historical experiments in collective security in several ways, as noted in chapter 3. The most significant difference is that NATO's Euro-Atlantic regional security project is being built on the foundation of a strong alliance, which is itself based on a superpower's commitments. The prospective new Allies are understandably more interested in the collective defense capabilities and commitments at the heart of the "old" NATO than in the collective security roles of the "new" NATO.

The Alliance's post–Cold War goal of "projecting stability" is, in a sense, an ambition to extend NATO's "security space" eastward, not only to new Allies, but to all states throughout the Euro-Atlantic region, including Russia and Ukraine. The limits to this process remain to be discovered. Eventually, the question of solvency is bound to arise in the U.S. Congress and other national legislatures: How many commitments can the Alliance afford to assume? The multiplicity of commitments— twenty-seven PfP security consultation pledges as well as general "security is indivisible" declarations regarding the Euro-Atlantic region— suggests that the risk of overextension may be greater than that of excessive caution.

Actual demands for crisis management interventions and peace operations (much less for collective defense) might become less probable, however, if PfP initiatives in transparency and cooperation promote international understanding and make armed clashes of interests less conceivable. Nonetheless, serious gaps could emerge—between the material requirements for security assistance and the Alliance's ability to meet them, and between the expectations created by the Alliance's Article 4–type commitments to PfP Partners and the Alliance's ability to muster the political will and staying power required to honor those commitments if and when challenges arise.

The limits to the process of making NATO the foundation for the construction of a European peace order through the Alliance's new roles will be discovered as events unfold in the Balkans and in Central and Eastern Europe—particularly with regard to Russian politics and

Russia's relations with its "Near Abroad" (as Moscow calls the other former Soviet republics).

Aside from the uncertainties about the challenges that may arise "in the field"—that is, in the areas most subject to conflict and turmoil in the Euro-Atlantic region—questions may arise about the Alliance's political will to honor "security is indivisible" commitments. Whether the Allies and Partners will have what Martin Wight once called "the moral solidarity"[12] necessary to uphold collective security principles in every case of aggression is doubtful, in view of the fact that Alliance arrangements for crisis management and peace operations (including CJTF and PfP) are already conceived and organized on the assumption that only coalitions of the willing would act in specific contingencies.

In practice, as suggested in chapter 4, NATO's collective security protection will in all likelihood depend on a consensus, explicit or implicit, of the major powers. In the absence of such consensus (as in Bosnia during 1992–95), little effective action will be taken. If intervention in a crisis in the Euro-Atlantic region cannot be undertaken without Russia's concurrence (as in, for example, Tajikistan, or elsewhere in the former Soviet republics of the Caucasus or Central Asia), the universalistic aspirations of "security is indivisible" pledges will not be fulfilled. In other words, the Alliance's realization of Kantian and Wilsonian ideals remains a distant prospect, despite the many reaffirmations of their relevance by the Allies and their partners in PfP and the EAPC.

No examination of the appeal of collective security can overlook Woodrow Wilson's arguments for an end to fear and competition in power relations among states. In 1917 Wilson declared, "The question upon which the whole future peace and policy of the world depends is this: Is the present war a struggle for a just and secure peace, or only for a new balance of power? If it be only a struggle for a new balance of power, who will guarantee, who can guarantee, the stable equilibrium of the new arrangement? Only a tranquil Europe can be a stable Europe. There must be, not a balance of power, but a community of power; not organized rivalries, but an organized common peace."[13] Wilson's eloquence in setting forth an attractive vision of collective security has never been surpassed.

Martin Wight nonetheless contends that Wilson presented a false alternative to the balance of power. Unless Wilson's "community of power" signifies a federation, Wight argues, "it is a chimera."

> International politics have never revealed, nor do they today, a habitual recognition among states of a community of interest overriding their separate interest, comparable to that which normally binds individuals within the state. And where conflicts of interest between organized groups are insurmountable, the only principle of order is to try to maintain, at the price of perpetual vigilance, an even distribution of power. The alternatives are either universal anarchy, or universal dominion.[14]

Wight acknowledged that the concept of "an even distribution of power" raises the questions of how, precisely, power is distributed and of the continuing competition for advantage.[15] In practice, states normally hedge against risks by building military postures and alliance frameworks for deterrence and defense, while simultaneously seeking to cooperate with other states and thereby to diminish the likelihood of conflict, to the extent that this can be done without excessive cost to their vital interests. Unless or until a sense of common interest and shared loyalty overcomes the prominence and distinctness of the interests dividing states, no country or alliance can be indifferent to power relationships and the balance of power.[16] According to Wight, "All that history authorizes us to be sure of is that the balance of power lasts only so long as someone is ready to take risks to maintain it, and that international order will in the end be brought about only by those who are prepared to make sacrifices to construct and enforce it."[17]

In other words, despite the theoretical attractions of a Kantian or Wilsonian collective security arrangement, in which commitments to the "security is indivisible" principle would be honored consistently, such a consensus on the requirements of international order cannot be expected in the foreseeable future in the Euro-Atlantic region, much less the world as a whole. As Inis Claude once put it, "it appears that it is *too early* for the realization of the collective security ideal. Considering the subjective requirements of collective security, the doctrine is premature; neither statesmen nor their peoples have undergone the transformations in attitude and outlook, in loyalty and commitment, which are demanded by the theory of collective security."[18]

The Alliance's first priority must therefore remain collective defense, with due attention to the need to preserve what the Alliance's 1991 Strategic Concept called "the strategic balance within Europe."[19] In practice, this means remaining attentive to Russia's power potential and to other power centers that could, in some circumstances, threaten the security of the Alliance.

Keeping the importance of collective defense in mind means that the Allies have no responsible choice other than to grapple with the risks implicit in balance-of-power policymaking. This approach to international politics has had such a negative reputation since the First World War that some experts and politicians have continued the Kantian and Wilsonian tradition of contrasting it with collective security. However, it should be recalled that past attempts to build international order along Kantian or Wilsonian lines failed for multiple reasons that remain pertinent today, as noted in the Introduction—naïveté about the decision making of real governments, which prefer to assess their interests and options in specific cases, rather than following through with univeralist commitments; the absence of the other projected conditions for the order's success, such as democracy and the rule of law in all the participating states; the continuing struggle over rival visions of national self-determination; and, indeed, the enduring nature of international politics, which involves power competitions as well as shared interests and values. As James Goodby has rightly pointed out, the practical constraints of international politics mean that combined action in support of collective security is likely to be undertaken only on a selective basis, and such efforts will have to "coexist with national policies aimed at maintaining a power equilibrium."[20]

While collective security rhetoric has tarnished the reputation of balance-of-power politics, recognizing the inescapable reality of power politics may be less risky than attempting to eliminate war entirely. It should be recalled that Kant and Wilson are simply the most famous proponents of eradicating war and establishing international order through what later came to be known as collective security, and that the basic ideas have been intermittently subjected to critical analysis for centuries. For example, in a perceptive critique of the Wilsonian design, Robert Osgood contrasted it with the balance-of-power doctrine of Christian Wolff, an eighteenth-century German theorist who dissented from then-contemporary proposals for such an approach to collective security:

> Far from subscribing to Wilson's conception of collective security, Wolff stated that it was neither necessary nor desirable that all states should participate in a war against a disturber of the peace. In order to *mitigate* war he put his faith in the prevailing balance-of-power system, by which states entered war or remained neutral as their special interests dictated, and not in the theoretical system Wilson envisioned, which was designed to *abolish* war by obliging states to employ or withhold force as the impartial application of legal rules might prescribe.[21]

Wolff's approach is consistent with what Martin Wight and other students of the history of ideas have called the Grotian approach to international politics and the balance of power—rather than trying to eliminate war completely, the aim is to prevent it and, failing that, to contain its consequences.[22] Before World War I, balance-of-power politics was widely seen as essential to ensure national independence, make states conscious of their interdependence, and put international law on a realistic foundation. As Wight notes, "This conception of the balance of power as a guarantee of national independence sank deep into the European consciousness in the eighteenth century, and although it came under attack in the nineteenth, it was not discredited until Wilson and 1918."[23] Even in the eighteenth century, however, national independence was in fact guaranteed only to major powers and other states strong or fortunate enough to keep it. When Austria, Prussia, and Russia partitioned the Polish state into nonexistence in 1772–95, they asserted that their action had preserved peace. The partitions of Poland underscored how balance-of-power politics can fail to preserve the independence of weaker states.[24]

Such failures and disastrous losses in major wars furnished the impetus to seek "something better" than the balance of power, a more reliable method of defending interests—such as peace—that should be seen, in principle at least, as common to all states. However, the difficulty with the Kantian and Wilsonian model of international order is that, despite its enduring attractions, it does not offer a genuine alternative to balance-of-power politics; it is illusory, a fateful mirage, given that the conditions that might make it work are not available, and that (in part because of the absence of those conditions) governments will not behave as the model demands.

Although collective security of the Kantian or Wilsonian type is, at least for the foreseeable future, a nonexistent alternative to balance-of-power politics, collective security of the major-power-consensus type and actions by states and coalitions in support of collective security outside a major-power consensus implicitly acknowledge the continuing reality of power relationships in international politics. While the interactions of national policies in a balance-of-power system may result in wars and other upheavals, such outcomes are not foreordained. The practical consequences, despite the inevitable risks and uncertainties, depend in large part on the acumen of policymakers. As Michael Wheeler has noted, "Balance-of-power politics does not preordain any final result. It leaves considerable room for initiative, innovation, and above all political skill."[25] President Truman's secretary of state, Dean Acheson, elaborated on this point in a letter he wrote to Hans Morgenthau in 1957: "There is not in foreign policy the self-starting, energizing, and directing force of an all-embracing interest. Responsibility, will, and direction must come from the devisers of policy."[26] Given the enduring realities of balance-of-power politics, aspirations to promote collective security can provide a basis for some, but not all, choices by U.S. and Allied policymakers as they strive for, to use Kissinger's phrase, "the patient accumulation of partial successes."[27]

Although deeds (for example, investments, exercises, and actual operations, such as IFOR and SFOR) are generally more telling than words, one of the most significant indicators of the Alliance's future direction will be the choices made regarding its May 1997 commitment to "examine" its 1991 Strategic Concept, the most recent statement of the Alliance's fundamental purposes and operational missions. As part of the NATO-Russia Founding Act, the Alliance announced that "NATO member States have decided to examine NATO's Strategic Concept to ensure that it is fully consistent with Europe's new security situation and challenges."[28]

Justifications for what may in practice become a rewrite instead of simply a review of the Strategic Concept are not hard to find.[29]

First, NATO has adopted new policies and pursued many new initiatives since 1991, including PfP, efforts to counter the proliferation of weapons of mass destruction, CJTF, the European Security and Defense

Identity, the NATO-Russia Founding Act, the NATO-Ukraine Charter, the EAPC, and the enlargement process.

Second, international circumstances have changed—for instance, the European Community is now the European Union, with a more ambitious agenda for widening and deepening European integration, including monetary union for many of its members. The CSCE has become the OSCE, with some limited but genuine enhancements in its capabilities for mediation and conflict resolution. The USSR has dissolved into an array of successor states, linked by a tenuous network of multilateral and bilateral treaties, and dominated for the most part by Russia.

Third, NATO has undertaken demanding operations in the former Yugoslavia: the various activities such as embargo and no-fly-zone enforcement in support of UNPROFOR in 1992–95; Operation Deliberate Force in mid-1995; and, since late 1995, multiple responsibilities under the auspices of IFOR and then SFOR. NATO strategy obviously needs to reflect such changes.

Some observers are nonetheless concerned that Russia may attempt to influence the review of NATO's Strategic Concept, even though the formal procedural arrangements offer it little chance to do so. Given its declared agenda, Moscow may try to move the Strategic Concept away from collective defense and promote its long-standing plan to subordinate NATO to the OSCE. With or without Russian encouragement, the exercise could also legitimize the behavior of Allies inclined to make further defense budget cuts and to concentrate on capabilities more suitable for crisis management and peace operations than for collective defense.

Preserving the Alliance's core function of collective defense in the Strategic Concept review is imperative. As the Dutch ambassador to the United States, Joris Michael Vos, pointed out in February 1998, NATO's "commitment to collective defense and the trans-Atlantic link, and adherence to the nuclear [policy] paragraphs [in the 1991 Strategic Concept], should be maintained. These represent the heart of the organization, and changing them would alter NATO's essence and purpose irrevocably."[30]

An issue of significant concern is the fate of the 1991 Strategic Concept's call to "preserve the strategic balance within Europe."[31] Because the Strategic Concept was approved a month before the collapse of the Soviet Union, it uses the word "Soviet" in discussing what must be considered in defining the European strategic balance: "Even in a non-adversarial and co-operative relationship, Soviet military capability and build-up potential, including its nuclear dimension, still constitute the most significant factor of which the Alliance has to take account in maintaining the strategic balance in Europe."[32]

Some observers contend that such language could be seen as antagonistic to Russia and might complicate prospects for constructive NATO-Russia cooperation because it singles out the country and implies that it could become a threat to NATO in some circumstances. Others judge, however, that retaining some "strategic balance" language is essential to demonstrate that the Alliance is committed to balanced relations with Russia, and cannot rule out the risk of unforeseen political changes in the country, which has yet to establish a stable democracy.

Nonetheless, the Alliance may choose to find other ways to refer discreetly to its continuing collective defense function. In May 1997, German minister of defense Volker Rühe used the following formula: "The Alliance has made it clear from the beginning in its negotiations with Russia that the political strategy of the Alliance includes two core elements, cooperation and reassurance, that is, cooperation and the capability for defense as an insurance against unforeseen developments."[33] An even more circumspect solution, suggested by some European observers, might be simply to refer in general terms to the goal of "strategic stability" or (borrowing from the Alliance's July 1997 Madrid Declaration) to "improving the security and stability environment for nations in the Euro-Atlantic area."[34]

THE CONTINUING CENTRAL ROLE OF THE UNITED STATES

The most important determinants of the future of security in Europe will be (a) the steadfastness of U.S. engagement in European security, with regard to crisis contingencies demanding intervention and long-term stabilization, such as Bosnia, as well as collective defense and Euro-Atlantic cooperation, including a measured and prudent process of Alliance enlargement; (b) the evolution of Russian politics and policy with regard to the "Near Abroad" and neighbors further to the west and south; and (c) the political and social cohesion and economic health of the European Union and its partners in Central and Eastern Europe.

The course of U.S. policy, however, is likely to be the single most influential factor. The great preponderance of military power and the considerable political and economic influence the United States currently enjoys may enable the Alliance to cope with the potential contradictions involved in keeping NATO a collective defense organization while also making it an instrument for an increasing number of activities in support of collective security.

Some European analysts are nonetheless concerned about the degree to which the new Euro-Atlantic security structure depends on the United States—specifically, its capabilities, discernment, political will, and staying power. As it stands, the structure is that of an inverted pyramid. At its base is the United States. The Alliance rests on the foundation of U.S. commitments. On top of the Alliance stand the various structures it has established since the end of the Cold War—the Partnership for Peace, the Euro-Atlantic Partnership Council, and the special consultation mechanisms with Russia and Ukraine.

The new Euro-Atlantic security structure relies above all on the steadfastness of U.S. commitments, and some Europeans are worried that this could also be a source of weakness: excessive dependence on a single power acting as Atlas, with much of the structure on his shoulders. They are concerned by signs of U.S. hesitation with regard to upholding NATO's new collective security functions—above all, the divisions within the U.S. administration and Congress in 1996–97 about staying the course in Bosnia and looking beyond the initial December 1996–June 1998 schedule for SFOR's deployment to follow-on stabilization measures. President Clinton's December 1997 announcement (with significant Congressional support) that U.S. forces will remain in Bosnia beyond the June 1998 deadline was particularly appreciated in the Alliance because the president said that it would be an "error" to specify another departure deadline. U.S. forces will now participate in a NATO-led stabilization effort indefinitely, with the scope and nature of their tasks contingent on the achievement of concrete results in what may well be a protracted endeavor.[35]

Contentious policy debates and signs of hesitation are tolerable as long as U.S. credibility remains high with regard to the Alliance's core function of collective defense. However, that credibility could be jeopardized, some fear, by an open-ended NATO enlargement process that downplays the significance of collective defense and increasingly high-lights collective security purposes. The differences among political leaders in the United States over NATO's future also furnish grounds for concern. Some of the senators who voted against NATO enlargement in April 1998 expressed dismay about the extent to which the Alliance has increasingly been oriented toward operations in support of collective security, such as peacekeeping. Indeed, some of the senators who voted for NATO enlargement have expressed similar reservations about this trend. For example, Senator Jesse Helms (R-North Carolina) has declared that applicants may find "that we are not inviting new nations into the NATO that won the cold war but rather into a diluted NATO converted from a well-defined military alliance into a nebulous 'collective security arrangement.'"[36]

The United States was drawn into serving as the stabilizer, pacifier, and balancer of Europe because Soviet control over East-Central Europe encouraged West European, and then Western, defense cooperation. As Uwe Nerlich observed in 1979, "The American engagement was caused by Soviet actions and policies; indeed the very simplicity of the bipolar confrontation was presumably a prerequisite for this departure from American traditions. In a more complex and diffused competitive environment internal American pressures to stay out might have been decisive."[37]

The security environment in the Euro-Atlantic region has become, to use Nerlich's terms, "more complex and diffused" since the end of the Cold War, and some analysts wonder whether this will have any impact on the sustainability of U.S. commitments in Europe. As noted in chapter 4, with reference to Bosnia, the policy of the United States has been one of conflict-containment and caution about involvement in any operations that could result in large-scale U.S. fatalities, partly because of concern that such fatalities could jeopardize long-standing U.S. security commitments in Europe.

The Atlantic Alliance historically has enjoyed a high level of approval and legitimacy in America's political discourse; and, to a significant extent, this remains the case today. A tendency to regard U.S. alliances as Cold War political structures of little obvious contemporary utility has nonetheless emerged. In October 1995, Secretary of Defense William Perry was asked, "What's so sacred about NATO?" In reply,

Secretary Perry used a long-term regional stabilization argument: "There are still 20,000 nuclear weapons in the former Soviet Union. And the political and the economic recovery going on in those countries is extremely fragile. . . . So we have a very strong interest in the security and stability of Europe. NATO, in my judgment, is the linchpin of maintaining that stability."[38]

This argument relies on assessments of probable consequences of specific policies. The assessments amount to judgments, based on historical precedents and political intuition, that are ultimately unprovable, short of withdrawing U.S. forces and commitments and observing the evolution of events. Such assessments, however, are likely to strike some Americans as abstract and speculative projections about what might happen in the distant future in remote regions that appear to be sufficiently peaceful at present; therefore, they may not persuade Americans reluctant to accept the continuing obligations they imply.

It is unclear whether and to what extent U.S. political leaders will be persuaded by arguments contending that U.S. forces and security commitments in Europe play a major role in preventing or postponing arms races and power competitions and conflicts among major powers in the Euro-Atlantic region. The argument for continued engagement is that U.S. commitments are essential to sustain collective defense institutions that deter coercion and aggression, enable Western governments to take combined action effectively, and discourage the renationalization of defense policies and possible nuclear proliferation.[39] Despite the force of such arguments, American politicians and commentators may ask whether lessening the long-term possibility of major-power regional rivalries and wars is worth the expense and security risks for the United States.

Some Europeans have highlighted the risks of instability, even in Western Europe, in the event of a U.S. withdrawal. In 1992, Manfred Wörner, then NATO's secretary general, said, "If the United States disengages, I foresee a certain temptation for Western European nations to revert to past patterns of power politics."[40] In this regard, one should recall the Alliance's "internal" functions in support of international security (discussed in chapter 2). If European analysts such as Josef Joffe are correct about the NATO framework and U.S. commitments and leadership having solved the security dilemma in relations among the major states of Western Europe, an erosion of that framework could lead to a breakdown of the European Union.[41]

Another prominent argument in the region holds that the United States remains engaged in European security affairs precisely because it could not afford the consequences of disengagement. "The consequences of a return to endemic European instability could not be ignored by the United States. . . . Every security problem which touches on the military great power Russia, every crisis which has even the remotest nuclear dimension, and every conflict which threatens escalation on NATO territory thus will force the United States to become engaged."[42]

François Heisbourg, a prominent French analyst in security affairs, has described U.S. leadership in NATO since the end of the Cold War, and notably with regard to the former Yugoslavia, as *"à éclipses"* (that is, by fits and starts, something that comes and goes) and *"aléatoire"* (uncertain, risky, random), based on the impression that America's vital interests are no longer intrinsically at stake in every European crisis. According to Heisbourg, the end of the steady U.S. leadership of NATO during the Cold War, with the potential for more U.S. selectivity in taking action to deal with European security challenges, means that France cannot rely on NATO alone and must strive to build up the ESDI within NATO.[43]

To what extent can NATO tolerate unpredictable and intermittent U.S. involvement in non–Article 5 operations without profoundly weakening the Alliance and the projected Euro-Atlantic security order? Contingent U.S. involvement in non–Article 5 operations might be sufficient under the following conditions:

- the United States continues to uphold collective defense and the NATO structure as a whole with a high level of consistency and credibility;

- the United States participates in some crisis management and peace operations, demonstrating at least the selective applicability of the U.S. commitment to collective security principles and the genuine possibility of U.S. action in specific cases; and

- the United States provides the necessary tools for European-led operations using the Alliance's CJTF for the contingencies the Europeans feel capable of handling—the so-called Petersberg tasks, such as humanitarian relief, peacekeeping, and crisis-management interventions, including peacemaking.[44]

CJTF mechanisms and associated arrangements for the release, monitoring, and return of NATO assets and capabilities in WEU-led operations are still under development, but their practical success in specific cases will depend critically on U.S.-European consensus regarding the necessity for action and the cogency of the political-military strategies developed by the European Allies.

It is intriguing and noteworthy that Richard Holbrooke, who has probably been the single most influential architect of U.S. policy regarding both NATO enlargement and the Dayton Accords, has justified long-term U.S. engagement in European security not with Wilsonian rhetoric but in more traditional balance-of-power terms: "It took some time to realize that we are still part of the balance of power in Europe. . . . We are needed now to counteract tribal nationalism and bring stability in the vast land mass from the eastern German border to the western Russian border, where so many overlapping territorial claims and potential conflicts lurk."[45]

Maintaining U.S. engagement in European security will require effort, persuasion, and recognition of the magnitude of U.S. responsibilities, because proponents of isolationist and unilateralist approaches can still exert considerable influence in American politics, given the right issues and circumstances. The Alliance's future depends above all on the United States. Without a continuing U.S. engagement, NATO will have no credibility, cohesion, or future. It is therefore imperative to construct a definition of the Alliance's purposes that meets the collective defense and other security challenges at hand, and that conforms to the interests of the United States and the other Allies. In view of the difficulty of precisely codifying in advance how to respond to all the potential new challenges facing the Alliance, both Article 5 and non–Article 5, and the political-military pitfalls in attempting to do so (for example, precluding options and exposing or even exacerbating intra-Alliance divergences of policy and interests), the wisest course may well be to define a broad conceptual framework that will offer the Allies enough flexibility to devise "variable-geometry" responses to specific contingencies.

The Need for Lucidity in Pursuing a Two-Track Policy

As Martin Wight once pointed out, security—in contrast with power—need not be a "relational concept," whereby "the security of one power is in inverse ratio to that of others. . . . Security consists in other factors besides national power: the strength and reliability of allies, and the absence of conflicting interests, for example. . . . Security, like prosperity, is an objective towards which all powers can, conceivably, move simultaneously."[46] However, the movement of a multiplicity of powers in this direction depends on a high level of mutual trust and a solid consensus on the requirements of international order—a sense of commonality of interests and purposes that may take decades to build and that is normally found only within a nation or a federation.

Given the absence of a sense of common interest and community in the Euro-Atlantic region (and pending the development of such a sense), the United States and its Allies will have little choice but to pursue a two-track policy with perseverance and full awareness of the potential pitfalls—pursuing collective security aspirations to the extent that this is feasible and prudent, but maintaining a collective defense posture as a hedge in case those aspirations cannot be fulfilled. The challenge is to find a *via media* that maintains collective defense capabilities in good order, given the risk of future threats to Alliance security, while seeking to deepen cooperation and transparency in security matters and to contain the risks inherent in emerging or ongoing rivalries. It is imperative to pursue opportunities for constructive cooperation with Russia while hedging against the continuing risk of grave setbacks in that country's political development.

In criticizing the NATO-Russia Founding Act, Henry Kissinger wrote as follows: "The Founding Act seeks to graft a system of collective security on top of an alliance system. This has never worked no matter how cleverly legal points are argued."[47]

Kissinger is right about the general theoretical point. As discussed in chapter 1, no system of collective security in the Kantian or Wilsonian sense has ever worked as its proponents claimed it would, whether grafted on top of an alliance system or not. Kissinger is also right with regard to the rhetoric employed by the Alliance. Since 1990–91, the Allies have declared repeatedly that "security is indivisible" in the Euro-

Atlantic region and that NATO's goal is "a stable security environment in Europe, based on the growth of democratic institutions and commitment to the peaceful resolution of disputes, in which *no* country would be able to intimidate or coerce *any* European nation or to impose hegemony through the threat or use of force."[48] In the Founding Act that Kissinger questions, the rhetoric is even more ambitious, as noted at the beginning of chapter 3. Moreover, the United States in particular has at times raised the possibility of including Russia in NATO, a step that would be consistent with an attempt to transform the Alliance into an inclusive collective security system along Kantian or Wilsonian lines.

The generally negative European reactions to the notion of Russian membership in NATO (discussed in chapter 3) suggest, however, that the situation is more complex than Kissinger's formulation implies. The Alliance is far from having achieved a consensus on the aim of creating "a system of collective security" or, as Kissinger puts it, "grafting" such a system on top of its collective defense arrangements. Inis Claude's distinction between a "system" of collective security and an "ideology" of collective security is instructive in this regard.[49] Instead of undertaking the construction of a Wilsonian-style collective security system, the Allies have accepted the potent influence of the general ideology; rhetorically, at least, they have endorsed many of its principles, such as the idea that "security is indivisible."

For several years now, the Allies have been struggling to define a prudent and sustainable adaptation of their purposes and institutions to defend their interests in a substantially changed international security environment. The Allies have given lip-service to rhetoric that implies that all the Allies and PfP Partners should intervene in every case of aggression and injustice. In fact, all the Allies and many PfP members have participated in IFOR and SFOR in Bosnia. The institutional adaptations—such as CJTF for coalitions of the willing—and other principles (such as "case-by-case" caveats) imply, however, that many of the Allies see non–Article 5 missions in support of collective security as tasks in the long run for only some self-designated Allies, and only then in selected cases. Bosnia has been the sole example to date of a NATO-led peacekeeping operation, and it should be kept in mind that years of bitter European-American (and intra-European) disputes within the Alliance preceded the Dayton Accords and the subsequent military stabilization arrangements.

In terms of their operational practice and the guidelines for their decision making, the Allies evidently envisage going no further than collective security in the major-power-consensus sense of the term. Rather than creating a comprehensive "system" of collective security, the Allies are gradually adapting their military and institutional instruments, so that they can be applied to operations in support of collective security when selected Allies choose to undertake them and the Alliance as a whole is prepared to offer a political endorsement. In practice, the Allies are likely to remain cautious about intervening in conflicts beyond the Alliance's territory. NATO's updated decision-making guidelines use terms such as "case-by-case," "selective," and "coalitions of the willing"— unlike the universally binding political and moral commitments of a Kantian or Wilsonian system of collective security. In crisis management and peace operations under OSCE or UN Security Council mandates, the Allies have noted, "Participation in any such operation or mission will remain subject to decisions of member states in accordance with national constitutions."[50]

In short, the participation of specific Allies in any non–Article 5 operation is optional, in contrast with the obligatory nature of a Kantian or Wilsonian system of collective security. Rather than yield decision-making authority to PfP members, the Alliance intends to retain full authority over NATO-led crisis management and peace operations, including decisions about whether to invite specific PfP members to contribute. Far from being universal throughout the Euro-Atlantic region, the practical commitments to action that the Allies have undertaken to date have been limited to the Balkans, particularly Bosnia, and the sustainability of this engagement depends on many factors— above all, continued U.S. leadership. Since August 1997, as discussed in chapter 4, NATO has also been engaged, with selected PfP Partners, in efforts to help restore stability in Albania. Furthermore, since March 1998 the Alliance has been taking measures to respond to Albania's external security concerns with regard to Kosovo, and this may lead to more extensive PfP activities in both Albania and the Former Yugoslav Republic of Macedonia, if not actual military intervention in Kosovo.

The struggle within the Alliance about how to reconcile collective security aspirations with continuing collective defense commitments will in all likelihood continue for several years. Both of NATO's new roles draw inspiration from the collective security tradition, and each contains the potential for serious setbacks. Hence, as the Allies struggle to give practical meaning to their various obligations and aspirations, they might ponder the following approaches to NATO's new roles.

The Alliance enlargement process should be incremental, prudently limited, and carried forward at a cautious and deliberate pace, lest Alliance cohesion and effectiveness be undermined. The SFOR operation should be continued to give the Dayton Accords a reasonable multi-year chance of success; failure to do so could create a crippling "Bosnia syndrome" and hamper the Alliance's ability to undertake future crisis management and peacekeeping operations.

The Alliance's core collective defense mission and the supporting institutions, including the integrated military structure and defense planning system, must be retained, because they constitute the basis for the Alliance's cohesion and its several valuable internal functions in support of international security, including the promotion of stability in relations among the major Western powers and the avoidance of a renationalization of defense policies (discussed in chapter 2).

With collective defense assured, the Alliance can serve as a solid foundation for cultivating cooperative relations with former adversaries and other non-NATO countries in the Euro-Atlantic region. Cooperative structures and activities such as PfP can furnish an improved basis for undertaking non–Article 5 missions, including crisis management and peace operations, with the participation of PfP members. The result, however, will not be a collective security system in the Kantian or Wilsonian sense. As long as some of the Allies hold that NATO-led or -endorsed operations in support of collective security can be undertaken solely with UN Security Council or OSCE mandates, the major-power-consensus approach to collective security will prevail in Alliance decision making. Moreover, power relationships will continue to play a preponderant role in international politics, including Alliance decision making (discussed in chapter 3).

While the ideas legitimizing crisis management and peace operations will almost certainly reflect the collective security tradition, the

Allies will have to recognize the risks and limits inherent in certain ideas. For example, trying to act on the principle that "security is indivisible" with regard to every case of aggression or internal conflict in the Euro-Atlantic region probably would exceed the resources and political will of the Allies, particularly with regard to conflicts in the former Soviet Union. Moreover, depending on the OSCE and the UN Security Council as the only entities capable of legitimizing an intervention in support of collective security could hamper the Alliance's ability to act in cases where the gravity of the injustice and the magnitude of the threat to Allied interests demand immediate action. The Allies have not yet been able to agree on whether they would be prepared to act in support of collective security when and if a major-power-consensus endorsement in the form of a Security Council or OSCE mandate is not available. Such a contingency could arise if Russian (or, in the Security Council, Chinese) interests differed with the interests of the Allies, and the Alliance were convinced that collective action had to be taken (discussed in chapter 4).

Inis Claude's hypothesis may be correct: interest in collective security (or, in an attenuated form, a concert of the major powers) may be greatest following the end of a general war, such as the Napoleonic Wars, the two World Wars, or the Cold War. Yet the aspirations to establish such arrangements for preventing future wars or major-power confrontations are usually accompanied by a reluctance to acknowledge the probability of future polarities and power competitions.

The only secure foundation for the Allies to investigate opportunities for constructive cooperation in support of collective security throughout the Euro-Atlantic region is collective defense. The core commitment on which the Alliance's cohesion is built remains Article 5, the collective defense pledge; and the commitment that the European Allies have cared about most is that of the United States. Opinion polls have shown that, during the Cold War, the major West European Allies (Britain, France, Germany, and Italy) generally had more confidence in the reliability of the United States as an ally in collective-defense contingencies than they had in one another.

After analyzing a large number of surveys, Stephen Szabo concluded in 1988 that

Trust in the United States as an ally has been consistently high through-out Europe from the 1950s through the 1980s. . . . Trust in the U.S. as an ally was substantially higher than trust in the other European nations or in NATO. In fact little trust existed in allies other than the U.S. . . . The United States was the overwhelming choice as the nation most likely to come to the aid of these nations and with the exception of 31 percent of the French citing the British, no other ally received substantial mention.[51]

In a similar poll conducted in April 1998, "Asked which country 'we could count on most' during a time of crisis, Britons (82%) and Germans (56%) are far more likely to name the United States than name a European ally. . . . In France, more say they would count on Germany (44%) than either the U.S. (31%) or Britain (14%), and few Britons (3%) or Germans (16%) name France. . . . Half in France (50%) and majorities in Britain (67%) and Germany (60%) say that NATO is 'still essential' in the post-Cold War world."[52] These findings about German views reflect the country's unification; Germans from the for-mer German Democratic Republic (Communist-ruled East Germany) continue to have views regarding NATO (and the European Union) that are distinctly more negative than those of West Germans.[53]

The importance of the Alliance's collective defense function for maintaining peace and stability in Europe cannot be overstated. Joffe's analysis of how U.S. engagement through the Alliance cleared away the competitive "self-help" dynamic in relations among the Western Euro-pean powers remains quite pertinent. As Joffe pointed out, "Once the issue of security [in NATO Europe's interstate relations] was dispatched, collective gain could overwhelm the logic of rivalry and relative gain."[54]

In Joffe's analysis, dispatching "the issue of security" depended on the engagement of the United States as the guarantor and organizer of secu-rity among the NATO European powers, so they no longer feared each other and could work together in common tasks under U.S. leadership —above all, collective defense against a common threat. However, that common threat has become more ambiguous; and the common task of collective defense has received less attention as the focus has shifted to the Alliance's new roles, despite the Alliance's repeated reaffirma-tions that collective defense continues to be its central function.

NATO's new roles of cooperation with non-Allies and crisis management and peace operations are entirely appropriate, to be sure, to the extent that the Alliance can perform constructive work in these domains without jeopardizing its core purpose of collective defense, which is the ultimate foundation of its political and strategic cohesion. The risk resides in undermining Alliance cohesion and effectiveness; the Alliance could suddenly discover in a serious confrontation with Russia or other powers that it had excessively neglected collective defense. Alternatively, the Alliance might increasingly be relegated to an OSCE-like role, while the major Allies turn to other arrangements for the defense of their core national security interests.

In both new roles—cooperation with former adversaries and other non-NATO countries, and crisis management and peace operations—an essential question is how to maintain the robustness and centrality of collective defense while the Alliance and Alliance-led institutions (such as PfP and the EAPC) devote more attention to collective security activities. An erosion of collective defense as the central and primary purpose of the Alliance could lead to two damaging consequences: renationalization of defense policies and a simultaneous breakdown of the basis for stability in Europe. Renationalization is the shorthand expression for the possibility that member states could become less confident in NATO as the vehicle for ensuring their national security, and more likely to seek other means of security, such as strengthened national military capabilities (including nuclear weapons, in some cases) and alliance arrangements outside the NATO framework. As noted in chapter 2, NATO's positive "internal" functions on behalf of international security depend on the Alliance's collective defense orientation.

If certain trends went too far—if, in the eyes of major Allies, NATO and its associated bodies, such as PfP and the EAPC, began to look like a "mini-UN," "a latter-day League of Nations," or a "peacock alliance—all show and no go," with vague collective security obligations for virtually all of the Euro-Atlantic region—the Allies, particularly the stronger ones capable of a measure of self-reliance, would start to discount NATO and focus on other means to ensure their national security.[55] What has given NATO credibility has been its manifest commitment to its bedrock role of collective defense.

In short, the central challenge is containing the impact of NATO's new roles on the Alliance's central purpose—collective defense—within manageable bounds. The new roles will be politically sustainable in the long term only if they support the core security interests of the Allies. These roles may well be politically sustainable if their net impact is positive: that is, if they improve the general international security environment in Europe by promoting transparency and cooperation, notably with regard to crisis management and peace operations.

The long-term sustainability of the new roles could be jeopardized, however, under two conditions: if they increasingly entailed a shift to "collective security" in the Kantian or Wilsonian sense and gradually undermined the Alliance's collective defense function, or if the Allies and their PfP Partners discovered, in grappling with crises and conflicts in the Euro-Atlantic region, further practical limits to their declaratory consensus on "collective security"–style commitments that imply "security is indivisible." The Allies must exercise caution and selectivity in directing NATO's resources (including its political capital) toward new "collective security"–related missions lest they break down Alliance cohesion and undermine NATO's capabilities and credibility as an instrument of collective defense.

NATO's collective defense function remains relevant for several purposes:

- as a hedge against the unforeseen in Russia, and with regard to third parties, such as Iran and Iraq;
- as the basis for the Alliance's internal functions, including the containment of potential mistrust and rivalry among the European member states; and
- as a means to enable the Alliance to perform collective security functions, calling upon the integrated military structure, the command, control, communications, and logistical arrangements, and the political cohesion and patterns of cooperation developed for collective-defense purposes.

Despite the widespread tendency in Western countries to compartmentalize discussions of NATO enlargement and Bosnia, the highest-profile NATO issues since the end of the Cold War, they are understandably linked in the minds of officials and experts in the countries striving to build a closer relationship with the Alliance. The failures of the EU, the CSCE/OSCE, and the UN in dealing with the conflicts in the former Yugoslavia strengthened East European interest in NATO membership. As Jonathan Eyal has observed, the Alliance "not merely claimed to be the only meaningful security institution, but actually proved itself as such in the first post-communist crisis. Those who still wonder why the east Europeans became so obsessed with NATO membership should search through the annals of the Yugoslav saga."[56]

NATO's collective defense function might return to the foreground if powers outside the Euro-Atlantic region threatened a NATO Ally. During the 1990–91 Gulf War, for example, Iraq might have attacked Turkey. Within the Euro-Atlantic region, the most plausible potential threat to the Allies remains Russia. The anti-Western rhetoric of some Russian politicians may be designed to advance domestic political agendas; but such pronouncements, particularly in the post-Yeltsin era, could have external political effects and create a self-fulfilling prophecy of antago-nism with the West. Depending on the nature and gravity of the circum-stances, NATO might have to undertake deterrence and collective defense measures, such as augmenting its existing forces, deploying Allied forces to Poland, taking in additional allies, or extending a declaratory umbrella of protection over threatened states.

Preparations to conduct collective-security operations (and the actual conduct of such operations) may serve collective defense purposes as well as NATO's larger objectives regarding stability and security in the Euro-Atlantic region:

- effective crisis interventions and peace operations may lower the risk that collective defense contingencies will arise, because they may contain conflicts that could spill over into Article 5 threats to NATO Allies;
- peacekeeping exercises and other cooperative activities with non-NATO countries may help to sustain the Alliance, including its collec-tive defense potential; and
- these activities may provide reassurance to states not in the Alliance.

The linkage between NATO's goal of building cooperative security structures throughout the Euro-Atlantic region and its role in leading peacekeeping operations such as SFOR in Bosnia has become obvious. The Allies cannot have credibility regarding the grand Euro-Atlantic regional project if they do not demonstrate determination and staying power in Bosnia and other peace support operations.

Although it is likely to suffer through further political crises as it works out the practical applications and proper boundaries of its new roles, NATO must meet this challenge. NATO remains the single most effective institution for combining the political-military assets of the major Western powers, and its effectiveness must be preserved—for collective defense, above all, but also to enable it to conduct selected operations in support of collective security.

APPENDIX 1

The North Atlantic Treaty

Washington D.C., April 4, 1949

The Parties to this Treaty reaffirm their faith in the purposes and principles of the Charter of the United Nations and their desire to live in peace with all peoples and all governments.

They are determined to safeguard the freedom, common heritage and civilisation of their peoples, founded on the principles of democracy, individual liberty and the rule of law. They seek to promote stability and well-being in the North Atlantic area. They are resolved to unite their efforts for collective defence and for the preservation of peace and security. They therefore agree to this North Atlantic Treaty:

ARTICLE 1

The Parties undertake, as set forth in the Charter of the United Nations, to settle any international dispute in which they may be involved by peaceful means in such a manner that international peace and security and justice are not endangered, and to refrain in their international relations from the threat or use of force in any manner inconsistent with the purposes of the United Nations.

ARTICLE 2

The Parties will contribute toward the further development of peaceful and friendly international relations by strengthening their free institutions, by bringing about a better understanding of the principles upon which these institutions are founded, and by promoting conditions of stability and well-being. They will seek to eliminate conflict in their international economic policies and will encourage economic collaboration between any or all of them.

ARTICLE 3

In order more effectively to achieve the objectives of this Treaty, the Parties, separately and jointly, by means of continuous and effective self-help and mutual aid, will maintain and develop their individual and collective capacity to resist armed attack.

ARTICLE 4

The Parties will consult together whenever, in the opinion of any of them, the territorial integrity, political independence or security of any of the Parties is threatened.

ARTICLE 5

The Parties agree that an armed attack against one or more of them in Europe or North America shall be considered an attack against them all and consequently they agree that, if such an armed attack occurs, each of them, in exercise of the right of individual or collective self-defence recognised by Article 51 of the Charter of the United Nations, will assist the Party or Parties so attacked by taking forthwith, individually and in concert with the other Parties, such action as it deems necessary, including the use of armed force, to restore and maintain the security of the North Atlantic area.

Any such armed attack and all measures taken as a result thereof shall immediately be reported to the Security Council. Such measures shall be terminated when the Security Council has taken the measures necessary to restore and maintain international peace and security (1).

ARTICLE 6

For the purpose of Article 5, an armed attack on one or more of the Parties is deemed to include an armed attack:

- on the territory of any of the Parties in Europe or North America, on the Algerian Departments of France, (2) on the territory of Turkey or on the Islands under the jurisdiction of any of the Parties in the North Atlantic area north of the Tropic of Cancer;

• on the forces, vessels, or aircraft of any of the Parties, when in or over these territories or any other area in Europe in which occupation forces of any of the Parties were stationed on the date when the Treaty entered into force or the Mediterranean Sea or the North Atlantic area north of the Tropic of Cancer.

ARTICLE 7

This Treaty does not affect, and shall not be interpreted as affecting in any way the rights and obligations under the Charter of the Parties which are members of the United Nations, or the primary responsibility of the Security Council for the maintenance of international peace and security.

ARTICLE 8

Each Party declares that none of the international engagements now in force between it and any other of the Parties or any third State is in conflict with the provisions of this Treaty, and undertakes not to enter into any international engagement in conflict with this Treaty.

ARTICLE 9

The Parties hereby establish a Council, on which each of them shall be represented, to consider matters concerning the implementation of this Treaty. The Council shall be so organised as to be able to meet promptly at any time. The Council shall set up such subsidiary bodies as may be necessary; in particular it shall establish immediately a defence committee which shall recommend measures for the implementation of Articles 3 and 5.

ARTICLE 10

The Parties may, by unanimous agreement, invite any other European State in a position to further the principles of this Treaty and to contribute to the security of the North Atlantic area to accede to this Treaty. Any State so invited may become a Party to the Treaty by depositing its instrument of accession with the Government of the United States of America. The Government of the United States of America will inform each of the Parties of the deposit of each such instrument of accession.

ARTICLE 11

This Treaty shall be ratified and its provisions carried out by the Parties in accordance with their respective constitutional processes. The instruments of ratification shall be deposited as soon as possible with the Government of the United States of America, which will notify all the other signatories of each deposit. The Treaty shall enter into force between the States which have ratified it as soon as the ratifications of the majority of the signatories, including the ratifications of Belgium, Canada, France, Luxembourg, the Netherlands, the United Kingdom and the United States, have been deposited and shall come into effect with respect to other States on the date of the deposit of their ratifications.

ARTICLE 12

After the Treaty has been in force for ten years, or at any time thereafter, the Parties shall, if any of them so requests, consult together for the purpose of reviewing the Treaty, having regard for the factors then affecting peace and security in the North Atlantic area, including the development of universal as well as regional arrangements under the Charter of the United Nations for the maintenance of international peace and security.

ARTICLE 13

After the Treaty has been in force for twenty years, any Party may cease to be a Party one year after its notice of denunciation has been given to the Government of the United States of America, which will inform the Governments of the other Parties of the deposit of each notice of denunciation.

ARTICLE 14

This Treaty, of which the English and French texts are equally authentic, shall be deposited in the archives of the Government of the United States of America. Duly certified copies will be transmitted by that Government to the Governments of other signatories.

FOOTNOTES :

1. The definition of the territories to which Article 5 applies was revised by Article 2 of the Protocol to the North Atlantic Treaty on the accession of Greece and Turkey and by the Protocols signed on the accession of the Federal Republic of Germany and of Spain.

2. On January 16, 1963, the North Atlantic Council heard a declaration by the French Representative who recalled that by the vote on self-determination on July 1, 1962, the Algerian people had pronounced itself in favour of the independence of Algeria in co-operation with France. In consequence, the President of the French Republic had on July 3, 1962, formally recognised the independence of Algeria. The result was that the *"Algerian departments of France"* no longer existed as such, and that at the same time the fact that they were mentioned in the North Atlantic Treaty had no longer any bearing. Following this statement the Council noted that insofar as the former Algerian Departments of France were concerned, the relevant clauses of this Treaty had become inapplicable as from July 3, 1962.

APPENDIX 2

Partnership for Peace
Framework Document

Ministerial Meeting of the North Atlantic Council/North Atlantic Cooperation Council, NATO Headquarters, Brussels, 10–11 January 1994

1. Further to the invitation extended by the NATO Heads of State and Government at their meeting on 10th/11th January, 1994, the member states of the North Atlantic Alliance and the other states subscribing to this document, resolved to deepen their political and military ties and to contribute further to the strengthening of security within the Euro-Atlantic area, hereby establish, within the framework of the North Atlantic Cooperation Council, this Partnership for Peace.

2. This Partnership is established as an expression of a joint conviction that stability and security in the Euro-Atlantic area can be achieved only through cooperation and common action. Protection and promotion of fundamental freedoms and human rights, and safeguarding of freedom, justice, and peace through democracy are shared values fundamental to the Partnership.

   In joining the Partnership, the member States of the North Atlantic Alliance and the other States subscribing to this Document recall that they are committed to the preservation of democratic societies, their freedom from coercion and intimidation, and the maintenance of the principles of international law.

   They reaffirm their commitment to fulfill in good faith the obligations of the Charter of the United Nations and the principles of the Universal Declaration on Human Rights; specifically, to refrain from the threat or use of force against the territorial integrity or political independence of any State, to respect existing borders and to settle disputes by peaceful means. They also reaffirm their commitment to the Helsinki Final Act and all subsequent CSCE documents and to the fulfillment of the commitments and obligations they have undertaken in the field of disarmament and arms control.

3. The other states subscribing to this document will cooperate with the North Atlantic Treaty Organization in pursuing the following objectives:

   a. facilitation of transparency in national defence planning and budgeting processes;
   b. ensuring democratic control of defence forces;
   c. maintenance of the capability and readiness to contribute, subject to constitutional considerations, to operations under the authority of the UN and/or the responsibility of the CSCE;
   d. the development of cooperative military relations with NATO, for the purpose of joint planning, training, and exercises in order to strengthen their ability to undertake missions in the fields of peacekeeping, search and rescue, humanitarian operations, and others as may subsequently be agreed;
   e. the development, over the longer term, of forces that are better able to operate with those of the members of the North Atlantic Alliance.

4. The other subscribing states will provide to the NATO Authorities Presentation Documents identifying the steps they will take to achieve the political goals of the Partnership and the military and other assets that might be used for Partnership activities. NATO will propose a programme of partnership exercises and other activities consistent with the Partnership's objectives. Based on this programme and its Presentation Document, each subscribing state will develop with NATO an individual Partnership Programme.

5. In preparing and implementing their individual Partnership Programmes, other subscribing states may, at their own expense and in agreement with the Alliance and, as necessary, relevant Belgian authorities, establish their own liaison office with NATO Headquarters in Brussels. This will facilitate their participation in NACC/Partnership meetings and activities, as well as certain others by invitation. They will also make available personnel, assets, facilities and capabilities necessary and appropriate for carrying out the agreed Partnership Programme. NATO will assist them, as appropriate, in formulating and executing their individual Partnership Programmes.

6. The other subscribing states accept the following understandings:

- those who envisage participation in missions referred to in paragraph 3(d) will, where appropriate, take part in related NATO exercises;

- they will fund their own participation in Partnership activities, and will endeavour otherwise to share the burdens of mounting exercises in which they take part;

- they may send, after appropriate agreement, permanent liaison officers to a separate Partnership Coordination Cell at Mons (Belgium) that would, under the authority of the North Atlantic Council, carry out the military planning necessary to implement the Partnership programmes;

- those participating in planning and military exercises will have access to certain NATO technical data relevant to interoperability;

- building upon the CSCE measures on defence planning, the other subscribing states and NATO countries will exchange information on the steps that have been taken or are being taken to promote transparency in defence planning and budgeting and to ensure the democratic control of armed forces;

- they may participate in a reciprocal exchange of information on defence planning and budgeting which will be developed within the framework of the NACC/Partnership for Peace.

7. In keeping with their commitment to the objectives of this Partnership for Peace, the members of the North Atlantic Alliance will:

- develop with the other subscribing states a planning and review process to provide a basis for identifying and evaluating forces and capabilities that might be made available by them for multinational training, exercises, and operations in conjunction with Alliance forces;

- promote military and political coordination at NATO Headquarters in order to provide direction and guidance relevant to Partnership activities with the other subscribing states, including planning, training, exercises and the development of doctrine.

8. NATO will consult with any active participant in the Partnership if that Partner perceives a direct threat to its territorial integrity, political independence, or security.

APPENDIX 3

Founding Act on Mutual Relations, Cooperation and Security between NATO and the Russian Federation

Paris, 27 May 1997

The North Atlantic Treaty Organization and its member States, on the one hand, and the Russian Federation, on the other hand, hereinafter referred to as NATO and Russia, based on an enduring political commitment undertaken at the highest political level, will build together a lasting and inclusive peace in the Euro-Atlantic area on the principles of democracy and cooperative security.

NATO and Russia do not consider each other as adversaries. They share the goal of overcoming the vestiges of earlier confrontation and competition and of strengthening mutual trust and cooperation. The present Act reaffirms the determination of NATO and Russia to give concrete substance to their shared commitment to build a stable, peaceful and undivided Europe, whole and free, to the benefit of all its peoples. Making this commitment at the highest political level marks the beginning of a fundamentally new relationship between NATO and Russia. They intend to develop, on the basis of common interest, reciprocity and transparency a strong, stable and enduring partnership.

This Act defines the goals and mechanism of consultation, cooperation, joint decision-making and joint action that will constitute the core of the mutual relations between NATO and Russia.

NATO has undertaken a historic transformation—a process that will continue. In 1991 the Alliance revised its strategic doctrine to take account of the new security environment in Europe. Accordingly, NATO has radically reduced and continues the adaptation of its conventional and nuclear forces. While preserving the capability to meet the commitments undertaken in the Washington Treaty, NATO has expanded and will continue to expand its political functions, and taken on new missions of peacekeeping and crisis management in support of the United Nations (UN) and the Organisation for Security and Cooperation in Europe (OSCE), such as in Bosnia and Herzegovina, to address new security challenges in close association with other countries and international organisations. NATO is in the process of developing the European Security and Defence Identity (ESDI) within the Alliance. It will continue to develop a broad and dynamic pattern of cooperation with OSCE participating States in particular through the Partnership for Peace and is working with Partner countries on the initiative to establish a Euro-Atlantic Partnership Council. NATO member States have decided to examine NATO's Strategic Concept to ensure that it is fully consistent with Europe's new security situation and challenges.

Russia is continuing the building of a democratic society and the realisation of its political and economic transformation. It is developing the concept of its national security and revising its military doctrine to ensure that they are fully consistent with new security realities. Russia has carried out deep reductions in its armed forces, has withdrawn its forces on an unprecedented scale from the countries of Central and Eastern Europe and the Baltic countries and withdrawn all its nuclear weapons back to its own national territory. Russia is committed to further reducing its conventional and nuclear forces. It is actively participating in peacekeeping operations in support of the UN and the OSCE, as well as in crisis management in different areas of the world. Russia is contributing to the multinational forces in Bosnia and Herzegovina.

I. Principles

Proceeding from the principle that the security of all states in the Euro-Atlantic community is indivisible, NATO and Russia will work together to contribute to the establishment in Europe of common and comprehensive security based on the allegiance to shared values, commitments and norms of behaviour in the interests of all states. NATO and Russia will help to strengthen the Organisation for Security and Cooperation in Europe, including developing further its role as a primary instrument in preventive diplomacy, conflict prevention, crisis management, post-conflict rehabilitation and regional security cooperation, as well as in enhancing its operational capabilities to carry out these tasks. The OSCE, as the only pan-European security organisation, has a key role in European peace and stability. In strengthening the OSCE, NATO and Russia will cooperate to prevent any possibility of returning to a Europe of division and confrontation, or the isolation of any state.

Consistent with the OSCE's work on a Common and Comprehensive Security Model for Europe for the Twenty-First Century, and taking into account the decisions of the Lisbon Summit concerning a Charter on European security, NATO and Russia will seek the widest possible cooperation among participating States of the OSCE with the aim of creating in Europe a common space of security and stability, without dividing lines or spheres of influence limiting the sovereignty of any state.

NATO and Russia start from the premise that the shared objective of strengthening security and stability in the Euro-Atlantic area for the benefit of all countries requires a response to new risks and challenges, such as aggressive nationalism, proliferation of nuclear, biological and chemical weapons, terrorism, persistent abuse of human rights and of the rights of persons belonging to national minorities and unresolved territorial disputes, which pose a threat to common peace, prosperity and stability.

This Act does not affect, and cannot be regarded as affecting, the primary responsibility of the UN Security Council for maintaining international peace and security, or the role of the OSCE as the inclusive and comprehensive organisation for consultation, decision-making and cooperation in its area and as a regional arrangement under Chapter VIII of the United Nations Charter.

In implementing the provisions in this Act, NATO and Russia will observe in good faith their obligations under international law and international instruments, including the obligations of the United Nations Charter and the provisions of the Universal Declaration on Human Rights as well as their commitments under the Helsinki Final Act and subsequent OSCE documents, including the Charter of Paris and the documents adopted at the Lisbon OSCE Summit.

To achieve the aims of this Act, NATO and Russia will base their relations on a shared commitment to the following principles:

- development, on the basis of transparency, of a strong, stable, enduring and equal partnership and of cooperation to strengthen security and stability in the Euro-Atlantic area;

- acknowledgment of the vital role that democracy, political pluralism, the rule of law, and respect for human rights and civil liberties and the development of free market economies play in the development of common prosperity and comprehensive security;

- refraining from the threat or use of force against each other as well as against any other state, its sovereignty, territorial integrity or political independence in any manner inconsistent with the United Nations Charter and

with the Declaration of Principles Guiding Relations Between Participating
States contained in the Helsinki Final Act;

- respect for sovereignty, independence and territorial integrity of all states
  and their inherent right to choose the means to ensure their own security,
  the inviolability of borders and peoples' right of self-determination as enshrined in the Helsinki Final Act and other OSCE documents;
- mutual transparency in creating and implementing defence policy and military doctrines;
- prevention of conflicts and settlement of disputes by peaceful means in
  accordance with UN and OSCE principles;
- support, on a case-by-case basis, of peacekeeping operations carried out
  under the authority of the UN Security Council or the responsibility of the
  OSCE.

II. MECHANISM FOR CONSULTATION AND COOPERATION, THE NATO-RUSSIA PERMANENT JOINT COUNCIL

To carry out the activities and aims provided for by this Act and to develop
common approaches to European security and to political problems, NATO and
Russia will create the NATO-Russia Permanent Joint Council. The central objective
of this Permanent Joint Council will be to build increasing levels of trust, unity
of purpose and habits of consultation and cooperation between NATO and
Russia, in order to enhance each other's security and that of all nations in the
Euro-Atlantic area and diminish the security of none. If disagreements arise,
NATO and Russia will endeavour to settle them on the basis of goodwill and
mutual respect within the framework of political consultations.

The Permanent Joint Council will provide a mechanism for consultations,
coordination and, to the maximum extent possible, where appropriate, for joint
decisions and joint action with respect to security issues of common concern.
The consultations will not extend to internal matters of either NATO, NATO
member States or Russia.

The shared objective of NATO and Russia is to identify and pursue as many
opportunities for joint action as possible. As the relationship develops, they
expect that additional opportunities for joint action will emerge.

The Permanent Joint Council will be the principal venue of consultation
between NATO and Russia in times of crisis or for any other situation affecting
peace and stability. Extraordinary meetings of the Council will take place in
addition to its regular meetings to allow for prompt consultations in case of
emergencies. In this context, NATO and Russia will promptly consult within

the Permanent Joint Council in case one of the Council members perceives a threat to its territorial integrity, political independence or security.

The activities of the Permanent Joint Council will be built upon the principles of reciprocity and transparency. In the course of their consultations and cooperation, NATO and Russia will inform each other regarding the respective security-related challenges they face and the measures that each intends to take to address them.

Provisions of this Act do not provide NATO or Russia, in any way, with a right of veto over the actions of the other nor do they infringe upon or restrict the rights of NATO or Russia to independent decision-making and action. They cannot be used as a means to disadvantage the interests of other states.

The Permanent Joint Council will meet at various levels and in different forms, according to the subject matter and the wishes of NATO and Russia. The Permanent Joint Council will meet at the level of Foreign Ministers and at the level of Defence Ministers twice annually, and also monthly at the level of ambassadors/permanent representatives to the North Atlantic Council.

The Permanent Joint Council may also meet, as appropriate, at the level of Heads of State and Government.

The Permanent Joint Council may establish committees or working groups for individual subjects or areas of cooperation on an ad hoc or permanent basis, as appropriate.

Under the auspices of the Permanent Joint Council, military representatives and Chiefs of Staff will also meet; meetings of Chiefs of Staff will take place no less than twice a year, and also monthly at military representatives level. Meetings of military experts may be convened, as appropriate.

The Permanent Joint Council will be chaired jointly by the Secretary General of NATO, a representative of one of the NATO member States on a rotation basis, and a representative of Russia.

To support the work of the Permanent Joint Council, NATO and Russia will establish the necessary administrative structures.

Russia will establish a Mission to NATO headed by a representative at the rank of Ambassador. A senior military representative and his staff will be part of this Mission for the purposes of the military cooperation. NATO retains the possibility of establishing an appropriate presence in Moscow, the modalities of which remain to be determined.

The agenda for regular sessions will be established jointly. Organisational arrangements and rules of procedure for the Permanent Joint Council will be worked out. These arrangements will be in place for the inaugural meeting of the Permanent Joint Council which will be held no later than four months after the signature of this Act.

The Permanent Joint Council will engage in three distinct activities:

- consulting on the topics in Section III of this Act and on any other political or security issue determined by mutual consent;
- on the basis of these consultations, developing joint initiatives on which NATO and Russia would agree to speak or act in parallel;
- once consensus has been reached in the course of consultation, making joint decisions and taking joint action on a case-by-case basis, including participation, on an equitable basis, in the planning and preparation of joint operations, including peacekeeping operations under the authority of the UN Security Council or the responsibility of the OSCE.

Any actions undertaken by NATO or Russia, together or separately, must be consistent with the United Nations Charter and the OSCE's governing principles.

Recognizing the importance of deepening contacts between the legislative bodies of the participating States to this Act, NATO and Russia will also encourage expanded dialogue and cooperation between the North Atlantic Assembly and the Federal Assembly of the Russian Federation.

III. AREAS FOR CONSULTATION AND COOPERATION

In building their relationship, NATO and Russia will focus on specific areas of mutual interest. They will consult and strive to cooperate to the broadest possible degree in the following areas:

- issues of common interest related to security and stability in the Euro-Atlantic area or to concrete crises, including the contribution of NATO and Russia to security and stability in this area;
- conflict prevention, including preventive diplomacy, crisis management and conflict resolution taking into account the role and responsibility of the UN and the OSCE and the work of these organisations in these fields;
- joint operations, including peacekeeping operations, on a case-by-case basis, under the authority of the UN Security Council or the responsibility of the OSCE, and if Combined Joint Task Forces (CJTF) are used in such cases, participation in them at an early stage;
- participation of Russia in the Euro-Atlantic Partnership Council and the Partnership for Peace;
- exchange of information and consultation on strategy, defence policy, the military doctrines of NATO and Russia, and budgets and infrastructure development programmes;

- arms control issues;
- nuclear safety issues, across their full spectrum;
- preventing the proliferation of nuclear, biological and chemical weapons, and their delivery means, combating nuclear trafficking and strengthening cooperation in specific arms control areas, including political and defence aspects of proliferation;
- possible cooperation in Theatre Missile Defence;
- enhanced regional air traffic safety, increased air traffic capacity and reciprocal exchanges, as appropriate, to promote confidence through increased measures of transparency and exchanges of information in relation to air defence and related aspects of airspace management/control. This will include exploring possible cooperation on appropriate air defence related matters;
- increasing transparency, predictability and mutual confidence regarding the size and roles of the conventional forces of member States of NATO and Russia;
- reciprocal exchanges, as appropriate, on nuclear weapons issues, including doctrines and strategy of NATO and Russia;
- coordinating a programme of expanded cooperation between respective military establishments, as further detailed below;
- pursuing possible armaments-related cooperation through association of Russia with NATO's Conference of National Armaments Directors;
- conversion of defence industries;
- developing mutually agreed cooperative projects in defence-related economic, environmental and scientific fields;
- conducting joint initiatives and exercises in civil emergency preparedness and disaster relief;
- combating terrorism and drug trafficking;
- improving public understanding of evolving relations between NATO and Russia, including the establishment of a NATO documentation centre or information office in Moscow.

Other areas can be added by mutual agreement.

IV. POLITICAL-MILITARY MATTERS

NATO and Russia affirm their shared desire to achieve greater stability and security in the Euro-Atlantic area.

The member States of NATO reiterate that they have no intention, no plan and no reason to deploy nuclear weapons on the territory of new members, nor any need to change any aspect of NATO's nuclear posture or nuclear policy —and do not foresee any future need to do so. This subsumes the fact that NATO has decided that it has no intention, no plan, and no reason to establish nuclear weapon storage sites on the territory of those members, whether through the construction of new nuclear storage facilities or the adaptation of old nuclear storage facilities. Nuclear storage sites are understood to be facilities specifically designed for the stationing of nuclear weapons, and include all types of hardened above or below ground facilities (storage bunkers or vaults) designed for storing nuclear weapons.

Recognising the importance of the adaptation of the Treaty on Conventional Armed Forces in Europe (CFE) for the broader context of security in the OSCE area and the work on a Common and Comprehensive Security Model for Europe for the Twenty-First Century, the member States of NATO and Russia will work together in Vienna with the other States Parties to adapt the CFE Treaty to enhance its viability and effectiveness, taking into account Europe's changing security environment and the legitimate security interests of all OSCE participating States. They share the objective of concluding an adaptation agreement as expeditiously as possible and, as a first step in this process, they will, together with other States Parties to the CFE Treaty, seek to conclude as soon as possible a framework agreement setting forth the basic elements of an adapted CFE Treaty, consistent with the objectives and principles of the Document on Scope and Parameters agreed at Lisbon in December 1996.

NATO and Russia believe that an important goal of CFE Treaty adaptation should be a significant lowering in the total amount of Treaty-Limited Equipment permitted in the Treaty's area of application compatible with the legitimate defence requirements of each State Party. NATO and Russia encourage all States Parties to the CFE Treaty to consider reductions in their CFE equipment entitlements, as part of an overall effort to achieve lower equipment levels that are consistent with the transformation of Europe's security environment.

The member States of NATO and Russia commit themselves to exercise restraint during the period of negotiations, as foreseen in the Document on Scope and Parameters, in relation to the current postures and capabilities of their conventional armed forces—in particular with respect to their levels of forces and deployments—in the Treaty's area of application, in order to avoid developments in the security situation in Europe diminishing the security of any State Party. This commitment is without prejudice to possible voluntary decisions by the individual States Parties to reduce their force levels or deployments, or to their legitimate security interests.

The member States of NATO and Russia proceed on the basis that adaptation of the CFE Treaty should help to ensure equal security for all States Parties irrespective of their membership of a politico-military alliance, both to preserve and strengthen stability and continue to prevent any destabilizing increase of forces in various regions of Europe and in Europe as a whole. An adapted CFE Treaty should also further enhance military transparency by extended information exchange and verification, and permit the possible accession by new States Parties.

The member States of NATO and Russia propose to other CFE States Parties to carry out such adaptation of the CFE Treaty so as to enable States Parties to reach, through a transparent and cooperative process, conclusions regarding reductions they might be prepared to take and resulting national Treaty-Limited Equipment ceilings. These will then be codified as binding limits in the adapted Treaty to be agreed by consensus of all States Parties, and reviewed in 2001 and at five-year intervals thereafter. In doing so, the States Parties will take into account all the levels of Treaty-Limited Equipment established for the Atlantic-to-the-Urals area by the original CFE Treaty, the substantial reductions that have been carried out since then, the changes to the situation in Europe and the need to ensure that the security of no state is diminished.

The member States of NATO and Russia reaffirm that States Parties to the CFE Treaty should maintain only such military capabilities, individually or in conjunction with others, as are commensurate with individual or collective legitimate security needs, taking into account their international obligations, including the CFE Treaty.

Each State-Party will base its agreement to the provisions of the adapted Treaty on all national ceilings of the States Parties, on its projections of the current and future security situation in Europe.

In addition, in the negotiations on the adaptation of the CFE Treaty, the member States of NATO and Russia will, together with other States Parties, seek to strengthen stability by further developing measures to prevent any potentially threatening build-up of conventional forces in agreed regions of Europe, to include Central and Eastern Europe.

NATO and Russia have clarified their intentions with regard to their conventional force postures in Europe's new security environment and are prepared to consult on the evolution of these postures in the framework of the Permanent Joint Council.

NATO reiterates that in the current and foreseeable security environment, the Alliance will carry out its collective defence and other missions by ensuring the necessary interoperability, integration, and capability for reinforcement rather than by additional permanent stationing of substantial combat forces.

Accordingly, it will have to rely on adequate infrastructure commensurate with the above tasks. In this context, reinforcement may take place, when necessary, in the event of defence against a threat of aggression and missions in support of peace consistent with the United Nations Charter and the OSCE governing principles, as well as for exercises consistent with the adapted CFE Treaty, the provisions of the Vienna Document 1994 and mutually agreed transparency measures. Russia will exercise similar restraint in its conventional force deployments in Europe.

The member States of NATO and Russia will strive for greater transparency, predictability and mutual confidence with regard to their armed forces. They will comply fully with their obligations under the Vienna Document 1994 and develop cooperation with the other OSCE participating States, including negotiations in the appropriate format, inter alia within the OSCE to promote confidence and security.

The member States of NATO and Russia will use and improve existing arms control regimes and confidence-building measures to create security relations based on peaceful cooperation.

NATO and Russia, in order to develop cooperation between their military establishments, will expand political-military consultations and cooperation through the Permanent Joint Council with an enhanced dialogue between the senior military authorities of NATO and its member States and of Russia. They will implement a programme of significantly expanded military activities and practical cooperation between NATO and Russia at all levels. Consistent with the tenets of the Permanent Joint Council, this enhanced military-to-military dialogue will be built upon the principle that neither party views the other as a threat nor seeks to disadvantage the other's security. This enhanced military-to-military dialogue will include regularly-scheduled reciprocal briefings on NATO and Russian military doctrine, strategy and resultant force posture and will include the broad possibilities for joint exercises and training.

To support this enhanced dialogue and the military components of the Permanent Joint Council, NATO and Russia will establish military liaison missions at various levels on the basis of reciprocity and further mutual arrangements.

To enhance their partnership and ensure this partnership is grounded to the greatest extent possible in practical activities and direct cooperation, NATO's and Russia's respective military authorities will explore the further development of a concept for joint NATO-Russia peacekeeping operations. This initiative should build upon the positive experience of working together in Bosnia and Herzegovina, and the lessons learned there will be used in the establishment of Combined Joint Task Forces.

The present Act takes effect upon the date of its signature.

NATO and Russia will take the proper steps to ensure its implementation in accordance with their procedures.

The present Act is established in two originals in the French, English and Russian language.

The Secretary General of NATO and the Government of the Russian Federation will provide the Secretary General of the United Nations and the Secretary General of the OSCE with the text of this Act with the request to circulate it to all members of their Organisations.

APPENDIX 4

Charter on a Distinctive Partnership between the North Atlantic Treaty Organization and Ukraine

Madrid, 9 July 1997

I. Building an Enhanced NATO-Ukraine Relationship

1. The North Atlantic Treaty Organization (NATO) and its member States and Ukraine, hereinafter referred to as NATO and Ukraine,

   - building on a political commitment at the highest level;

   - recognizing the fundamental changes in the security environment in Europe which have inseparably linked the security of every state to that of all the others;

   - determined to strengthen mutual trust and cooperation in order to enhance security and stability, and to cooperate in building a stable, peaceful and undivided Europe;

   - stressing the profound transformation undertaken by NATO since the end of the Cold War and its continued adaptation to meet the changing circumstances of Euro-Atlantic security, including its support, on a case-by-case basis, of new missions of peacekeeping operations carried out under the authority of the United Nations Security Council or the responsibility of the OSCE;

- welcoming the progress achieved by Ukraine and looking forward to further steps to develop its democratic institutions, to implement radical economic reforms, and to deepen the process of integration with the full range of European and Euro-Atlantic structures;

- noting NATO's positive role in maintaining peace and stability in Europe and in promoting greater confidence and transparency in the Euro-Atlantic area, and its openness for cooperation with the new democracies of Central and Eastern Europe, an inseparable part of which is Ukraine;

- convinced that an independent, democratic and stable Ukraine is one of the key factors for ensuring stability in Central and Eastern Europe, and the continent as a whole;

- mindful of the importance of a strong and enduring relationship between NATO and Ukraine and recognizing the solid progress made, across a broad range of activities, to develop an enhanced and strengthened relationship between NATO and Ukraine on the foundations created by the Joint Press Statement of 14 September 1995;

- determined to further expand and intensify their cooperation in the framework of the Euro-Atlantic Partnership Council, including the enhanced Partnership for Peace programme;

- welcoming their practical cooperation within IFOR/SFOR and other peacekeeping operations on the territory of the former Yugoslavia;

- sharing the view that the opening of the Alliance to new members, in accordance with Article 10 of the Washington Treaty, is directed at enhancing the stability of Europe, and the security of all countries in Europe without recreating dividing lines;

are committed, on the basis of this Charter, to further broaden and strengthen their cooperation and to develop a distinctive and effective partnership, which will promote further stability and common democratic values in Central and Eastern Europe.

II. Principles for the Development of NATO-Ukraine Relations

2. NATO and Ukraine will base their relationship on the principles, obligations and commitments under international law and international instruments, including the United Nations Charter, the Helsinki Final Act and subsequent OSCE documents. Accordingly, NATO and Ukraine reaffirm their commitment to:

- the recognition that security of all states in the OSCE area is indivisible, that no state should pursue its security at the expense of that of another state, and that no state can regard any part of the OSCE region as its sphere of influence;
- refrain from the threat or use of force against any state in any manner inconsistent with the United Nations Charter or Helsinki Final Act principles guiding participating States;
- the inherent right of all states to choose and to implement freely their own security arrangements, and to be free to choose or change their security arrangements, including treaties of alliance, as they evolve;
- respect for the sovereignty, territorial integrity and political independence of all other states, for the inviolability of frontiers, and the development of good-neighbourly relations;
- the rule of law, the fostering of democracy, political pluralism and a market economy;
- human rights and the rights of persons belonging to national minorities;
- the prevention of conflicts and settlement of disputes by peaceful means in accordance with UN and OSCE principles.

3. Ukraine reaffirms its determination to carry forward its defence reforms, to strengthen democratic and civilian control of the armed forces, and to increase their interoperability with the forces of NATO and Partner countries. NATO reaffirms its support for Ukraine's efforts in these areas.

4. Ukraine welcomes NATO's continuing and active adaptation to meet the changing circumstances of Euro-Atlantic security, and its role, in cooperation with other international organizations such as the OSCE, the European Union, the Council of Europe and the Western European Union in promoting Euro-Atlantic security and fostering a general climate of trust and confidence in Europe.

III. Areas for Consultation and/or Cooperation between NATO and Ukraine

5. Reaffirming the common goal of implementation of a broad range of issues for consultation and cooperation, NATO and Ukraine commit themselves to develop and strengthen their consultation and/or cooperation in the areas described below. In this regard, NATO and Ukraine reaffirm their commitment to the full development of the EAPC and the enhanced PfP. This includes Ukrainian participation in operations, including

peacekeeping operations, on a case-by-case basis, under the authority of the UN Security Council, or the responsibility of the OSCE, and, if CJTF are used in such cases, Ukrainian participation in them at an early stage on a case-by-case basis, subject to decisions by the North Atlantic Council on specific operations.

6. Consultations between NATO and Ukraine will cover issues of common concern, such as:

- political and security related subjects, in particular the development of Euro-Atlantic security and stability, including the security of Ukraine;
- conflict prevention, crisis management, peace support, conflict resolution and humanitarian operations, taking into account the roles of the United Nations and the OSCE in this field;
- the political and defence aspects of nuclear, biological and chemical non-proliferation;
- disarmament and arms control issues, including those related to the Treaty on Conventional Armed Forces in Europe (CFE Treaty), the Open Skies Treaty and confidence and security building measures in the 1994 Vienna Document;
- arms exports and related technology transfers;
- combating drug-trafficking and terrorism.

7. Areas for consultation and cooperation, in particular through joint seminars, joint working groups, and other cooperative programmes, will cover a broad range of topics, such as:

- civil emergency planning, and disaster preparedness;
- civil-military relations, democratic control of the armed forces, and Ukrainian defence reform;
- defence planning, budgeting, policy, strategy and national security concepts;
- defence conversion;
- NATO-Ukraine military cooperation and interoperability;
- economic aspects of security;
- science and technology issues;
- environmental security issues, including nuclear safety;
- aerospace research and development, through AGARD;
- civil-military coordination of air traffic management and control.

8. In addition, NATO and Ukraine will explore to the broadest possible degree the following areas for cooperation:

- armaments cooperation (beyond the existing CNAD dialogue);
- military training, including PfP exercises on Ukrainian territory and NATO support for the Polish-Ukrainian peacekeeping battalion;
- promotion of defence cooperation between Ukraine and its neighbours.

9. Other areas for consultation and cooperation may be added, by mutual agreement, on the basis of experience gained.

10. Given the importance of information activities to improve reciprocal knowledge and understanding, NATO has established an Information and Documentation Centre in Kyiv. The Ukrainian side will provide its full support to the operation of the Centre in accordance with the Memorandum of Understanding between NATO and the Government of Ukraine signed at Kyiv on 7 May 1997.

IV. Practical Arrangements for Consultation and Cooperation between NATO and Ukraine

11. Consultation and cooperation as set out in this Charter will be implemented through:

- NATO-Ukraine meetings at the level of the North Atlantic Council at intervals to be mutually agreed;
- NATO-Ukraine meetings with appropriate NATO Committees as mutually agreed;
- reciprocal high level visits;
- mechanisms for military cooperation, including periodic meetings with NATO Chiefs of Defence and activities within the framework of the enhanced Partnership for Peace programme;
- a military liaison mission of Ukraine will be established as part of a Ukrainian mission to NATO in Brussels. NATO retains the right reciprocally to establish a NATO military liaison mission in Kyiv.

Meetings will normally take place at NATO Headquarters in Brussels. Under exceptional circumstances, they may be convened elsewhere, including in Ukraine, as mutually agreed. Meetings, as a rule, will take place on the basis of an agreed calendar.

12. NATO and Ukraine consider their relationship as an evolving, dynamic process. To ensure that they are developing their relationship and implementing the provisions of this Charter to the fullest extent possible, the North Atlantic Council will periodically meet with Ukraine as the NATO-Ukraine Commission, as a rule not less than twice a year. The NATO-Ukraine Commission will not duplicate the functions of other mechanisms described in this Charter, but instead would meet to assess broadly the implementation of the relationship, survey planning for the future, and suggest ways to improve or further develop cooperation between NATO and Ukraine.

13. NATO and Ukraine will encourage expanded dialogue and cooperation between the North Atlantic Assembly and the Verkhovna Rada.

V. Cooperation for a More Secure Europe

14. NATO Allies will continue to support Ukrainian sovereignty and independence, territorial integrity, democratic development, economic prosperity and its status as a non-nuclear weapon state, and the principle of inviolability of frontiers, as key factors of stability and security in Central and Eastern Europe and in the continent as a whole.

15. NATO and Ukraine will develop a crisis consultative mechanism to consult together whenever Ukraine perceives a direct threat to its territorial integrity, political independence, or security.

16. NATO welcomes and supports the fact that Ukraine received security assurances from all five nuclear-weapon states parties to the Treaty on the Non-Proliferation of Nuclear Weapons (NPT) as a non-nuclear weapon state party to the NPT, and recalls the commitments undertaken by the United States and the United Kingdom, together with Russia, and by France unilaterally, which took the historic decision in Budapest in 1994 to provide Ukraine with security assurances as a non-nuclear weapon state party to the NPT.

Ukraine's landmark decision to renounce nuclear weapons and to accede to the NPT as a non-nuclear weapon state greatly contributed to the strengthening of security and stability in Europe and has earned Ukraine special stature in the world community. NATO welcomes Ukraine's decision to support the indefinite extension of the NPT and its contribution to the withdrawal and dismantlement of nuclear weapons which were based on its territory.

Ukraine's strengthened cooperation with NATO will enhance and deepen the political dialogue between Ukraine and the members of the Alliance on a broad range of security matters, including on nuclear issues. This will contribute to the improvement of the overall security environment in Europe.

17. NATO and Ukraine note the entry into force of the CFE Flank Document on 15 May 1997. NATO and Ukraine will continue to cooperate on issues of mutual interest such as CFE adaptation. NATO and Ukraine intend to improve the operation of the CFE treaty in a changing environment and, through that, the security of each state party, irrespective of whether it belongs to a political-military alliance. They share the view that the presence of foreign troops on the territory of a participating state must be in conformity with international law, the freely expressed consent of the host state or a relevant decision of the United Nations Security Council.

18. Ukraine welcomes the statement by NATO members that "enlarging the Alliance will not require a change in NATO's current nuclear posture and, therefore, NATO countries have no intention, no plan and no reason to deploy nuclear weapons on the territory of new members nor any need to change any aspect of NATO's nuclear posture or nuclear policy—and do not foresee any future need to do so."

19. NATO member States and Ukraine will continue fully to implement all agreements on disarmament, non-proliferation and arms control and confidence-building measures they are part of.

The present Charter takes effect upon its signature.

The present Charter is established in two originals in the English, French and Ukrainian languages, all three texts having equal validity.

Notes

1. INTRODUCTION

1. Joint Declaration of Twenty-Two States, Paris, November 19, 1990, par. 3, in Adam Daniel Rotfeld and Walter Stützle, eds., *Germany and Europe in Transition* (New York: Oxford University Press, 1991), 217–18.

2. North Atlantic Council, Strategic Concept, November 7, 1991, par. 37.

3. Maxim Litvinov, Note to the Allies, February 25, 1920, from A. U. Pope, *Maxim Litvinov* (1943), p. 234, in *The Oxford Dictionary of Quotations,* 4th ed., 423.

4. North Atlantic Cooperation Council, Statement on Dialogue, Partnership and Cooperation, December 20, 1991, par. 2.

5. "The Covenant of the League of Nations," Appendix I, in Inis L. Claude, Jr., *Swords into Plowshares: The Problems and Progress of International Organization,* 4th ed. (New York: McGraw-Hill, 1984), 456–57.

6. Henry A. Kissinger, *Diplomacy* (New York: Simon and Schuster, 1994), 247–49.

7. Inis L. Claude, Jr., *Power and International Relations* (New York: Random House, 1962), 114; emphasis in the original.

8. Article 22 of the League's Covenant called for various "peoples not yet able to stand by themselves under the strenuous conditions of the modern world" to be "entrusted to advanced nations" under a "mandate" system.

9. Claude, *Power and International Relations,* 116.

10. The first use of the phrase cited in the *Oxford English Dictionary* is attributed to Winston Churchill in a 1934 parliamentary debate: "The great principle of collective security . . . is the only principle that will induce hon. Gentlemen opposite to make any preparation for the defense of this island." *Oxford English Dictionary,* 2d ed., 3:478.

11. Martin Wight, *Systems of States,* ed. Hedley Bull (London: Leicester University Press, 1977), 149.

12. Ibid., 111, 149.

13. For a valuable survey, see Sylvester John Hemleben, *Plans for World Peace through Six Centuries* (Chicago: University of Chicago Press, 1943). Hemleben's study begins (p. 3) with the pioneering proposal, written in 1305–07 by Pierre Dubois, an adviser to King Philip le Bel of France, for a council of kings and an international court of arbitration to enforce peace within Christendom, including "concerted military action against the offending nation." See also Elizabeth York, *Leagues of Nations: Ancient, Mediaeval, and Modern* (London: Swarthmore Press, 1919); Walter Alison Phillips, *The Confederation of Europe: A Study of the European Alliance, 1813–1823, as an Experiment in the International Organization of Peace* (London: Longmans, Green and Co., 1920), 18–33; and Claude, *Power and International Relations,* 106–7.

14. John Donne, "Meditation XVII," Devotions upon Emergent Occasions (1624), in *The Oxford Dictionary of Quotations,* 4th ed., 253.

15. Immanuel Kant, "Eternal Peace: A Philosophical Essay," first published in 1795, in Kant, *Eternal Peace and Other International Essays,* trans. W. Hastie (Boston: The World Peace Foundation, 1914), 77, 84, 86.

16. Immanuel Kant, "The Principle of Progress," first published in 1793, in Kant, *Eternal Peace,* 64, 65.

17. Kant, "Eternal Peace," 98.

18. Woodrow Wilson, "An Address to the Senate," January 22, 1917, in Arthur S. Link, ed., *The Papers of Woodrow Wilson* (Princeton: Princeton University Press, 1982), 40:536–37.

19. Woodrow Wilson, "At Reno, Nevada," September 22, 1919, in *War and Peace: Presidential Messages, Addresses, and Public Papers (1917–1924),* 2 vols., ed. Ray Stannard Baker and William E. Dodd (New York: Harper and Brothers, 1927), 2:328.

20. This discussion of the ideas shared by Kant and Wilson is indebted to Gerhard Beestermöller, *Die Völkerbundsidee: Leistungsfähigkeit und Grenzen der Kriegsächtung durch Staatensolidarität* (Stuttgart: Verlag W. Kohlhammer, 1995), 94–142. Beestermöller points out that while Wilson appears never to have quoted Kant, Wilson studied Kant and was in close contact with American peace society leaders, who considered Kant one of their most important intellectual forebears. According to Warren F. Kuehl, "Of all the early planners for an international organization, Kant had the greatest influence upon American thinkers." Warren F. Kuehl, *Seeking World Order: The United States and International Organization to 1920* (Nashville, Tenn.: Vanderbilt University Press, 1969), 10. Regarding Wilson's study of Kant, see Josephus Daniels, *The Life of Woodrow Wilson, 1856–1924* (Westport, Conn.: Greenwood Press, 1971; first published by John C. Winston, Chicago, 1924), 47.

21. The term "League of Nations" was proposed by Goldsworthy Lowes Dickinson, a Cambridge University professor, in his article, "The War and the Way Out," *Atlantic Monthly,* December 1914, an article that was brought to the attention of President Wilson. Thomas J. Knock, "Woodrow Wilson and the Origins of the League of Nations" (Ph.D. diss., Department of History, Princeton University, October 1982), 61–73.

22. Wilson, "An Address to the Senate," 535–36.

23. Woodrow Wilson, "Address Delivered at Mount Vernon," July 4, 1918, in Wilson, *War and Peace,* 1:234.

24. In current usage, as employed in this discussion, the concepts of popular sovereignty and constitutional government, with the rule of law and respect for individual rights, are among the essential elements of democracy. As suggested earlier, however, Kant favored the term "republican" for the rightful form of constitutional government for all states in his design for international order, and held that what he called a "democracy" was necessarily despotic. Unfortunately, as Hans Reiss has pointed out, Kant did not always employ these terms consistently. Kant nonetheless emphasized his support for principles that are, in current usage, considered aspects of democracy, such as the rule of law and respect for law. "There can also be no doubt as to his basic plea for separation of powers and his conviction that the sovereign authority should rest in the people or its representatives." Hans Reiss, introduction to *Political Writings,* by Immanuel Kant, 2d ed., edited by Hans Reiss and translated by H. B. Nisbet (Cambridge: Cambridge University Press, 1991), 30.

25. Woodrow Wilson, "The Fourteen Points Speech, Address Delivered at a Joint Session of the Two Houses of Congress," January 8, 1918, in Wilson, *War and Peace,* 1:159.

26. Kant, "Eternal Peace," 84–85.

27. Woodrow Wilson, "For Declaration of War Against Germany, Address Delivered at a Joint Session of the Two Houses of Congress," April 2, 1917, in Wilson, *War and Peace,* 1:16.

28. Woodrow Wilson, "Speech at the Coliseum, St. Louis, Missouri," September 5, 1919, in ibid., 1:645.

29. Outside the context of the League of Nations, one of the contrasts between Kant and Wilson concerns intervention. Whereas Kant opposed any military intervention in the internal affairs of foreign states, Wilson was in practice an interventionist who sent U.S. troops into Cuba, the Dominican Republic, Haiti, Mexico, and Russia—despite the moral reservations he expressed at times about the principle of intervention.

30. Raymond J. Sontag, *A Broken World, 1919–1939* (New York: Harper and Row, 1971), 12.

336 NOTES TO PAGES 13-14

31. Wilson, "An Address to the Senate," 539.

32. League of Nations Covenant, Article 8. Kant also argued that no national debts should be contracted with regard to a state's external affairs, because such debts could support and encourage interstate rivalries and facilitate the conduct of wars.

33. Perhaps the best source on Wilson's role (and that of other national representatives) is Florence Wilson, *The Origins of the League Covenant: Documentary History of Its Drafting* (London: Leonard and Virginia Woolf at the Hogarth Press, under the auspices of the Association for International Understanding, 1928).

34. League of Nations Covenant, Articles 10, 12, and 16.

35. ibid., Article 5.

36. Sontag, *A Broken World,* 13.

37. Woodrow Wilson, "Presentation of the Covenant of the League of Nations, Address before the Third Plenary Session of the Peace Conference," February 14, 1919, in Wilson, *War and Peace,* 1:425–26, 429; emphasis in the original.

38. Woodrow Wilson, "Speech at the Armory, Tacoma, Washington," September 13, 1919, in Wilson, *War and Peace,* 2:169. In fairness to Wilson, it should also be noted that he predicted "with absolute certainty that within another generation there will be another world war if the nations of the world do not concert the method by which to prevent it" and that such a war would involve "methods of explosive destruction unheard of even during this war," including the delivery of "tons of explosives upon helpless cities." For the former judgment, see Woodrow Wilson, "Speech at the Auditorium, Omaha, Nebraska," September 8, 1919, in Wilson, *War and Peace,* 2:36–37; for the latter, see "Speech at the Auditorium, Denver, Colorado," September 25, 1919, 391–92 of the same volume.

39. As Wight has observed, the notion that "'Man is born free, [yet] everywhere he is in chains', is the Rousseauite paradox. . . . If he was born free, how does he come to be in chains? How did the golden age of natural man decline into the *ancien régime* of the Bourbons and Habsburgs? It is because men, who manage to be exceptions to the rule that all are naturally good and free, have put him in chains." Martin Wight, *International Theory: The Three Traditions,* ed. Gabriele Wight and Brian Porter (London: Leicester University Press for the Royal Institute of International Affairs, 1991), 27.

40. Martin Wight, "The Balance of Power and International Order," in Alan James, ed., *The Bases of International Order: Essays in Honour of C.A.W. Manning* (London: Oxford University Press, 1973), 109–110. With regard to the Enlightenment critique of the balance of power, see also Claude, *Power and International Relations,* 85–87.

41. Treaty of Utrecht cited in Wight, "The Balance of Power and International Order," 98.

42. Treaty of Chaumont cited in Phillips, *The Confederation of Europe,* 74–75.

43. Vattel cited in Quincy Wright, *A Study of War* (Chicago: University of Chicago Press, 1942), 2:750.

44. Friedrich von Gentz (*Fragments Upon the Balance of Power in Europe)* cited in Claude, *Power and International Relations,* 130.

45. Wight, *International Theory,* 166. Wight cites Brougham's *An Enquiry into the Colonial Policy of the European Powers* for this passage.

46. Ibid., 154. Wight cites the following source for this passage: William Gladstone, "Right Principles of Foreign Policy," November 27, 1879, in E. R. Jones, ed., *Selected Speeches on British Foreign Policy, 1738–1914* (London: Oxford University Press, 1924), 372.

47. Edward V. Gulick, *Europe's Classical Balance of Power* (Ithaca: Cornell University Press, 1955), 307–308.

48. Quincy Wright, *The Study of International Relations* (New York: Appleton-Century-Crofts, 1955), 163, cited in Claude, *Power and International Relations,* 133.

49. Martin Wight, *Power Politics,* ed. Hedley Bull and Carsten Holbraad (London: Leicester University Press for the Royal Institute of International Affairs, 1978), 208. See also Claude, *Power and International Relations,* 154–55. Wight points out, however, that there is some evidence (notably in certain comments by Mussolini at the 1938 Munich Conference) that the sanctions against Italy came close to working. Wight, "The Balance of Power and International Order," 110.

50. Claude, *Power and International Relations,* 165.

51. Secretary of State Cordell Hull, address to joint meeting of both houses of Congress, November 18, 1943, in Leland M. Goodrich and Marie J. Carroll, eds., *Documents on American Foreign Relations,* vol. 6, *July 1943–June 1944* (Boston: World Peace Foundation, 1945), 14.

52. UN Information Organizations and U.S. Library of Congress, *Documents of the United Nations Conference on International Organization,* cited in Claude, *Power and International Relations,* 159.

53. According to Article 51 of the UN Charter, "Nothing in the present Charter shall impair the inherent right of individual or collective self-defense if an armed attack occurs against a Member of the United Nations, until the Security Council has taken the measures necessary to maintain international peace and security."

54. The tendency to equate collective security with collective defense has been a continuing source of confusion, because it implies that any alliance organized for self-defense and balance-of-power purposes is a collective security arrangement.

55. The range of instruments available to the international community for collective security intervention is concisely discussed by Willem van Eekelen in *The Security Agenda for 1996: Background and Proposals,* CEPS Paper no. 64 (Brussels: Centre for European Policy Studies, 1995), 18–19. Van Eekelen bases his discussion on Robert A. Pastor, "Forward to the Beginning: Widening the Scope for Global Collective Action," in Laura W. Reed and Carl Kaysen, eds., *Emerging Norms of Justified Intervention* (Cambridge, Mass.: Committee on International Security Studies, American Academy of Arts and Sciences, 1993).

56. In December 1994, the Conference on Security and Cooperation in Europe (CSCE) was renamed the Organization for Security and Cooperation in Europe (OSCE).

57. Ernst B. Haas, "Types of Collective Security: An Examination of Operational Concepts," *American Political Science Review* 49 (March 1955): 40.

58. Ibid., 41.

59. Ibid., 61. For a similar judgment, see Robert E. Osgood, "Woodrow Wilson, Collective Security, and the Lessons of History," in Earl Latham, ed., *The Philosophy and Policies of Woodrow Wilson* (Chicago: University of Chicago Press, 1958), 191.

60. Wight, "The Balance of Power and International Order," 113. Wight's quotation refers to an official British analysis: *A Commentary on the Charter of the United Nations,* Miscellaneous No. 9 (1945), Cmd. 6666, par. 87.

61. Thomas Hobbes, *Leviathan,* ed. Richard Tuck (Cambridge: Cambridge University Press, 1991; first published in 1651), 230.

62. Inis L. Claude, Jr., "Collective Security after the Cold War," in Gary L. Guertner, ed., *Collective Security in Europe and Asia* (Carlisle Barracks, Penn.: Strategic Studies Institute, U.S. Army War College, 1992), 13–15. The pattern of recurring interest in plans to secure an enduring peace after major wars has been identifiable since the origins of the modern states-system during the fourteenth and fifteenth centuries. As Hemleben notes, among other examples, the wars of Louis XIV encouraged William Penn and the Abbé de Saint-Pierre to devise their proposals, and the wars of the Austrian Succession and the French Revolution furnished the background for Rousseau and Kant, respectively. Hemleben, *Plans for World Peace through Six Centuries,* 182.

63. Wight, *Systems of States,* 62.

64. Claude, *Power and International Relations,* 203.

65. Wight, *International Theory,* 262.

66. Claude, *Power and International Relations,* 201, 204. Claude also maintains (pp. 192–198) that various developments in the 1940s and 1950s (and subsequently)—in military technology, the distribution of power, alliance patterns, and methods of carrying out aggression—have made the realization of traditional collective security designs even more difficult to achieve than was the case during the initial decades of the twentieth century.

67. Much of the scholarly literature on collective security in the post–Cold War period has concentrated on explaining the pitfalls of the Kantian and Wilsonian approach. See, for example, Mark P. Lagon, "The Illusions of Collective Security," *The National Interest,* Summer 1995, 50–55; Richard K. Betts, "Systems for Peace or Causes of War? Collective Security, Arms Control, and the New Europe," *International Security* 17 (Summer 1992): 5–43; Josef Joffe, "Collective Security and the Future of Europe: Failed Dreams and Dead Ends," *Survival* 34 (Spring 1992): 36–50; and Richard Russell, "The Chimera of Collective Security in Europe," *European Security* 4 (Summer 1995): 241–55.

68. Max Jakobson, "Collective Security in Europe Today," *Washington Quarterly,* Spring 1995, 62.

69. James E. Goodby, "Can Collective Security Work? Reflections on the European Case," in Chester A. Crocker and Fen Osler Hampson, with Pamela Aall, eds., *Managing Global Chaos: Sources of and Responses to International Conflict* (Washington, D.C.: United States Institute of Peace Press, 1996), 237.

70. James E. Goodby, "Collective Security in Europe after the Cold War," *Journal of International Affairs* 46 (Winter 1993): 309.

71. Goodby, "Can Collective Security Work?" 241.

72. Wight, "The Balance of Power," in Herbert Butterfield and Martin Wight, eds., *Diplomatic Investigations: Essays in the Theory of International Politics* (Cambridge, Mass.: Harvard University Press, 1966), 150–51. Wight discusses nine meanings of the term in international history.

73. For a discussion of continuing value, see Andrew W. Marshall, "Arms Competitions: The Status of Analysis," in Uwe Nerlich, ed., *The Western Panacea: Constraining Soviet Power through Negotiation,* vol. 2 of *Soviet Power and Western Negotiating Policies* (Cambridge, Mass.: Ballinger Publishing Co., 1983). Not all arms and power competitions lead to war, of course. The nonviolent dénouement of the U.S.-Soviet and broader East-West (and NATO–Warsaw Pact) competition illustrates this principle. In this case, the competition ended because of the exhaustion and collapse of one of the antagonists. The intermittent British-French competition during the nineteenth century, from the Napoleonic Wars to Fashoda (1898), provides an example of a different type. With the turn of the century, London and Paris increasingly subordinated their competition to shared concern regarding Germany's power and ambitions. In other words, the antagonists shifted their attention to a third party.

74. This categorization of motives in war was proposed by Wight, following the suggestions of "Hobbes, who was himself adapting the motives of Athenian imperialism described by Thucydides." In Wight's view, "rational apprehension of future evil . . . is the prime motive of international politics. . . . It is worth remembering that the motive of fear prompts preventive war as well as defensive war, and that in the majority of wars between great powers the aggressor's motive has been preventive." Wight, *Power Politics*, 138–39.

75. Claude, *Power and International Relations,* 59.

76. Wight, *Power Politics,* 43.

77. Kissinger, *Diplomacy,* 242, 226.

2. NATO during the Cold War and Its Aftermath

1. Shevardnadze testimony to the Supreme Soviet International Affairs Committee, in TASS, September 20, 1990, cited in John Van Oudenaren, *Détente in Europe: The Soviet Union and the West since 1953* (Durham, N.C.: Duke University Press, 1991), 363–64.

2. Nikolai Portugalov, *Der Spiegel,* October 8, 1990, in *Foreign Broadcast Information Service* (hereafter, FBIS)/*Soviet Union,* October 10, 1990, cited in Van Oudenaren, *Détente in Europe,* 364.

3. Two-thirds of U.S. military installations in Europe have been closed, and U.S. military personnel in Europe have been pared from 341,000 in 1989 to 109,000 today. The U.S. nuclear presence has been reduced by more than 80 percent since 1991, and the only U.S. nuclear weapons remaining in Europe are a reduced number of gravity bombs for U.S. and Allied dual-capable aircraft.

4. The Soviet ideological justification for such interventions was the claim that the USSR's duty to protect "the socialist community" and "the world revolutionary movement" by force overrode "bourgeois" concepts such as sovereignty and national self-determination. The most famous articulation of this argument, a 1968 article in *Pravda* defending the suppression of the "Prague Spring" by the Soviet Union and four of its Warsaw Pact allies (Bulgaria, East Germany, Hungary, and Poland), became known as the Brezhnev Doctrine. For extended excerpts from this article, see Sergei Kovalev, "Sovereignty and the International Duties of Socialist Countries," *Pravda,* September 26, 1968, in Alvin Z. Rubinstein, ed., *The Foreign Policy of the Soviet Union,* 3d ed. (New York: Random House, 1972), 302–5. For a comprehensive analysis of the origins and history of this Soviet policy, see Robert A. Jones, *The Soviet Concept of 'Limited Sovereignty' from Lenin to Gorbachev* (London: Macmillan, 1990).

5. The Treaty of Dunkirk referred specifically to the possibility of a future German threat in addition to establishing a mutual defense obligation.

6. The essential role of British and French statesmen (such as Ernest Bevin, Georges Bidault, and Robert Schuman) in organizing the Atlantic Alliance has been examined in recent studies such as Alan Bullock, *The Life and Times of Ernest Bevin,* vol. 3, *Foreign Secretary, 1945–1951* (London: William Heinemann, 1983), 529–31, 540–43, 582–85, 632–33, 644–45, 857; Theodore C. Achilles, "The Omaha Milkman: The Role of the United States in the Negotiations," and Claude Delmas, "A Change of Heart: Concerns behind the Discussions in France," both in Nicholas Sherwen, ed., *NATO's Anxious Birth: The Prophetic Vision of the 1940s* (London: C. Hurst and Co., 1985). Historians differ regarding the extent to which (and for how long) British officials took seriously the idea of organizing a West European–based "Third Force" supported by the United States in arrangements short of a formal alliance. For background, see John W. Young and John Kent, "British Policy Overseas: The 'Third Force' and the Origins of NATO—In Search of a New Perspective," in Beatrice Heuser and Robert O'Neill, eds., *Securing Peace in Europe, 1945–62: Thoughts for the Post–Cold War Era* (London: Macmillan, 1992).

7. Harry S. Truman, *Memoirs,* vol. 2, *Years of Trial and Hope* (Garden City, N.Y.: Doubleday and Co., 1956), 249.

8. The phrase "entangling alliances" has customarily been attributed to President George Washington as a part of his Farewell Address on September 19, 1796, even though his actual words were as follows: "Why, by interweaving our destiny with that of any part of Europe, entangle our peace and prosperity in the toils of European ambition, rivalship, interest, humour, or caprice? 'Tis our true policy to steer clear of permanent alliances, with any portion of the foreign world." Washington's Farewell Address quoted in Walter Millis, ed., *American Military Thought* (Indianapolis: Bobbs-Merrill Co., 1966), 68. It was, in fact, President Thomas Jefferson who urged his fellow citizens to avoid "entangling alliances," in his First Inaugural Address on March 4, 1801. Jefferson's First Inaugural Address quoted in John Bartlett, *Familiar Quotations,* ed. Emily Morison Beck, 15th ed. (Boston: Little Brown and Co., 1980), 389.

9. Dean Acheson, testimony to U.S. Senate, *North Atlantic Treaty,* hearings before the Committee on Foreign Relations (Washington, D.C.: U.S. Government Printing Office, 1949), 47.

10. Robert E. Osgood, *NATO: The Entangling Alliance* (Chicago: University of Chicago Press, 1962), 68–69; and Doris M. Condit, *The Test of War, 1950–1953,* vol. 2 of *History of the Office of the Secretary of Defense* (Washington, D.C.: U.S. Government Printing Office, 1988), 307–9.

11. Jules Moch cited in Edward Fursdon, *The European Defence Community: A History* (London: Macmillan, 1980), 91.

12. The EDC in fact was never directly voted on in the French National Assembly, nor was a full-scale debate held. The EDC was defeated on a procedural motion before such a debate could be held. For details, see ibid., 295–7.

13. Two agreements in the mid-1950s probably also contributed to (and reflected) the political stability of Europe during the Cold War: the 1954 London Memorandum of Understanding on the "Free Territory of Trieste" and the 1955 Austrian State Treaty. For background on the former, see Ettore Greco, "Italy, the Yugoslav Crisis and the Osimo Agreements," *The International Spectator,* January/March 1994, 13–31. On the latter, see Audrey Kurth Cronin, *Great Power Politics and the Struggle over Austria, 1945–1955* (Ithaca, N.Y.: Cornell University Press, 1986).

14. For a useful analysis of national differences in foreign policy within the Warsaw Pact, see Edwina Moreton, "Foreign Policy Goals," in David Holloway and Jane M. O. Sharp, eds., *The Warsaw Pact: Alliance in Transition?* (London: Macmillan, 1984), especially the discussion of Romania (pp. 149–151).

15. Article IV of the Brussels Treaty, as amended and signed at Paris, October 23, 1954. This article was not in the original 1948 Brussels Treaty, of course, because NATO had not yet been established. In practice, the parties to the Brussels Treaty began to rely on the Alliance promptly after its establishment, particularly after Allied Command Europe became operational in 1951.

16. For a discussion of Soviet ideology and propaganda about military-technical innovation during the Cold War (at times the Soviets claimed credit for being the first to develop ICBMs and certain other capabilities, and at other times portrayed the United States as the sole "engine of the arms race," with the USSR in a purely reactive mode), see David S. Yost, *Soviet Ballistic Missile Defense and the Western Alliance* (Cambridge, Mass.: Harvard University Press, 1988), 71–80.

17. Gorbachev speech on Moscow television, May 8, 1985, in *FBIS/ Soviet Union, Daily Report,* May 9, 1985, R17.

18. Nikita Khrushchev, speech to Western diplomats at a reception in Moscow, November 18, 1956, in *The Times* (London), November 19, 1956, in *The Oxford Dictionary of Quotations,* 4th ed., 395.

19. R. Craig Nation, *Black Earth, Red Star: A History of Soviet Security Policy, 1917–1991* (Ithaca, N.Y.: Cornell University Press, 1992), 233.

20. For a first-rate study of Soviet articulations of this ideology, see Peter H. Vigor, *The Soviet View of War, Peace and Neutrality* (London: Routledge and Kegan Paul, 1975).

21. No reasonably comprehensive history of NATO exists. An excellent source on the Alliance's early period remains Osgood's *NATO: The Entangling Alliance.* An illuminating survey for the period up through the 1970s is Alfred Grosser, *The Western Alliance: European-American Relations Since 1945,* trans. Michael Shaw (London: Macmillan, 1980). A useful one-volume survey of the Alliance's history through the end of the Cold War is Richard L. Kugler, *Commitment to Purpose: How Alliance Partnership Won the Cold War* (Santa Monica, Calif.: Rand Corporation, 1993).

22. Of the vast literature on this subject, three books deserve particular mention: David N. Schwartz, *NATO's Nuclear Dilemmas* (Washington, D.C.: Brookings Institution, 1983); Jane E. Stromseth, *The Origins of Flexible Response: NATO's Debate over Strategy in the 1960s* (London: Macmillan, 1988); and Ivo H. Daalder, *The Nature and Practice of Flexible Response: NATO Strategy and Theater Nuclear Forces since 1967* (New York: Columbia University Press, 1991). For further background, including a discussion of key questions about extended deterrence and limited nuclear operations that were never fully answered during the Cold War, see David S. Yost, "The History of NATO Theater Nuclear Force Policy: Key Findings from the Sandia Conference," *Journal of Strategic Studies* 15 (June 1992): 228–61.

23. For a useful discussion of the first topic, with an extensive bibliography, see Simon Duke, *The Burdensharing Debate: A Reassessment* (London: Macmillan, 1993). For an exceptionally valuable analysis of the second topic, see Eliot A. Cohen, "Toward Better Net Assessment: Rethinking the European Conventional Balance," *International Security* 13 (Summer 1988). Finally, with regard to arms control, an ambitious and influential collection of analyses communicated its basic message in the volume titles: Uwe Nerlich, ed., *Soviet Power and Western Negotiating Policies,* vol. 1, *The Soviet Asset: Military Power in the Competition over Europe,* and vol. 2, *The Western Panacea: Constraining Soviet Power through Negotiation* (Cambridge, Mass.: Ballinger Publishing Co., 1983).

24. For the first number, see Robert S. Norris and William M. Arkin, "U.S. Nuclear Weapon Locations, 1995," *Bulletin of the Atomic Scientists,* November/December 1995, 74–75. For the second, see Alan Riding, "NATO Will Cut Atom Weapons for Aircraft Use," *New York Times,* October 18, 1991, A1.

25. *Enhancing Alliance Collective Security: Shared Roles, Risks and Responsibilities in the Alliance,* A Report by NATO's Defense Planning Committee, December 1988, par. 36. It should be noted that the United Kingdom provided its own nuclear gravity bombs for its dual-capable aircraft, and that all British air-delivered nuclear weapons were phased out in early 1998.

26. North Atlantic Council, Strategic Concept, par. 56.

27. Ibid., par. 55, 57.

28. The U.S. nuclear arsenal available to uphold U.S. security commitments includes forces in addition to those actually based in Europe. The U.S. nuclear posture includes Ohio-class nuclear-powered submarines equipped with ballistic missiles, Minuteman III and MX Peacekeeper intercontinental ballistic missiles, B-52 and B-2 bombers, nuclear-armed Tomahawk sea-launched cruise missiles, and bombs for tactical aircraft in addition to those in Europe. Since the withdrawal of its last air-delivered bombs in early 1998, the United Kingdom's nuclear forces have consisted solely of nuclear-powered submarines equipped with ballistic missiles. Since the deactivation of its intermediate-range missile force on the Plateau d'Albion in 1996, France's operational nuclear forces have consisted solely of nuclear-powered submarines equipped with ballistic missiles, plus aircraft equipped with air-launched missiles. For details, see International Institute for Strategic Studies, *The Military Balance 1997/98* (London: Oxford University Press for the International Institute for Strategic Studies, 1997), 18, 50, 70.

29. In one case, the French are excluded by the "allies concerned" formula (par. 57) and in another by the reference to "European Allies involved in collective defense planning in nuclear roles" (par. 56). For background, see David S. Yost, "Nuclear Weapons Issues in France," in John C. Hopkins and Weixing Hu, eds., *Strategic Views from the Second Tier: The Nuclear Weapons Policies of France, Britain, and China* (San Diego, Calif.: Institute on Global Conflict and Cooperation, University of California, San Diego, 1994), especially 24–28.

30. Par. 8 of the communiqué regarding the December 1962 U.S.-British summit at Nassau. The communiqué is reproduced in Andrew J. Pierre, *Nuclear Politics: The British Experience with an Independent Strategic Force, 1939–70* (London: Oxford University Press, 1972), 346–47.

31. See, among other sources, Shaun R. Gregory, *Nuclear Command and Control in NATO: Nuclear Weapons Operations and the Strategy of Flexible Response* (London: Macmillan, 1996).

32. "Mr. Churchill's Address Calling for United Effort for World Peace," *New York Times,* March 6, 1946, 4.

33. Phrases used in NATO communiqués of September 17, 1949; December 14–16, 1953; and December 16–19, 1957, in *Texts of Final Communiqués, 1949–1974* (Brussels: NATO Information Service, 1975), 39, 79, 109.

34. The Harmel Report, named after the Belgian Foreign Minister, is available under its formal title, "The Future Tasks of the Alliance," Report of the Council, Annex to the Final Communiqué of the Ministerial Meeting, December 13–14, 1967, in ibid., 198–202.

35. North Atlantic Council communiqué of December 15–16, 1955, in ibid., 95.

36. For example, see North Atlantic Council communiqué of December 16–19, 1957, in ibid., 109.

37. North Atlantic Council declaration of December 11–14, 1956, in ibid., 102.

38. North Atlantic Council communiqué of December 15–16, 1966, in ibid., 178.

39. North Atlantic Council communiqué of May 2–3, 1957, in ibid., 106.

40. North Atlantic Council communiqué of June 13–14, 1967, in ibid., 189.

41. North Atlantic Council declaration of December 4–5, 1969, in ibid., 231.

42. This brief discussion omits national differences within the Alliance during the Cold War regarding how to pursue peaceful changes in the European political order. Among other sources, see Charles R. Planck, *The Changing Status of German Reunification in Western Diplomacy, 1955–1966* (Baltimore: Johns Hopkins University Press, 1967); Bennett Kovrig, *The Myth of Liberation: East-Central Europe in U.S. Diplomacy and Politics since 1941* (Baltimore: Johns Hopkins University Press, 1973); Lincoln Gordon et al., *Eroding Empire: Western Relations with Eastern Europe* (Washington, D.C.: Brookings Institution, 1987); and David S. Yost, *Alternative Structures of European Security,* Working Paper no. 81 (Washington,. D.C.: International Security Studies Program, Woodrow Wilson International Center for Scholars, 1987).

43. For a valuable account by a U.S. participant in the negotiations, see John J. Maresca, *To Helsinki: The Conference on Security and Cooperation in Europe, 1973–1975* (Durham, N.C.: Duke University Press, 1985). Maresca's book includes the full text of the Helsinki Final Act as an appendix.

44. Ibid., 158.

45. For a detailed discussion, see ibid., especially 46, 121, and 156–60.

46. For background regarding Soviet efforts to attribute more legal standing to the Helsinki Final Act than it has, see Van Oudenaren, *Détente in Europe,* 323–27.

47. The metaphor refers to the myth of Yalta, the notion that Churchill, Roosevelt, and Stalin met at Yalta in the Crimea in February 1945 to divide up Europe. According to the myth, Roosevelt and Churchill agreed that the Soviet Union should dominate Eastern Europe. According to the French version of the myth, advanced repeatedly by General de Gaulle, this came about because France was not represented at Yalta. In fact, the U.S.-drafted Declaration on Liberated Europe approved at the Yalta conference called for national self-determination through free and democratic elections. Europe was divided by Soviet military power and Moscow's determination to retain control of the territories it occupied, not by any agreement at Yalta. See Reiner Marcowitz, "Yalta, the Myth of the Division of the World," in Cyril Buffet and Beatrice Heuser, eds., *Haunted by History: Myths in International Relations* (Providence, R.I.: Berghahn Books, 1998), 80–91; and Richard F. Fenno, Jr., ed., *The Yalta Conference* (Lexington, Mass.: D.C. Heath and Co., 1972). The latter includes the key conference documents, including the Declaration on Liberated Europe.

48. Among other sources, see Harold S. Russell, "The Helsinki Declaration: Brobdingnag or Lilliput?" *American Journal of International Law* 70 (April 1976): 242–72.

346 NOTES TO PAGES 39–42

49. For a discussion of this attitude, see Ronald Steel, "The West Has Its Own Stake in the Eastern Status Quo," *Los Angeles Times,* January 17, 1982, part IV, pp. 1, 3.

50. Helmut Schmidt quoted in Timothy Garton Ash, *The Polish Revolution: Solidarity* (New York: Charles Scribner's Sons, 1984), 317.

51. Giulio Andreotti quoted in James M. Markham, "For Both East and West, Two Germanys is Better," *New York Times,* September 23, 1984, part IV, p. 5.

52. Milovan Djilas, *The New Class: An Analysis of the Communist System* (New York: Frederick A. Praeger, 1957).

53. Peter Rudolf, "Managing Strategic Divergence: German-American Conflict over Policy Towards Iran," in Peter Rudolf and Geoffrey Kemp, *The Iranian Dilemma: Challenges for German and American Foreign Policy* (Washington, D.C.: American Institute for Contemporary German Studies, Johns Hopkins University, 1997), 3.

54. For general background, see Charles Gati, *The Bloc that Failed: Soviet–East European Relations in Transition* (Bloomington: Indiana University Press, 1990). For detailed discussions, see "Romania and Bulgaria: Those southeastern laggards," *The Economist,* October 19, 1996, 54–56; Albert P. Melone, "The Struggle for Judicial Independence and the Transition Toward Democracy in Bulgaria," *Communist and Post-Communist Studies* 29, no. 2 (1996); and Thomas Carothers, "Romania: Projecting the Positive," *Current History,* March 1996.

55. Kissinger quoted in Michael Charlton, *The Eagle and the Small Birds: Crisis in the Soviet Empire: From Yalta to Solidarity* (Chicago: University of Chicago Press, 1984), 139–40.

56. X [George F. Kennan], "The Sources of Soviet Conduct," in Hamilton Fish Armstrong, ed., *The Foreign Affairs Reader* (New York: Harper and Brothers for the Council on Foreign Relations, 1947), 475, 477, 481, 483.

57. Pierre Hassner, "Recurrent Stresses, Resilient Structures," in Robert W. Tucker and Linda Wrigley, eds., *The Atlantic Alliance and Its Critics* (New York: Praeger, 1983), 91.

58. Zbigniew Brzezinski, *The Grand Failure: The Birth and Death of Communism in the Twentieth Century* (New York: Scribner's, 1989); Jacob Kipp, "Alternative Politico-Military Futures," in John Hemsley, ed., *The Lost Empire: Perceptions of Soviet Policy Shifts in the 1990s* (London: Brassey's, 1991), 67–87; Vladimir Bukovsky, "The Political Condition of the Soviet Empire," and Charles Wolf, Jr., "The Costs and Benefits of the Soviet Empire," both in Henry S. Rowen and Charles Wolf, Jr., eds., *The Future of the Soviet Empire* (London: Macmillan, 1988); Z [Martin Malia], "To the Stalin Mausoleum," *Daedalus* 119 (Winter 1990).

59. The most far-sighted analysis was probably Andrei Amalrik's *Will the Soviet Union Survive Until 1984?* (New York: Harper and Row, 1971). While Amalrik overstated the likelihood of a Sino-Soviet war as a factor in the USSR's collapse, he perceptively drew attention to widespread social demoralization, the regime's self-isolation and immobilism, and the frustrations of non-Russian nationalities.

60. Bukovsky, "The Political Condition," 29.

61. In December 1988, Gorbachev told the General Assembly of the United Nations, "We in no way aspire to be the bearer of ultimate truth." Senator Daniel Patrick Moynihan called this "the most astounding statement of surrender in the history of ideological struggle." (Moynihan letter in *The National Interest,* Winter 1995/96, 111.)

62. Myron Rush, "Fortune and Fate," *The National Interest,* Spring 1993, 22, 25.

63. Adam Ulam, letter in the *Washington Post Book World*, February 9, 1997, 14.

64. Adam Ulam, "Charting the Communist Course," *Washington Post Book World,* January 5, 1997, 1, 14.

65. Charles Fairbanks, "The Nature of the Beast," *The National Interest,* Spring 1993, 50, 54.

66. For a penetrating analysis, see Ernest Gellner, "Homeland of the Unrevolution," *Daedalus* 122 (Summer 1993): especially 145–47.

67. Peter Reddaway, "The Role of Popular Discontent," *The National Interest,* Spring 1993, 63.

68. Roman Laba, "How Yeltsin's Exploitation of Ethnic Nationalism Brought Down an Empire," *Transition* 2, no. 1 (January 12, 1996): 5.

69. Anders Aslund, "Suddenly and Peacefully," *The National Interest,* Spring 1997, 109.

70. Ibid., 108.

71. Vladimir Kontorovich, "The Economic Fallacy," *The National Interest,* Spring 1993, 43.

72. Jacob Kipp, "The Other Side of the Hill: Soviet Military Foresight and Forecasting," in Derek Leebaert and Timothy Dickinson, eds., *Soviet Strategy and New Military Thinking* (New York: Cambridge University Press, 1992), 265.

73. *Report of Secretary of Defense Caspar W. Weinberger to the Congress on the FY 1987 Budget, FY 1988 Authorization Request and FY 1987–1991 Defense Programs,* February 5, 1986 (Washington, D.C.: Government Printing Office, 1986), 85–88.

74. Peter Schweizer, *Victory: The Reagan Administration's Secret Strategy that Hastened the Collapse of the Soviet Union* (New York: Atlantic Monthly Press, 1994), xviii.

75. Gellner, "Homeland of the Unrevolution," 148.

76. Ulam, letter in the *Washington Post Book World,* 14.

77. Schweizer, *Victory,* 282.

78. Milton Bearden quoted in David Wise, "The CIA's Midlife Crisis," *Washington Post National Weekly Edition,* September 22, 1997, 21.

79. See, for example, George F. Kennan, "The G.O.P. Won the Cold War? Ridiculous," *New York Times,* October 28, 1992, and the letter in response by Richard Pipes, November 6, 1992.

80. Van Oudenaren, *Détente in Europe,* 366.

81. "Gorbachev at Stanford: Excerpts from Address," *New York Times,* June 5, 1990, A6.

82. Francis X. Clines, "Warsaw Pact Pronounces the End of Ideological Conflict with West," *New York Times,* June 8, 1990, A1, A4.

83. According to Article 11 of the Warsaw Treaty of Friendship, Cooperation, and Mutual Assistance of May 14, 1955, "In the event of the establishment of a system of collective security in Europe and the conclusion for that purpose of a General European Treaty concerning collective security, a goal which the Contracting Parties shall steadfastly strive to achieve, the present Treaty shall cease to have effect as from the date on which the General European Treaty comes into force." Gorbachev also proposed, as another arrangement of interest to the Soviet Union, that the soon-to-be-united Germany have membership in both NATO and the Warsaw Pact.

84. Jiri Dienstbier quoted in Walter S. Mossberg, "Concept of a 'European Peace Order' Challenges U.S. Efforts to Retain NATO," *Wall Street Journal,* March 12, 1990, A6.

85. Philip Revzin and Walter S. Mossberg, "Europe Will Rely Less on U.S. for Security, More on Own Devices," *Wall Street Journal,* May 4, 1990, A1, A8.

86. Foreign Minister Hans-Dietrich Genscher, speech at WEU meeting, March 23, 1990, text furnished by the German Information Center, New York, 3–4.

87. Joint Declaration of Twenty-Two States, Paris, November 19, 1990, par. 3, in Rotfeld and Stützle, eds., *Germany and Europe in Transition,* 217–18.

88. Charter of Paris for a New Europe, November 21, 1990, in ibid., 219–30.

89. Marc Fisher, "Kremlin Blocks Center Set Up to Prevent Conflict," *International Herald Tribune,* June 20, 1991, 1, 4. The ideas expressed by the German Chancellor, Helmut Kohl, in opening this meeting of CSCE foreign ministers are noteworthy because Kohl went beyond commending the goals outlined in the November 1990 Charter of Paris: "Quoting the philosopher Immanuel Kant, Mr. Kohl said European countries should form a 'multinational state' that 'would ultimately encompass all nations of the world.'"

90. President Vaclav Havel, statement at the headquarters of the North Atlantic Treaty Organization, March 21, 1991, text furnished by the NATO Press and Information Service, 2–3, 5–6, 8.

91. Jozsef Antall quoted in Celestine Bohlen, "Tensions in Other Countries Raise Concerns in Hungary," *New York Times,* October 13, 1991, 6.

92. Uwe Nerlich, "Western Europe's Relations with the United States," *Daedalus* 108 (Winter 1979): 88.

93. Josef Joffe, *The Limited Partnership: Europe, the United States, and the Burdens of Alliance* (Cambridge, Mass.: Ballinger Publishing Co., 1987), 178, 183–84.

94. Robert Art, "Why Western Europe Needs the United States and NATO," *Political Science Quarterly* 111, no. 1 (1996): 38.

95. Michael Rühle and Nick Williams, "Why NATO Will Survive," *Comparative Strategy* 16 (January/March 1997): 113.

96. Rodric Braithwaite, "Bringing Russia In," *Prospect,* June 1997, 36.

97. Ismay quoted in Timothy Garton Ash, *In Europe's Name: Germany and the Divided Continent* (London: Vintage, 1994), 389. According to a British scholar interviewed in June 1997, Ismay made the statement to backbench Conservative M.P.s in 1951, long before the Federal Republic of Germany joined NATO in 1955.

98. Fursdon, *The European Defense Community,* 321–22.

99. Catherine McArdle Kelleher, "The Defense Policy of the Federal Republic of Germany," in Douglas J. Murray and Paul R. Viotti, eds., *The Defense Policies of Nations: A Comparative Study* (Baltimore: Johns Hopkins University Press, 1982), 269.

100. This "German question" rationale for maintaining NATO was articulated, along with two others—the residual Russian uncertainties and the combination of risks of religious fanaticism, political and economic instability, and the proliferation of missiles and weapons of mass destruction in the Muslim world on Europe's southern and eastern periphery—in Brian Beedham's survey, "Defence: As the Tanks Rumble Away," *The Economist,* September 1, 1990.

101. President George Bush, "Remarks to Citizens in Mainz, West Germany," May 31, 1989, *Weekly Compilation of Presidential Documents,* June 5, 1989, 812–13.

102. Alexander Moens, "American Diplomacy and German Unification," *Survival* 33 (November/December 1991): 542.

103. Paul Wolfowitz, then the under secretary of defense for policy, remarks at the conference on "Future of European Security," Prague, April 25, 1991, text released by the Office of the Assistant Secretary of Defense for Public Affairs, 5.

104. Josef Joffe, "One Answer to the German Question," *U.S. News and World Report,* June 11, 1990, 33.

105. Unnamed Italian official cited in Russell Watson, Margaret Garrard Warner, and Michael Meyer, "Losing Out in Europe?" *Newsweek*, May 14, 1990, 27.

106. Christoph Bertram, "Visions of Leadership: Germany," in Steven Muller and Gebhard Schweigler, eds., *From Occupation to Cooperation: The United States and United Germany in a Changing World Order* (New York: W. W. Norton and Co., 1992), 61.

107. Margaret Thatcher, speech at the College of Europe, Bruges, Belgium, September 20, 1988, quoted in Nicholas Wood, "Thatcher Hits at 'Identikit' European Union," *The Times* (London), September 21, 1988, 1.

108. Margaret Thatcher, *The Downing Street Years* (London: Harper-Collins Publishers, 1993), 791; see also 792–99 and 813–15.

109. Helmut Kohl, "An Anchor in an Unstable Europe," *Financial Times* (London), January 4, 1993, 52.

110. Margaret Gowing, *Independence and Deterrence: Britain and Atomic Energy 1945–1952* (London: Macmillan, 1974), 1:184–85, quoted in John Roper, "Nuclear Policies: Different Approaches to Similar Objectives," in Yves Boyer, Pierre Lellouche, and John Roper, eds., *Franco-British Defence Co-operation: A New Entente Cordiale?* (London: Routledge, 1989), 5–6.

111. For an authoritative account of the origins of France's nuclear weapons program, see Dominique Mongin *La Bombe atomique française 1945–1958* (Paris: Librairie Générale de Droit et de Jurisprudence, 1997).

112. Charles de Gaulle, press conference of November 10, 1959, in *Discours et messages*, vol. 3, *Avec le renouveau, Mai 1958–Juillet 1962* (Paris: Plon, 1970), 134.

113. This discussion is based in part on David S. Yost, *U.S. Nuclear Weapons in Europe: Prospects and Priorities,* Future Roles Series Paper no. 7 (Livermore, Calif.: Sandia National Laboratories, December 1996). For a discussion of the Turkish case, see Duygu Bazoglu Sezer, "Turkey's New Security Environment, Nuclear Weapons and Proliferation," *Comparative Strategy* 14 (April–June 1995).

114. Walter B. Slocombe, "The Future of U.S. Nuclear Weapons in a Restructured World," in Patrick J. Garrity and Steven A. Maarenen, eds., *Nuclear Weapons in the Changing World: Perspectives from Europe, Asia, and North America* (New York: Plenum Press, 1992), 63.

115. Major Mark N. Gose, USAF, "The New Germany and Nuclear Weapons: Options for the Future," *Airpower Journal* 10 (Special Edition 1996): 67–78.

116. Ibid., 75, 78.

117. John S. Duffield, "NATO's Functions after the Cold War," *Political Science Quarterly* 109 (Winter 1994–95): 775.

118. Wight, *Power Politics,* 222–23.

119. Michael M. Harrison, *The Reluctant Ally: France and Atlantic Security* (Baltimore: Johns Hopkins University Press, 1981), 21.

120. *NATO Handbook* (Brussels: NATO Office of Information and Press, October 1995), 112–13.

121. Stephen J. Flanagan, "NATO and Central and Eastern Europe: From Liaison to Security Partnership," *Washington Quarterly,* Spring 1992, 149.

122. Wight, *Power Politics,* 134.

123. France provided a noteworthy example of dissent with its refusal to participate in the NATO declarations of 1968 and 1970 that responded to Warsaw Pact proposals and that led to the negotiations concerning Mutual and Balanced Force Reductions (MBFR). Indeed, France consistently refused to participate in these negotiations, held from 1973 to 1989, which concluded without an agreement. For background, see David S. Yost, "France," in Fen Hampson, Harald von Riekhoff, and John Roper, eds., *The Allies and Arms Control* (Baltimore: Johns Hopkins University Press, 1992), 168–69.

124. Admiral Jonathan T. Howe, "NATO and the Gulf crisis," *Survival* 33 (May/June 1991): 255. Admiral Howe was then Commander in Chief of Allied Forces in NATO's southern region.

125. General John Galvin, statement before the Senate Committee on Armed Services, March 7, 1991, 6–7.

126. Robert B. McCalla, "NATO's Persistence after the Cold War," *International Organization* 50 (Summer 1996): 464, 470.

127. In Walter Slocombe's words, "Collective defense is both cheaper and stronger than national defense." Walter B. Slocombe, under secretary of defense for policy, prepared statement before the Senate Foreign Relations Committee, October 28, 1997, in *The Debate on NATO Enlargement,* hearings before the Committee on Foreign Relations, U.S. Senate, 105th Cong., 1st sess., October 7, 9, 22, 28, 30 and November 5, 1997 (Washington, D.C.: Government Printing Office, 1998), 139.

128. *NATO Handbook,* 115.

129. Since the end of the Cold War and the establishment of cooperative institutions with former adversaries and other non-NATO countries in the Euro-Atlantic area, the Alliance has sponsored seminars and other activities regarding economic questions such as the conversion of defense industries to civilian purposes and improved control over military budgets and expenditures.

130. Article 13 of the North Atlantic Treaty indicates that after the treaty has been in force for twenty years (that is, after 1969), an Ally may withdraw by giving a year's notice of its intention to do so. No Ally has exercised this option. In 1966, when France chose to withdraw from the integrated military structure, it affirmed its intention to remain part of the Alliance.

131. *NATO Handbook,* 119–20.

132. Interviews with NATO sources in Brussels, early 1998.

133. *NATO Handbook,* 120–21, 125.

134. According to calculations furnished to the author by NATO sources in early 1998, the three commonly funded budgets amounted to 0.34 percent in 1997—that is, approximately one-third of one percent of total defense spending by NATO governments, based on late-1996 exchange rates. In fiscal year 1997, the U.S. share of the three commonly funded budgets—military, civil, and infrastructure (Security Investment Program)—was "about $470 million," an amount equivalent to "about 25 percent of the total funding for these budgets." Henry L. Hinton, Jr., assistant comptroller general, National Security and International Affairs Division, U.S. General Accounting Office, "NATO Enlargement: Cost Implications for the United States Remain Unclear," testimony before the Senate Committee on Appropriations, GAO/T-NSIAD-98-50, October 23, 1997, 1.

135. Interviews with NATO sources in Brussels, early 1998.

136. For discussions of the inefficiencies and cost savings involved in collaborative projects, see Keith Hartley, "Industrial Policies in the Defense Sector," in Keith Hartley and Todd Sandler, eds., *Handbook of Defense Economics* (Amsterdam: Elsevier Science B.V., 1995), especially 1:475–78; and Todd Sandler and Keith Hartley, *The Economics of Defense* (Cambridge: Cambridge University Press, 1995), 234–38.

137. Keith Hartley, *NATO Arms Co-operation: A Study in Economics and Politics* (London: George Allen and Unwin, 1983), 21–22; emphasis in the original.

138. Andrew W. Marshall, *Determinants of NATO Force Posture,* P-3280 (Santa Monica, Calif.: Rand Corporation, January 1966), 11.

139. Ibid., 16.

140. Secretary of Defense Caspar Weinberger, *Annual Report for Fiscal Year 1983* (Washington, D.C.: U.S. Government Printing Office, 1982), II-7. For a more extensive discussion of the notion of "additivity," see David S. Yost, "Beyond MBFR: The Atlantic to the Urals Gambit," *Orbis* 31 (Spring 1987): 132–33. The judgment that the Warsaw Pact's arms procurement arrangements were more efficient relied mainly on the notion of economies of scale through large production runs. In the Warsaw Pact, however, there was no profit motive to encourage manufacturers to seek cost-reduction efficiencies in production, or any market-competition incentive to maintain high quality control.

141. Robert W. Komer, adviser to the secretary of defense for NATO affairs, address to the Atlantic Treaty Association Assembly, Washington, D.C., October 12, 1979, Department of Defense News Release No. 501-79, p. 4, cited in Thomas A. Callaghan, Jr., "Nuclear Parity Requires Conventional Parity," in David S. Yost, ed., *NATO's Strategic Options: Arms Control and Defense* (New York: Pergamon Press, 1981), 184.

142. Giovanni Battista Ferrari, "NATO's New Standardization Organization Tackles an Erstwhile Elusive Goal," *NATO Review* 43 (May 1995): 34.

143. In constant prices, Greece's defense spending as a percentage of GDP in 1994–97 exceeded that of the United States. Average U.S. defense spending as a percentage of GDP exceeded that of all other Allies during the periods 1980–84, 1985–89, and 1990–94. In the period 1975–79, Greece's defense spending as a percentage of GDP exceeded that of the United States. For details, see table 3 in "Financial and Economic Data Relating to NATO Defence," NATO Press and Media Service, Press Release M-DPC-2(97)147, December 2, 1997.

144. The United Kingdom had phased out conscription by 1963. In February 1996, French president Jacques Chirac announced that France would make the transition to entirely professional armed forces by 2002. The German government has continued to support conscription, but pressures to shift to an all-volunteer force are growing.

145. Duke, *The Burdensharing Debate,* 3.

146. Jane M. O. Sharp, "Summary and Conclusions," in Jane M. O. Sharp, ed., *Europe after an American Withdrawal: Economic and Military Issues* (New York: Oxford University Press, 1990), 49.

147. Klaus Knorr, "Burden-Sharing in NATO: Aspects of U.S. Policy," *Orbis* 29 (Fall 1985): 520. See also James B. Steinberg, "Rethinking the Debate on Burden-Sharing," *Survival* 29 (January/February 1987).

148. Mancur Olson and Richard Zeckhauser, "An Economic Theory of Alliances," *Review of Economics and Statistics* 48 (August 1966): 266–79.

149. James C. Murdoch, "Military Alliances: Theory and Empirics," in Hartley and Sandler, eds., *Handbook of Defense Economics,* 1:91, 95, 100, and 106. For a concise exposition of the joint product model in relation to NATO, see Todd Sandler and John F. Forbes, "Burden Sharing, Strategy, and the Design of NATO," *Economic Inquiry* 18 (July 1980): 425–44.

150. Madeleine K. Albright, prepared statement before the Senate Armed Services Committee, April 23, 1997, 1.

151. John Duffield, "The North Atlantic Treaty Organization: Alliance Theory," in Ngaire Woods, ed., *Explaining International Relations since 1945* (London: Oxford University Press, 1996), 344.

152. Ibid., 345.

153. Madrid Declaration on Euro-Atlantic Security and Cooperation, published at the meeting of the North Atlantic Council in Madrid, July 8, 1997, par. 8.

154. North Atlantic Council, London Declaration on a Transformed North Atlantic Alliance, July 6, 1990, par. 1–2.

155. North Atlantic Council, London Declaration, par. 6–8.

156. North Atlantic Council, Rome Declaration on Peace and Cooperation, November 8, 1991, par. 11.

157. North Atlantic Council, Strategic Concept, par. 24–25.

158. Michael Legge, "The Making of NATO's New Strategy," *NATO Review* 39 (December 1991): 12. For further background on the revision of NATO strategy, including the "catalytic" impact of the "Wittmann Paper" prepared by Dr. Klaus Wittmann, a German colonel then serving on the International Military Staff, see Rob de Wijk, *NATO on the Brink of the New Millennium: The Battle for Consensus* (Washington, D.C.: Brassey's, 1997), 13–47.

159. North Atlantic Council declaration, January 11, 1994, par. 13.

160. Ibid., par. 14.

161. See the Glossaries for a concise description of PfP and a list of PfP members.

162. North Atlantic Council, final communiqué, December 1, 1994, par. 19.

163. NATO press release, "The Mediterranean Dialogue," July 8, 1997.

164. North Atlantic Council, Strategic Concept, par. 10.

165. North Atlantic Council, Rome Declaration, par. 4–5. See also the Strategic Concept, especially par. 47.

166. North Atlantic Council communiqué, June 4, 1992, par. 4, 11.

167. North Atlantic Council communiqué, December 17, 1992, par. 4–5.

168. North Atlantic Council declaration, January 11, 1994, par. 7, 9.

169. NATO has nonetheless specified that "The employment of CJTFs for Article 5 operations is also not excluded." Final communiqué of the North Atlantic Council in defense ministers session, December 18, 1996, par. 15.

170. The fourteen Partner countries that participated in IFOR were Albania, Austria, Bulgaria, the Czech Republic, Estonia, Finland, Hungary, Latvia, Lithuania, Poland, Romania, Russia, Sweden, and Ukraine. The other four participants were Egypt, Jordan, Malaysia, and Morocco. SFOR includes Slovenia, an additional Partner country, and Ireland, which has not joined PfP.

171. Final communiqué of the North Atlantic Council in defense ministers session, December 18, 1996, par. 7–8.

172. North Atlantic Council, London Declaration, par. 3.

173. North Atlantic Council communiqué, December 18, 1990, par. 5.

174. North Atlantic Council communiqué, June 7, 1991, par. 1.

175. North Atlantic Council, Rome Declaration, par. 6– 7.

176. North Atlantic Council declaration, January 11, 1994, par. 4–6.

177. Ibid., par. 6.

178. North Atlantic Council communiqué, December 18, 1990, par. 15.

179. North Atlantic Council communiqué, June 7, 1991, par. 7.

180. North Atlantic Council, Rome Declaration, par. 18.

181. North Atlantic Council, Strategic Concept, par. 50–51.

182. North Atlantic Council declaration, January 11, 1994, par. 17.

183. Final communiqué of the North Atlantic Council in defense ministers session, June 13, 1996, par. 21.

184. United Kingdom Ministry of Defence, *Statement on the Defence Estimates 1996* (London: Her Majesty's Stationery Office, 1996), 18, table 3.

185. North Atlantic Council, Strategic Concept, par. 21.

186. Ibid., par. 14.

187. Secretary of Defense Dick Cheney, statement before the Senate Armed Services Committee, January 31, 1992, text furnished by the Department of Defense, 21–22. The expression "non-MIRVed" means without multiple independently targeted reentry vehicles—that is, separate warheads containing nuclear weapons aimed at distinct targets—on submarine-launched and intercontinental ballistic missiles (SLBMs and ICBMs).

188. Remarks as delivered by Secretary of Defense Les Aspin at National Defense University, March 25, 1993, transcript furnished by the Office of the Assistant Secretary of Defense for Public Affairs, 2.

189. Secretary of Defense Les Aspin, *Report on the Bottom-Up Review* (Washington, D.C.: Department of Defense, October 1993), 5, 26.

190. Walter B. Slocombe, under secretary of defense for policy, remarks to the Atlantic Council, June 14, 1996, text furnished by the Department of Defense, 15.

191. Secretary of State Madeleine K. Albright, prepared statement before the Senate Foreign Relations Committee, October 7, 1997, in *The Debate on NATO Enlargement,* 13. Deputy Secretary of State Strobe Talbott has used a similar formulation, noting that "among the contingencies for which NATO must be prepared is that Russia will abandon democracy and return to the threatening patterns of international behavior that have sometimes characterized its history, particularly during the Soviet period." Strobe Talbott, "Why NATO Should Grow," *New York Review of Books,* August 10, 1995, 28.

192. Christopher Donnelly, *Red Banner: The Soviet Military System in Peace and War* (London: Jane's Information Group Ltd., 1988), 44.

193. Vladimir Shlapentokh, "Russia: Privatization and Illegalization of Social and Political Life," *Washington Quarterly,* Winter 1996, 84.

194. Jacob W. Kipp, "The Zhirinovsky Threat," *Foreign Affairs,* May/June 1994, 72–86.

195. Andrei Kozyrev, "Partnership or Cold Peace?" *Foreign Policy,* no. 99 (Summer 1995): 4–5.

196. Sergey Rogov cited in indirect discourse in Theresa Hitchens and Anton Zhigulsky, "Hard-Line Russians Tout Nukes to Match West," *Defense News,* November 20–26, 1995, 1, 36.

197. Alexei G. Arbatov, *The Russian Military in the 21st Century* (Carlisle Barracks, Penn.: Strategic Studies Institute, U.S. Army War College, June 3, 1997), 9–10.

198. For authoritative surveys of these problems, see C. J. Dick, *The Russian Army: Present Plight and Future Prospects,* Occasional Brief no. 31 (Camberley, England: Conflict Studies Research Centre, Royal Military Academy Sandhurst, November 1994), and M. J. Orr, *The Current State of the Russian Armed Forces* (Camberley, England: Conflict Studies Research Centre, Royal Military Academy Sandhurst, November 1996). See also Anatol Lieven, "Russia's Military Nadir: The Meaning of the Chechen Debacle," *The National Interest,* Summer 1996, 24–33.

199. Vladimir Shlapentokh, "The Enfeebled Army: A Key Player in Moscow's Current Political Crisis," *European Security* 4 (Autumn 1995): 417–37.

200. C. J. Dick, *A Bear Without Claws: The Russian Army in the Nineties* (Camberley, England: Conflict Studies Research Centre, Royal Military Academy Sandhurst, June 1996), 7.

201. Deborah Yarsike Ball, "The Unreliability of the Russian Officer Corps: Reluctant Domestic Warriors," in Kathleen C. Bailey and M. Elaine Price, eds., *Director's Series on Proliferation* (Livermore, Calif.: Lawrence Livermore National Laboratory, November 17, 1995), 29.

202. Stuart D. Goldman, *Russian Conventional Armed Forces: On the Verge of Collapse?* (Washington, D.C.: Congressional Research Service, Library of Congress, September 4, 1997), 34, 36.

203. Stephen J. Blank, *Energy and Security in Transcaucasia* (Carlisle Barracks, Penn.: Strategic Studies Institute, U.S. Army War College, September 7, 1994), 8.

204. Paul Felgengauer, "The Russian Army and the East-West Military Balance: Self-Deception and Mutual Misunderstanding Did Not End with the Cold War," *Segodnya,* August 18, 1995, extracts published in *The National Interest,* Winter 1995–96, 116.

205. Bruce G. Blair, "Russian Control of Nuclear Weapons," in George Quester, ed., *The Nuclear Challenge in Russia and the New States of Eurasia* (Armonk, N.Y.: M.E. Sharpe, 1995), 60–61.

206. Ken Alibek, "Russia's Deadly Expertise," *New York Times,* March 27, 1998, A19. See also Goldman, *Russian Conventional Armed Forces,* 17.

207. Malcolm Rifkind, British secretary of state for defense, speech in Paris on September 30, 1992, text furnished by the British Ministry of Defence, 5.

208. David Omand, "Nuclear Deterrence in a Changing World: The View from a UK Perspective," *RUSI Journal,* June 1996, 17.

209. John Deutch, deputy secretary of defense, comments at press conference, news release by the Office of the Assistant Secretary of Defense for Public Affairs, September 22, 1994, 7.

210. Adam Michnik, interview reproduced in *The National Interest,* Spring 1998, 128.

211. Zbigniew Brzezinski, *The Grand Chessboard: American Primacy and Its Geostrategic Imperatives* (New York: Basic Books, 1997), 118–19.

212. Final communiqué of the North Atlantic Council in defense ministers session, June 13, 1996, par. 23.

213. Ibid., par. 25.

214. Ibid., par. 21.

3. COOPERATION WITH FORMER ADVERSARIES

1. "The Future Tasks of the Alliance," report of the Council, annex to the final communiqué of the ministerial meeting, December 13–14, 1967, par. 8 and 9, in *Texts of Final Communiqués,* 200.

2. North Atlantic Council, Strategic Concept, par. 16.

3. Ibid., par. 19.

4. Ibid., par. 21; emphasis added.

5. North Atlantic Council communiqué, December 10, 1996, par. 4.

6. Madeleine K. Albright, "Enlarging NATO," *The Economist,* February 15, 1997, 22.

7. Albright, prepared written submission, April 23, 1997, 1.

8. Founding Act on Mutual Relations, Cooperation and Security between the North Atlantic Treaty Organization and the Russian Federation, signed at Paris, May 27, 1997, 2–3; emphasis added. See also the Madrid Declaration, par. 21.

9. Although Spain recently decided to participate fully in this structure, France remains outside the integrated military structure.

10. The Soviet representative to the first meeting of the NACC made the following statement, which was included in a note to the communiqué regarding the meeting: "We proceed from the assumption that the agreements concerning the contacts in the framework of the North Atlantic Cooperation

Council which is being created today are valid for the sovereign states which are becoming legal successors of the Soviet Union." He later asked that "all references to the Soviet Union be excluded from the text of the Statement." North Atlantic Cooperation Council, Statement on Dialogue, Partnership and Cooperation, December 20, 1991, note 1.

11. Ibid., par. 4–5.

12. Jonathan Eyal, "NATO's Enlargement: Anatomy of a Decision," *International Affairs* 73 (October 1997): 701.

13. *NATO Handbook,* 46, 49.

14. In order to signify their vague disapproval of NACC, it seems, the French at the outset used a faintly ridiculous, even sarcastic, acronym—COCONA—for the Conseil de Coopération Nord-Atlantique (North Atlantic Cooperation Council). Within months, however, French officials shifted to an inoffensive neutral acronym—CCNA. To understand the significance of the original acronym, it should be noted that most of the meanings in French of *coco* are less than entirely dignified. The acronym COCONA conveyed accurately the opinion some French observers expressed about the NACC: that it was a "political gadget" of doubtful seriousness.

15. In September 1994, President Mitterrand allowed Minister of Defense François Léotard to attend an informal meeting of NATO defense ministers in Seville, Spain, but did not permit the chief of staff of the armed forces, Admiral Jacques Lanxade, to accompany Léotard. In October 1995, President Jacques Chirac allowed both Minister of Defense Charles Millon and General Jean-Philippe Douin, the chief of staff of the armed forces, to attend the informal meeting of NATO defense ministers in Williamsburg, Virginia.

16. This discussion of the evolution of the NACC's activities is based on the author's interviews in Brussels, and on Robert Weaver, "NACC's Five Years of Strengthening Cooperation," *NATO Review* 45 (May–June 1997): 24–26.

17. North Atlantic Council declaration, January 11, 1994, par. 14.

18. In October 1996, Malta became the first and only country (so far) to withdraw from PfP. The new Labour government elected that month had argued in opposition that PfP membership was incompatible with Malta's policy of neutrality, because NATO is a "military alliance." At the same time, the new government emphasized its wish "not only to maintain diplomatic relations with NATO but to explore other avenues and modalities of future bilateral and possibly also multilateral cooperation in the field of security." Press release of October 31, 1996, furnished by the Embassy of Malta, Washington, D.C.

19. North Atlantic Council declaration, January 11, 1994, par. 14. According to Article 4 of the North Atlantic Treaty, "The Parties will consult together whenever, in the opinion of any of them, the territorial integrity, political independence or security of any of the Parties is threatened."

20. For the latter term, see Eyal, "NATO's Enlargement," 702.

21. Nick Williams, "Partnership for Peace: Permanent Fixture or Declining Asset?" *Survival* 38 (Spring 1996): 99.

22. Nick Williams, *The Future of Partnership for Peace* (Sankt Augustin bei Bonn: Konrad-Adenauer-Stiftung, April 1996), 18.

23. North Atlantic Council communiqué, December 10, 1996, par. 8.

24. Williams, "Partnership for Peace," 103.

25. Ibid., 103–4.

26. Prepared statement by Secretary of Defense William S. Cohen before the Senate Committee on Armed Services, April 23, 1997, 7–8.

27. Wolfowitz, remarks at the conference on "Future of European Security," 3–4, 6.

28. President George Bush, "The President's News Conference in Rome, Italy," November 8, 1991, *Weekly Compilation of Presidential Documents,* November 11, 1991, 1605.

29. Secretary of State James A. Baker III, "US Commitment to Strengthening Euro-Atlantic Cooperation," intervention before the NACC, December 20, 1991, *U.S. Department of State Dispatch,* December 23, 1991, 903–4.

30. Ronald D. Asmus, "Germany and America: Partners in Leadership?" *Survival* 33 (November/December 1991): 563; and Henry A. Kissinger, "The Atlantic Alliance Needs Renewal in a Changed World," *International Herald Tribune,* March 2, 1992, 5.

31. In NATO Europe, support for enlargement has been most visible in Germany. When the NATO enlargement debate began in the Alliance in late 1993, it was difficult to identify supporters outside Germany and the United States. Most European NATO experts and officials expressed reservations about U.S. and German interest in enlargement. According to a German scholar, "Apart from Germany, it is hard to find any other European NATO member with a genuine interest in expanding the alliance to the East." Peter Rudolf, "The Future of the United States as a European Power: The Case of NATO Enlargement," *European Security* 5 (Summer 1996): 179.

32. James A. Baker III, "Expanding to the East: A New NATO," *Los Angeles Times,* December 5, 1993, part M, p. 2; Zbigniew Brzezinski, "A Bigger —and Safer—Europe," *New York Times,* December 1, 1993, A23; and Henry A. Kissinger, "Not This Partnership," *Washington Post,* November 24, 1993, A17.

33. Senator Richard Lugar quoted in Stephen S. Rosenfeld, "NATO's Last Chance," *Washington Post,* July 2, 1993, A19.

34. Ronald D. Asmus, Richard L. Kugler, and F. Stephen Larrabee, "Building a New NATO," *Foreign Affairs,* September/October 1993, especially 35–36.

35. James M. Goldgeier, "NATO Expansion: The Anatomy of a Decision," *Washington Quarterly,* Winter 1998, 88.

36. Talbott memo to Christopher, October 17, 1993, reported in Michael Dobbs, "Wider Alliance Would Increase U.S. Commitments," *Washington Post,* July 5, 1995, A1, A16; and Michael R. Gordon, "U.S. Opposes Move to Rapidly Expand NATO Membership," *New York Times,* January 2, 1994, A1, A7, both cited in Goldgeier, "NATO Expansion," 90.

37. According to Goldgeier's interviews, "many of Talbott's colleagues" say the new deputy secretary of state reassessed his position after he considered "the broader European landscape and the needs of the Central and Eastern Europeans," whereas "several" of his colleagues "argue that he opposed expansion, lost, and then sought to ensure that both the expansion track and the NATO-Russia track would proceed in tandem." See Goldgeier, "NATO Expansion," 96.

38. Ibid., 100.

39. Ibid., 99.

40. Peter Rudolf, "The USA and NATO Enlargement," *Aussenpolitik* 47, no. 4 (1996): 341.

41. North Atlantic Council declaration, January 11, 1994, par. 12–13.

42. "Clinton Hints NATO Would Defend East From Attack," *International Herald Tribune,* January 13, 1994, p 1.

43. Eyal, "NATO's Enlargement," 704.

44. North Atlantic Council communiqué, December 1, 1994, par. 6.

45. *Study on NATO Enlargement* (Brussels: North Atlantic Treaty Organization, September 1995), par. 3.

46. North Atlantic Council, Madrid Declaration, par. 6.

47. President Clinton quoted in John F. Harris, "Clinton Vows Wider NATO in 3 Years," *Washington Post,* October 23, 1996, A1, A17.

48. Ibid.

49. Among the most useful journal articles, see Ronald D. Asmus, Richard L. Kugler, and F. Stephen Larrabee, "NATO Expansion: The Next Steps," *Survival* 37 (Spring 1995); Michael E. Brown, "The Flawed Logic of NATO Expansion," *Survival* 37 (Spring 1995); Michael Mandelbaum, "Preserving the New Peace: The Case Against NATO Expansion," *Foreign Affairs,* May/June 1995; William E. Odom, "NATO's Expansion: Why the Critics Are Wrong," *The National Interest,* Spring 1995; Adam Garfinkle, "NATO Enlargement: What's the Rush?" *The National Interest,* Winter 1996/1997; and Owen Harries, "The Dangers of Expansive Realism," *The National Interest,* Winter

1997/1998. Of the book-length discussions, see Michael Mandelbaum, *The Dawn of Peace in Europe* (New York: Twentieth Century Fund Press, 1996), especially chapter 3.

50. Jeremy D. Rosner, "NATO Enlargement: What Will the Congress and Public Say?" *Armed Forces Journal International,* April 1997, 10.

51. Eric Schmitt, "Senate Approves Expansion of NATO in Bipartisan Vote; Clinton Pleased by Decision," *New York Times,* May 1, 1998, A1, A8.

52. Jeremy D. Rosner, "NATO Enlargement's American Hurdle," *Foreign Affairs,* July/August 1996, 14–15.

53. Fred C. Iklé, "How to Ruin NATO," *New York Times,* January 11, 1995, A21.

54. Smith quoted in Eric Schmitt, "Senate Abruptly Opens Debate on NATO," *New York Times,* March 18, 1998, A12.

55. Inhofe quoted in Eric Schmitt, "Senators Reject Bid to Limit Costs of Enlarging NATO," *New York Times,* April 29, 1998, A1, A12.

56. Warner quoted in Eric Schmitt, "Senate Rejects Bid to Create a NATO Unit to Resolve Conflicts," *New York Times,* April 30, 1998, A14.

57. Schmitt, "Senate Approves Expansion of NATO."

58. Nunn quoted in Rosner, "NATO Enlargement's American Hurdle," 14.

59. George F. Kennan, "A Fateful Error," *New York Times,* February 5, 1997, A23.

60. Wellstone quoted in Schmitt, "Senate Rejects Bid to Create a NATO Unit."

61. Moynihan quoted in Eric Schmitt, "Senate Jousting Starts a Debate on Widening NATO," *New York Times,* April 28, 1998, A1, A8.

62. Smith quoted in "Words of Warning in the NATO Battle: Senators Tilt at Europe's Future," excerpts from the Senate debate, *New York Times,* April 29, 1998, A12.

63. Linder quoted in Rosner, "NATO Enlargement's American Hurdle," 15.

64. Ted Galen Carpenter in "Expanding NATO: An Exchange between Odom and his Critics," *The National Interest,* Summer 1995, 103. See also Ted Galen Carpenter, *Beyond NATO: Staying Out of Europe's Wars* (Washington, D.C.: Cato Institute, 1994).

65. Harkin quoted in Schmitt, "Senators Reject Bid to Limit Costs."

66. Craig quoted in Schmitt, "Senate Rejects Bid to Create a NATO Unit."

67. Ashcroft quoted in ibid.

68. Warner quoted in "Words of Warning in the NATO Battle."

69. Peter Rodman, "4 More for NATO," *Washington Post,* December 13, 1994, A27. See also Charles Krauthammer, "NATO's Hedge Against Russia," *Sacramento Bee,* April 21, 1998, B7.

70. Senator Jesse Helms, "The Madrid Summit—New Members, Not New Missions," in *The Debate on NATO Enlargement,* 4.

71. Odom, "NATO's Expansion," 45.

72. William E. Odom, "History Tells Us The Alliance Should Grow," *Washington Post,* July 6, 1997, C3.

73. Vaclav Havel, "NATO's Quality of Life," *New York Times,* May 13, 1997, A21.

74. Richard Holbrooke, "America, a European Power," *Foreign Affairs,* March/April 1995, 41–42.

75. Secretary of State Madeleine K. Albright, prepared statement before the Senate Foreign Relations Committee, October 7, 1997, in *The Debate on NATO Enlargement,* 15.

76. These points are drawn from a survey of arguments prepared by Karsten Voigt, a Social Democratic Party member of the Bundestag, in *The Enlargement of the Alliance,* draft special report of the working group on NATO enlargement, North Atlantic Assembly, November 1994, 2–4.

77. Rühe's Alastair Buchan Memorial Lecture in London, on March 26, 1993, is usually cited in this regard: Volker Rühe, "Shaping Euro-Atlantic Policies: A Grand Strategy for a New Era," *Survival* 35 (Summer 1993): 129–37.

78. See the discussion of the German enlargement debate in Rudolf, "The Future of the United States as a European Power," 179–81.

79. Volker Rühe, "The New NATO," lecture at Johns Hopkins University's Paul H. Nitze School of Advanced International Studies, American Institute for Contemporary German Studies, Washington, D.C., April 30, 1996, text furnished by the German Ministry of Defense, 7–8.

80. This paragraph is based on the author's interviews in Bonn, May 1997.

81. Karsten Voigt quoted in Jane Perlez, "Rare Candor About NATO: A Curb on United Germany," *New York Times,* December 7, 1997, 14.

82. Eyal, "NATO's Enlargement," 703.

83. See in particular, Holger H. Mey, "New Members—New Mission: The Real Issues Behind the New NATO Debate," *Comparative Strategy* 13, no. 2 (1994); Karl-Heinz Kamp, "The Folly of Rapid NATO Expansion," *Foreign Policy,* no. 98 (Spring 1995); and Josef Joffe, "Is There Life after Victory? What NATO Can and Cannot Do," *The National Interest,* Fall 1995.

84. Karl-Heinz Kamp and Peter Weilemann, *Germany and the Enlargement of NATO,* Occasional Paper in European Studies 97/23 (Washington, D.C.: Center for Strategic and International Studies, September 1997), 4.

85. Ibid., 3.

86. Deutsche Presse Agentur dispatch, "Grosse Mehrheit für Erweiterung der NATO im Deutschen Parlament," March 26, 1998; "Grosse Mehrheit im Bundestag für die Ost-Erweiterung der Nato," *Frankfurter Allgemeine Zeitung,* March 27, 1998; and "Bundestag/NATO," in *Nachrichtenspiegel Inland,* Presse und Informationsamt der Bundesregierung, March 27, 1998.

87. For specific references to Juppé's several statements in late 1993, see Pascal Boniface, "Le débat français sur l'élargissement de l'Otan," *Relations Internationales et Stratégiques,* no. 27 (Autumn 1997): 37–38.

88. François Léotard in *Les Echos,* January 7, 1994, cited in ibid., 38.

89. Alain Juppé, speech at the Institut des Hautes Études de Défense Nationale, January 21, 1994, in *Propos sur la Défense,* no. 40 (January–February 1994): 74–75.

90. Hervé de Charette, press conference after North Atlantic Council meeting, May 30, 1995, in *Propos sur la Défense,* no. 51 (May–June 1995): 38.

91. Boniface, "Le débat français," 41–42.

92. Paul-Marie de la Gorce, "L'OTAN aux portes de la Russie," *Le Monde Diplomatique,* July 1997, 10–11.

93. Boniface, "Le débat français," 36.

94. For examples, see Guillaume Parmentier, "OTAN: pas d'élargissement sans réforme," *Le Monde,* May 19, 1995; and Nicole Gnesotto, "Élargissement de l'OTAN: une responsabilité européenne," *Politique Étrangère* 62 (Spring 1997).

95. Boniface, "Le débat français," 35–36.

96. Eyal, "NATO's Enlargement," 708.

97. This paragraph is based on the author's interviews in Paris, December 1996–January 1997 and May 1997.

98. Michel Rocard, "Otan: attention, danger!" *L'Express,* March 13, 1997, 94.

99. Michel Rocard, "Otan: danger," *Le Monde,* April 19, 1997, 14. See also Michel Rocard, "Ce qu'il ne faut pas faire," *L'Express,* July 3, 1997, 70. François Heisbourg, the highly respected former director of the International Institute for Strategic Studies, expressed similar reservations in his article, "At This Point, Only Washington Can Slow the Reckless Pace," *International Herald Tribune,* November 28, 1996.

100. For quotations from Giscard d'Estaing, Séguin, and others, see Boniface, "Le débat français," 44–45.

101. Hubert Védrine, "Défense: l'Europe sous tutelle," *Le Point,* April 12, 1997, 23.

102. For the full debate in the National Assembly, see *Journal Officiel de la République Française, Débats Parlementaires, Assemblée Nationale,* June 11, 1998, 4891–4908.

103. Eyal, "NATO's Enlargement," 709.

104. For a useful brief survey of the ratification process and political considerations in all sixteen NATO nations, see Sean Kay and Hans Binnendijk, "After the Madrid Summit: Parliamentary Ratification of NATO Enlargement," *Strategic Forum,* no. 107 (March 1997). For a recent discussion of the issues associated with Turkey's application for EU membership, see Stephen Kinzer, "U.S. Presses European Union To Be Friendlier to Turkey," *New York Times,* May 1, 1998, A13.

105. See Stephen S. Rosenfeld, "Taking the U.S. for a Sucker?" *Washington Post,* August 1, 1997; and Stephen S. Rosenfeld, "Freeloaders? Not Us," *Washington Post,* August 8, 1997, A21.

106. The "Danish footnotes" refers to the many statements Denmark attached to paragraphs in Alliance communiqués dealing with intermediate-range nuclear forces (INF) issues during the early and mid-1980s. The term is not entirely accurate, because Greece attached many such reservations as well, often joining with Denmark. Some NATO observers regretted such reservations, because they considered them a sign of division within the Alliance that might weaken the U.S. position in negotiations with Moscow and even encourage anti-nuclear protest movements in the West.

107. North Atlantic Council communiqué, June 3, 1996, par. 13.

108. Cohen, prepared statement, April 23, 1997, 6.

109. Albright, prepared written submission, April 23, 1997, 5.

110. Secretary of State Warren Christopher, speech in Stuttgart, September 6, 1996, text from USIS Wireless File.

111. Cohen, prepared statement, April 23, 1997, 11–12.

112. Slocombe, remarks to the Atlantic Council, 8–9.

113. Ronald Asmus and Stephen Larrabee have suggested using PfP and subregional cooperative frameworks, for instance in the Baltic region, to create "strategic homes" for the countries left out of the first round of NATO enlargement. Ronald D. Asmus and F. Stephen Larrabee, "NATO and the Have-Nots: Reassurance after Enlargement," *Foreign Affairs,* November/December 1996.

114. North Atlantic Council, Madrid Declaration, par. 8.

115. Albright, prepared statement, October 7, 1997, in *The Debate on NATO Enlargement,* 13–14.

116. Eyal, "NATO's Enlargement," 714.

117. Kamp and Weilemann, *Germany and the Enlargement of NATO,* 9.

118. North Atlantic Council, defense ministers, December 18, 1996, par. 28.

119. Slocombe, remarks to the Atlantic Council, 12.

120. Gerhard Wettig, "Post-Soviet Central Europe in International Security," *European Security* 3 (Autumn 1994): 478.

121. Natalie Nougayrède, "Les tendances dictatoriales de la Biélorussie inquiètent les Polonais," *Le Monde,* April 23, 1997, 3.

122. Eyal, "NATO's Enlargement," 716.

123. North Atlantic Council communiqué, June 3, 1996, par. 13.

124. Henry A. Kissinger, "Helsinki Fiasco," *Washington Post,* March 30, 1997, C7.

125. It is noteworthy that James Goldgeier, after extensive interviews with administration officials, concluded that President Clinton's motives involved several considerations other than an explicit concern with collective defense: "For Clinton, the appeal by the Central Europeans to erase the line drawn for them in 1945, the need to demonstrate U.S. leadership at a time when others questioned that leadership, the domestic political consequences of the choice, and his own Wilsonian orientation toward spreading liberalism combined by the second half of 1994—if not earlier—to produce a presidential preference favoring expansion." Goldgeier, "NATO Expansion," 100–101.

126. Robert E. Hunter, "Enlargement: Part of a Strategy for Projecting Stability into Central Europe," *NATO Review* 43 (May 1995): 3–8.

127. Talbott, "Why NATO Should Grow," 28.

128. Cohen, prepared statement, April 23, 1997, 2–3.

129. Albright, "Enlarging NATO," 22.

130. Albright, prepared written submission, April 23, 1997, 8.

131. Ibid., 4.

132. Cohen, prepared statement, April 23, 1997, 6.

133. Ibid., 9.

134. North Atlantic Council, Strategic Concept, par. 21.

135. Slocombe, remarks to the Atlantic Council, 15.

136. Slocombe, prepared statement before the Senate Foreign Relations Committee, October 28, 1997, in *The Debate on NATO Enlargement,* 139.

137. North Atlantic Council, defense ministers, December 18, 1996, par. 28.

138. Eyal, "NATO's Enlargement," 708–709.

139. Zbigniew Brzezinski and Anthony Lake, "For a New World, a New NATO," *New York Times,* June 30, 1997, 19.

140. Stephen S. Rosenfeld, "Guilt and the National Interest," *Washington Post,* July 11, 1997, A23.

141. Michael Dobbs, "West Making Amends, Albright Tells Czechs," *Washington Post,* July 15, 1997, A13. See also David S. Broder, "Spare Us the Guilt Trips About NATO," *Washington Post,* July 20, 1997, C9.

142. Jim Hoagland, ". . . And the Gatsby Syndrome," *Washington Post,* July 6, 1997, C7.

143. Rudolf, "The USA and NATO Enlargement," 343.

144. Goldgeier, "NATO Expansion," 95.

145. R. W. Apple, Jr., "Road to Approval Is Rocky, and the Gamble Is Perilous," *New York Times,* May 15, 1997.

146. Dole quoted in Harris, "Clinton Vows Wider NATO."

147. Jean Chretien quoted in John F. Harris, "Tape Catches Choice Words About Clinton," *Washington Post,* July 10, 1997, A24.

148. Some Europeans, especially the French, interviewed by the author in late 1997 also deplored the prominence of U.S. defense industry personnel in the campaign for NATO enlargement in the United States. For background on this aspect of the NATO enlargement debate, see Katharine Q. Seelye, "Arms Contractors Spend to Promote an Expanded NATO," *New York Times,* March 30, 1998, A1.

149. Marcel Déat, a French Socialist politician and journalist, wrote a notorious article with this title in the newspaper *L'Oeuvre* during the period in which he advocated compromising with Nazi Germany (in 1939–1940). He collaborated with the Nazis during the war and took refuge in Italy after France's liberation in 1944. The phrase implies doubt about the wisdom of honoring France's commitment to defend Poland by alluding to one of Nazi Germany's demands—an end to the Danzig corridor that linked that city (Gdansk) to the rest of Poland and thereby separated East Prussia from the rest of Germany.

150. Founding Act on Mutual Relations, 8.

151. The observations in the preceding paragraphs are based on the author's interviews with expert observers in London, Paris, Bonn, and Brussels in May–June 1997.

152. Slocombe, remarks to the Atlantic Council, 14–15.

153. Albright, "Enlarging NATO," 23.

154. Albright, prepared written submission, April 23, 1997, 9.

155. Albright, prepared statement, October 7, 1997, in *The Debate on NATO Enlargement,* 16.

156. Albright, "Enlarging NATO," 23; emphasis in the original.

157. Albright, prepared written submission, April 23, 1997, 7.

158. Talbott, "Why NATO Should Grow," 30.

159. Albright, "Enlarging NATO," 23.

160. The mass public in Russia evidently has other preoccupations. Opinion poll findings vary, but most report a relatively low level of interest and concern regarding NATO enlargement. According to one poll, 37 percent of the Russians oppose NATO's invitation to the Czech Republic, Hungary, and Poland, 14 percent support it, and 49 percent have no opinion or do not care. See, among other sources, Michael R. Gordon, "Russian Public's Yawn Reduces Risk of Backlash Over NATO," *International Herald Tribune,* May 29, 1997, 1, 6.

161. Tom Angelakis, *Russian Elites' Perceptions of NATO Expansion: The Military, Foreign Ministry, and Duma,* Briefing Paper no. 11 (Brussels: International Security Information Service, May 1997), 1–2. See also Anatol Lieven, "Russian Opposition to NATO Expansion," *The World Today* 51 (October 1995): 196–99; and Alexander A. Sergounin, "Russian Domestic Debate on NATO Enlargement: From Phobia to Damage Limitation," *European Security* 6 (Winter 1997): 55–71.

162. Vladimir Lukin, chairman of the International Affairs Committee of the State Duma, *Izvestiya,* May 12, 1995, in *FBIS/Central Eurasia, Daily Report,* May 12, 1995, 22.

163. "Yeltsin's Secret Letter on NATO Expansion," published in full in an unofficial translation in the Prague newspaper *Mlada Fronta Dnes,* December 2, 1993, in *FBIS/Central Eurasia, Daily Report,* December 3, 1993, 6.

164. Jim Hoagland, "Gorbachev on Tour," *Washington Post,* October 11, 1996, A21.

165. Eyal, "NATO's Enlargement," 699.

166. Philip Zelikow and Condoleezza Rice, *Germany Unified and Europe Transformed: A Study in Statecraft* (Cambridge, Mass.: Harvard University Press, 1995), 172–85. Zelikow and Baker are also cited in Michael R. Gordon, "Did Gorbachev Get U.S. NATO Pledge?" *International Herald Tribune,* May 26, 1997, 6.

167. Tatiana Parkhalina, "Of Myths and Illusions: Russian Perceptions of NATO Enlargement," *NATO Review* 45 (May/June 1997): 11–15.

168. Lukin in *FBIS/Central Eurasia, Daily Report,* May 12, 1995, 23.

169. Vladimir P. Lukin, "Our Security Predicament," *Foreign Policy,* no. 88 (Fall 1992): 75.

170. North Atlantic Council, December 10, 1996, par. 10.

171. Lukin in *FBIS/Central Eurasia, Daily Report,* May 12, 1995, 22.

172. This discussion of Russian PfP activities is based in part on the author's interviews with NATO observers in October and December 1997.

173. Yeltsin and Udovenko cited in Sophie Shihab, "La Russie veut couper court à toute nouvelle extension de l'Alliance atlantique," *Le Monde,* March 26, 1997, 2.

174. Agence France-Presse, "M. Eltsine menace de revenir sur l'accord Russie-OTAN," *Le Monde,* May 21, 1997, 5.

175. Founding Act on Mutual Relations, 3.

176. This is, to be sure, a reference to the myth of Yalta. As noted in chapter 2, Britain and the United States did not agree with the Soviet Union on a division of Europe into spheres of influence at Yalta, and the USSR never implemented the commitments to free elections in Eastern Europe it made at Yalta.

177. Anton Surikov, Defense Research Institute, *Special Institute Staff Suggests Russia Oppose NATO and the USA,* October 1995, ADVAB 1017 (Sandhurst, England: Conflict Studies Research Centre, Royal Military Academy, April 1996), 3, 5–7. This is a translation of the widely discussed article in *Segodnya* on October 20, 1995.

178. Lukin in *FBIS/Central Eurasia, Daily Report,* May 12, 1995, 23.

179. *Study on NATO Enlargement*, par. 27.

180. Perry quoted in "Eastward Expansion of NATO: The Key to Future Stability," *International Herald Tribune,* October 5, 1995, cited in Rudolf, "The Future of the United States as a European Power," 191.

181. North Atlantic Council communiqué, December 10, 1996, par. 10.

182. Slocombe, remarks to the Atlantic Council, 14.

183. North Atlantic Council in defense ministers session, December 18, 1996, par. 38.

184. William Drozdiak, "Russian Defense Chief Jolts NATO With a Warning," *International Herald Tribune,* December 19, 1996.

185. Cohen, prepared statement, April 23, 1997, 13.

186. Walter B. Slocombe, under secretary of defense for policy, remarks on the dedication of the Geneva Center for Security Policy auditorium to the memory of Joe Kruzel, January 10, 1997, text furnished by the Department of Defense, 9.

187. Cohen, prepared statement, April 23, 1997, 12.

188. Ibid., 13.

189. Founding Act on Mutual Relations, 7.

190. Ibid., 8.

191. Henry A. Kissinger, "NATO: Make It Stronger, Make it Larger," *Washington Post,* January 14, 1997, A15.

192. Joint statements by, and news conference with, Presidents Clinton and Yeltsin at summit in Helsinki, Finland, March 21, 1997, transcript by Federal News Service, 18.

193. Cohen, prepared statement, April 23, 1997, 13–14.

194. Founding Act on Mutual Relations, 4–5.

195. Henry A. Kissinger, "The Dilution of NATO," *Washington Post,* June 8, 1997, C8.

196. Williams, "Partnership for Peace," 107; emphasis in the original.

197. These judgments are based on the author's interviews with NATO observers in late 1997 and early 1998.

198. William Drozdiak, "The Next Step for NATO: Handling Russia," *Washington Post National Weekly Edition,* May 11, 1998, 15. See also Michael R. Gordon, "Uneasy Friendship: Expanding NATO Courts Russia," *New York Times,* May 28, 1998, A12.

199. *Study on NATO Enlargement,* par. 27.

200. Javier Solana, speech at the Royal Institute of International Affairs, London, March 4, 1997, text furnished by the NATO Press and Media Service, 4.

201. Ibid., 4–6.

202. Rühe quoted in Thom Shanker, "Bonn Rebuffs U.S. over NATO Role for Russia," *Chicago Tribune,* September 10, 1994, 2.

203. Rühe quoted in Rick Atkinson, "Allies Seek New Ties to Bind NATO; German and U.S. Defense Ministers Differ on Russian Membership," *Washington Post,* September 10, 1994, A16.

204. Perry quoted in Shanker, "Bonn Rebuffs U.S.," 2.

205. President Clinton's news conference of March 7, 1997, transcript in the *Washington Post,* March 8, 1997, A11.

206. Goldgeier, "NATO Expansion," 97.

207. Ibid., 90.

208. Talbott, "Why NATO Should Grow," 27.

209. Ibid., 30.

210. Rudolf, "The USA and NATO Enlargement," 342.

211. Michael Rühle and Nick Williams, "Partnership for Peace after NATO Enlargement," *European Security* 5 (Winter 1996): 527.

212. North Atlantic Council, Strategic Concept, par. 21.

213. Rühle and Williams, "Why NATO Will Survive," 114.

214. Kissinger, "Helsinki Fiasco," C7.

215. Volker Rühe, speech to the Yomiuri International Economic Society, Tokyo, May 28, 1997, text furnished by the German Ministry of Defense, 15.

216. This concern has been raised despite the geographical limitations on the Article 5 obligation specified in Article 6 of the North Atlantic Treaty. Article 6 indicates that "an armed attack on one or more of the Parties" would include attacks on the territory of any of the Allies in Europe, North America, or Turkey (including "islands under the jurisdiction of any of the Parties in the North Atlantic area north of the Tropic of Cancer") or on the "forces, vessels, or aircraft" of any of the Allies "when in or over these territories or any other area in Europe in which occupation forces of any of the Parties were stationed on the date when the Treaty entered into force or the Mediterranean Sea or the North Atlantic area north of the Tropic of Cancer."

217. Havel, "NATO's Quality of Life," A21.

218. On Malenkov, see J. M. Mackintosh, *Strategy and Tactics of Soviet Foreign Policy* (London: Oxford University Press, 1962), 85–87. For Yeltsin, see *Pravda*, December 23, 1991, summarized in *Current Digest of the Soviet Press* 43, no. 51 (1991): 21–22; "Yeltsin's Secret Letter," 6; and the discussion in Goldgeier, "NATO Expansion," 88. For Rybkin's proposal during a radio interview on October 20, 1996, see the *BBC Summary of World Broadcasts,* October 22, 1996.

219. The preceding discussion of Russian membership issues is based on the author's interviews with security analysts in Europe in 1996–97 and early 1998.

220. Ronald Steel, "Playing Loose with History," *New York Times,* May 26, 1997, 23. For a similar view, see Charles A. Kupchan, "Clinton's Next Step on NATO," *Washington Post National Weekly Edition,* September 8, 1997, 21.

221. Kissinger, "NATO: Make It Stronger," A15.

222. North Atlantic Council, June 3, 1996, par. 2.

223. North Atlantic Council, December 10, 1996, par. 1.

224. Ibid., par. 11.

225. Charter on a Distinctive Partnership between the North Atlantic Treaty Organization and Ukraine, Madrid, July 9, 1997, par. 12.

226. Ibid., par. 1.

227. Ibid., par. 6, 8, 14, 15.

228. Sherman W. Garnett, "The Role of Security Assurances in Ukrainian Denuclearization," in Virginia I. Foran, ed., *Missed Opportunities? The Role of Security Assurances in Nuclear Non-Proliferation* (Washington, D.C.: Carnegie Endowment for International Peace, forthcoming), p. 2 of manuscript, cited with the author's permission.

229. Sherman W. Garnett, "The Sources and Conduct of Ukrainian Security Policy: November 1992 to January 1994," in George Quester, ed., *The Nuclear Challenge in Russia and the New States of Eurasia* (Armonk, N.Y.: M.E. Sharpe, 1995), 146. See also Sherman W. Garnett, *Keystone in the Arch: Ukraine in the Emerging Security Environment of Central and Eastern Europe* (Washington, D.C.: Carnegie Endowment for International Peace, 1997).

230. France's statement regarding Ukraine's accession to the NPT as a non-nuclear-weapons state was transmitted to the Ukrainian foreign minister at the CSCE meeting in Budapest on December 5, 1994. It reaffirms UN Charter and CSCE pledges and the positive and negative security assurances extended to all non-nuclear-weapons states party to the NPT. See the statement by Alain Juppé, then France's foreign minister, at his news conference in Budapest, December 5, 1994, in *Propos sur la Défense,* no. 48 (December 1994): 34–35. For the full text of France's statement on Ukraine's accession to the NPT, see *PPNN Briefing Book,* vol. 2, *Treaties, Agreements and Other Relevant Documents,* 6th ed., compiled and edited by Emily Bailey, Richard Guthrie, Darryl Howlett, and John Simpson (Southampton, UK: Mountbatten Centre for International Studies, University of Southampton on behalf of the Programme for Promoting Nuclear Nonproliferation, 1998), p. L-8; the December 1994 Memorandum on Security Assurances signed by the leaders of Britain, Russia, Ukraine, and the United States may be found on p. L-6 of this volume.

231. Garnett, "The Role of Security Assurances," 19–20.

232. Ibid., 16.

233. Surikov, *Special Institute Staff Suggests Russia Oppose NATO and the USA,* 9.

234. Deputy Secretary of State Strobe Talbott quoted in Steven Erlanger, "For U.S. Russia-Watchers, Bipartisan Fear Over Future," *New York Times,* June 17, 1996, 9.

235. Slocombe, remarks to the Atlantic Council, 11–12.

236. *Study on NATO Enlargement,* par. 34 and 36.

237. Ibid., par. 9.

238. North Atlantic Council in defense ministers session, June 13, 1996, par. 22.

239. Cohen, prepared statement, April 23, 1997, 8.

240. Vernon Penner, "Partnership for Peace," *Strategic Forum,* no. 97 (December 1996).

241. NATO press release, "The Enhanced Partnership for Peace Programme," Madrid, July 8, 1997.

242. Secretary of State Warren Christopher, speech in Stuttgart, September 6, 1996, text from USIS Wireless File.

243. North Atlantic Council, December 10, 1996, par. 9.

244. NATO press release, "The Euro-Atlantic Partnership Council," Madrid, July 8, 1997.

245. Basic Document of the Euro-Atlantic Partnership Council, May 30, 1997, par. 3.

246. Chairman's summary of the meetings of the North Atlantic Cooperation Council and the Euro-Atlantic Partnership Council, Sintra, Portugal, May 30, 1997, par. 3.

247. Basic Document of the Euro-Atlantic Partnership Council, May 30, 1997, par. 4.

248. North Atlantic Council, Madrid Declaration, par. 10.

249. Solana, speech at the Royal Institute of International Affairs, 2.

250. Although the Federal Republic of Yugoslavia's membership in the OSCE was suspended in 1992, it is still considered an OSCE member-state.

251. North Atlantic Council communiqué, January 11, 1994, par. 10.

252. North Atlantic Council, Rome Declaration, par. 2.

253. North Atlantic Cooperation Council, Statement on Dialogue, Partnership and Cooperation, December 20, 1991, par. 2; emphasis added.

254. North Atlantic Council, Strategic Concept, par. 21; emphasis added.

255. Ibid., par. 19.

256. Slocombe, remarks to the Atlantic Council, 12.

257. Cohen, prepared statement, April 23, 1997, 4, 12, and 14.

258. Simon Lunn quoted in William Drozdiak, "Baltic States Fear Being Wallflowers at NATO's Expansion Party," *Washington Post,* October 13, 1996, A45.

259. Paul A. Goble quoted in Steven Erlanger, "U.S. to Back Baltic Membership in NATO, but Not Anytime Soon," *New York Times,* January 12, 1998, A1, A8.

260. Daniel Vernet, "OTAN, l'alliance des paradoxes," *Le Monde,* July 14, 1997, 1, 11. According to Max Jakobson, a Finnish diplomat, "A cynic reading the fine print might conclude that NATO membership will be available to the countries of Central and Eastern Europe when they no longer need it." Jakobson, "Collective Security in Europe Today," 65.

261. Henry A. Kissinger, "The All-European Security System," *Baltimore Sun,* April 16, 1990, 15A.

262. Kissinger, "Helsinki Fiasco," C7.

263. Whether the Alliance should consider itself politically or legally bound to receive UN or OSCE mandates to undertake non–Article 5 operations, particularly involving the use of force, is discussed in chapter 4.

264. Rühle and Williams, "Partnership for Peace," 523.

265. Ibid., 527.

266. North Atlantic Council declaration, January 11, 1994, par. 14.

267. Rühle and Williams, "Partnership for Peace," 527–28.

268. John S. Duffield, "Why NATO Persists," in Kenneth W. Thompson, ed., *NATO and the Changing World Order: An Appraisal by Scholars and Policymakers* (Lanham, Md.: University Press of America, 1996), 117.

269. Robert Hunter, then U.S. permanent representative on the North Atlantic Council, speech at the Marshall Legacy Symposium, Washington, D.C., January 10, 1996, transcript furnished by Federal Document Clearing House, Inc., 8.

270. Williams, *The Future of Partnership for Peace,* 24; emphasis in the original.

271. Charles A. Kupchan, "Reviving the West," *Foreign Affairs,* May/June 1996, 97–98, 100.

272. Charles A. Kupchan, "Strategic Visions," *World Policy Journal,* Fall 1994, 119–20, 122.

273. North Atlantic Council, Strategic Concept, par. 19.

274. de Wijk, *NATO on the Brink of the New Millennium,* 143–44.

275. Ibid.

276. Wight, *Power Politics,* 232.

277. Mancur Olson, *The Logic of Collective Action* (Cambridge, Mass.: Harvard University Press, 1965).

278. Charles A. Kupchan and Clifford A. Kupchan, "Concerts, Collective Security, and the Future of Europe," *International Security* 16 (Summer 1991): 138–39.

279. Interviews in London, Paris, Brussels, and Bonn, May–June 1997.

280. Ambassador Robert E. Hunter, "New NATO Members Will Be Producers of Security," address to the Pilgrims Society in London, September 19, 1994, text furnished by the U.S. Information Service, U.S. Embassy, Brussels, 4.

281. Wight, *Power Politics,* 200.

282. Woodrow Wilson, "At the Guildhall, London," December 28, 1918, in Wilson, *War and Peace,* 1:342.

283. Solana, speech at the Royal Institute of International Affairs, 2.

284. Hull, address to joint meeting of both houses of Congress, 14.

285. Another historical analogy that deserves consideration is the Congress of Vienna. After the Congress, it has been pointed out, the victors— and the restored monarchy in France—generally wanted to maintain their power against popular revolutionary movements. Since the fall of the Soviet empire, the Western powers have been interested in maintaining democracy and preventing a return to dictatorial rule in the former Communist states.

286. Partnership for Peace Framework Document, January 11, 1994, in *NATO Handbook,* 267.

287. Chairman's summary of the meetings of the North Atlantic Cooperation Council and the Euro-Atlantic Partnership Council, par. 4.

288. League of Nations Covenant, Article 8, par. 6.

289. Partnership for Peace Framework Document, in *NATO Handbook,* 266.

290. League of Nations Covenant, Articles 12, 13, and 15.

291. For an authoritative overview, see Dorn Crawford, *Conventional Armed Forces in Europe (CFE): A Review and Update of Key Treaty Elements* (Washington, DC: U.S. Arms Control and Disarmament Agency, December 1997).

292. League of Nations Covenant, Article 8, par. 1–2.

293. Wight, *Power Politics,* 66–67.

294. Ibid., 206–7.

295. League of Nations Covenant, Article 10. In practice, of course, League members generally failed to honor this commitment, most notoriously with regard to Italian aggression against Abyssinia.

296. Alan Cowell, "Germans Protest as Unemployment Hits Postwar Record," *New York Times,* February 6, 1998, A9.

297. During the ten-year period 1986–1995, Italy's defense spending averaged 54.75 percent of France's, 61.11 percent of Britain's, and 59.17 percent of the Federal Republic of Germany's. These calculations were made on the basis of the constant price figures (in millions of U.S. dollars at 1990 prices) published in the *SIPRI Yearbook 1996: Armaments, Disarmament and International Security* (New York: Oxford University Press for the Stockholm International Peace Research Institute, 1996), 365.

298. de Wijk, *NATO on the Brink of the New Millennium,* 136.

299. Richard R. Burt, statement before the Senate Foreign Relations Committee, May 3, 1995, in *NATO's Future: Problems, Threats, and U.S. Interests,* hearings before the Committee on Foreign Relations, U. S. Senate, 104th Cong., 1st sess., April 27 and May 3, 1995 (Washington, D.C.: Government Printing Office, 1995), 62. This statement is reminiscent of President Bush's May 1989 description of the United States and the Federal Republic of Germany as "partners in leadership" (cited in chapter 2).

300. James Gow, *Triumph of the Lack of Will: International Diplomacy and the Yugoslav War* (London: Hurst and Co., 1997), 261.

301. David Owen, *Balkan Odyssey* (London: Indigo, 1996), 296–99.

302. For a thorough analysis of the formation and functioning of the Contact Group, with a chronology of its meetings, including the topics discussed and which nations were represented at each session, see Francine Boidevaix, *Une diplomatie informelle pour l'Europe: Le Groupe de Contact Bosnie* (Paris: Fondation pour les Études de Défense, 1997).

303. Owen, *Balkan Odyssey,* 339.

304. Boidevaix, *Une diplomatie informelle,* 120.

305. See, among other sources, Pierre Bocev, "Otan: un sommet qui divise les alliés," *Le Figaro,* February 7, 1997; "OTAN: Washington refuse un sommet à cinq à Paris," *Le Monde,* February 7, 1997, 5; and Michel Rosten, "Le front atlantique est perturbé," *La Libre Belgique,* February 8–9, 1997.

306. For background, see the essays by Peter Lomas entitled simply "Sweden" and "Switzerland" in Harald Müller, ed., *How Western European Nuclear Policy Is Made: Deciding on the Atom* (New York: St. Martin's Press, 1991).

4. CRISIS MANAGEMENT AND PEACE OPERATIONS

1. For a valuable analysis of this question during the Cold War period, see Douglas Stuart and William Tow, *The Limits of Alliance: NATO Out-of-Area Problems Since 1949* (Baltimore: Johns Hopkins University Press, 1990).

2. Manfred Wörner, "The Security Policy of the Federal Republic of Germany in the 1980s," *AEI Foreign Policy and Defense Review* 4, nos. 3–4 (1983): 45.

3. Howe, "NATO and the Gulf crisis."

4. Thatcher, *The Downing Street Years,* 813.

5. North Atlantic Council, Strategic Concept, par. 10.

6. Despite the tendency during the Cold War to focus on the immense force concentrations on the inter-German border, the Alliance was always attentive to the security requirements of other Allies directly adjacent to Warsaw Pact territory—Greece, Norway, and Turkey.

7. North Atlantic Council, Strategic Concept, par. 47.

8. Ibid., par. 9, 47.

9. Ibid., par. 36.

10. According to prevailing usage, a non–Article 5 operation is one in support of collective security and an Article 5 operation is one dedicated to collective defense. The Allies, however, could conduct a collective defense operation outside Article 5—for example, by choosing to defend one or more of their number outside the geographical area specified by Article 6, or by defending a third party that is not an Ally.

11. North Atlantic Council in defense ministers session, June 13, 1996, par. 1.

12. "The Situation in Yugoslavia," statement issued by the heads of state and government participating in the meeting of the North Atlantic Council in Rome on November 7–8, 1991, par. 1, 4.

13. Jacques Poos on the ITN News, June 28, 1991, cited in Gow, *Triumph of the Lack of Will,* 48, 50.

14. See, among other sources on the origins of the conflicts in the former Yugoslavia, Warren Zimmermann, "The Last Ambassador: A Memoir of the Collapse of Yugoslavia," *Foreign Affairs,* March/April 1995. In addition to the book by James Gow cited in the preceding note, the following books are specially noteworthy: Robert D. Kaplan, *Balkan Ghosts: A Journey through History* (London: Macmillan, 1993); Noel Malcolm, *Bosnia: A Short History* (London: Macmillan, 1994); Owen, *Balkan Odyssey;* Laura Silber and Allan Little, *The Death of Yugoslavia* (London: Penguin Books and BBC Books, 1995); and Dick A. Leurdijk, *The United Nations and NATO in Former*

Yugoslavia, 1991–1996: Limits to Diplomacy and Force (The Hague: Nether-lands Atlantic Commission and Netherlands Institute of International Rela-tions "Clingendael," 1996).

15. The term "Bosniak" has historic standing, and is often used by scholars dissatisfied with the inconsistency involved in not routinely calling the Croats "the Catholics" or the Serbs "the Orthodox" while calling the Bosniaks "the Muslims." According to Timothy Garton Ash, the term "Bosniak" was "revived by the Bosnian government to describe the national-ity of the non-Serb, non-Croat citizens of Bosnia. . . . 'Muslim' immediately suggests to the Western reader a kind of religious identity and culture which really does not seem to be characteristic of much of this population." Timothy Garton Ash, "Bosnia in Our Future," *The New York Review of Books,* Decem-ber 21, 1995, 27–31.

16. North Atlantic Council communiqué, December 17, 1992, par. 5.

17. Among the best sources on the impact of the conflict in the former Yugoslavia on NATO and other European security institutions, see Nicole Gnesotto, *Lessons of Yugoslavia,* Chaillot Paper no. 14 (Paris: Institute for Security Studies, Western European Union, March 1994); Gerd Koslowski, "Bosnia: Failure of the Institutions and of the Balance of Power in Europe," *Aussenpolitik* 47, no. 4 (1996); Gregory L. Schulte, "Former Yugoslavia and the New NATO," *Survival* 39 (Spring 1997); Gregory L. Schulte, "Bringing Peace to Bosnia and Change to the Alliance," *NATO Review* 45 (March 1997); Martin A. Smith, *On Rocky Foundations: NATO, the UN and Peace Operations in the Post–Cold War Era,* Peace Research Report no. 37 (Bradford, England: Department of Peace Studies, University of Bradford, September 1996).

18. Statement of General George A. Joulwan, commander in chief, U.S. European Command, before the House Armed Services Committee, March 23, 1994, 5.

19. Stephanie Anderson, "EU, NATO, and CSCE Responses to the Yugoslav Crisis: Testing Europe's New Security Architecture," *European Security* 4 (Summer 1995): 349.

20. de Wijk, *NATO on the Brink of the New Millennium,* 111.

21. Associated Press, "NATO Agrees on Plan to Extend Bosnia Force," *New York Times,* February 19, 1998, A6.

22. NATO press release, "NATO's Role in Bringing Peace to the Former Yugoslavia," Madrid, July 8, 1997.

23. Eagleburger quoted in David Binder, "U.S. May Loosen Yugoslav Embargo," *New York Times,* October 1, 1992, A3.

24. Lawrence Eagleburger on *The MacNeil/Lehrer NewsHour,* April 11, 1994, transcript furnished by Strictly Business, Overland Park, Kansas, 10.

25. Christopher quoted in *International Herald Tribune,* May 29–30, 1993, cited in Anderson, "EU, NATO, and CSCE Responses," 348–49.

26. Transcript of remarks by President Clinton on Bosnia, May 21, 1993, U.S. Newswire online.

27. Interviews in Washington, D.C., July 1994.

28. Interviews in Brussels with NATO observers, May–June 1997.

29. "Bosnia: Peace at last, at least for now," *The Economist,* November 25, 1995, 23–25.

30. Ibid., 25.

31. Stephen Engelberg, "How Events Drew U.S. Into Balkans," *New York Times,* August 19, 1995.

32. The Allies had invested a great deal of effort in preparing for the emergency withdrawal contingency. The operation probably would have been called Determined Effort, in accordance with "OPLAN 40104." In June 1995, General John Shalikashvili, then the chairman of the Joint Chiefs of Staff, said that an UNPROFOR evacuation operation could require up to 22 weeks and 83,000 troops, including about 10,000 U.S. troops. (Associated Press dispatch, June 8, 1995.) Walter Slocombe, under secretary of defense for policy, described OPLAN 40104 as a "preplanned withdrawal operation" with "sufficient flexibility" that could support "an emergency extraction of all or part of UNPROFOR." Slocombe said, "We simply cannot leave our allies in the lurch when our help could be critical. The assurance of U.S. and NATO help in a hypothetical evacuation from Bosnia is an important element in persuading UNPROFOR-contributing nations to keep their troops in Bosnia." Walter B. Slocombe, prepared statement before the Senate Foreign Relations Committee and the House International Relations Committee, June 12, 1995, text provided by the Federal News Service, 3. For an authoritative discussion of the impact of OPLAN 40104 on U.S. decision making about Bosnia, see Richard Holbrooke, *To End a War* (New York: Random House, 1998), 65–68. While Holbrooke indicates that the plan called for 20,000 U.S. troops, some sources hold that the United States was committed to furnish "around 25,000" troops; see, for example, Leurdijk, *The United Nations and NATO in Former Yugoslavia,* 64–67.

33. Richard Holbrooke quoted in Michael Dobbs, "Holbrooke's Parting Shot—For Now," *Washington Post,* March 3, 1996, C1. In Holbrooke's interview with Dobbs, this conversation is mistakenly dated July 15, 1995. In Holbrooke's book, the date of President Chirac's visit to Washington is indicated correctly as June 14, 1995, and the process by which Holbrooke and Christopher informed President Clinton of the degree of U.S. commitment to assist in conducting a withdrawal operation is described in greater detail. Moreover, according to Holbrooke's account in his book, he told President

Clinton about the degree of U.S. commitment after the French president left, and the information came as a "surprise" to Clinton. See Holbrooke, *To End a War,* 67–68.

34. Final communiqué of the Defense Planning Committee and the Nuclear Planning Group, December 9, 1993, par. 4; emphasis added.

35. Declaration of the heads of state and government participating in the meeting of the North Atlantic Council, Brussels, January 10–11, 1994, par. 6; emphasis added.

36. Ibid., par. 8–9.

37. North Atlantic Council communiqué, June 3, 1996, par. 7.

38. Slocombe, remarks to the Atlantic Council, 4.

39. North Atlantic Council in defense ministers session, final communiqué, June 12, 1997, par. 7.

40. Paul-Marie de la Gorce, "L'OTAN aux portes de la Russie," *Le Monde Diplomatique,* July 1997, 10–11.

41. North Atlantic Council in defense ministers session, June 13, 1996, par. 6, 9. The Combined Joint Planning Staff (CJPS) has been established on the basis of the Allied Command Europe (ACE) Reaction Forces Planning Staff (ARFPS), a body set up to implement the principles in the Alliance's 1991 Strategic Concept, including the shift away from preparations to meet a massive theatre-wide Soviet offensive to a greater emphasis on limited Article 5 contingencies on the flanks. The ARFPS was not part of SHAPE and reported directly to SACEUR, rather than the chief of staff of SHAPE. Similarly, the CJPS reports directly to SACEUR and SACLANT. While CJTF could be employed for both Article 5 and non–Article 5 contingencies, in practice the CJPS appears to be primarily oriented to preparing for the latter.

42. See, among other sources, Hans-Christian Hagman, "The Conceptual Evolution of NATO's CJTF," *Swedish Academy of War Sciences Proceedings and Journal* 200, no. 4 (September 1996): 129–42.

43. Report of the senior-level group on PfP enhancement, Sintra, Portugal, May 29, 1997, Enhanced Partnership for Peace section, par. 2; emphasis added.

44. Ibid., par. 2.

45. Sergio Balanzino, "Deepening Partnership: The Key to Long-Term Stability in Europe," *NATO Review* 45 (July–August 1997): 10–16.

46. For example, one of NATO's three major commands, Allied Command Channel, was disbanded; and the relevant British and Norwegian forces were reorganized in a new entity, Allied Forces Northwest, reporting to Allied Command Europe (ACE). Within Allied Forces Central Europe (AFCENT), two groupings (Air Forces Central Europe and Land Forces Central Europe) replaced five primary subcommands. See Larry Grossman, "NATO's New Strategy," *Air Force Magazine,* March 1992, 31.

47. North Atlantic Council in defense ministers session, final communiqué, December 2, 1997, par. 18.

48. North Atlantic Council, Strategic Concept, par. 22.

49. Slocombe, remarks to the Atlantic Council, 4.

50. North Atlantic Council, December 18, 1990, par. 5.

51. North Atlantic Council, June 7, 1991, par. 2. The North Atlantic Treaty is also known as the Washington Treaty.

52. "NATO's Core Security Functions in the New Europe," statement issued by the North Atlantic Council meeting in ministerial session in Copenhagen, June 7, 1991, par. 6–7.

53. North Atlantic Council, Strategic Concept, par. 21–22; and Rome Declaration, par. 6.

54. Western European Union, Council of Ministers, Bonn, June 19, 1992, "Petersberg Declaration," par. 4 of Part II, "On Strengthening WEU's Operational Role."

55. Slocombe, remarks to the Atlantic Council, 5.

56. North Atlantic Council, June 7, 1991, par. 3.

57. North Atlantic Council in defense ministers session, June 13, 1996, par. 8, 11, 35.

58. North Atlantic Council, December 10, 1996, par. 19.

59. Western European Union, Council of Ministers, Paris Declaration, May 13, 1997, par. 15, 17.

60. North Atlantic Council, Strategic Concept, par. 22.

61. One of the issues in this regard is known as the "back-door commitment" risk. All EU countries are eligible for membership in the WEU, which would provide them with a collective defense commitment from ten European NATO Allies. If the latter honored their WEU commitment to an EU member that was not a member of the Alliance, the United States could be drawn into a conflict, because of its commitments under the North Atlantic Treaty. Therefore, a number of the Allies, including the United States and the United Kingdom, have been firm in advocating a principle of "congruence"—that is, all full members of the WEU should be NATO members, as is the case at present. Some European and American observers have suggested that this principle might be a useful element in policymaking on NATO and EU enlargement.

62. For a discussion of this principle, see David S. Yost, "France and West European Defense Identity," *Survival* 33 (July/August 1991): especially 339–42. See also Philip H. Gordon, "Europe's Uncommon Foreign Policy," *International Security* 22 (Winter 1997/98): 89–96.

NOTES TO PAGES 212–215

63. Rick Atkinson and Bradley Graham, "As Europe Seeks Wider NATO Role, Its Armies Shrink," *Washington Post,* July 29, 1996, A1, A15.

64. Rick Atkinson, "With Deliberate Force in Bosnia," *Washington Post National Weekly Edition,* November 27–December 3, 1995, 6.

65. See, among other sources, Javier Solana's remarks at the SACLANT seminar in Lisbon, May 4–5, 1997; General Klaus Naumann's address to members of the U.S. Congress on June 23, 1997; and Admiral Ray's speech at the French National Assembly, January 23, 1997. The last is available in Arthur Paecht, ed., *Après la programmation, la nouvelle donne de la politique de défense, Actes du colloque* (Paris: M&M Conseil, 1997).

66. General Helge Hansen quoted in Detlef Puhl, "Nicht jeder im Bündnis muss alles können," *Stuttgarter Zeitung,* March 21, 1997.

67. Karl Feldmeyer, "Verteidigung oder Krisenintervention?" *Frankfurter Allgemeine Zeitung,* March 19, 1997.

68. For background on evolving German views regarding "out of area" and non–Article 5 security responsibilities, see Clay Clemens, "Opportunity or Obligation? Redefining Germany's Military Role Outside of NATO," *Armed Forces and Society* 19 (Winter 1993); Franz-Josef Meiers, "Germany: The Reluctant Power," *Survival* 37 (Autumn 1995); and Karl-Heinz Börner, "The Future of German Operations Outside NATO," *Parameters* 26 (Spring 1996).

69. Alan Cowell, "Germans Plan Combat Troops Outside NATO, A Postwar First," *New York Times,* December 14, 1996, 3.

70. North Atlantic Council, Madrid Declaration, par. 18.

71. North Atlantic Council in defense ministers session, final communiqué, June 12, 1997, par. 6.

72. Before the command structure reorganization finally approved by the North Atlantic Council in December 1997, and to be implemented over the next few years, there were three regional commands under SACEUR: AFNORTHWEST, held by a British officer; AFCENT, held by a German officer; and AFSOUTH, held by a U.S. officer.

73. Examples of this principle—commands reflecting force contributions —have been present since the beginning of the integrated military command structure, notably in the main subordinate commands in Allied Command Europe (ACE). Britain furnished the officer serving as CINCNORTH for the Allied forces in the northern region (AFNORTH) from 1951 to 1994, because Britain made the largest contribution of forces in that region. On the same principle, when AFNORTH was replaced by AFNORTHWEST in 1994, Britain received the CINCNORTHWEST billet. From the establishment of AFCENT (for Allied forces in the central region) in 1953 to 1966, France supplied the officer serving as CINCENT, because France had the largest number of forces in that region. After France withdrew from the integrated military structure in 1966, the Federal Republic of Germany had the largest number of forces assigned to the integrated military structure in the region, so Bonn provided the officer to serve as CINCENT. The United States has furnished an officer to serve as CINCSOUTH since 1951, because it has provided the greatest number of Allied forces in the southern region (AFSOUTH). From 1953 to 1967 there was a fourth main subordinate command in ACE known as AFMED, based in Malta, for Allied forces in the Mediterranean. The British supplied the officer serving as CINCAFMED, because Britain's fleet was then second only to that of the United States in the Mediterranean. Mainly because of cutbacks in British forces in the region, AFMED was disbanded in 1967. Since that time, COMNAVSOUTH, the commander of naval forces in the southern region, has been an Italian admiral, because—of the Allies in the integrated military structure—Italy provides the largest number of naval forces in the region, after the United States.

74. See the transcript of Chirac's interview with the German magazine *Focus,* September 15, 1997, available from the Service de Presse, Présidence de la République, 10.

75. Guillaume Parmentier, "Painstaking Adaptation to the New Europe: French and German Defence Policies in 1997," in *France and Japan in a Changing Security Environment,* Les Cahiers de l'IFRI no. 21 (Paris: Institut Français des Relations Internationales and Tokyo: Japan Institute of International Affairs, 1997), 30–31.

76. Deutsche Presse-Agentur dispatch, September 30, 1997.

77. For an authoritative discussion, see *Allied Command Structures in the New NATO* (Washington, D.C.: Institute for National Strategic Studies, National Defense University, April 1997).

78. Luc Rosenzweig and Daniel Vernet, "Le gouvernement juge inopportun un nouveau rapprochement avec l'OTAN," *Le Monde,* June 29–30, 1997, 2; Luc Rosenzweig and Daniel Vernet, "La France risque de se trouver isolée lors du sommet atlantique de Madrid," *Le Monde,* July 4, 1997, 4.

79. Alain Richard, speech at the Institut des Hautes Études de Défense Nationale, February 10, 1998, text furnished by the French Ministry of Defense, 6.

80. The British and the EU members with traditions of neutrality have consistently opposed such a merger, and it therefore appears most unlikely.

81. "Constructive abstention" means that, at least with regard to some types of decisions, EU countries may elect to abstain from voting—that is, they may choose not to block an operation conducted by a coalition of the willing in the EU's name while refraining from participating in policy implementation themselves. The EU's fundamental strategic choices are nonetheless to be made unanimously, as a general principle. Furthermore, as

Richard's comment suggests, if the states abstaining in this fashion represent more than a third of the total number of votes (state votes are to be weighted by other treaty provisions), no decision can be taken. The Amsterdam Treaty also provides for "qualified majority" voting in some policy implementation matters, but not with respect to "decisions having military or defense implications."

82. Richard, speech at the Institut des Hautes Études de Défense Nationale, 5–7.

83. Ibid., 7.

84. Gordon, "Europe's Uncommon Foreign Policy," 96.

85. North Atlantic Council in defense ministers session, June 13, 1996, par. 18.

86. Cohen quoted in Dana Priest, "Cohen Promises Senate Hearing Timely Troop Exit From Bosnia," *Washington Post,* January 23, 1997, A4.

87. Inge quoted in Susanne M. Schafer, "Cohen Issues Caution on Peace-keeping," *Washington Post,* January 25, 1997, A8.

88. Cook quoted in John F. Harris, "U.S. Renews Goals in Bosnia," *International Herald Tribune,* May 30, 1997, 1.

89. President Clinton's remarks on Bosnia, transcript in the *New York Times,* November 28, 1995, A6.

90. William E. Odom, "One Year? In Bosnia?" *New York Times,* December 5, 1995, 25.

91. President Clinton's remarks on Bosnia, in the *New York Times.*

92. GAO report summarized in Michael Dobbs, "In Bosnia, a Dubious Peace Process," *Washington Post,* May 2, 1997, A1, A25.

93. Cohen quoted in Steven Erlanger, "On Bosnia, Clinton Supports Albright Against Cohen View," *New York Times,* June 12, 1997, A1, A12.

94. Ivo Daalder, "Three Choices in Bosnia," *Washington Post,* July 18, 1997, A21.

95. North Atlantic Council, special declaration on Bosnia and Herzegovina issued by the heads of state and government, Madrid, July 8, 1997.

96. Ibid.

97. Richard Holbrooke, letter to the editor, *Foreign Affairs,* March/April 1997, 170. Holbrooke's statement apparently referred to the duress that Serbian leader Slobodan Milosevic applied to Radovan Karadzic to compel him to consent to the Dayton Accords, which were officially signed in Paris in December 1995 by Presidents Aliya Izetbegovic, Slobodan Milosevic, and Franjo Tudjman. Some observers speculate that Milosevic subsequently asked Karadzic to sign the Dayton Accords to indicate his acceptance of their terms.

98. Elaine Sciolino, "Soldiering On, Without an Enemy," *New York Times,* October 29, 1995, section 4, p. 4.

99. Associated Press, "U.S. Soldier Dies in Bosnia," *Washington Post,* August 5, 1997, A11.

100. William Drozdiak, "Mission to Bosnia: A Mixed 2 Years," *International Herald Tribune,* December 22, 1997, 5.

101. Holbrooke, letter to the editor, 171.

102. Drozdiak, "Mission to Bosnia," 5.

103. Tim Weiner, "Leak Caused NATO to Drop Bosnia Effort On Fugitives," *New York Times,* April 24, 1998, A8.

104. R. Jeffrey Smith, "A Plan to Nab Karadzic Is Foiled," *Washington Post National Weekly Edition,* April 27, 1998, 17.

105. Solomon quoted in Steven Erlanger, "Taking a Lesson From Cambodia," *New York Times,* July 13, 1997.

106. President Clinton's remarks on Bosnia, in the *New York Times.*

107. William E. Odom, "Putting Out the Balkan Fire," *Foreign Affairs,* November/December 1995, 152.

108. Cohen quoted in Erlanger, "On Bosnia, Clinton Supports Albright Against Cohen View," A1, A12.

109. Associated Press, "Two Chairmen Call for September 30 Bosnia Troop Pullout Deadline," *Washington Post,* March 22, 1997, A19.

110. Silber and Little, *The Death of Yugoslavia,* 131–32, 144–45.

111. For discussions of Tudjman's map, sketched on a restaurant menu in May 1995 at the request of a British politician, see Michael Evans, "Tudjman Mapped Out Future on City Menu," *The Times* (London), August 7, 1995; Stephen Engelberg, "Conflict in the Balkans: The Implications: To Peace or More War?" *New York Times,* August 8, 1995; and Thomas L. Friedman, "Foreign Affairs: Whose Balkan Menu?" *New York Times,* September 27, 1995, A23.

112. Charles G. Boyd, "Making Peace with the Guilty," *Foreign Affairs,* September/October 1995.

113. Holbrooke, letter to the editor, 170, 172.

114. Slocombe, remarks to the Atlantic Council, 17.

115. Bradley Graham, "House Backs June 1998 Funding Cutoff for U.S. Peacekeeping Troops in Bosnia," *Washington Post,* June 25, 1997, A6.

116. Helen Dewar, "Senate Presses for Bosnia Troop Pullout, but Does Not Deny Funds," *Washington Post,* July 12, 1997, A16.

117. Lee H. Hamilton, "The Crucial U.S. Role in Bosnia," *International Herald Tribune,* May 20, 1997, 8.

118. Cohen and Shalikashvili letter cited in Dewar, "Senate Presses for Bosnia Troop Pullout."

119. North Atlantic Council, special declaration on Bosnia and Herzegovina.

120. Clinton quoted in John F. Harris, "U.S. Troops May Stay On in Bosnia," *Washington Post,* July 13, 1997, A1.

121. Michael McCurry quoted in ibid.

122. Steven Komarow, "Cohen: No Pact to Keep U.S. Troops in Bosnia," *USA Today,* November 7, 1997, 20.

123. See, among other sources, Bradley Graham and John F. Harris, "White House Seeking Consensus On Size of Cuts in Bosnia Force," *Washington Post,* November 9, 1997, 27; Tracy Wilkinson, "In Bosnia, U.S. Creeps Deeper," *Los Angeles Times,* November 12, 1997; and Tyler Marshall and Tracy Wilkinson, "U.S. Team on Bosnia Takes Peacekeeping to the Limit," *Los Angeles Times,* November 12, 1997.

124. Cohen quoted in Steven Lee Myers, "U.S. Links Staying in Bosnia to Larger NATO Police Role," *New York Times,* December 3, 1997, A11.

125. North Atlantic Council in defense ministers session, final communiqué, December 2, 1997, par. 6.

126. Clinton quoted in Brian Knowlton, "U.S. Will Keep Its Troops In Bosnia Past June Cutoff," *International Herald Tribune,* December 19, 1997, 1, 12.

127. Steven Erlanger, "Flag-Waving in Bosnia," *International Herald Tribune,* December 17, 1997, 10.

128. Walter B. Slocombe, under secretary of defense for policy, hearing before the House International Relations Committee on prospects for implementation of Dayton Agreements and the new NATO mission in Bosnia, March 12, 1998, transcript furnished by Federal Document Clearing House, Inc., 38. According to interviews with NATO sources in early 1998, another reason was to avoid public ridicule, along the lines of "IFOR, SFOR, What For?" Two alternative names were suggested, not entirely in jest, to reflect the magnitude of the peacekeeping challenge: PFOR (Perpetual Force) and FOREVER.

129. Ibid., 23.

130. Ibid., 23, 26.

131. R. Jeffrey Smith and Bradley Graham, "NATO to Maintain Size of Bosnia Force in '98," *Washington Post,* March 4, 1998, 1.

132. Ambassador Robert Gelbard, the special representative of the president and the secretary of state for the implementation of the Dayton Peace Accords, hearing on prospects for implementation of Dayton Agreements, 19–20. Ambassador Gelbard's hope for Sarajevo to become once again "a truly multiethnic city" stands in contrast to Radovan Karadzic's notorious plan to divide the city into ethnic sectors with walls, "so that no ethnic groups will have to live or work together. . . . [O]ur vision of Sarajevo is like

Berlin when the wall was still standing." Karadzic cited in Zimmermann, "The Last Ambassador," 20.

133. Senator John McCain, "Get Our Troops Out of Bosnia," *Washington Quarterly,* Spring 1998, 7. See also Senator Kay Bailey Hutchison's (R-Texas) comments about the risk of "an unending commitment" in the absence of a clear strategy, in Steven Lee Myers, "Administration Decides to Reduce G.I. Force in Bosnia Slightly," *New York Times,* March 5, 1998, A13.

134. President Bill Clinton, letter to Congress, March 4, 1998, cited in Ernest Blazar, "Inside the Ring," *Washington Times,* March 5, 1998, 7.

135. Slocombe, hearing on prospects for implementation of Dayton Agreements, 29.

136. Schmitt, "Senate Approves Expansion of NATO."

137. President George Bush, speech on March 1, 1991, quoted in Ann Devroy and Guy Gugliotta, "Bush to 'Move Fast' on Mideast Peace; Cease-Fire Talks Delayed by 'Technical Details,'" *Washington Post,* March 2, 1991.

138. U.S. Department of Defense, *Conduct of the Persian Gulf War: Final Report to Congress* (Washington, D.C.: Government Printing Office, April 1992), xix, quoted in F. G. Hoffman, *Decisive Force: The New American Way of War* (Westport, Conn.: Praeger, 1996), 81.

139. Among other recent assessments of the challenges at hand, see David L. Bosco, "Reintegrating Bosnia: A Progress Report," *Washington Quarterly,* Spring 1998, 65–81; Charles G. Boyd, "Making Bosnia Work," *Foreign Affairs,* January/February 1998, 42–55; and Jane M. O. Sharp, "Dayton Report Card," *International Security* 22 (Winter 1997/98): 101–37.

140. Richard Morin, "Missing the Story on Bosnia," *Washington Post National Weekly Edition,* April 27, 1998, 35.

141. Rühe quoted in William Drozdiak, "At NATO, Unrest on Burden-Sharing Burbles Up," *International Herald Tribune,* December 16, 1997, 5.

142. Slocombe, hearing on prospects for implementation of Dayton Agreements, 23–24.

143. Neither Austria nor Romania is a member of NATO or the WEU, of course, but both are active participants in PfP.

144. North Atlantic Council communiqué, May 29, 1997, par. 11.

145. The two paragraphs discussing the Albanian case are based on interviews with NATO sources in late 1997 and early 1998.

146. Statistics about ethnic groups in the Balkans are controversial, but the proportions reported by Chris Hedges—ethnic Albanians making up 90 percent of the population in Kosovo and "about 25 percent" in FYROM—are widely accepted. See Chris Hedges, "Kosovo: Yet Another Act in the Balkan Tragedy," *New York Times,* April 30, 1998, A12; and Chris Hedges, "Macedonia's Albanians Are Restive," *New York Times,* May 11, 1998, A6.

147. Bush cited in John M. Goshko, "Bush Threatens 'Military Force' If Serbs Attack Ethnic Albanians," *Washington Post,* December 29, 1992, A10.

148. "Clinton Warns Serbian Leaders on Military Action in Kosovo," *Washington Post,* March 2, 1993, A14.

149. Gelbard and unnamed U.S. official quoted in Philip Shenon, "U.S. Says It Might Consider Attacking Serbs Over Kosovo," *New York Times,* March 13, 1998, A10.

150. Albright quoted in "U.S. Credibility On the Line," *Washington Post National Weekly Edition,* March 23, 1998, 24.

151. Teta and Solana quoted in Paul Ames, "NATO To Give Albania Extra Aid," March 12, 1998, Associated Press Online.

152. William Drozdiak, "NATO to Send More Aid to Albania, but No Troops," *International Herald Tribune,* March 12, 1998; Brooks Tigner, "Kosovo Fray Forces NATO's Hand," *Defense News,* March 16, 1998.

153. Steven Erlanger, "Yugoslavs Try to Outwit Albright Over Sanctions," *New York Times,* March 23, 1998, A8.

154. An explicit NATO role would carry a political weight distinct from the current participation in UNPREDEP by several Allies (including Belgium, Canada, Norway, Portugal, and the United States) as well as several non-NATO countries. For details about UNPREDEP's status and composition, see International Institute for Strategic Studies, *The Military Balance 1997/98,* 279. For the extension of UNPREDEP's mandate to February 1999 (and the authorization of an increase in its troop strength to 1,050), see UN Security Council Resolution 1186, adopted July 21, 1998.

155. Lazar Kitanoski cited in Kerin Hope, "Macedonia to Seek NATO Protection Force," *Financial Times* (London), March 13, 1998.

156. Interviews with NATO sources in Brussels in early 1998.

157. Partnership for Peace Invitation, issued by the North Atlantic Council, Brussels, January 10–11, 1994, in *NATO Handbook,* 265.

158. This judgment was expressed by a number of observers during the author's interviews in Europe in mid- to late 1997, in the context of security links and assurances to the Baltic states short of NATO membership.

159. With regard to U.S.-Baltic relations, see Erlanger, "U.S. to Back Baltic Membership in NATO"; and Steven Erlanger, "Clinton and 3 Baltic Leaders Sign Charter," *New York Times,* January 17, 1998, A4. Ulmanis is quoted in the latter article.

160. Daniel Vernet, "Une nouvelle Alliance pour une nouvelle Europe," *Le Monde,* May 25–26, 1997, 1, 14. According to Anton Surikov, a prominent Russian defense commentator, attempting to bring the Baltic states into the Alliance "could create a serious international crisis comparable with the Caribbean crisis of the 1960s"—that is, the 1962 Cuban missile crisis. Anton

Surikov, "Some Aspects of Russian Armed Forces Reform," *European Security* 6 (Autumn 1997): 55.

161. See, among other studies, Fiona Hill and Pamela Jewett, *"Back in the USSR": Russia's Intervention in the Internal Affairs of the Former Soviet Republics and the Implications for United States Policy Toward Russia* (Cambridge, Mass.: Strengthening Democratic Institutions Project, John F. Kennedy School of Government, Harvard University, January 1994); and John J. Maresca, "Post-Independence Decolonization: A Framework for Analyzing Russia's Relations with Neighbouring States," in James E. Goodby, ed., *Regional Conflicts: The Challenge to US–Russian Cooperation* (New York: Oxford University Press, 1995), 119–131.

162. As noted in chapter 3, the NATO-Ukraine Charter of July 1997 (see Appendix 4) calls for consultations "whenever Ukraine perceives a direct threat to its territorial integrity, political independence, or security." Charter on a Distinctive Partnership between the North Atlantic Treaty Organization and Ukraine, Madrid, July 9, 1997, par. 15.

163. North Atlantic Council, Strategic Concept, par. 21; emphasis added.

164. General George A. Joulwan, "When Ivan Meets GI Joe," *Washington Post,* April 28, 1996, C3.

165. Founding Act on Mutual Relations.

166. General John Galvin, statement before the Senate Committee on Armed Services, March 7, 1991, 6–7.

167. Paul Wolfowitz, statement before the Senate Committee on Armed Services, April 11, 1991, 24.

168. Robert B. Zoellick, *The New Europe in a New Age: Insular, Itinerant, or International? Prospects for an Alliance of Values,* Current Policy no. 1300 (Washington, D.C.: Bureau of Public Affairs, U.S. Department of State, September 21, 1990), 3.

169. de Wijk, *NATO on the Brink of the New Millennium,* 151.

170. See, for instance, John E. Peters and Howard Deshong, *Out of Area or Out of Reach? European Military Support for Operations in Southwest Asia* (Santa Monica, Calif.: Rand Corporation, 1995); Richard L. Kugler, *U.S.–West European Cooperation in Out-of-Area Military Operations: Problems and Prospects* (Santa Monica, Calif.: Rand Corporation, 1995); David Gompert and Richard Kugler, "Free-Rider Redux: NATO Needs to Project Power (and Europe Can Help)," *Foreign Affairs,* January/February 1995, 7–12; Ronald D. Asmus, Robert D. Blackwill, and F. Stephen Larrabee, "Can NATO Survive?" *Washington Quarterly,* Spring 1996, 79–101; and James A. Thomson, "A New Partnership: New NATO Military Structures," in David C. Gompert and F. Stephen Larrabee, eds., *America and Europe: A Partnership for a New Era* (Cambridge: Cambridge University Press, 1997).

171. Warren Christopher and William J. Perry, "NATO's True Mission," *New York Times,* October 21, 1997, A27.

172. Albright quoted in William Drozdiak, "Albright Urges NATO to Fight Arms of Mass Destruction," *International Herald Tribune,* December 17, 1997, 1, 10.

173. Cook quoted in ibid.

174. See, for example, the editorial, "Bigger NATO, safer world?" in *The Economist,* July 12, 1997, 14. Also see the speech by Karl Lamers, the foreign affairs spokesman of the Christian Democratic Union/Christian Social Union parliamentary group in the German Bundestag, given at the Royal Institute of International Affairs (Chatham House), London, January 20, 1998.

175. Joachim Krause, "Proliferation Risks and their Strategic Relevance: What Role for NATO?" *Survival* 37 (Summer 1995): 147.

176. Rühle and Williams, "Why NATO Will Survive," 112.

177. William Drozdiak, "Is NATO's Southern Flank Exposed?" *International Herald Tribune,* May 20, 1997, 1, 6.

178. Michael Rühle, "NATO and the Coming Proliferation Threat," *Comparative Strategy* 13 (July–September 1994): 317–18.

179. *Das Meinungsbild der Elite in Deutschland zur Aussen- und Sicherheitspolitik, Eine Studie im Auftrag des Liberalen Institutes der Friedrich-Naumann-Stiftung in Kooperation mit der Rand Corporation, USA* (Berlin: Infratest Burke Berlin, March 1996).

180. Albright quoted in Drozdiak, "Albright Urges NATO to Fight Arms of Mass Destruction."

181. John F. Sopko, "The Changing Proliferation Threat," *Foreign Policy,* no. 105 (Winter 1996–97): 3–20.

182. Ashton B. Carter and David B. Omand, "Countering the Proliferation Risks: Adapting the Alliance to the New Security Environment," *NATO Review* 44 (September 1996): 13.

183. Brad Roberts and Victor Utgoff, "Coalitions Against NBC-Armed Regional Aggressors: How Are They Formed, Maintained, and Led?" *Comparative Strategy* 16 (July–September 1997): 233–52.

184. "Yes, Help Russia, But Stop Magnifying Threats," *New York Times,* April 2, 1992, A22.

185. Claude, "Collective Security after the Cold War," 23.

186. Cheney quoted in David S. Broder, "With Cheney in Charge," *Washington Post,* February 27, 1991, A25.

187. NATO Defense Planning Committee and Nuclear Planning Group communiqué, November 29, 1995, par. 4.

188. Wight, "The Balance of Power and International Order," 106–7.

189. Wight, *Power Politics,* 214–15.

190. North Atlantic Council, declaration of the heads of state and government, Brussels, January 10–11, 1994, par. 7.

191. Craig R. Whitney, "Belgrade Suspended by European Security Group," *New York Times,* July 9, 1992, 13.

192. *The Challenges of Change,* Helsinki Document 1992 (Washington, D.C.: U.S. Arms Control and Disarmament Agency, July 10, 1992), par. 25.

193. North Atlantic Council, declaration of the heads of state and government, January 10–11, 1994, par. 7.

194. Some documents approved by the Allies have conveyed that impression, however, at least with respect to peacekeeping. In June 1993, a NACC Ad Hoc Group concluded, "Peacekeeping can be carried out only under the authority of the UN Security Council, or of the CSCE in accordance with the CSCE Document agreed in Helsinki in July 1992 and other relevant CSCE documents. . . . Peacekeeping requires a clear political objective and a precise mandate, as decided by the UN or the CSCE." (Report to Ministers by the NACC Ad Hoc Group on Cooperation in Peacekeeping, Athens, June 11, 1993, Part I, par. 2.) According to the December 1995 follow-up report, "Peacekeeping operations are carried out by the UN or, as appropriate, by the OSCE, with the consent of the principal parties to a conflict. . . . An operation, however, is not under any circumstances to become a peace enforcement operation without specific authorization from the UN Security Council." (Follow-on to the 1993 Athens Report on Cooperation in Peacekeeping, North Atlantic Cooperation Council, Brussels, December 6, 1995, par. 5.)

195. North Atlantic Council communiqué, May 30, 1995, par. 11.

196. For a useful analysis of a peacekeeping operation based entirely on sovereign decisions, without benefit of a UN Security Council mandate, see Mala Tabory, *The Multinational Force and Observers in the Sinai: Organization, Structure, and Function* (Boulder, Colo.: Westview Press, 1986).

197. Lt. Gen. William E. Odom, U.S. Army (ret.), director of national security studies, Hudson Institute, testimony before the House Committee on International Relations, June 20, 1996, prepared statement, 5–6.

198. Kissinger, "The Dilution of NATO," C9.

199. Michael Rühle, "Crisis Management in NATO," *European Security* 2 (Winter 1993): 497.

200. Willem Van Eekelen in *The Security Agenda for 1996: Background and Proposals,* CEPS Paper no. 64 (Brussels: Centre for European Policy Studies, 1995), 9n.

201. Wight, *International Theory,* 35.

202. Howe, "NATO and the Gulf crisis," 257.

203. Inis L. Claude, Jr., "The Collectivist Theme in International Relations," *International Journal* 24 (Autumn 1969): 655.

204. Ibid., 656.

205. It should not be forgotten, however, that the Alliance endured an abundance of discord during the Cold War over issues such as burden sharing, NATO strategy (especially with regard to nuclear deterrence), arms control, and political and economic relations with the Soviet Union and its allies.

206. Holger H. Mey, "New Members—New Mission: The Real Issues Behind the New NATO Debate," *Comparative Strategy* 13, no. 2 (1994): 226–28.

207. Until June 1995, the decline in French defense spending was much more gradual than the reductions in defense spending in Britain, Germany, and the United States. During the period from 1985 to 1994, for example, France's defense spending declined from 4.0 to 3.3 percent of GDP, while Germany's decreased from 3.2 to 1.8 percent of GDP. See Marc Aufrant, "Analyse économique des 'dépenses de défense' des principaux pays occidentaux," *Revue Française de Finances Publiques,* no. 54 (1996): 207–9. Since June 1995, French defense spending has declined substantially.

208. Talleyrand quoted in Wight, *Power Politics,* 199.

209. The distinction is analogous to the sometimes misleading distinction between high-intensity and low-intensity conflict; war is really a continuum of violence. To the extent that the distinction holds, both types of operations require purposeful political direction.

210. Observers such as Lord David Owen and Vitaly Churkin were concerned in early 1994 that NATO action outside explicit UN control might have this effect. See Silber and Little, *The Death of Yugoslavia,* 312, 328–29.

211. de Wijk, *NATO on the Brink of the New Millennium,* 143.

212. United Kingdom Ministry of Defence, *Statement on the Defence Estimates 1996* (London: Her Majesty's Stationery Office, 1996), 19, par. 165.

213. Ibid., 18, table 3.

214. Karl Kaiser and Klaus Becher, "Germany and the Iraq Conflict," in Nicole Gnesotto and John Roper, eds., *Western Europe and the Gulf* (Paris: Institute for Security Studies, Western European Union, 1992), 49–50.

215. Admiral T. Joseph Lopez, USN, letter to the editor, *Washington Post,* August 12, 1997, A18.

5. Prospects and Challenges

1. U.S. Secretary of State Warren Christopher, intervention at the meeting of the North Atlantic Council, NATO Headquarters, Brussels, December 1, 1994, in *U.S. Department of State Dispatch,* December 19, 1994, 830.

2. Slocombe, remarks to the Atlantic Council, 3; emphasis added.

3. North Atlantic Council communiqué, December 10, 1996, par. 24; emphasis added.

4. Javier Solana, speech at the Royal Institute of International Affairs, London, March 4, 1997, text furnished by the NATO Press and Media Service, 2.

5. Presidents Clinton and Yeltsin, joint statements and news conference, 18.

6. Albright, prepared statement before the Senate Foreign Relations Committee, October 7, 1997, in *The Debate on NATO Enlargement,* 17. Senator Arthur Vandenberg (R-Michigan) played a leading role in making the drafting and ratification of the North Atlantic Treaty possible in 1948–49. The June 1948 "Vandenberg Resolution" informed the Truman administration that the Senate supported efforts by the United States to devise "regional and other collective arrangements for individual and collective self-defense."

7. The Kantian and Wilsonian conceptions, it should be recalled, assume the establishment of a "community of power," such that any aggression would be dealt with on a "we among ourselves" basis. Balance-of-power conceptions and the major-power-consensus form of collective security (and operations in support of collective security outside a major-power consensus) imply an "us against them" situation of collective action against external parties.

8. Osgood, "Woodrow Wilson, Collective Security, and the Lessons of History," 190.

9. This discussion of centripetal and centrifugal forces is based on the author's interviews in Washington and Europe in late 1997 and early 1998.

10. North Atlantic Council, Strategic Concept, par. 37.

11. North Atlantic Council Declaration, January 11, 1994, par. 14. According to Article 4 of the North Atlantic Treaty, "The Parties will consult together whenever, in the opinion of any of them, the territorial integrity, political independence or security of any of the Parties is threatened."

12. Wight, *Power Politics,* 110.

13. Wilson, "An Address to the Senate," 535–36.

14. Wight, "The Balance of Power," 174–75. Compare Wight's assertion with Inis Claude's observation that "the alternatives to American isolationism" are limited to "participation in a balance of power system, in a collective security system in the Wilsonian sense, or in a movement to establish a world government either by conquest or by voluntary federation of the nations." Claude, *Power and International Relations,* 117.

15. In Wight's view, "it is the trouble about international politics that the distribution of power does not long remain constant and the Powers are usually in disagreement on its being an even distribution. Most arrangements of power favour some countries, which therefore seek to preserve the status quo, and justify it as being a true balance in the sense of an equilibrium; and are irksome to other countries whose policy is accordingly revisionist." Wight, "The Balance of Power," 154–55.

16. Wight's dismissal of the Wilsonian "community of power" as a "chimera" may have been an unconscious or deliberate rejoinder to Kant's assertion that "a lasting universal peace on the basis of the so-called balance of power in Europe is a mere chimera." Kant, "The Principle of Progress," 65. To be sure, Wight made no claim that the balance of power would provide "a lasting universal peace," only that it was the sole lucid basis for policy available. Even Kant expressed doubts at times about the feasibility of his design for enduring peace and international order, notably in his famous statement, "Nothing straight can be constructed from such warped wood as that which man is made of." Immanuel Kant, "Idea for a Universal History with a Cosmopolitan Purpose," first published in 1784, in Kant, *Political Writings,* 46.

17. Wight, "The Balance of Power and International Order," 115.

18. Claude, *Power and International Relations,* 198; emphasis in the original.

19. North Atlantic Council, Strategic Concept, par. 21.

20. Goodby, "Can Collective Security Work?" 241.

21. Osgood, "Woodrow Wilson, Collective Security, and the Lessons of History," 197; emphasis in the original.

22. For background, see Hedley Bull, Benedict Kingsbury, and Adam Roberts, eds., *Hugo Grotius and International Relations* (Oxford: Clarendon Press, 1992). For a discussion of Martin Wight's analysis of what he termed the Grotian, Machiavellian, and Kantian traditions, see David S. Yost, "Political Philosophy and the Theory of International Relations," *International Affairs* 70 (April 1994): 263–90.

23. Wight, *International Theory,* 166.

24. As Martin Wight observed regarding this case and comparable events, when major powers "impose their will," they "usually justify their action as enforcing peace and security. But these are among the ambiguous words of power politics: we must ask whose security is in question, and at whose expense it is purchased." Wight, *Power Politics,* 42.

25. Michael O. Wheeler, *Nuclear Weapons and the National Interest: The Early Years* (Washington, D.C.: National Defense University Press, 1989), 73.

26. Dean Acheson, letter to Hans J. Morgenthau, January 3, 1957, in *Among Friends: Personal Letters of Dean Acheson,* ed. David S. McLellan and David C. Acheson (New York: Dodd, Mead, and Co., 1980), 119.

27. Kissinger, *Diplomacy,* 835.

28. Founding Act on Mutual Relations, 2.

29. An important argument for a modest, rather than far-reaching, review is that the prospective new Allies—Poland, Hungary, and the Czech Republic—will be bound by the new Strategic Concept, but will not have participated fully in its elaboration. These three countries have participated in discussions with the Allies, but ultimately the new Strategic Concept is expected to be approved at sixteen rather than nineteen.

30. Joris Michael Vos quoted in Lisa Burgess, "Nuclear Policy Battle Looms as NATO Expansion Nears," *Defense News,* March 30, 1998, 42. The nuclear policy paragraphs in the 1991 Strategic Concept are discussed in chapter 2.

31. North Atlantic Council, Strategic Concept, par. 21.

32. Ibid., par. 14.

33. Volker Rühe, "Auf dem Weg zu einer neuen Sicherheitsordnung in Europa," *Frankfurter Allgemeine Zeitung,* May 27, 1997.

34. North Atlantic Council, Madrid Declaration, par. 4.

35. Knowlton, "U.S. Will Keep Its Troops In Bosnia."

36. Helms quoted in Alison Mitchell, "NATO Debate: From Big Risk to Sure Thing," *New York Times,* March 20, 1998, A1, A8.

37. Nerlich, "Western Europe's Relations with the United States," 88.

38. Perry quoted in Sciolino, "Soldiering On."

39. This argument is developed further in David S. Yost, "The Future of U.S. Overseas Presence," *Joint Force Quarterly*, no. 8 (Summer 1995).

40. Wörner cited in Alan Riding, "At East-West Crossroads, Western Europe Hesitates," *New York Times,* March 25, 1992, A6.

41. Josef Joffe, "Europe's American Pacifier," *Foreign Policy*, no. 54 (Spring 1984): 64–82; Joffe, *The Limited Partnership,* especially 178, 183, 184.

42. Rühle and Williams, "Why NATO Will Survive," 113.

43. François Heisbourg, "L'OTAN et le pilier européen," *Politique Internationale*, no. 71 (Spring 1996): 55–56, 63.

44. Western European Union, Council of Ministers, Bonn, June 19, 1992, "Petersberg Declaration," Part II, "On Strengthening WEU's Operational Role," par. 4.

45. Holbrooke quoted in Roger Cohen, "Over There: Why the Yanks Are Going. Yet Again," *New York Times,* November 26, 1995, section 4, pp. 1, 4.

46. Wight, *International Theory,* 129. This passage is drawn from Wight's discussion of the Rationalist, or Grotian, tradition of thinking about international relations, in contrast with the Realist, or Machiavellian, tradition.

47. Henry A. Kissinger, letter to the editor, *Washington Post,* July 12, 1997, A20.

48. North Atlantic Council, Strategic Concept, par. 21; emphasis added.

49. Claude, "The Collectivist Theme," 649.

50. North Atlantic Council, declaration of the heads of state and government, Brussels, January 10–11, 1994, par. 7.

51. Stephen F. Szabo, *West European Public Perceptions of Security Issues: A Survey of Attitudes in France, the FRG, Great Britain, and Italy over Three Decades* (Washington, D.C.: Office of Research, U.S. Information Agency, January 1989), 25. Szabo completed the study in July 1988; it was released to the public in January 1989.

52. Christopher Fleury, "In Time of Crisis, Britons and Germans Would Count on U.S. Most," *Opinion Analysis* (published by the Office of Research and Media Reaction, U.S. Information Agency, Washington, D.C.), May 12, 1998, 1–4.

53. For details, see Gebhard Schweigler, *The Legacy of History and Germany's Future Role in International Politics,* SWP-IP 2941 (Ebenhausen, Germany: Stiftung Wissenschaft und Politik, January 1996), 10–11.

54. Joffe, "Europe's American Pacifier," 73.

55. The critical phrases, such as "a latter-day League of Nations," came up in the author's interviews with U.S. and European observers in 1997 and 1998. In the same vein, a French critic of some current trends suggested that the Alliance might eventually have only a single office for its traditional functions, with the door labeled, "Collective Defense: No Russians Allowed."

56. Eyal, "NATO's Enlargement," 701.

Key Acronyms
Concepts and
Organizations in Brief

CFE—Conventional Armed Forces in Europe Treaty

The CFE Treaty was signed in 1990 by the NATO Allies and members of the Warsaw Treaty Organization, also known as the Warsaw Pact. Although the Warsaw Pact was dissolved in July 1991 and the Soviet Union disintegrated at the end of that year, the NATO Allies and the former Warsaw Pact states in East-Central Europe and most of the Soviet successor states with forces or territory in the treaty's geographical zone of application (with the exceptions of Estonia, Latvia, and Lithuania) continue to adhere to the treaty in adapted form. The treaty originally had twenty-two parties and now has thirty. The treaty sets ceilings for five categories of conventional military equipment (tanks, artillery, armored combat vehicles, attack helicopters, and combat aircraft) for groups of states as well as specific states in several zones in the "Atlantic-to-the-Urals" area. The treaty adaptation process continues in the framework of a Joint Consultative Group involving all the parties.

CJTF—Combined Joint Task Force

The CJTF concept was first officially approved at the January 1994 NATO summit in Brussels. The CJTF concept calls for the effective integration of forces from various armed services (hence, "joint") and various nations (hence, "combined"). The CJTF concept is being developed within the Alliance for multinational forces that could be employed flexibly and effectively in non–Article 5 crisis management and peacekeeping operations, as well as in

Article 5 (collective defense) contingencies. In accordance with agreed-upon procedures under the authority of the North Atlantic Council, CJTFs drawing on NATO assets could also be made available for operations undertaken under the leadership of the Western European Union.

EAPC—Euro-Atlantic Partnership Council

Established by the NATO Allies and PfP Partners (and Tajikistan) in May 1997, the EAPC provides a new framework for multilateral dialogue and cooperation. It replaced the North Atlantic Cooperation Council (NACC) in May 1997.

ESDI—European Security and Defense Identity

The ESDI is intended to enable all European Allies to make a more coherent and effective contribution to NATO, thereby forming a stronger "European pillar," and reinforcing the transatlantic link within the Alliance. The principal institutional manifestation of the ESDI for military operations is to be the Western European Union, on the accepted Alliance principle of "separable but not separate" capabilities for use by NATO or the WEU. Depending on North Atlantic Council decisions, the WEU might make use of CJTF and NATO assets. Another aspect of the ESDI is the aspiration evoked in the European Union's 1991 Maastricht Treaty—that the EU's Common Foreign and Security Policy in the long term will include "the eventual framing of a common defense policy, which might in time lead to a common defense." The Maastricht Treaty describes the WEU as "an integral part" of the EU's development, and stipulates that the foreign and security policies established in the EU will "respect the obligations of certain Member States under the North Atlantic Treaty and be compatible with the common security and defense policy established within that framework."

Euro-Atlantic area

The Euro-Atlantic area consists of the territory of all the states participating in the Organization for Security and Cooperation in Europe. In North America, it consists of the United States and Canada. In Eurasia, it consists of all of Europe, encompassing Turkey and the Caucasus, and all the territory of the former Soviet Union, including Siberian Russia and the former Soviet republics in Central Asia. The NATO Allies have repeatedly declared that "security is indivisible" in the Euro-Atlantic area, and states in this area are eligible to become PfP Partners and members of the Euro-Atlantic Partnership Council.

IFOR—Implementation Force

IFOR was deployed in Bosnia-Herzegovina from December 1995 to December 1996. Its mission was to ensure compliance with the military aspects of the Dayton Accords. All sixteen NATO nations participated in IFOR, as did eighteen non-NATO countries, including fourteen states in the Partnership for Peace (PfP). The Partner countries in IFOR were Albania, Austria, Bulgaria, the Czech Republic, Estonia, Finland, Hungary, Latvia, Lithuania, Poland, Romania, Russia, Sweden, and Ukraine. The other four participants were Egypt, Jordan, Malaysia, and Morocco.

NAC—North Atlantic Council

Comprised of representatives of the member countries, this deliberative forum was created by Article 9 of the North Atlantic Treaty and is the Alliance's highest decision-making body. It meets regularly in Brussels at the level of ambassadors, at least twice a year at the levels of foreign and defense ministers, and occasionally in summit session at the level of heads of state and government.

NACC—North Atlantic Cooperation Council

The NACC was established in December 1991 as a mechanism for dialogue between the NATO Allies and their former adversaries, the states that had been either members of the Warsaw Pact (which was dissolved in July 1991) or republics of the Soviet Union (which collapsed in December 1991). The NACC's accomplishments included the preparation of reports, notably those approved in June 1993 and December 1995, regarding principles for peacekeeping operations that might be undertaken in the Euro-Atlantic area. The NACC was replaced by the Euro-Atlantic Partnership Council in May 1997.

NATO—North Atlantic Treaty Organization

The North Atlantic Treaty, also known as the Washington Treaty, was signed in April 1949 and entered into force in August 1949. Since the end of the Cold War in 1989–91, the NATO Allies have recast the Alliance's roles and missions. While the Alliance retains its core function of collective defense, it has taken major steps to deepen and institutionalize cooperation with non-NATO countries in the Euro-Atlantic area by establishing the Partnership for Peace, the Euro-Atlantic Partnership Council, and special consultative bodies with Russia and Ukraine. Moreover, since 1992, the Alliance has undertaken significant activities in support of international security under the auspices of the United Nations, particularly in the Balkans.

NATO-Russia Permanent Joint Council (PJC)

The NATO-Russia PJC was established by the Founding Act, signed by the NATO Allies and Russia on May 27, 1997, in Paris. Under the terms of the Act, the PJC brings together representatives of the sixteen Allies and Russia and provides a venue for consultation and cooperation regarding political and security matters.

NATO-Ukraine Commission

Established under the terms of the July 1997 Charter on a Distinctive Partnership between NATO and Ukraine, the commission meets at least twice a year to examine progress in the development of the NATO-Ukraine relationship.

OSCE—Organization for Security and Cooperation in Europe

Known as the Conference on Security and Cooperation in Europe (CSCE) from 1972 to 1994, the OSCE was initially a process of dialogue on economic, political, and security affairs. This dialogue resulted in the definition of fundamental principles on human rights, economic relations, and international security and cooperation in the 1975 Helsinki Final Act. These principles have furnished the basis for subsequent review conferences. In November 1990 the CSCE heads of state and government adopted the Charter of Paris for a New Europe and established three institutions: a secretariat in Prague (later merged with the general secretariat in Vienna), a Conflict Prevention Center in Vienna, and an Office for Free Elections in Warsaw (later renamed the Office for Democratic Institutions and Human Rights). In July 1992 the CSCE decided to name a High Commissioner on National Minorities and to develop means for early warning and conflict prevention, including mediation and fact-finding missions. In December 1993 the CSCE established a Permanent Committee (later renamed the Permanent Council) for consultations and decision making. In December 1994 the member states decided to adopt the name OSCE and to strengthen the organization's capabilities for the oversight and conduct of activities in support of international security, including peacekeeping and conflict resolution.

PfP—Partnership for Peace

Set up in January 1994, PfP offers the Alliance's Partners the opportunity of cooperating with NATO in various programs, including military exercises and civil emergency relief, as well as in military operations such as IFOR and SFOR in Bosnia. In accordance with decisions taken in May 1997 by the North Atlantic

Council, PfP Partners are to have a greater role in planning and directing future PfP programs.

SACEUR and SACLANT—Supreme Allied Commander Europe and Supreme Allied Commander Atlantic

These are the two top-level commanders in the Alliance's integrated military structure, heading Supreme Headquarters Allied Powers Europe (SHAPE) and Allied Command Atlantic (ACLANT), respectively. Historically known as the Major NATO Commands, they are to be called Strategic Commands under the revised command structure approved by the North Atlantic Council in December 1997.

SFOR—Stabilization Force

The NATO-led SFOR has been deployed in Bosnia-Herzegovina since December 1996 in support of efforts to implement the November-December 1995 Dayton Accords. Replacing the Implementation Force (IFOR), SFOR is now scheduled to remain in Bosnia-Herzegovina past its original deadline of June 1998. All NATO countries and twenty non-NATO states, including fifteen PfP Partners, are taking part in SFOR. The contributors include all IFOR participants, plus Ireland and Slovenia, the latter a PfP Partner.

SHAPE—Supreme Headquarters Allied Powers Europe

Located near Mons, Belgium, this is the headquarters of Allied Command Europe (ACE).

WEU—Western European Union

Established in 1954 on the basis of the 1948 Treaty of Brussels, the WEU now numbers ten member countries, all of which are also members of NATO. By treaty, the WEU is a collective defense organization. In its 1992 Petersberg Declaration, however, the WEU declared that its forces could also be employed for "humanitarian and rescue tasks; peacekeeping tasks; [and] tasks of combat forces in crisis management, including peacemaking."

The Evolving Membership of Major European Security Organizations

EAPC—Euro-Atlantic Partnership Council

The EAPC replaced the North Atlantic Cooperation Council (NACC) in May 1997. Its membership is composed of all sixteen NATO Allies and all twenty-seven PfP Partners, plus Tajikistan, for a total of forty-four members.

EU—European Union

The original six participants in the 1951 European Coal and Steel Community (ECSC) were France, Italy, West Germany, and the Benelux countries (Belgium, the Netherlands, and Luxembourg). In 1957 these six countries signed the Treaty of Rome, founding the European Economic Community (EEC), as well as another treaty establishing the European Atomic Energy Community (EURATOM). In July 1967 these countries signed a "Merger Treaty" establishing a single Council and Commission for the "European Communities," effectively integrating the ECSC, the EEC, and EURATOM. The official term "European Communities" was never widely used, however. The enterprise was better known as the European Community (EC) or (incorrectly) the EEC until it became the European Union (EU) with the entry into force of the Maastricht Treaty in November 1993. The EC was expanded in 1973, with the accession of Denmark, Ireland, and the United Kingdom; in 1981, with the membership of Greece; and in 1986, with the accession of Spain and Portugal. Austria, Finland, and Sweden entered the EU in January 1995.

NACC—North Atlantic Cooperation Council

At its beginning in December 1991, the NACC had thirty-seven members: the sixteen NATO Allies, the fifteen successor states of the Soviet Union, and six other states that were formerly part of the Warsaw Pact (Albania, Bulgaria, Czechoslovakia, Hungary, Poland, and Romania). East Germany had become part of the Federal Republic of Germany in October 1990. The Czech Republic and Slovakia became separate states in January 1993, increasing the number of NACC members to thirty-eight. NACC observers included Austria, Finland, and Sweden. The NACC was replaced by the EAPC in May 1997.

NATO—North Atlantic Treaty Organization

The original twelve signatories of the 1949 North Atlantic Treaty, also known as the Treaty of Washington, were Belgium, Canada, Denmark, France, Iceland, Italy, Luxembourg, the Netherlands, Norway, Portugal, the United Kingdom, and the United States. In 1952, Greece and Turkey joined the Alliance, bringing the total to fourteen. In 1955, West Germany was admitted to the Alliance, followed in 1982 by Spain, for a total of sixteen Allies. Hungary, Poland, and the Czech Republic are expected to join NATO in 1998–99.

OSCE—the Organization for Security and Cooperation in Europe

Until December 1994, the OSCE was called the CSCE, the Conference on Security and Cooperation in Europe. From its origins in 1972–73 until 1990, the CSCE had thirty-five members: Austria, Belgium, Bulgaria, Canada, Cyprus, Czechoslovakia, Denmark, Finland, France, the German Democratic Republic (East Germany), the Federal Republic of Germany (West Germany), Greece, the Holy See, Hungary, Iceland, Ireland, Italy, Liechtenstein, Luxembourg, Malta, Monaco, the Netherlands, Norway, Poland, Portugal, Romania, San Marino, Spain, Sweden, Switzerland, Turkey, the Union of Soviet Socialist Republics, the United Kingdom, the United States, and Yugoslavia. In 1990, East Germany's participation ceased, because its territory became part of the Federal Republic of Germany. In 1991 Albania joined the CSCE. As a consequence of the disintegration of the Soviet Union in 1991 and the Yugoslav federation in 1991–92 and the separation of Slovakia and the Czech Republic in 1993, the membership of the OSCE (including the Federal Republic of Yugoslavia, joining Serbia and Montenegro) currently stands at fifty-five. The Soviet Union's successor states are as follows: Armenia, Azerbaijan, Belarus, Estonia, Georgia, Kazakstan, Kyrgyzstan, Latvia, Lithuania, Moldova, the Russian Federation, Tajikistan, Turkmenistan, Ukraine, and Uzbekistan.

(It should be noted that the Soviet annexation of the Baltic states was never recognized by the United States, the Federal Republic of Germany, or certain other NATO nations.) The successor states to the Yugoslav federation are the following: Bosnia and Herzegovina, Croatia, the Former Yugoslav Republic of Macedonia (FYROM), Slovenia, and the Federal Republic of Yugoslavia (Serbia and Montenegro). Although the membership of the Federal Republic of Yugoslavia in the OSCE was suspended in 1992, it is still considered an OSCE state.

PfP—Partnership for Peace

By the end of 1996, NATO had twenty-seven Partners in the PfP: Albania, Armenia, Austria, Azerbaijan, Belarus, Bulgaria, the Czech Republic, Estonia, Finland, Georgia, Hungary, Kazakstan, Kyrgyzstan, Latvia, Lithuania, the Former Yugoslavia Republic of Macedonia (FYROM), Moldova, Poland, Romania, Russia, Slovakia, Slovenia, Sweden, Switzerland, Turkmenistan, Ukraine, and Uzbekistan. Malta was a PfP Partner from April to October 1996. States that join NATO (as Poland, Hungary, and the Czech Republic are expected to do in 1998–99) will cease to be Partners and become Allies.

WEU—Western European Union

The original five signatories of the 1948 Brussels Treaty were France, the United Kingdom, and the Benelux countries (Belgium, the Netherlands, and Luxembourg). In 1954, the WEU was created on the basis of the Brussels Treaty, and Italy and West Germany joined. In 1988, Portugal and Spain signed protocols of accession, which entered into force in 1990. Greece was invited to join in 1992; and the process of accession was completed in March 1995, bringing the total of WEU members to ten. In 1992, Iceland, Norway, and Turkey (all NATO Allies but not members of the European Community) were made Associate Members of the WEU, with this status effective upon Greece's admittance to full membership in the WEU. Denmark and Ireland, as European Community members, were invited to become WEU members, but they chose to become WEU Observers. (As a NATO Ally, Denmark was also eligible for Associate Member status, but preferred to be an Observer.) After their accession to the European Union in 1995, Austria, Finland, and Sweden also became WEU Observers. In June 1992, the WEU established a Forum of Consultation for dialogue and cooperation with nine countries: Bulgaria, the Czech Republic, Estonia, Hungary, Latvia, Lithuania, Poland, Romania, and Slovakia. In May 1994, the Forum of Consultation was brought to an end, and these nine countries were made Associate Partners of the WEU. In June 1996,

Slovenia also became an Associate Partner of the WEU. At present, all full members of the WEU are also members of the EU and NATO.

WTO—The Warsaw Treaty Organization (also known as the Warsaw Pact)

The Warsaw Pact, the Soviet-led rival to NATO, began in 1955 with eight members: Albania, Bulgaria, Czechoslovakia, the German Democratic Republic (East Germany), Hungary, Poland, Romania, and the Soviet Union. Before its dissolution in 1991, only one state left the Warsaw Pact: Albania withdrew in 1968.

Index

Abkhazia
  possible nuclear weapons
    deployments in, 138
Abyssinia, Italian aggression in
    1935–1936, 16–17
ACE. *See* NATO military commands,
    Allied Command Europe
Acheson, Dean, 29, 284
ACLANT. *See* NATO military com-
    mands, Allied Command
    Atlantic
Ad Hoc Group on Cooperation in
    Peacekeeping, 95
Afghanistan
  CIA operations and collapse of
    Soviet Union, 46
  Soviet invasion of, 32, 45
AFSOUTH. *See* NATO military
    commands, Allied Forces
    Southern Europe
Albania
  applicant for NATO member-
    ship, 118
  concerns about Bosnian conflict
    spillover, 199, 227
  exercise of PfP emergency con-
    sultation rights, 236
  NATO assistance, 235, 236, 294

Operation Alba, 217, 235
  participation in IFOR, 195
  withdrawal from Warsaw Pact,
    31
Albright, Madeleine
  on Bosnian conflict, 196
  on European Allies' shirking
    responsibility, 246
  on global interests of NATO, 244
  on NATO and democratization,
    70
  on NATO enlargement, 109–110,
    118, 120–121, 125, 128
  on NATO's core mission of col-
    lective defense, 92, 273
  on Russian opposition to NATO
    enlargement, 131–132
  on Russian threat, 83
  warning about conflict in
    Kosovo, 236
Amsterdam Treaty, 217
Andorra, 162
Andreotti, Giulio, 39
Antall, Jozsef, 49
Arbatov, Alexei, 84
Armenia
  possible nuclear weapons
    deployments in, 138

Arms competition. *See also*
    Deterrence
    factor in Soviet collapse, 45, 46
    Iraqi programs for weapons of
        mass destruction, 80
    and risk of war, 24
    U.S.-Soviet, 44–45, 46
Arms control
    Bonn Conference on Arms
        Control Issues, 250
    Bosnia issue, 218
    Cold War issue, 33–34, 36
    disarmament, 11, 13
    NATO enlargement effects on,
        106, 115, 140
    NATO's emphasis on countering
        proliferation of weapons of
        mass destruction, 73, 79–81,
        89, 284
    NATO's role, 55–57, 60–61, 173
    Nuclear Non-Proliferation Treaty,
        68, 153
    OSCE role, 176
    PfP and League of Nations sup-
        port for, 178–179
    START II agreement, 106, 138
Arms embargo against former Yugo-
    slavia, 1, 193, 194, 195, 198
ARRC. *See* NATO military com-
    mands, Allied Command
    Europe Rapid Reaction Corps
Art, Robert, 51
Ashcroft, John, 108
Aslund, Anders, 44
Asmus, Ronald D., 101
Aspin, Les, 82, 97, 200
Association of the Hague
    (1681–83), 9
Austria
    and Hungary's NATO member-
        ship, 128
    neutrality of, 211
    observer status in NACC, 95

    participation in IFOR, 195
    participation in multinational
        intervention in Albania, 235
    participation in PfP, 97
    partition of Polish state, 283
    possible NATO membership,
        175
    WEU Council invitation to par-
        ticipate in WEU defense
        planning, 211
Azerbaijan
    decision to hold off on apply-
        ing for NATO member-
        ship, 118
    and Russian sphere of influence,
        241
    Russian support for Armenian
        forces fighting, 86

Baker, James, 100–101, 134
Baku, 86
Balance of power
    "balance-of-power politics," 24,
        26, 251, 283, 284
    Cold War issue, 33, 140
    and collective defense, 7, 23,
        26, 148, 209, 240, 282
    collective security's development
        from, 14–16, 23–26
    community of power *vs.*, 11, 16,
        280–281
    confusion of term, 24
    and Europe's peace from
        1815–1914, 24–25, 250, 251
    German-Russian rivalries, 109–
        110, 123
    Grotian approach, 283
    historical similarities to collective
        security theory, 14–16
    intra-Western, 52–55
    Kant and Wilson's repudiation
        of, 8, 11, 16, 24, 177, 251,
        280–281, 283–284

Balance of power *(cont.)*
NAC's statement on NATO's
role to preserve strategic
balance, 209
and NATO enlargement issues,
109, 114–115, 122–123, 148,
177–178
and partitions of Poland, 283
and "right of intervention," 250
and risk of war, 24
and Russian membership in
NATO, 148
and Strategic Concept, 282,
285–286
U.S. as part of Europe's balance, 281
Balkans. *See also specific countries,*
regions
NATO commitment to, 294
potential conflict, 128, 197, 234,
237, 240, 269, 272, 275, 279
Ball, Deborah, 85
Baltic states
admission to UN, 73
applicants for NATO membership, 118
Germany's support for NATO
membership, 110, 112
interest in NATO membership
as hedge against Russia,
164–165, 166
NACC discussions on withdrawal
of former Soviet troops, 96
NATO commitment to security
of, 238–239
NATO outreach to, 73
nonparticipation in CFE Treaty,
178
participation in IFOR, 195
PfP encouragement of regional
military cooperation, 98, 158
regaining independence from
Soviet Union, 73

role in collapse of Soviet Union,
43–44
Russian opposition to NATO
membership for, 121, 137,
138–139, 165
Russian threat to, 85–86, 128,
238, 240
Soviet refusal to recognize CSCE
standing to deal with, 49
Soviet territorial acquisition during World War II, 35
steps toward NATO membership,
120, 146
U.S. Charter of Partnership
with, 238
U.S. politics and NATO admission debate, 122, 129
U.S. refusal to recognize Soviet
acquisition of, 39
Becher, Klaus, 266
Belarus
possible nuclear weapons
deployments in, 138
Russian dominance of, 123
Belgium
Brussels Pact signatory, 28
facilities for U.S. nuclear-capable
forces, 34
possibility of multilateral alliances
for collective defense, 186
post–Cold War shift of NATO
investments from, 64, 261–262
support for French definition of
CJTF purposes, 202
support for NATO membership
for Romania, 127
view of Quad's preeminence in
NATO, 185
WEU membership, 31, 77
Berlin blockade, 28, 32
"Berlin Four." *See* The Quad
Berlin Wall
construction of, 36

Berlin Wall *(cont.)*
  fall of, 53, 72
Bertram, Christoph, 54
Biological and chemical weapons.
  See also Nuclear weapons;
  Weapons of mass destruction
  Iraqi programs for, 80
  NATO's emphasis on countering
    proliferation of, 73, 79–81,
    89, 284
  risks posed by interventions
    beyond Europe, 245–248
  Russian programs for, 86–87
Black Sea Fleet, 155
Boniface, Pascal, 113
Bonn Conference on Arms Control
  Issues, 250
Bosnia. *See also* Implementation
  Force; Stabilization Force
  arms control issue, 218
  arms embargo, 193, 194, 195,
    198
  as buffer zone, 226
  compared to Cambodian situa-
    tion, 225
  conflict's role in development of
    NATO's crisis management
    and peace operations, 190–
    191, 192–199, 249, 264, 272,
    276, 285, 293–294
  Contact Group, 184–185, 250
  and credibility of U.S. and
    NATO, 195, 197, 224, 227,
    249, 273, 301
  danger of "Bosnia syndrome,"
    295
  Dayton Accords, 1, 4, 76, 133,
    195, 197, 198, 219–234, 236,
    249, 273, 291, 294, 295
  European insistence on U.S. in-
    volvement, 217, 218
  factors in U.S. and NATO forces
    involvement, 197–198

  and major-power consensus on
    intervention, 22, 275, 280
  and NATO enlargement, 117,
    232, 299–300
  NATO infrastructure invest-
    ments in support of IFOR
    and SFOR, 64
  NATO peacekeeping operations,
    1–2, 4, 21, 22–23, 76–77, 89,
    190–192, 192–199, 218–234,
    249, 285
  NATO statement on (November
    1991), 193
  "one out, all out" view of, 218
  OSCE cooperation with NATO
    in, 93
  OSCE member not in EAPC or
    PfP, 162
  parties to conflict, 193
  PfP participation in IFOR and
    SFOR, 2, 21, 89, 98, 195
  phases of conflict, 194–195
  political sustainability of U.S.
    presence in, 222–224, 234, 288
  Russian involvement, 2, 21, 133,
    140, 195, 218, 227, 241, 275
  stakes for future of NATO, 227,
    249, 295, 301
  U.S. leadership in, 286, 294
  U.S.-European disagreements
    over, 195, 218, 272, 276,
    293–294
  war criminals issue, 221–223,
    224, 225, 230
Bosniaks
  commitment to Dayton goal of
    unified Bosnia, 221, 224, 226
  goal of self-determination, 193
  massacres in "safe areas" at
    Srebrenica and Zepa, 198
  and power sharing, 231
  U.S. support for, 133, 218
  and war crimes issue, 223

Bosnian Croats
  goals of, 221, 231
  parties to conflict, 193
  victories over Bosnian Serbs, 198
  and war crimes issue, 221–223,
    224, 225, 230
Bosnian Serbs
  attacks on Sarajevo markets,
    194–195, 198
  Croatian victories over, 198
  forced to accept Dayton
    Accords, 198, 222
  goals of, 221
  massacres of Bosniaks in "safe
    areas," 198
  parties to conflict, 193
  and return of refugees, 224
  taking of UNPROFOR hostages,
    198, 199
  war crimes issue, 221–223, 224,
    225, 230
Braithwaite, Rodric, 52
Brezhnev, Leonid, 41
Brezhnev Doctrine, 28, 45
Brougham, Lord Henry Peter, 15
Brussels Pact, 186
Brussels summit (January 1994),
  102–103, 113, 127, 201
Brussels Treaty, 28, 31, 32, 77, 209
Brzezinski, Zbigniew, 42, 88, 101
Buffer zones
  independent Bosnia as, 226
  and Russia, 132
Bukovsky, Vladimir, 42
Bulgaria
  applicant for NATO member-
    ship, 118
  democratization of, 41
  NATO outreach to, 73
  participation in IFOR, 195
Burden sharing
  in Bosnian conflict, 234
  and CJTF, 200

and "collective action" problem
  in economics, 174
and economic benefits of
  NATO, 63, 64, 68–70
NATO enlargement issue, 117,
  128
and nuclear weapons issues, 33
Burt, Richard, 184
Bush, George
  call for self-determination of Ger-
    many and Eastern Europe, 53
  on Gulf War ending "Vietnam
    syndrome," 232
  on NATO enlargement, 100
  view of Bosnian conflict, 196
  warning to Milosevic about
    conflict in Kosovo, 236
Bush administration
  definition of "Atlantic Forces"
    package, 242
  view of Bosnian conflict, 196
  view of ESDI, 204
  view of NATO enlargement,
    100–101

Cambodia
  Bosnia compared to Cambodian
    situation, 225
  Germany's participation in
    Cambodian operation, 213
Canada
  contributions to PfP, 100
  as "free-rider," 69
  military presence in Germany, 31
  participation in NATO, 28
  support for NATO membership
    for Romania, 127
  support for seeking mandate
    for crisis management and
    peace operations, 253, 254
Capabilities Coordination Cell, 205
Carpenter, Ted Galen, 107
Carter, Jimmy, 45

Cato Institute, 107
Caucasus and Central Asia
  potential conflict, 234, 248
  Russian concurrence necessary
    for intervention, 280
  Russian intervention, 85, 109, 241
  Turkish interest in, 86
Central Europe
  and competitive diplomacy,
    108, 109
  potential conflict, 49, 234, 269,
    272, 279
  prevention of German-Russian
    rivalries, 109, 123, 131
  Russian relations with, 274,
    279–280
  Russian threat, 86
  security vacuum as threat to
    stability, 105, 109, 111
Central Intelligence Agency, 46
Centrifugal and centripetal forces
  affecting NATO's future,
    276–278
CFE Treaty. See Conventional Armed
  Forces in Europe Treaty
Charter of Paris, 48, 162
Charter of Partnership, 238
Chechnya, 139
Cheney, Dick, 82, 249
China
  and Bosnia conflict, 185
  and non–UN-mandated "peace-
    keeping," 253
  and Russian membership for
    NATO, 149
  UN Security Council power over
    mandates, 254, 255, 258, 296
Chirac, Jacques, 114, 185, 199,
    204–205, 215
Chretien, Jean, 129
Christopher, Warren, 102, 118–119,
    158, 196, 199, 243, 269–270
Churchill, Winston, 35

CINCENT. See NATO military com-
  mands, Allied Forces Central
  Europe
Civil-emergency planning
  PfP mission, 156
  Russia's PfP participation in,
    136–137
CJTFs. See Combined Joint Task
  Forces
Claude, Inis, Jr.
  on balance of power and peace
    of Europe from 1815–1914,
    25
  on collective security, 7–8,
    21, 22, 249, 258, 259, 281,
    293, 296
  on UN and collective security, 17
  on U.S. policy of "selective anti-
    aggression," 249
Clinton, Bill
  advocate of NATO enlargement,
    101, 102, 103, 104
  announcement U.S. forces
    would remain in Bosnia, 230
  on Bosnia mission as NATO
    priority, 273
  on Dayton Accords, 219–220
  on IFOR role in Bosnian con-
    flict, 218–219
  politics and Bosnian conflict,
    198
  politics and NATO enlargement
    debate, 129
  on possible Russian member-
    ship in NATO, 147
  on threat of spread of ethnic
    conflict in former Soviet
    Union, 249
  view of Bosnian conflict, 196–
    197, 199, 218–219, 225, 229,
    230, 231, 273
  warning to Milosevic about
    conflict in Kosovo, 236

Clinton administration
downplaying NATO's collective
defense function to avoid
antagonizing Russia, 124–
127, 132
interest in NATO enlargement,
101–102, 103, 104–110,
129, 148
retention of "Atlantic Forces"
package, 242
view of Bosnian conflict, 196–
199, 231–234, 287
view of ESDI, 204
view of possible Russian membership in NATO, 147, 148
"Coalitions of the willing," 2, 3, 72,
76, 78, 159–160, 162, 167,
173, 190, 200, 205, 206, 217,
235, 243, 244, 245, 248, 250,
260, 263, 277, 280, 293
Cobden, Richard, 14
Cohen, William
discussion of collective defense
and collective security, 164
downplaying NATO's collective
defense function to avoid
antagonizing Russia, 125–126
on NATO enlargement, 119,
141–142
on NATO-Russia Permanent
Joint Council, 143
on PfP enhancement, 156–157
on U.S. bilateral contributions
to PfP, 99–100
on U.S. involvement in Bosnia,
218, 221, 226, 227, 228, 229
Cold War
arms control issues, 33–34, 36
events marking end of, 72
factors in Soviet empire's collapse, 41–47
meaning of crisis management
for NATO during, 189–190

NATO collective defense policy
during, 1, 3, 32–35, 189–190,
276
NATO policies for peaceful
change during, 35–47
NATO-UN relations, 194
nuclear deterrence issues, 32–35
political and strategic stalemate
in Europe during, 31–32, 190
stalemate in UN Security Council
during, 257
"Collective action" problem, 174–175
Collective defense
Article 5 commitment in North
Atlantic Treaty, 29, 61, 81,
156, 157, 162, 166, 168, 169,
189, 267
and balance of power, 7, 23,
26, 209, 240, 282
changing nature of, 264,
265–267
core purpose of NATO, 1, 3, 26,
74, 93, 148, 149, 191, 192,
209, 269, 273, 282, 285, 295,
296, 297, 298, 299
de facto downgrading of, 272–
278, 298
dilemmas in combining with
collective security, 88–90,
163–187
distinguished from collective
security, 5–9
as foundation for collective
security operations, 206
and limited subregional contingencies, 265–267, 274
and NATO enlargement, 124–
131, 186–187
NATO shift of priorities away
from collective defense, 260,
272–278, 297, 298
and NATO-Russia Founding
Act, 141–144

Collective defense *(cont.)*
  post–Cold War redefining of, 73, 79–81, 265–267
  prospect of Article 4–like commitments leading to, 240
  relationship to crisis management and peace operations, 191, 259–264
  relevance of NATO's collective defense function, 81–88, 299
  two-track policy combining collective defense and collective security, 292–301
  UN Charter's Article 51 right to individual and collective self-defense, 20, 255, 256, 257
Collective security. *See also* Crisis management and peace operations; "Security is indivisible" concept
  Article 4–like PfP consultation pledges, 97–98, 162, 180, 237, 239, 240, 262, 271, 279
  contrast between concepts of, 17–20
  "cooperative security" compared with, 173
  development from balance of power, 14–16, 23–26
  dilemmas in combining with collective defense, 88–90, 163–187
  distinct from balance of power, 8, 11, 16, 24
  distinguished from collective defense, 5–9
  following general war, 21, 296
  historical perspective on, 9–20, 176–182, 296
  interventions without major-power consensus, 20, 24, 182–187, 296, 298
  Kantian and Wilsonian approach, 7–9, 10–18, 93, 149, 167, 169, 170, 172, 173, 177, 181, 240, 241, 249, 250, 259, 270, 271, 275, 280, 281, 282–284, 292, 293, 294, 299
  League of Nations commitment compared to PfP and EAPC, 178–182
  major-power-consensus approach, 9, 18–20, 22–23, 24, 167, 172, 173, 176, 181, 240–241, 250, 251, 256, 269, 270, 274–275, 280, 284, 294, 296
  NATO enlargement emphasis on, 124–125, 130–131, 132, 163–166
  NATO's new roles and, 1–4, 20–26, 292–301
  NATO's shift of priorities from collective defense to, 166, 167, 260, 272–278, 297, 298
  "non–Article 5 missions" as shorthand for collective security missions, 2
  practical limits to NATO's assumption of collective security functions, 278–286
  two-track policy combining collective defense and collective security, 292–301
Combined Joint Planning Staff, 205
Combined Joint Task Forces, 284. *See also* Implementation Force; Stabilization Force
  components of, 203
  cost benefits of, 68
  decision-making formula, 201
  defining as instrument for both Article 5 and non–Article 5 missions, 199–200, 202–205, 210, 262
  French approval of, 204

Combined Joint Task Forces *(cont.)*
  French interest in, 114
  French participation in, 216
  French proposal for non–Article
    5 tasks use only, 202–203
  French resentment of NATO and
    U.S. control of, 201, 204–205
  North Atlantic Council decision
    to establish, 201–202
  PfP cooperation with, 207
  possibility of PfP participation
    in, 169
  possibility of use under EAPC
    command, 160
  proposal for, 200
  purpose of, 2, 3, 76, 78–79, 200,
    203–204
  and redefining of NATO's com-
    mand structure, 2, 3, 72, 121
  "separable but not separate"
    capabilities, 200, 201, 202,
    205, 207
Commissariat à l'Énergie Atom-
    ique, 55
Commonwealth of Independent
    States, 154, 155. *See also
    specific countries*
Communism
  atrophy of ideological legitimacy
    as factor in Soviet collapse, 42
  European communists' support
    for developing OSCE rather
    than NATO enlargement,
    112, 116
  historical determinism ideology,
    32, 40
  Warsaw Pact as instrument of, 28
  West's shifting views of during
    Cold War, 36–41
  West's view of at time of inva-
    sion of South Korea, 30
"Community of power" *vs.* balance
    of power, 11, 16, 280–281

Concert of Europe, 24–25, 250,
    251, 270
Conference of National Armaments
    Directors, 65
Conference on Security and Coop-
    eration in Europe. *See also*
    Organization for Security
    and Cooperation in Europe
  assumption that mandate is
    necessary for NATO inter-
    vention, 251, 252, 253
  Conflict Prevention Center,
    48, 49
  failure in former Yugoslavia, 300
  French concern about NACC's
    potential impact on, 96
  Helsinki Final Act, 37–39, 45,
    48, 137, 154, 162
  ineffectiveness against Soviet
    pressures, 49
  mandate for EU action in con-
    flict in former Yugoslavia,
    193
  NATO's support for peacekeep-
    ing efforts, 1, 3, 76
  origination of, 37
  proposals for all-European col-
    lective security system based
    on, 48–49
  replacement by OSCE, 3, 285
  and "security is indivisible" con-
    cept, 3, 6, 48
Confidence building. *See also*
    Transparency of military
    capabilities and plans
  CSCE measures for, 37, 38
  OSCE role, 176
  purpose of NATO-established
    institutions, 3, 163, 173
  Stockholm conference on, 38
Conflict Prevention Center, 48, 49
Congress of Vienna, 25, 270
Conscription, 67, 213, 214

Consensus building
    antinomy between inclusiveness
        and effectiveness, 173–176
    disadvantages to decision mak-
        ing by consensus, 159
    and EAPC and PfP, 159–160, 161,
        162, 167
    and intervention in Albania, 217
    major-power-consensus
        approach to collective secu-
        rity, 9, 18–20, 22–23, 24, 167,
        172, 173, 176, 213, 240–241,
        250, 251, 256, 269, 270, 274–
        275, 280, 284, 294, 296
    and NATO-Russian Council, 143
    and OSCE, 176
    rationale for NATO enlargement,
        124
Contact Group, 184–185, 250
Containment of conflict
    NATO role, 262, 270–271, 275,
        300
    U.S. policy toward Bosnia, 288
Contract with America, 129
Conventional Armed Forces in
        Europe (CFE) Treaty, 60–61,
        178–179
Cook, Robin, 218, 244
"Cooperative security," 93, 164,
        172–173, 191, 270, 300–301
Coordination of Western security
        policies, 60–62, 276
Council of Europe, 180
Council of the Baltic Sea States, 238
Council on Foreign Relations, 171
Craig, Larry, 108
Credibility of NATO
    and Bosnia conflict, 195, 224,
        227, 273, 301
    and NATO enlargement, 186,
        287–288, 298
    and U.S. engagement in NATO,
        291

Crimea, 138, 156
Crisis management and peace
        operations
    assumption that UN or OSCE
        approval is necessary for
        NATO intervention, 251–259,
        271
    Bosnian conflict, 1–2, 4, 21,
        22–23, 76–77, 89, 190–191,
        192–199, 218–234, 249, 264,
        272, 276, 285, 293–294
    and CJTFs, 2, 3, 76, 78–79,
        199–200, 202–205, 262
    complex relationship with col-
        lective defense, 259–264
    contingencies beyond Bosnia,
        234–248
    contingencies beyond Europe,
        241–245
    contingencies in the former
        Soviet Union, 239–241
    contingent U.S. involvement
        and, 290–291
    and credibility of NATO, 186, 195,
        227, 287–288, 291, 298, 301
    and ESDI, 79, 207–217
    historical perspective, 250–251
    implications for NATO cohesion
        and collective defense, 191,
        259–267, 271–272, 279,
        298–301
    major powers' responsibility for,
        213–214, 250
    meaning of crisis management
        for NATO during Cold War,
        189–190
    meaning of crisis management
        for NATO since the Cold
        War, 190–191, 192
    NACC approach to, 99
    NATO declaration of willing-
        ness to support peacekeep-
        ing operations, 3, 76

Crisis management and peace
operations *(cont.)*
NATO shift of priorities from
collective defense to, 166,
167, 260, 272–278, 297, 298
"NATO-minus-plus" formula,
205
new institutions for, 199–207
"non–Article 5 missions" as
shorthand for collective
security missions, 2
PfP role, 97, 156–157, 159, 161,
162
practical limits and risks, 239,
248–259
rationale for, 262, 270–271
as rationale for NATO enlargement, 104, 124
reassessments of security requirements, 191–192
U.S. capabilities' superiority to
NATO, 68, 202, 212
use of NATO assets, 200–201,
202, 205, 206, 207
"variable-geometry" responses
to specific contingencies,
203, 291
Croatia
Bosnia as buffer zone for, 226
Bosnian conflict, 198, 219, 221,
226, 230–231
Germany's influence on, 184
OSCE member not in EAPC or
PfP, 162
parties to Bosnia conflict, 193
CSCE. *See* Conference on Security
and Cooperation in Europe
Cuban missile crisis, 32, 36
Cyprus
Bosnia compared to, 196, 231
Gulf War involvement, 61, 242
OSCE member not in EAPC or
PfP, 162

Czech Republic
applicant for NATO membership, 101, 104, 112, 118, 120,
121, 232
candidate for European Union,
146
French support for NATO membership, 113, 116
German support for NATO
membership, 112
NACC membership, 95
NATO membership as righting
of an injustice, 128
participation in IFOR, 195
PfP encouragement of regional
military cooperation in, 98
possible effects of NATO membership on Quad influence,
186
U.S. Congress attempt to tie
NATO membership to Bosnia
issue, 232
U.S. support for NATO membership, 105
view of possible NATO membership for Russia, 149–150
Czechoslovakia
collapse of Communist regime,
192
democratization of, 41
NATO outreach to, 73
Soviet intervention, 28, 31, 32, 190
Soviet territorial acquisition
during World War II, 35
support for all-European security organization, 48

Daalder, Ivo, 221
Daley, Richard, 129
"Danish footnotes," 117
Dayton Accords
Bosniaks' commitment to goal of
unified Bosnia, 221, 224, 226

Dayton Accords *(cont.)*
Clinton's description of, 219–220
goals of, 195
Holbrooke's U.S. policy role, 291
IFOR and SFOR goal of implementation, 76, 218, 229, 230–231, 295
London Peace Implementation Conference, 250
McCain on insufficiency as "mission," 231
Milosevic crucial to success of, 236
NATO's role in, 1, 4, 294
nonimplementation and the sustainability of operations such as IFOR and SFOR, 222–224
nonimplementation of certain nonmilitary aspects of, 220–222
prospects for a prolonged peace-enforcement operation, 224–234
Russian view of as U.S. muscle-flexing, 133
signed under duress, 198, 220, 222
and U.S. and NATO credibility, 197, 224, 227, 249, 273, 301
war criminals issue, 221–223, 224, 225, 230
de Charette, Hervé, 113
de Gaulle, Charles, 55, 56, 183
de la Gorce, Paul-Marie, 113–114, 204
de St. Pierre, Abbé, 9
de Vattel, Emmerich, 15
de Wijk, Rob, 172–173, 184, 263
Decolonization conflicts
and Article 6 of North Atlantic Treaty, 189
Defense Group on Proliferation, 89

Defense "hawks"
and NATO enlargement debate, 105–106, 108
Defense planning
coordination of Western security policies, 60–62, 276
denationalization of, 57–60, 149, 276
and PfP enhancement, 157, 262
transparency in, 3, 21, 58, 97, 98, 103, 109, 141, 142, 157, 163, 173, 178, 279, 292, 299
use of NATO defense planning system for both Article 5 and non–Article 5 operations, 262
Defense Planning Committee, 58–59, 158
Defense Research Institute, 155
Defense spending
burden sharing, 33, 63, 64, 68–70, 117, 128, 174, 200, 234
and "collective action" problem in economics, 174
commonly funded NATO activities as percentage of, 64–65
economic benefits of NATO, 62–70, 276
joint product model, 70
and NATO enlargement, 127
NATO shift of resources from collective defense to PfP and peacekeeping, 166, 167, 260
procurement programs, 64, 65, 66
public-good model, 69, 70
reduced spending of Allies, 62, 127, 175–176, 260, 274
U.S. spending compared to other Allies, 67, 212, 215
Democracies. *See also* Democratization
disposition toward peace in Kantian thinking, 10, 12, 14

Democracies *(cont.)*
NATO's role in encouraging and legitimizing, 70–72, 124
political solidarity of, 10, 12, 14, 70–71
Democratization
as criterion for NATO membership, 71–72, 128, 175
CSCE as a demand for movement toward, 38, 45
and détente, 37, 39
factor in Soviet collapse, 41, 45, 46
and NATO-Russia Founding Act, 93, 165–166
NATO's role in promoting, 70–72, 124, 164, 182, 240, 270
purpose of NATO-established institutions, 163, 165
as rationale for NATO enlargement, 71–72, 103, 109, 110, 124, 128, 131, 151, 175, 182
as route to peace, 10, 21, 25
in Russia, 88, 130, 186
U.S. interest in, 155
West's concern about destabilization of Eastern Europe, 39
Denationalization of defense planning, 57–60, 149, 276
Denmark
and Baltic states, 238
contributions to PfP, 100
as "free-rider," 69
interest in WEU-led operations, 210
participation in multinational intervention in Albania, 235
Desert Storm. *See* Gulf War
Détente
Cold War issue, 36–37, 39, 272
definition, 37
German view of end of Cold War as result of, 41

Deterrence. *See also* Balance of power
as hedge against risk, 281
NATO Cold War policy, 28, 32–35, 36, 192
nuclear deterrence, 33–34, 87, 134, 138–139, 247
as purpose of NATO, 36, 209, 240
rapid reaction forces for, 192
Russia-NATO deterrence relationship, 87, 105, 108–109, 134–135, 138–139, 148, 240, 300
U.S. "extended deterrence," 33
Deutch, John, 87
DGP. *See* Senior Defense Group on Proliferation
Dick, Charles, 85
Die Zeit, 54
Dienstbier, Jiri, 48
Dilemmas in combining collective defense with collective security, 163–187
Diplomacy
need for open, 11, 12
need to forestall competitive diplomacy, 109
OSCE role in preventive, 93
Disarmament, 11, 13. *See also* Arms control
Disaster relief, 137, 156, 259
Djilas, Milovan, 40
Dole, Bob, 129
Donne, John, 10
Donnelly, Christopher, 83
Duffield, John, 57, 70–71, 169

Eagleburger, Lawrence, 196
EAPC. *See* Euro-Atlantic Partnership Council
East Germany. *See* German Democratic Republic

Eastern Europe
  potential conflicts, 49, 234, 269, 272, 279
  Russian relations with, 122, 274, 279–280
Economic issues. *See also* Defense spending
  during Cold War, 40
  and collapse of Soviet Union, 42, 44, 45, 46
  CSCE's Helsinki Final Act provision on cooperation, 37
  economic reform in Russia, 87–88
  European economic integration movement, 29, 51, 62, 78, 103–104, 285
  factor in League of Nations' failure, 181–182
  NATO's role in supplying economic benefits to Allies, 62–70, 276
  pre-war conditions, 191
  promoting reform as part of "cooperative security," 270
  unemployment, 182
Economic sanctions
  Cold War issue, 40, 45
  as collective security intervention, 18
  against Serbia and Montenegro, 193, 194
  against Soviet Union after invasion of Afghanistan, 45
The Economist, 197, 198
EDC. *See* European Defense Community
Egypt
  NATO outreach to, 75
  participation in IFOR and SFOR, 89, 195
Eisenhower, Dwight, 30, 58, 183
Election monitoring
  OSCE role, 93

EMERCOM. *See* Russia, Ministry for Civil Defense, Emergencies, and Elimination of Consequences of Natural Disasters
Enlargement of NATO. *See* NATO enlargement
Enlightenment's perspective on collective security, 10, 12, 14, 177, 250–251
ESDI. *See* European Security and Defense Identity
Estonia. *See* Baltic states
Ethnic factors
  and collapse of Soviet Union, 42, 44
  ethno-nationalism as pre-war condition, 191
  OSCE role in protecting minority rights, 93, 176
  potential conflicts, 234, 235, 238, 249
  precedent of Bosnian conflict, 199
  and Ukraine-Russian relations, 155, 240
  U.S. as counter to ethno-nationalism in Europe, 291
  and U.S. support for NATO enlargement, 104, 122, 129
EU. *See* European Union
EUCOM. *See* United States, European Command
Euro-Atlantic area
  definition, 3
  NATO's zone of special interest, 5, 234, 244
Euro-Atlantic Partnership Council
  adoption of NACC workplan, 159
  and collective security, 167, 186, 238, 279, 280, 298
  compared to League of Nations, 178–182

Euro-Atlantic Partnership Council
(cont.)
  dependence on U.S. commit-
    ments, 280
  disadvantages to decision mak-
    ing by consensus, 159–160
  establishment of, 73, 75, 91, 94,
    97, 158–159
  French participation, 96
  limitations of, 161, 186
  membership, 401
  as pathway to NATO member-
    ship, 120
  principles of inclusiveness and
    self-differentiation, 159
  purpose of, 91, 163
  replacement of NACC, 2, 91, 97,
    158–159
  speculation of replacement
    of NAC's decision-making
    authority, 206
  time and personnel constraints,
    163
Eurocorps, 186
Europe. See also specific countries
  challenge of building a peace-
    ful political order, 91–94
  de Vattel's view of as republic, 15
  economic integration move-
    ment, 29, 51, 62, 78,
    103–104, 285
  NATO's role in resolving
    intra–West European security
    dilemmas, 50–52, 276
  opposition to NATO member-
    ship for Russia, 149–150
  relative peace from 1815 to 1914,
    24–25
  security vacuum as threat to
    stability, 105, 109, 111
  U.S. strategic interest in, 155,
    197, 208
Europe des Patries concept, 54

European Coal and Steel Commu-
  nity, 51, 62
European Community
  Bosnia peace efforts, 193
  Council of Ministers, 193
  Intergovernmental Conferences
    on Political Union and
    Economic and Monetary
    Union, 78
  replacement by EU, 285
European Defense Community
  France's proposal of, 30, 52
European Security and Defense
  Identity
  CJTFs as response to, 2, 200, 205
  Eastern European countries'
    interest in, 186
  establishment efforts, 72, 77–79,
    207–217, 284–285, 290
  French support for, 114, 116,
    202, 203, 204–205, 207, 208,
    211, 290
  obstacles to building, 210–214
  and "Petersberg tasks," 79, 209,
    213, 217, 278, 290–291
  progress in building within
    NATO, 205, 214–215
  proposals for making responsi-
    ble for non–Article 5 tasks
    only, 209–210
  reasons for interest in, 77
  "separable but not separate"
    capabilities, 200, 201, 202,
    205, 207
  U.S. support for, 204–205, 228
  use of NATO assets, 200, 201,
    202, 207, 208, 209–210
European Union
  Amsterdam Treaty, 217
  commitment to security of
    Baltic states, 238
  Common Foreign and Security
    Policy, 211, 217

European Union (cont.)
    as determinant of future security in Europe, 286
    Eastern European candidates for, 146, 186
    and economic aims of NATO, 63
    economic integration movement, 29, 51, 62, 78, 103–104, 285
    and ESDI establishment efforts, 207, 211
    failure of efforts in former Yugoslavia, 220, 300
    membership, 401
    and NATO enlargement, 93, 117
    NATO's role in development of, 51, 62
    participation in Contact Group, 184, 185
    possible connection to NATO membership, 175
    possible merger with WEU, 217
    replacement of EC, 285
    support for Euro-Atlantic security structures, 180, 182
    and U.S. engagement in Europe, 290
Exit strategies, 233
"Extended deterrence," 33
Eyal, Jonathan, 117, 121, 127–128, 300

Fairbanks, Charles, 43
Federal Republic of Germany. See Germany, Federal Republic of
Federal Republic of Yugoslavia. See Montenegro; Serbia
Felgengauer, Paul, 86
Finland
    and Baltic states, 238
    decision to hold off on applying for NATO membership, 118
    neutrality of, 138, 211
    observer status in NACC, 95, 96

Finland (cont.)
    participation in IFOR, 195
    participation in PfP, 97
    Soviet territorial acquisition during World War II, 35
    war in 1939–1940, 139
    WEU Council invitation to participate in WEU defense planning, 211
Flanagan, Stephen, 59
Former Yugoslav Republic of Macedonia. See Macedonia
Forward defense concept, 191–192, 267
France
    approval of CJTF concept, 204
    CJTF proposal for non–Article 5 tasks only, 202–203
    confidence in U.S. reliability, 296–297
    debate on NATO enlargement, 112–116
    decolonization conflicts, 189
    defense spending, 65, 67, 68, 70
    disagreements over Bosnia, 218
    distinction between North Atlantic Treaty and NATO's military structure, 59
    EDC proposal, 30, 52
    and European competitive diplomacy, 109
    and European Union, 186
    flexible capabilities for out-of-area use, 244
    Four Power rights regarding German question, 39, 183
    Gulf War involvement, 61, 242
    interest in ESDI, 114, 116, 202, 203, 204–205, 207, 208, 209–210, 211, 290
    interest in NATO's internal adaptation, 114
    intervention in Rwanda, 256

France *(cont.)*
  and League of Nations, 13, 16–17, 181
  major-power responsibilities for crisis management and peace operations, 205, 213
  National Front, 182
  nonparticipation in NATO integrated air defense forces, 60
  nuclear weapons program, 33, 34–35, 55–56, 68
  opposition to PfP enhancement, 157–158
  outward expansion and European peace, 25
  participation in CJTFs, 216
  participation in EAPC meetings, 96
  participation in Joint Committee on Proliferation, 61
  participation in multinational intervention in Albania, 235
  participation in UNPROFOR, 193, 197, 263
  political polarization, 182
  possibility of multilateral alliances for collective defense, 186
  the Quad's preeminence in NATO, 183–187, 250
  Rapid Reaction Force development, 198
  reluctance to endorse establishment of NACC, 95–96
  resentment of NATO control of CJTFs, 201, 204–205
  resistance of returning to NATO integrated military structure, 113–114, 216
  role in establishing NATO, 28
  and Russia, 257–258
  security assurances to Ukraine, 153–154
  support for EU membership for Poland, Hungary, and Czech Republic, 186
  support for NATO membership for Poland, Hungary, and Czech Republic, 116
  support for NATO membership for Romania, 113, 114–115, 127
  use of NATO assets for UN-authorized activities related to Iraq, 190
  view of European officers' role in NATO, 215–216
  view of German reunification, 53, 54
  view of NATO's and ESDI's roles, 209–210
  view of necessity of UN or OSCE mandates for non–Article 5 operations, 253, 264
  view of U.S. role in NATO, 113–114, 116, 208, 211, 214, 215–216, 290
  WEU membership, 31, 77
  willingness to relax sanctions against Iraq and to trade with Iran, 246
  withdrawal from NATO's integrated military structure, 96, 158, 183
  withdrawal from Somalia, 224
"Free-rider" behavior, 69, 174, 278. *See also* Burden sharing
FRG. *See* Germany, Federal Republic of
FYROM. *See* Macedonia

Galvin, John, 61, 242
Garnett, Sherman, 153, 154–155
Gelbard, Robert, 230, 236
Gellner, Ernest, 45
Genscher, Hans-Dietrich, 48, 134

Georgia
  possible nuclear weapons deployments in, 138
  and Russian influence, 239, 241
German Democratic Republic
  and NATO forward defense concept, 191–192
  Soviet intervention, 31, 32, 190
  support for all-European collective security system, 48
Germany
  Allied state-building efforts in, 219
  approval of NATO enlargement, 112
  and Baltic states, 238
  confidence in U.S. reliability, 296–297
  conscription, 213, 214
  contributions to PfP, 100
  debate on NATO enlargement, 110–112
  defense spending, 68
  democratization of, 70
  disagreements over Bosnia, 218
  and ESDI, 77
  and European competitive diplomacy, 109
  facilities for U.S. nuclear-capable forces, 34
  and failure of League of Nations, 16
  flexible capabilities for out-of-area use, 244
  geography of and NATO enlargement issues, 110–111
  Gulf War involvement, 61, 242
  and intra-Western balance of power, 52–55
  limitations on crisis management and peace operations participation, 213–214
  moral duty to support NATO enlargement, 110, 112, 129
  NATO enlargement as prevention of German-Russian rivalries, 109–110, 123, 131
  NATO's role in reassuring Germany's neighbors and allies, 52–55, 276
  nonparticipation in Operation Alba, 217
  nuclear weapons program possibility, 56–57, 187
  participation in IFOR and SFOR, 213, 214, 234
  participation in PfP, 158
  participation in reinforcement to signal NATO's commitment to defense of Turkey, 266
  possible bilateral or multilateral alliances for collective defense, 186
  post–Cold War shift of NATO investments from, 64, 261–262
  the Quad's preeminence in NATO, 183–187, 250
  renationalization of defense policy, 149
  responsibility for fate of Central and Eastern Europe as result of Molotov-Ribbentrop Pact, 110
  reunification and obsolescence of NATO forward defense concept, 192
  reunification as goal of NATO, 36, 37, 39, 92
  reunification treaty conditioned on nonexpansion of NATO, 133–134
  Russian view of NATO enlargement as attempt by Germany to resume expansion, 138

Germany *(cont.)*
  satisfaction with two Germanies, 39
  Soviet territorial acquisition during World War II, 35
  support for NATO enlargement, 101, 110–112, 121
  support for seeking mandate for crisis management and peace operations, 253, 254
  unemployment, 182
  U.S. *vs.* European views of reunification, 53
  view of end of Cold War as result of détente, 41
  view of European officers' role in NATO, 215–216
  willingness to relax sanctions against Iraq and to trade with Iran, 246
  willingness to take action against a WMD "proliferant," 246
  withdrawal of Soviet troops, 27
Germany, Federal Republic of
  foreign military presence in, 27, 31
  NATO admission, 31, 183
  NATO forward defense concept, 191–192
  "out-of-area" deployments out of question, 189–190
  proposals to establish armed forces, 30–31, 52–53
  the Quad's preeminence in NATO, 183–187, 250
  reunification as goal of NATO, 36, 37, 39, 92
  support for all-European collective security system, 48
  WEU membership, 31, 77
Gibbon, Edward, 42
Giscard d'Estaing, Valéry, 116, 183

Gladstone, William, 15–16
Glasnost, 43
"Global NATO" concept, 243–245
Goble, Paul, 165
Goldgeier, James, 102, 129
Gompert, David, 243
Goodby, James, 23, 282
Gorbachev, Mikhail
  call for all-European security system, 47
  "gentlemen's agreement" on NATO enlargement and German reunification, 133–134
  on historical determinism ideology, 32
  role in collapse of Soviet Union, 42–44, 45
Gordon, Philip, 217
Gose, Mark, 57
Gow, James, 184
Gowing, Margaret, 55
Gravity bombs
  U.S. nuclear weapons in Europe, 33–34
Great Britain
  confidence in U.S. reliability, 296–297
  contributions to PfP, 100
  decolonization conflicts, 189
  defense spending, 67, 68, 70
  disagreement over Bosnia, 218
  and European competitive diplomacy, 109
  facilities for U.S. nuclear-capable forces, 34
  flexible capabilities for out-of-area use, 244
  Four Power rights regarding German question, 39, 183
  Gulf War involvement, 61, 242
  and League of Nations, 16–17, 181

Great Britain *(cont.)*
major-power responsibilities for crisis management and peace operations, 213
military and nuclear presence in Europe, 31, 52
NATO collective security policy endorsement, 81
nonparticipation in Operation Alba, 217
nuclear weapons program, 33, 34–35, 55, 56, 68
outward expansion and European peace, 25
participation in UNPROFOR, 193, 197, 263
possible multilateral alliances for collective defense, 186
the Quad's preeminence in NATO, 183–187, 250
Rapid Reaction Force development, 198
role in establishing NATO, 28
and Russia, 257–258
signatory to Memorandum on Security Assurances, 153
view of German reunification, 53, 54
view of NATO enlargement, 117
view of Russia-NATO deterrence relationship, 87
WEU membership, 31, 77
Greece
concerns about Bosnian conflict spillover, 199
defense spending, 67, 260
facilities for U.S. nuclear-capable forces, 34
Gulf War involvement, 61, 242
NATO admission, 31
NATO mediation in Greek-Turkish disputes, 51–52, 118

NATO membership despite military dictatorship, 71
participation in multinational intervention in Albania, 235
post–Cold War shift of NATO investments to, 64
potential involvement in Kosovo or FYROM, 235
support for NATO membership for Romania, 127
Grotian approach to international politics, 283
Group on Defense Matters, 96
"Guadeloupe Four." *See* The Quad
Gulf War
Alliance cohesion and subregional collective defense contingencies, 266
fear of Iraqi attack on Turkey, 61, 81, 190, 266, 300
and "global NATO" concept, 243
mandate for, 190, 256, 257
NATO Allies' contributions, 190, 242
and NATO's emphasis on countering WMD proliferation, 79
and NATO's role in coordination of Western security policies, 61–62
unique circumstances for collective security action, 242, 249, 257
U.S. and "Vietnam syndrome," 232–233
and use of Atlantic Forces, 242
Gulick, Edward, 16

Haas, Ernst B., 19
Haiti, 214
Hamilton, Lee, 228, 231–232
Hansen, Helge, 213
Harkin, Tom, 108

Harmel Report, 36, 39–40, 48, 74, 92
Hartley, Keith, 66
Hassner, Pierre, 42
Havel, Vaclav
    Czech Republic interest in NATO
        membership, 101, 128
    rise to power, 41
    support for all-European secu-
        rity structure, 48, 49
    view of NATO membership for
        Russia, 149–150
    view of security vacuum as
        threat, 109
Heisbourg, François, 290
Helms, Jesse, 108–109, 288
Helsinki Final Act, 37–39, 45, 48,
    137, 154, 162
Helsinki summit (March 1997), 167,
    216
Henry IV, 9
Hoagland, James, 128–129
Hoare-Laval Pact, 182
Hobbes, Thomas, 19
Holbrooke, Richard, 102, 109, 199,
    222, 223, 227, 291
Holocaust Memorial Museum, 101,
    128
Holy See, 162, 185
Honecker, Erich, 39
Howe, Jonathan, 257
Hull, Cordell, 17, 178
Human rights
    and Dayton Accords, 220
    Helsinki Final Act provisions
        for, 37–38, 45
    Kissinger's role in negotiations
        for CSCE's human rights
        provisions, 38
    OSCE role in, 93, 176
Humanitarian aid. *See also* Crisis
    management and peace
    operations
    to Albania, 236

CJTFs and, 2, 290–291
disaster relief, 137, 156, 259
ESDI's support for, 79
NATO efforts, 2, 3, 259
PfP's support for, 3, 97, 156,
    236
and UN or OSCE mandate, 254,
    256
UNPROFOR operation in
    Bosnia, 194, 199
U.S. support for, 290–291
and WEU, 209
Hungary
    applicant for NATO member-
        ship, 104, 112, 118, 120,
        121, 146
    candidate for European Union,
        146
    French support for NATO mem-
        bership, 113, 116
    German support for NATO
        membership, 112
    importance of NATO member-
        ship to Ukraine, 123
    isolation and NATO enlarge-
        ment, 128
    and NATO membership for
        Romania, 114, 115
    NATO outreach to, 73
    participation in Albania inter-
        vention, 235
    participation in IFOR, 195
    PfP encouragement of regional
        military cooperation in, 98
    possible effects of NATO mem-
        bership on Quad influence,
        186
    Soviet attempts to prevent join-
        ing of alliance, 49
    Soviet intervention, 36, 190
    suggested U.S. presence in as
        back-up support for Bosnia,
        228

Hungary (cont.)
  U.S. Congress attempt to tie
    NATO membership to Bosnia
    issue, 232
  U.S. Senate approval of NATO
    membership for, 105
Hunter, Robert, 169–170, 177
Hutchison, Kay Bailey, 105, 106

Iceland
  as "free-rider," 66, 69
  interest in WEU-led operations,
    210
  medical support to IFOR and
    SFOR, 196
ICFY. See International Conference
    on Former Yugoslavia
IFOR. See Implementation Force
Iklé, Fred, 105
Implementation Force. See also
    Stabilization Force
  casualties, 222, 224
  countries participating, 195, 278,
    293
  establishment of, 1, 4, 76
  as example of shift in NATO
    priorities to collective secu-
    rity, 270, 272, 284, 285
  Germany's participation in, 213,
    214
  and "global NATO" concept, 243
  goals of, 218–219
  ineffectiveness of, 218
  mandate for, 240
  Mediterranean Dialogue mem-
    bers' participation, 89
  NACC member participation, 76
  NATO infrastructure investments
    in support of, 64
  and "NATO-minus-plus" con-
    cept, 205
  NATO's first "out-of-area" deploy-
    ment, 193, 195

  North Atlantic Council's author-
    ity over, 160
  PfP participation, 2, 21, 76, 89,
    98, 195, 206, 293
  political sustainability of U.S.
    presence in Bosnia, 222–
    224, 288
  replacement by SFOR, 195
  Russian participation in, 2, 21,
    133, 195, 241, 275
  solidarity of, 278, 293
  U.S. participation, 196–199, 212
India, 253
Individual Partnership Programs
  and NATO, 97, 99
  and Russia, 136
INF Treaty. See Intermediate-range
    Nuclear Forces Treaty
Inge, Peter, 218
Inhofe, James, 106
Inspection
  and balance-of-power system,
    15
  UN efforts in Iraq, 246
Intermediate-range Nuclear Forces
    Treaty, 33
Internal functions of NATO in sup-
    port of international security,
    289, 295, 298, 299
  coordination of Western security
    policies, 60–62, 276
  encouraging and legitimizing
    democratic forms of govern-
    ment, 70–72, 276
  limiting nuclear proliferation in
    Europe, 55–57, 276
  maintaining U.S. engagement in
    European security, 50, 276
  promoting denationalization of
    defense planning, 57–60, 276
  as rationale for enlargement, 124
  reassuring Germany's neighbors
    and allies, 52–55, 276

Internal functions of NATO in support of international security *(cont.)*
 resolving intra–West European security dilemmas, 52–52, 276
 supplying economic benefits to Allies, 62–70, 276
International Atomic Energy Agency, 80
International Conference on Former Yugoslavia, 184, 193
International Criminal Tribunal, 221
International Institute for Strategic Studies, 54
International Monetary Fund, 231
International order, concepts of.
 See also specific concepts, including Balance of power
 collective defense *vs.* collective security, 5–9
 historical perspective, 9–20
 importance of to NATO, 20–26
 rule of law, 11, 19, 20
Interoperability. *See* Standardization and interoperability
IPPs. *See* Individual Partnership Programs
Iran, 246, 299
Iraq
 Allies' willingness to relax sanctions, 246
 Gulf War, 61, 79, 81, 190, 232, 243, 300
 post–Gulf War UN activities relating to, 190, 246
 and relevance of NATO's collective defense function, 299
 U.S. dual containment policy, 246
 weapons of mass destruction programs, 79–80
Ireland
 neutrality of, 71, 211

OSCE member not in EAPC or PfP, 162
 participation in Contact Group, 185
 participation in NACC Ad Hoc Group on Cooperation in Peacekeeping, 95
 participation in SFOR, 76, 196
 WEU Council invitation to participate in WEU defense planning, 211
Ismay, Lord Hastings, 52
Isolationism
 influence in American politics, 291
 and NATO enlargement debate, 105, 107–108
 and U.S. membership in NATO, 29, 105
Israel
 Gulf War involvement, 61, 242
 NATO outreach to, 75
Italy
 aggression against Abyssinia in 1935–1936, 16–17
 Allied state-building efforts in, 219
 Andreotti's comment on necessity of two German states, 39
 confidence in U.S. reliability, 296–297
 de facto membership in Contact Group, 185, 250
 democratization of, 70
 facilities for U.S. nuclear-capable forces, 34
 Gulf War involvement, 61, 242
 leadership of multinational intervention in Albania, 217, 235
 possibility of multicultural alliance for collective defense, 186

Italy *(cont.)*
   post–Cold War shift of NATO
     investments to, 64
   support for Romania's member-
     ship in NATO, 117, 127
   support for Slovenia's member-
     ship in NATO, 117
   view of Quad's preeminence in
     NATO, 183, 184, 185
   WEU membership, 31, 77

Jakobson, Max, 23
Japan
   Allied state-building efforts in,
     219
   U.S. mutual defense pledge, 233
Joffe, Josef, 50–51, 53, 289–290, 297
John Paul II, 45
Joint Committee on Proliferation,
   80–81
Joint Declaration of Paris (1990),
   6, 163
Jordan
   NATO outreach to, 75
   participation in IFOR and SFOR,
     89, 195
Joulwan, George, 241
Juppé, Alain, 112

Kaiser, Karl, 266
Kaliningrad
   and NATO membership for
     Poland, 237–238
   possible nuclear weapons de-
     ployments in, 138
Kamp, Karl-Heinz, 121
Kant, Immanuel
   collective security approach,
     7–9, 10–18, 93, 149, 167, 169,
     170, 172, 173, 177, 181, 240,
     241, 249, 250–251, 259, 270,
     271, 275, 280, 281, 282–284,
     292, 293, 294, 299

   differences and similarities with
     thinking of Wilson, 11–13
   "Eternal Peace" essay, 9
   predicting advent of democratic
     peace, 135
   view of democracies and inter-
     national order, 10, 12, 14
Karadzic, Radovan, 222, 223
Kelleher, Catherine, 53
Kennan, George, 41–42, 106–107
Khrushchev, Nikita, 32
Kinkel, Klaus, 112
Kipp, Jacob, 42, 45
Kissinger, Henry
   on balance of power, 25, 284
   criticism of NATO-Russia
     Founding Act, 143–144,
     292–293
   on distinction between collec-
     tive security and collective
     defense, 7
   NATO enlargement advocate,
     101
   on NATO-Russian relations,
     142–144, 145, 148, 151
   role in negotiations of CSCE's
     human rights provisions, 38
   suggestion of major-power
     grouping with OSCE, 255
   view of Cold War, 41
   view of NATO enlargement and
     creation of European divid-
     ing lines, 123–124, 166–167
Kitanoski, Lazar, 236, 237
Knorr, Klaus, 69
Kohl, Helmut, 53, 54–55, 112, 129,
   134
Komer, Robert, 67
Kontorovich, Vladimir, 44–45
Kosovo
   potential conflict, 199, 227,
     235–236, 275, 294
   U.S. warnings to Serbs about, 236

Kozyrev, Andrei, 84, 136
Krause, Joachim, 244
Kugler, Richard, 101, 243
Kupchan, Charles, 171–172
Kuwait, 79, 190, 232, 256

Laba, Roman, 44
Lake, Anthony, 102, 128
Larrabee, F. Stephen, 101, 243
Latvia. *See* Baltic states
Le Monde, 165
Le Pen, Jean-Marie, 182
League of Nations
  and collective security concept,
    6–7, 8, 9, 11, 12–14, 16–17,
    18, 19, 22, 177, 249–250,
    251, 270
  compared to PfP and EAPC,
    178–182
  Covenant compared to PfP
    Framework Document,
    178–182
  Covenant compared to UN
    Charter, 17, 19
  failure of, 16–17
  Fourteen Points, 12, 13
  "lessons learned" and devel-
    opment of major-power-
    consensus approach, 18
League of the Hellenes, 22
Lefort, Jean-Claude, 116
Legge, Michael, 74
Léotard, François, 113
Liberal internationalists
  and NATO enlargement debate,
    105, 106–107, 108
Libya, 246
Liechtenstein, 162
Linder, John, 107
Lithuania. *See* Baltic states
Litvinov, Maxim, 6
London and Paris agreements of
  1954, 31

London Declaration (July 1990),
  73, 75, 78, 80
Lopez, T. Joseph, 267
Louis XIV, 14–15
Lugar, Richard, 101
Lukin, Vladimir, 133, 135, 136, 139
Lunn, Simon, 164–165
Luxembourg
  Brussels Pact signatory, 28, 186
  foreign minister's comments on
    Yugoslav problem as Euro-
    pean problem, 193
  as "free-rider," 66, 69
  NATO's shift of resources from,
    64, 261–262
  possible multilateral alliances
    for collective defense, 186
  WEU membership, 31, 77

Maastricht Treaty, 78, 79, 184
Macedonia
  applicant for NATO member-
    ship, 118
  concerns about Bosnian con-
    flict spillover, 199, 227, 235,
    237, 275
  ethnic Albanians in, 235
  participation in PfP, 97
  PfP activities in, 294
  plan for stationing NATO forces
    in, 236–237
  United Nations Preventive
    Deployment Force in,
    236–237
  U.S. peacekeeping forces in, 194
Macmillan, Harold, 183
Madrid Declaration (July 1997), 71,
  120, 159, 286
Madrid summit (July 1997), 104,
  112, 120, 127
Major-power interactions outside
  formal institutions, 20, 24,
  182–187, 296, 298

Major-power-consensus approach to collective security, 9, 18–20, 22–23, 24, 167, 172, 173, 176, 181, 213, 240–241, 250, 251, 256, 269, 270, 274–275, 280, 284, 294, 296
Malaysia, 195
Malenkov, Georgi, 150
Malia, Martin, 42
Malta, 162
Manhattan Project, 55
Marshall, Andrew, 66
Massigli, René, 52
Mauritania, 75
Mazzini, Giuseppe, 14
McCain, John, 231
McCalla, Robert, 62
McCurry, Michael, 229
Mediation and crisis resolution
    as collective security intervention, 18
    and intra-Alliance security problems, 51–52
    NATO enlargement and need for, 118
    OSCE role, 176, 285
    PfP compared to League of Nations, 178
    U.S. role, 51–52
Mediterranean Dialogue
    members' participation in IFOR and SFOR, 89
    NATO outreach initiative, 75
Memorandum on Security Assurances (December 1994), 153–154
Mey, Holger, 259–260
Michnik, Adam, 88
Millon, Charles, 113
Milosevic, Slobodan, 198, 226, 236
Minority and border disputes
    and NATO enlargement, 109, 110, 114, 115

OSCE role in protecting minority rights, 93, 176
    potential conflicts, 234, 235, 238, 240, 249
    and Romania, 114, 115
    and Ukraine, 155, 240
Mitterrand, François, 96, 114, 116
Mladic, Ratko, 198, 223
Moch, Jules, 30
Moldova, 85
Molotov-Ribbentrop Pact, 110
Monaco, 162
Monnet, Jean, 51
Montenegro
    economic sanctions against, 193
    OSCE member not in EAPC or PfP, 162
Moral issues. See also Crisis management and peace operations; Human rights
    collective security and international morality, 8, 13–14, 18, 19, 280, 294
    Germany's responsibility for fate of Europe and NATO enlargement issue, 110, 112, 129
    guilt as factor in NATO enlargement, 128–129
    moral power of enlightened public opinion, 10–11, 12, 13–14, 25
Morgenthau, Hans, 284
Morocco
    NATO outreach to, 75
    participation in IFOR and SFOR, 89, 195
Most Holy League of Venice (1454), 9
Moynihan, Daniel Patrick, 107
Multinational Protection Force, 217, 235
Munich agreement (1938), 128, 182

NACC. *See* North Atlantic Cooperation Council
NACOSA. *See* NATO, Integrated
Communications and Infor-
mation Systems Operating
and Support Agency
Nagorno-Karabakh war, 86, 96
National Security Agency, 109
Nationalism
ethno-nationalism and collapse
of Soviet Union, 42, 44
as hindrance to all-European
security structure, 49
as pre-war condition, 191
U.S. as counter to ethno-
nationalism in Europe, 291
NATO
Central Europe Operating
Agency, 64
Central Europe Pipeline System,
64
civilian secretariat and activities, 65
collective defense as core purpose of, 1, 3, 26, 74, 93, 148,
149, 191, 192, 209, 269, 273,
282, 285, 295, 296, 297,
298, 299
Defense Planning Committee,
58–59, 158
Economic Committee, 63
future prospects and challenges,
269–301
importance of international
order concepts to, 20–26
Information and Documentation
Center, 152
Integrated Communications and
Information Systems Operating and Support Agency, 64
internal functions in support of
international security, 50–72,
124, 276, 289, 295, 298, 299

International Military Staff, 205
Maintenance and Supply Organization, 64
membership, 402
new roles and responsibilities,
1–4, 72–90
post–Cold War reassessments
of security requirements,
191–192
predictions of demise, 27, 208,
276
prospects and challenges, 88–
90, 269–301
reconciling traditional and new
roles, 88–90, 269–301
risk of "OSCE-ization" of, 151,
175–176, 186, 298
Standing Group, 183
survival after Cold War, 47–72
two-track policy combining collective defense and collective
security, 292–301
NATO cooperation with former adversaries, 2, 3, 72, 73–75. *See
also specific countries and
cooperative organizations*
antinomy between inclusiveness
and effectiveness, 173–176
challenges of, 91–94, 163–166,
298–300
historical perspective, 176–182
risks for Alliance cohesion and
effectiveness, 166–173
NATO enlargement
Allies' debates on, 102–104
antinomy between inclusiveness and effectiveness,
173–176
and burden sharing, 117, 128
and collective defense obligations, 124–131
danger of alliances outside of
NATO, 186–187

NATO enlargement *(cont.)*
democratization as rationale for,
15, 103, 109, 110, 124, 131,
164, 175, 182
French debate on, 112–116
German debate on, 110–112
German reunification treaty
conditioned on nonexpan-
sion of NATO, 133–134
guilt as factor in, 128–129
Holbrooke's U.S. policy role, 291
implications for "also-rans,"
118–121, 138, 148
inclusiveness *vs.* effectiveness,
173–176
link with Bosnia, 299–300
"open-door" policy, 118–121,
131, 175
potential impact on Alliance
cohesion, 117–118, 295
and the Quad, 184
rationales for, 103–104
and Russia, 110, 120, 121–124,
125–127, 130, 131–151
Russian membership possibility,
132, 145–151
security vacuum as threat to
stability, 105, 109, 111
and U.S. credibility, 287–288
U.S. debate on, 104–110
U.S. views on, 100–102, 103,
104–110, 124–127, 128, 129,
137–138, 148, 164, 175, 261
NATO headquarters, Brussels
proposal for PfP military liaison
mission, 157
proposal for Russian military
liaison mission, 140–141
NATO integrated military structure,
59–60, 93, 203, 204, 205,
207, 216
French resistance to, 96,
113–114, 158, 183, 203, 205

NATO military commands
Airborne Early Warning Force,
60, 194
Allied Command Atlantic,
140–141
Allied Command Europe, 30, 215
Allied Command Europe Rapid
Reaction Corps, 265
Allied Forces Central Europe, 213
Allied Forces Southern Europe,
215, 216, 267
Northern Army Group, 194
restructuring of, 2, 114, 121,
199, 207, 216, 273
Standing Naval Force Channel,
59
Standing Naval Force Mediter-
ranean, 59–60
NATO Military Committee
Capabilities Coordination Cell
support to, 205
and CJTFs, 202
comments by chairman on
U.S. involvement in NATO,
212, 216
French participation, 158
PfP participation, 157
Standing Group, 183
NATO-Albania Clearing House, 235
NATO-Russia Founding Act
and collective security, 93, 241
compared with NATO-Ukraine
Charter, 152
French view of, 149
intention to respect all pertinent
international agreements, 142
Kissinger's criticism of, 143–144,
292–293
NATO outreach initiative, 285
and NATO's collective defense,
130, 141, 142, 143–144, 165
negotiations, 141–142
and nuclear weapons, 141–142

NATO-Russia Founding Act *(cont.)*
  possible threats to implementation of, 137, 144, 145
  and reexamination of NATO's Strategic Concept, 284
  signing of, 74–75, 165
  Solana's role in, 185
  text of, 313–323
NATO-Russia Permanent Joint Council
  establishment of, 2, 74–75
  fear of damage to U.S. relations with NATO Europe, 144
  fear of Russian influence in NATO via, 143–144, 145, 238
  and hierarchy of NATO-sponsored security structures, 161
  major-power consultations outside of, 185
  purpose of, 2, 88, 91, 163, 181, 241
  and Russian distrust, 145
  time and personnel constraints, 163
NATO-Ukraine Charter
  consultation pledge, 240
  NATO outreach initiative, 75, 285
  and NATO-Ukraine relations, 152–153
  text of, 325–331
NATO-Ukraine Commission
  establishment of, 2, 75, 152
  and hierarchy of NATO-sponsored security structures, 161
  meetings with NAC, 152
  purpose of, 91, 163, 181
  time and personnel constraints, 163
Naumann, Klaus, 212–213, 216
Nerlich, Uwe, 50, 288
Netherlands
  Brussels Pact signatory, 28, 186
  facilities for U.S. nuclear-capable forces, 34
  flexible capabilities for out-of-area use, 244
  Ministry of Defense, 172
  objection to Contact Group, 184
  possible multilateral alliances for collective defense, 186
  post–Cold War shift of NATO investments from, 64, 261–262
  Rapid Reaction Force development, 198
  view of Quad's preeminence in NATO, 185
  WEU membership, 31, 77
New York Times, 165, 232, 249
Nigeria, 253
Non–Article 5 missions. *See* Crisis management and peace operations
North Atlantic Assembly, 164–165
North Atlantic Cooperation Council
  Ad Hoc Group on Cooperation in Peacekeeping, 95
  compared to PfP, 98–99
  establishment of, 2, 94–97
  France's reluctance to endorse establishment of, 95–96
  inclusion of PfP members in meetings, 96, 97
  mechanism for cooperation, 73–74
  member participation in IFOR and SFOR, 73–74
  membership, 402
  NATO attempt to institutionalize cooperative relations with former adversaries, 2, 94–97
  replacement by EAPC, 73, 75, 91, 97, 159
  Russian preference for over PfP, 160

North Atlantic Cooperation Council
(cont.)
and "security is indivisible"
concept, 6, 163–164
U.S. aims for, 100–101
North Atlantic Council, 177, 238
Albania's exercise of PfP consultation rights, 236
call for war criminal trials,
221–222
and CJTFs, 201–202, 204
on commitment to NATO-Russia
partnership, 140
consultations with and use of
NATO assets, 201, 204, 206,
207, 211
control of IFOR and SFOR, 160
and EAPC, 158–159, 160–161
and ESDI, 209, 211, 216
French participation, 96
"Group on Defense Matters"
name for NACC meetings
not approved by, 96
and hierarchy of NATO-sponsored security structures, 161
liaison with NATO-Russia Permanent Joint Council, 143
mandate for crisis management
and peace operations, 256
and NATO command structure,
60, 68
on NATO enlargement, 92, 123
outreach to Mediterranean
countries, 75
and PfP, 74, 97, 99, 157, 206–207
Policy Coordination Group,
205, 206
policy on weapons of mass
destruction, 80, 81, 246
on primacy of NATO, 209
Russian refusal to approve PfP
IPP or program for NATO-
Russia cooperation, 136

North Atlantic Council (cont.)
SFOR mandate extended indefinitely on basis of NAC decisions, 195, 218
on shift of priorities to PfP and
information activities in
Moscow and Kyiv, 273
special relationship for Russia
and Ukraine, 151–152
statement of long-term interest
in Bosnia, 228, 229
Study on NATO Enlargement,
103–104, 124
support for cooperative all-
European security structures,
92, 123
North Atlantic Treaty, 35, 62, 209
Article 2 on economic cooperation, 63
Article 4 similarity to NATO
consultation pledges to PfP,
97–98, 162, 180, 237, 239,
240, 262, 271
Article 5 commitment to mutual
defense, 7, 29, 61, 81, 156,
157, 162, 166, 168, 169,
189, 267
Article 6 interpretation and
out-of-area operations, 189,
244, 267
Article 10 statement on membership, 71, 103, 137–138, 150
Article 11 on countries' respective constitutional processes,
29
French distinction between
Treaty and NATO military
structure, 59
NATO enlargement and 50th
anniversary of, 104
no reference to specific adversaries, 81
and nuclear nonproliferation, 55

North Atlantic Treaty *(cont.)*
  preamble's reference to democracy, liberty, and rule of law, 70
  text of, 303–307
  U.S. commitment to, 28–29
  U.S. ratification of, 105
North Atlantic Treaty Organization. *See* NATO
North Korea
  invasion of South Korea in 1950, 29–30
Norway
  conscription, 213
  and ESDI, 210
  interest in WEU-led operations, 210
  view of Quad's preeminence in NATO, 185
Nuclear Non-Proliferation Treaty, 68, 153
Nuclear Planning Group, 34, 35, 56, 58, 143
Nuclear Posture Review, 87
Nuclear weapons
  "Danish footnotes" to nuclear controversies, 117
  deterrence, 33, 34, 87, 134, 138–139, 247
  in former Soviet Union, 289
  France's program, 33, 34–35, 55–56, 68
  German program possibility, 56–57
  Great Britain's program, 33, 34–35, 55, 56, 68
  INF Treaty, 33
  NATO's role in limiting proliferation of, 55–57, 73, 79–81, 89, 276, 284
  Nuclear Non-Proliferation Treaty, 68, 153
  Quick Reaction Alert program, 60

and renationalization of defense capabilities, 187, 298
  risks posed by interventions beyond Europe, 245–248
  Russian nuclear threat, 86–87, 109, 138–139, 140, 145, 148, 289
  Russian-NATO deterrence relationship, 87, 105, 108–109, 134–135, 138–139, 148, 240, 300
  START II agreement, 106, 138
  Strategic Concept and nuclear policy, 34, 35, 80, 285–286
  on territory of new NATO allies, 141–142
  Turkey program possibility, 56
  Ukraine as non–nuclear-weapon state, 153–154
  U.S. weapons in Europe, 27, 33–34, 50, 56, 57, 60, 68, 87
  West Germany's renunciation of production of, 31
Nunn, Sam, 106

Odom, William, 109, 219, 225–226, 255
OECD. *See* Organization for Economic Cooperation and Development
Olson, Mancur, 174
Omand, David, 87
Open diplomacy, 11, 12
Operation Alba, 217, 235
Operation Deliberate Force, 1, 195, 197, 198, 212, 233, 285
Operation Joint Endeavor. *See* Implementation Force
Operation Provide Comfort, 190
Operation Southern Watch, 190
Opinion polls. *See* Public opinion polls
Organization for Economic Cooperation and Development, 63

Organization for Security and Co-operation in Europe, 154, 180, 185, 278. *See also* Conference on Security and Cooperation in Europe
  assumption that UN or OSCE approval is necessary for NATO intervention, 192, 251–259
  compared to PfP, 98
  cooperation with NATO, 3, 93, 142
  failure of Bosnian conflict efforts, 220
  insufficiency for primary security, 170, 174, 176
  mandate for non–Article 5 contingencies, 18, 20, 104, 162, 167, 173, 181, 192, 251–259, 270, 271, 294
  mediation and crisis resolution role, 176, 285
  membership, 402–403
  NATO offer of support for peacekeeping activities, 3, 76
  and NATO-Russia Founding Act, 142, 241
  and new NATO institutions, 91
  relationship with PfP, 158, 160, 161–163
  replacement of CSCE, 3, 285
  responsibilities, 93
  strengthening through "security committee," 255
  support for developing OSCE rather than NATO enlargement, 112, 116, 133, 139, 150, 160
  weaknesses of, 176
"OSCE-ization" of NATO, risk of, 141, 175–176, 186, 298
Osgood, Robert, 276, 282–283

Ostpolitik, end of Cold War and, 39, 41
Owen, David, 184

Pakistan
  aid to Afghanistan against Soviets, 45
Paris Conference, 250
Parkhalina, Tatiana, 135
Parmentier, Guillaume, 215–216
PARP. *See* Planning and Review Process
Partnership for Peace
  accomplishments of, 98–99, 118, 156
  Albania's exercise of emergency consultation rights, 236
  collective security approach, 138, 167, 298
  compared to League of Nations, 178–182
  compared to NACC, 98–99
  compared to OSCE, 98
  cooperation on weapons proliferation issues, 89
  Coordination Cell (Mons, Belgium), 99, 157
  and crisis management and peace operations, 2, 3, 190, 280, 294, 295, 298
  criticisms of, 98
  dependence on U.S. commitments, 287
  disagreements involving, 90
  enhancement of, 98, 119, 121, 139, 155–163, 161
  establishment of, 2, 74, 97–100, 284
  funding of, 65, 99–100, 157
  and "global NATO" concept, 243
  Individual Partnership Programs, 97, 99, 136
  limitations of, 161

Partnership for Peace *(cont.)*
membership, 175, 403
Military Cooperation Program, 95
Military liaison proposals, 140–141, 157
NATO consultation pledges, 3, 97–98, 162, 168–169, 180, 236, 237, 239, 240, 262, 279
and NATO enlargement, 94, 98, 103, 120, 139, 155–156, 159
NATO outreach to former adversaries, 2, 72, 74, 94, 163
NATO's forward engagement as reassurance for, 267
North Atlantic Council's decision-making authority, 206
participation in Albania intervention, 235, 294
participation in CJTFs, 204, 207
participation in IFOR and SFOR, 2, 21, 76, 89, 98, 195, 293
participation in NACC meetings, 96, 97
participation in NATO defense planning system, 262
participation in NATO-led operations at NATO's invitation only, 206–207
Partnership Staff Elements, 207
as pathway to NATO membership, 94, 98, 103, 120, 155
purposes of, 2, 91, 94, 97, 163
relationship with OSCE, 158, 160, 161–163
risks for NATO cohesion and effectiveness, 166–173
Russian participation in, 123, 134–137, 151, 239
Russian reluctance to legitimize agenda, 140
Russian withdrawal possibility, 145

self-differentiation among Partners, 98–99, 159
Ukraine participation in, 152
Partnership Framework Document compared to League of Nations Covenant, 178–182
extension of, 157
text of, 309–311
PCG. *See* North Atlantic Council, Policy Coordination Group
"Peace is indivisible" concept. *See* "Security is indivisible" concept
Peacekeeping operations. *See* Crisis management and peace operations
Penn, William, 9
Perry, William, 139–140, 147, 243, 288–289
Persian Gulf War. *See* Gulf War
"Petersberg tasks," 79, 209, 213, 217, 278, 290–291
PfP. *See* Partnership for Peace
PJC. *See* NATO-Russia Permanent Joint Council
Planning and Review Process, 89, 99, 157, 262
Poland
applicant for NATO membership, 101, 104, 112, 118, 120, 121, 146, 166
and Baltic states, 238
candidate for European Union, 146
and collective defense concept, 3
democratization of, 41, 46
deployment of Allied forces to as deterrence measure, 300
French support for NATO membership, 113, 116
German support for NATO membership, 112

Poland *(cont.)*
importance of NATO membership to Ukraine, 123
imposition of martial law, 39,
190
NATO admission and expiation
of German guilt, 129
NATO membership and risk of
Russian complaints, 237–238
NATO outreach to, 73
participation in Albania intervention, 235
participation in IFOR, 195
participation in PfP, 158
partitions of, 283
PfP encouragement of regional
military cooperation in, 98
possible effects of NATO membership on Quad influence,
186
Solidarity movement, 38, 45
Soviet territorial acquisition
during World War II, 35
U.S. Congress attempt to tie
NATO membership to Bosnia
issue, 232
U.S. Senate approval of NATO
membership for, 105
view of NATO membership for
Russia, 151
view of NATO-Russia Permanent
Joint Council, 161
Polish-American Congress, 101
Poos, Jacques, 193
Portugal
decolonization conflicts, 189
Gulf War involvement, 61, 242
NATO membership, 71
support for NATO membership
for Romania, 127
WEU membership, 32
Portugalov, Nikolai, 27
Procurement programs, 64, 65, 66

Progress toward peaceful world
order, 11, 12
Prussia, 25, 283
PSEs. *See* Partnership for Peace,
Partnership Staff Elements
Public opinion
desire to avoid casualties in crisis
management and peace op-
erations, 222, 224, 261
moral power of, 10–11, 12,
13–14, 25
Public opinion polls
European Allies' confidence in
U.S. reliability, 296–297
on German interest in a national
nuclear force, 56–57
on German participation in
preventive strike by NATO
against nuclear weapons
development, 246
on U.S. involvement in Bosnia,
222, 234

QRA. *See* Quick Reaction Alert
program
The Quad (United States, Great
Britain, France, Germany)
and Dayton Accords, 250
main responsibilities in crisis
management and peace
operations, 213–214, 250
preeminence in NATO, 183–
187, 250
Quadruple Alliance (1718), 9
Quick Reaction Alert program, 60

Radio Free Europe/Radio Liberty,
165
Rapid reaction forces, 192, 198,
228, 244, 265
Ray, Norman, 212–213
Reagan, Ronald, 44–45, 150
Reddaway, Peter, 43–44

Renationalization of defense policies, 59, 135, 149, 186–187, 289, 295, 298

Republika Srpska, 221, 230

Rice, Condoleezza, 134

Richard, Alain, 216–217

Rifkind, Malcolm, 87

Rocard, Michel, 115

Rodionov, Igor, 141

Rodman, Peter, 108

Rogov, Sergey, 84

Romania

  applicant for NATO membership, 112, 118, 120, 146

  Cold War relations with West, 31–32

  countries supporting NATO membership, 127

  democratization of, 41

  French support for NATO membership, 113, 114–115, 127

  Italian support for NATO membership, 117, 127

  NATO outreach to, 73

  participation in IFOR, 195

  participation in multinational intervention in Albania, 235

  PfP encouragement of regional military cooperation in, 98

  Soviet attempts to prevent joining of alliance, 49

  Soviet territorial acquisition during World War II, 35

  as symbol for deficiencies of NATO enlargement process, 128

Rome Declaration (November 1991), 64, 76, 78, 80, 163

Roosevelt, Franklin D., 17

Rosati, Dariusz, 123

Rosenfeld, Stephen S., 128

Rosner, Jeremy, 105, 106

Rowen, Henry, 42

Rudolf, Peter, 41

Rühe, Volker, 101, 110–111, 112, 146–147, 148–149, 213–214, 216, 234, 286

Rühle, Michael, 51, 168–169, 170, 244–246, 255–256, 257

Rush, Myron, 42–43

Russia. *See also* NATO-Russia Permanent Joint Council; Soviet Union

  Academy of Sciences, 135

  and Bosnia conflict, 2, 21, 133, 140, 195, 218, 227, 240, 241, 275

  cooperation on WMD proliferation issues, 89

  democratization, 88, 130, 186

  and EAPC, 160, 161

  Eastern Europeans' perception of threat of, 122–124, 164–165, 166

  economic reform, 87–88

  efforts to reassert influence, 238, 239

  European opposition to NATO membership for, 149–150

  former Soviet republics as Russia's "Near Abroad," 280, 285, 286

  French proposal for Quad and Russia meetings on enlargement, 185

  French view of NATO's deterrent effect on, 115–116

  influence in Baltic region, 238–239

  influence on former republics, 280, 285, 286

  influence on Strategic Concept review, 285

  Institute of the USA and Canada, 84

Russia *(cont.)*
justification of interventions as "peacekeeping," 253
military deterioration, 84–85, 274
military liaison proposal, 140–141
Ministry for Civil Defense, Emergencies, and Elimination of Consequences of Natural Disasters, 137
multilateral alliances for collective defense, 285
NATO enlargement as prevention of German-Russian rivalries, 109–110, 123, 131
NATO membership possibility, 132, 145–151
NATO view of post–Cold War Russian threat, 81–88, 108–109, 122–123, 125–127, 130, 140, 164–165, 282, 298, 299, 300
NATO-Russia relations, 73–75, 120, 121–124, 131–151, 271
and NATO's goal of projecting stability, 279
nuclear threat, 86–87, 109, 138–139, 140, 145, 148, 289
opposition to NATO enlargement, 94, 120, 121–124, 132–135, 137–139, 155, 166
and OSCE security committee, 255
outward expansion and European peace, 25
participation in Contact Group, 184
participation in IFOR and SFOR, 2, 21, 133, 195, 241, 275
participation in PfP, 123, 135–137, 158
partition of Polish state, 283
post–Cold War threat, 300

risk of NATO enlargement leading to confrontation with, 120, 121–124, 130–131
"special relationship" with NATO, 93, 122–123, 151–152, 287
support for developing OSCE rather than NATO enlargement, 133, 139, 150
and UN Security Council mandates, 110, 253, 254, 258, 296
U.S. treatment of as superpower, 144
U.S. view of NATO's deterrent effect on, 105, 108–109
U.S. view of post–Cold War threat, 82–83, 87, 108–109, 125–127
U.S. view of what Russians should think of NATO enlargement, 131–132
view of NATO membership for former republics, 137–139
Rwanda, French intervention, 256
Rybkin, Ivan, 150

SACEUR. *See* Supreme Allied Commander, Europe
SACLANT. *See* Supreme Allied Commander, Atlantic
San Marino, 162
Sandler, Todd, 70
Sarajevo, siege of, 194–195, 197, 198
Saudi Arabia, 45
Schmidt, Helmut, 39
Schweizer, Peter, 46
SDI. *See* Strategic Defense Initiative
Security Investment Program, 64
"Security is indivisible" concept
as collective security concept, 11, 15, 22
foundations of, 15
and League of Nations, 6–8

"Security is indivisible" concept
(cont.)
and NATO, 3, 21, 163–164, 172,
174–175, 180, 237, 270, 275,
279, 280, 281, 296, 299
in NATO-Russia Founding Act,
93, 241
and PfP, 167, 168, 174–175
post–Cold War declaration by
NATO and Warsaw Pact, 48
practical limitations to, 235,
240, 241, 248–251, 260,
299
in Strategic Concept, 278
U.S. support for, 100
Séguin, Philippe, 116
Self-determination
Baltic states, 43
Bosniaks' goal, 193
Bush call for self-determination
for Germany and Eastern
Europe, 53
Kantian vs. Wilsonian view of,
12–13, 251
Kosovo, 235
role in collapse of Soviet Union,
43–44
as route to peace, 10, 14, 25
Russian support for "great
power" sphere-of-influence
arrangement rather than, 134
Self-differentiation
in EAPC, 159
in PfP, 98–99, 159
Senior Defense Group on Prolifer-
ation, 80–81, 245, 247
Senior Political-Military Group on
Proliferation, 80
"Separable but not separate" assets,
200, 201, 202, 205, 207
Serbia. See also Bosnia; Kosovo
economic sanctions against,
193, 194

Milosevic's abandonment of
Bosnian Serbs, 198
OSCE member not in EAPC or
PfP, 162
parties to Bosnia conflict, 193
and partition of Bosnia, 221,
222
siege of Sarajevo, 194–195, 197,
198
view of independent Bosnia,
219, 226
Sevastopol, 155
SFOR. See Stabilization Force
Shalikashvili, John, 228
SHAPE. See Supreme Headquarters
Allied Powers Europe
Shevardnadze, Eduard, 27
Shlapentokh, Vladimir, 83
Shoigu, Sergei, 137
Slocombe, Walter
on Bosnia, 140, 227, 230,
231–232, 234
on challenges facing NATO, 272
on CJTFs, 204
on "cooperative security" as one
of NATO's principles, 164
on ESDI within NATO, 210
on NATO enlargement, 119
on NATO-Russian cooperation,
140, 141, 227
on NATO's collective defense
function against Russia, 82–
83, 126–127
on nuclear weapons in Europe,
56
on PfP, 155
on U.S. strategic interest in
Europe, 208
Slovakia
applicant for NATO membership,
118, 146
candidate for European Union,
146

Slovakia *(cont.)*
and Hungary's NATO membership, 128
NACC membership, 95
PfP encouragement of regional
military cooperation in, 98
Slovenia
applicant for NATO membership, 112, 118, 120
and Hungary's NATO membership, 128
Italy's support for NATO membership, 117
observer status in NACC, 95
participation in PfP, 97
participation in SFOR, 76, 196
Smith, Robert, 106, 107, 108, 232
Solana, Javier, 146, 177–178, 185,
212–213, 236, 273
Solomon, Richard, 225
Somalia, humanitarian intervention
Germany's participation in, 213
withdrawal of France and United
States from, 224
Sopko, John, 247
South Korea
Allied state-building efforts in,
219
invasion by North Korea in 1950,
29–30
Soviet Union. *See also* Russia; *specific countries*
Berlin blockade, 28, 32
Cuban missile crisis, 32, 36
factors in collapse of, 41–47
and failure of League of
Nations, 16
former Soviet republics as Russia's
"Near Abroad," 280, 285, 286
Helsinki Final Act interpreta-
tion, 38–39
historical determinism ideology,
32, 40

invasion of Afghanistan, 32, 45
invasion of Czechoslovakia,
31, 32
NACC membership of former
Soviet republics, 95
NATO Cold War policies, 1, 3,
32–47, 81, 189–190, 276
NATO outreach to former Soviet
republics, 2, 73–75, 88–89
not named by NATO as specific
adversary, 81
potential conflicts in former
Soviet republics, 239–241,
269, 272
as stimulus for NATO cohesion,
32
and Strategic Concept defining
of strategic balance, 285
suppression of Hungarian uprising, 36
territorial acquisitions in World
War II, 35, 38–39
view of NATO as equivalent
to Warsaw Pact, 27–28
withdrawal of troops from
Germany, 27
Spain
burden sharing, 65
democratization of, 70
Gulf War involvement, 61, 242
NATO admission, 32
objection to Contact Group, 184
participation in multinational
intervention in Albania, 235
participation in NATO integrated
air defense forces, 60
support for French defining of
CJTF purposes, 202
support for NATO membership
for Romania, 127
WEU membership, 32
Spence, Floyd, 226
Srebrenica massacre, 198

Stabilization Force, 1–2, 4, 273
  activation of, 76
  Bosnia beyond SFOR, 218–234, 301
  casualties, 222, 224
  countries participating, 196, 278, 293
  European insistence on U.S. involvement in successor operation, 217, 218
  as example of shift in NATO priorities to collective security, 270, 272, 284, 285
  follow-on also called SFOR, 230
  future dilemmas, 220–234
  Germany's participation, 213, 214
  mandate extended indefinitely, 195, 218, 228–230, 233–234
  mandate for, 240
  Mediterranean Dialogue members' participation, 89
  mission of, 76–77
  NATO infrastructure investments in support of, 64
  and "NATO-minus-plus" concept, 205
  North Atlantic Council's authority over, 160
  number of troops, 196, 219, 230
  PfP participation, 21, 89, 98, 206
  political sustainability of U.S. presence in Bosnia, 222–224, 234, 288
  replacement of IFOR, 195
  Russian participation in, 133, 241
  solidarity of, 278, 293
  U.S. Congress attempt to end U.S. participation in, 228, 232
  U.S. participation, 196–199, 212, 218–220, 225, 226, 228–234, 287
Stalin, Joseph, 28, 36

Standardization and interoperability
  economic benefits of, 65–66, 67
  as means of collective defense, 130, 142
  and NATO support for crisis management and peace operations, 206
  and PfP, 3, 98, 99, 207
  in Warsaw Pact, 67
"Star Wars." See Strategic Defense Initiative
START II agreement, 106, 138
Steel, Ronald, 151
Stockholm conference on confidence-building measures, 38
Strait of Hormuz, 245
Strategic Concept (November 1991)
  and nuclear defenses, 34, 35, 80, 285–286
  on risks to Allied security, 75, 191, 265, 285–286
  and "security is indivisible," 278
  statement of purposes, 74, 81, 92, 126, 148, 164, 172, 192, 282
  Strategy Review Group, 74
  use of word "Soviet," 285–286
Strategic Concept review
  French participation in, 216
  as indicator of NATO's future direction, 4, 284
  preserving NATO's core function of collective defense, 285
  Russian influence on, 285
Strategic Defense Initiative, 44, 45, 46, 150
Study on NATO Enlargement, 103–104, 124
Süddeutsche Zeitung, 53
Suez Canal, 245
Supreme Allied Commander, Atlantic
  French proposal for European officer as, 215

Supreme Allied Commander,
    Atlantic *(cont.)*
  and integrated military structure,
    60, 202, 205, 215
Supreme Allied Commander, Europe
  Eisenhower's appointment as, 30
  European Deputy specifications,
    214
  French proposal for European
    officer as, 215
  and integrated military structure,
    59–60, 202, 205, 215, 216
  role in mediating Greek-Turkish
    disputes, 51
Supreme Headquarters Allied
    Powers Europe
  and CJTF planning, 202, 203, 205
  establishment of, 30
  PfP Partnership Coordination
    Cell located near, 99
  proposal for PfP military liaison
    mission, 157
  proposal for Russian military
    liaison mission, 140–141
  staff integration, 58
Surikov, Anton, 138–139, 155
Sweden
  and Baltic states, 238
  consideration of nuclear
    weapons program, 187
  neutrality of, 71, 211
  observer status in NACC, 95
  participation in IFOR, 195
  participation in NACC meetings,
    96
  participation in PfP, 97
  possible NATO membership, 175
  WEU Council invitation to par-
    ticipate in WEU defense
    planning, 211
Switzerland
  consideration of nuclear wea-
    pons program, 187

  neutrality of, 71
  observer status in NACC, 95
  participation in Albania inter-
    vention, 235
  participation in PfP, 97, 98
Szabo, Stephen, 296–297

Tajikistan
  nonparticipation in PfP, 97
  Russian influence on, 239, 241,
    280
Talbott, Strobe, 102, 124, 132, 147
Talleyrand, Charles-Maurice, 260
Technology
  factor in collapse of Soviet
    Union, 44–45, 46
Technology transfers
  Cold War issue, 40
  multinational programs and, 65
Territorial defense. *See* Collective
    defense
Terrorism
  NATO as framework for fight-
    ing, 247
Teta, Perikli, 236
Thatcher, Margaret, 54, 191
"Third Dimension" programs, 95
Thomson, James, 243
Transparency of military capabili-
    ties and plans
  and collective security tradition,
    21, 178
  and ESDI, 209
  and NATO, 21, 58, 141, 142,
    163, 173, 292, 299
  and NATO-established institu-
    tions, 163
  and NATO-Russia relations, 141,
    142
  and PfP, 3, 97, 98, 178, 279
  as rationale for NATO enlarge-
    ment, 103
Treaty of Chaumont (1814), 15

Treaty of Dunkirk, 28
Treaty of London (1518), 9
Treaty of Utrecht (1713), 15
Treaty of Versailles, 12, 134, 179, 270
Trilateral Statement (January 1994), 153
Truman, Harry, 28–29, 284
Truman administration
  support for North Atlantic Treaty, 105
Tudjman, Franjo, 184, 226
Tunisia, 75
Turkey
  concerns about Bosnian conflict spillover, 199
  defense spending, 260
  and ESDI, 210
  facilities for U.S. nuclear-capable forces, 34
  fear of Iraqi attack during Gulf War, 61, 81, 190, 266, 300
  Germany's participation in reinforcement, 266
  Gulf War involvement, 61, 81, 190, 242, 266, 300
  interest in joining European Union, 117, 120
  interest in WEU-led operations, 210
  modernization and democratization of, 88
  NATO mediation in Greek-Turkish disputes, 118
  NATO membership, 31, 71
  nuclear weapons program possibility, 56
  participation in multinational intervention in Albania, 235
  possible nuclear program, 187
  potential involvement in Kosovo or FYROM, 235
  support for NATO membership for Romania, 127
  threat of Russian military intervention, 86
  U.S. mediation in Greek-Turkish disputes, 51–52
  use of NATO assets for UN-authorized activities relating to Iraq, 190

Udovenko, Gennadiy, 137
Ukraine. See also NATO-Ukraine Commission
  as buffer zone to Russia, 132
  cooperation on WMD proliferation issues, 89
  decision to hold off on applying for NATO membership, 118
  democratization, 146, 166
  minority issues, 155, 240
  NATO consultation pledges, 240
  NATO membership as "strategic objective" of, 137
  and NATO's goal of projecting stability, 279
  participation in IFOR and SFOR, 2, 195
  participation in PfP, 152, 158
  PfP encouragement of regional military cooperation in, 98
  and Russian influence, 123, 155
  Russian opposition to NATO membership for, 137, 138, 155
  Russian threat to, 240
  "special relationship" with NATO, 93, 94, 123, 148, 151–155, 279, 287
  U.S. assistance to, 154
Ulam, Adam, 43, 46
Ulmanis, Guntis, 238
United Kingdom. See Great Britain
United Nations
  admission of Baltic states, 73

United Nations *(cont.)*
    assumption that UN or OSCE approval is necessary for NATO intervention, 192, 251–259
    Charter compared with League of Nations Covenant, 17
    Charter's Article 51 right to individual and collective self-defense, 20, 255, 256, 257
    Cold War relations with NATO, 194
    and collective security concept, 17, 19–20, 23
    economic sanctions against Serbia and Montenegro, 193
    establishment of, 17
    Gulf War operations, 79
    insufficiency for primary security, 170, 174
    International Conference on Former Yugoslavia, 184
    Iraq-related operations, 190
    mandates for IFOR and SFOR, 240
    mandates for non–Article 5 contingencies, 19, 20, 162, 167, 181, 240, 254, 270, 271, 275, 294, 295, 296
    and Memorandum on Security Assurances, 154
    and NATO enlargement, 93
    and NATO-Russia Founding Act, 142
    OSCE compared to, 176
    peacekeeping efforts in former Yugoslavia, 1–2, 4, 21, 22–23, 76–77, 89, 193–194, 197–198, 199
    recognition of OSCE as regional arrangement in terms of Charter, 150

    Russia and UN Security Council mandates, 239, 253, 254
    Security Council and major-power consensus, 17, 19–20, 23, 239, 253, 254
    strengthening peacekeeping operations as rationale for NATO expansion, 104
    support for NATO, 180
United Nations Preventive Deployment Force, 236–237
United Nations Protection Force
    Bosnia involvement, 193–194, 197–198, 199
    composition of, 193, 263
    hostages taken by Bosnian Serbs, 198, 199
    hypothetical case of Russian attack on, 263
    NATO support for, 194, 195, 285
    Russian chartering of aircraft to, 137
    staffing of, 197
    U.S. support for, 194, 197, 199
United Nations Special Commission on Iraq, 80, 246
United States
    aid to Afghanistan against Soviets, 45
    Atlantic Forces, 242, 244
    and Baltic states, 238–239
    Bosnia involvement, 194, 199, 208, 212, 218, 224–234, 248–249, 288
    burden sharing, 68, 70
    capabilities' superiority to NATO, 202, 212
    central role in NATO, 286–291
    and China, 257–258
    CJTF proposal, 200
    commitment to NATO, 28–29
    as counterbalance to German power, 52–54

United States (cont.)
  debate on NATO enlargement, 104–110
  and defining of CJTF purposes, 202, 203, 204–205
  Defense Department support for PfP rather than NATO enlargement, 102
  "dual containment" policy to isolate Iran and Iraq, 246
  East Asia and Middle East conflicts and Article 6 of North Atlantic Treaty, 189
  and ESDI, 204–205, 208, 211, 228, 278
  European Allies' confidence in reliability of, 296–297
  European Command, 242
  and European cooperation and economic integration, 29, 51
  Europe-U.S. disagreements over Bosnia, 195, 218, 272, 276, 293–294
  and failure of League of Nations, 16
  Four Power rights regarding German question, 39, 183
  French view of interference in ESDI, 208
  French view of role in NATO, 113–114, 116
  General Accounting Office report on Dayton Accords, 220–221
  and "global NATO" concept, 243–245
  as guarantor of NATO's collective defense pledges, 68, 130, 181, 287, 297
  insistence on possibility of Russian membership in NATO, 148, 150
  major-power responsibilities for crisis management and peace operations, 213
  military and nuclear presence in Europe, 27, 31, 33–34, 50–52, 56, 57, 60, 68, 87, 134–135, 197
  moral and emotional considerations in supporting NATO enlargement, 128, 129
  NATO enlargement as political issue, 121–122, 129
  and NATO's integrated military structure, 203
  as part of bilateral alliances for collective defense, 186
  participation in IFOR and SFOR, 196–199, 212, 218–220, 225, 226, 228–234
  and PfP, 99–100, 158, 181
  policy on foreign military engagements, 233, 248–249
  potential involvement in Kosovo or FYROM, 235–236
  the Quad's preeminence in NATO, 183–187, 250
  refusal to recognize Soviet territorial acquisitions, 39
  role in resolving intra–West European security dilemmas, 50–51
  and Russia, 133, 144, 257–258
  strategic interest in Europe, 155, 197, 208
  superiority of capabilities, 68, 202, 212
  support for NATO inclusiveness, 120–121, 175, 176
  treatment of Russia as superpower, 144
  two-track policy combining collective defense and collective security, 292–301

United States *(cont.)*
  and Ukraine, 153, 154
  use of assets for crisis manage-
    ment and peace operations,
    190, 200–201
  view of cause of end of Cold
    War, 41
  view of ethnic conflicts, 248–249
  view of NATO enlargement,
    100–102, 103, 104–110, 120–
    122, 124–127, 128, 129, 137–
    138, 148, 164, 175, 261
  view of post–Cold War Russian
    threat, 82–83, 87, 108–109,
    125–127
  Wilson's view of special leader-
    ship role, 12
  withdrawal from Somalia, 224
United States Institute of Peace, 225
UNPREDEP. *See* United Nations
    Preventive Deployment
    Force
UNPROFOR. *See* United Nations
    Protection Force

Van Eekelen, Willem, 256, 257
Van Oudenaren, John, 46–47
Vandenberg, Arthur, 273
"Variable-geometry" responses,
    203, 291
Védrine, Hubert, 116, 149
Vernet, Daniel, 165, 239
Vienna Document 1994, 142
Vietnam syndrome, 232–233
Vietnam War, 197, 232–233
Voigt, Karsten, 111
von Gentz, Friedrich, 15
Vos, Joris Michael, 285

Walesa, Lech
  Poland's interest in NATO
    membership, 101, 128
  rise to power, 41

War
  arms competitions and, 24
  collective security as pact
    against, 7, 11
  Grotian approach, 283
  increase in vulnerability and, 24
  interest in collective security
    greatest following, 21, 296
War criminals, 221–223, 224, 225,
    230
War of the Spanish Succession,
    14–15
Warner, John, 106, 108
Warsaw Pact
  call for all-European security
    system at end of Cold War,
    47–48
  disbanding of, 94
  establishment of, 31
  membership, 404
  NATO outreach to former
    members, 2, 73–75
  Paris Declaration that NATO
    and Warsaw Pact are "no
    longer adversaries," 73
  Soviet view of NATO as equi-
    valent to, 27–28
Warsaw Treaty (1955), 48
Washington Treaty. *See* North
    Atlantic Treaty
Weapons of mass destruction. *See
    also* Biological and chemical
    weapons; Nuclear weapons
  Iraqi programs, 80
  NATO's emphasis on countering
    proliferation of, 73, 79–81,
    89, 284
  risks posed by interventions
    beyond Europe, 245–248
  Russian threat, 86–87, 109, 138–
    139, 140, 145, 148
  West Germany's renunciation of
    production of, 31

Weilemann, Peter, 121
Weinberger, Caspar, 67
Wellstone, Paul, 107
West Germany. *See* Germany,
    Federal Republic of
Western European Union
    Cold War role, 77
    connection with NATO mem-
        bership, 175
    Council of Ministers, 209,
        210–211
    economic sanctions against
        Serbia and Montenegro,
        193, 194
    and ESDI, 2, 190, 207–217
    establishment of, 77
    French support for WEU rather
        than NATO enlargement, 113
    insufficient consensus for Alba-
        nian intervention, 235
    membership, 31, 71, 403–404
    and NATO enlargement, 93
    NATO support for WEU-led
        operations, 72, 77–79, 200,
        201, 202, 204, 205, 207–208,
        210, 211, 215, 228, 243, 291
    "Petersberg tasks," 209, 213, 217,
        278, 290–291
    possible merger with EU, 217
    post–Cold War role, 72, 77–79
    support for NATO, 180
    use of CJTFs, 200, 201, 202, 204,
        205, 207, 215
WEU. *See* Western European Union
Wheeler, Michael, 284
Wight, Martin
    on "balance of power," 24, 177,
        250, 251, 281, 283
    on collective security, 7, 9, 14,
        15, 22, 177, 280, 281, 292
    on Concert of Europe, 25
    on effectiveness *vs.* inclusiveness,
        173–174

on League of Nations, 17, 179,
    251
on "right of intervention," 250
on rule of law in international
    relations, 19, 20
on UN Security Council mecha-
    nism, 19, 257
Williams, Nick, 51, 98, 99, 144–145,
    168–169, 170, 244–245
Wilson, Woodrow. *See also* League
    of Nations
collective security approach,
    7–9, 10–18, 93, 149, 167, 169,
    170, 172, 173, 177, 181, 240,
    241, 249, 250–251, 259, 270,
    271, 275, 280, 281, 282–284,
    292, 293, 294, 299
"community of power" replac-
    ing balance of power, 11, 16,
    280–281
differences and similarities with
    thinking of Kant, 11–13
Fourteen Points, 13
repudiation of balance-of-power
    systems, 8, 11, 16, 24, 177,
    251, 280–281, 283–284
WMD. *See* Weapons of mass
    destruction
Wolf, Charles, Jr., 42
Wolff, Christian, 282–283
Wolfowitz, Paul, 100, 242
Wörner, Manfred, 189–190, 289
Wright, Quincy, 16

Yakovlev, Alexander, 42
Yalta conference, 36, 128
Yeltsin, Boris, 44, 84, 85, 88, 133,
    137, 143, 147, 150
Yugoslavia, former. *See also spe-
    cific countries*
arms control issue, 218
arms embargo, 193, 194, 195, 198
Bosnia beyond SFOR, 218–234

Yugoslavia, former *(cont.)*
Cold War relations with West, 31
compared to Cambodian situation, 225
conflict's role in development of NATO's crisis management and peace operations, 190–191, 192–199, 249, 264, 272, 276, 285, 293–294
and credibility of U.S. and NATO, 195, 227, 301
danger of "Bosnia syndrome," 295
Dayton Accords, 1, 4, 76, 133, 195, 197, 198, 219–234, 236, 249, 273, 291, 294, 295
European insistence on U.S. involvement, 217, 218
factors in U.S. and NATO forces involvement, 197–198
future dilemmas for SFOR, 218–234
International Conference on Former Yugoslavia, 184
and major-power consensus, 22, 275, 280
Mediterranean Dialogue members' participation in NATO peacekeeping efforts, 89
and NATO enlargement, 117, 232, 299–300
NATO infrastructure investments in support of IFOR and SFOR, 64

NATO peacekeeping operations, 1–2, 4, 21, 22–23, 76–77, 89, 190–191, 192–199, 218–234, 249, 285
NATO statement on (November 1991), 193
NATO view of risks to Allies' security, 75–76
"one out, all out" view of, 218
OSCE cooperation with NATO, 93
parties to conflict, 193
PfP participation in IFOR and SFOR, 2, 21, 89, 98, 195
phases of conflict, 194–195
political sustainability of U.S. presence in Bosnia, 222–224, 234, 288
stakes for future of NATO, 227, 249, 295, 301
U.S.-European disagreements over, 195, 218, 272, 276, 293–294
war criminals issue, 221–223, 224, 225, 230

Zelikow, Philip, 134
Zepa massacre, 198
Zhirinovsky, Vladimir, 84
Zoellick, Robert, 243
Zuganov, Gennadi, 84

David S. Yost is a professor of international relations at the Naval Postgraduate School in Monterey, California. He worked in the Department of Defense, primarily in the Office of Net Assessment, during 1984–86, under the auspices of a fellowship from the Council on Foreign Relations. He has been a fellow at the Smithsonian Institution, a visiting scholar at Johns Hopkins University; a Fulbright fellow in Paris; and a visiting professor and research associate at the Centre des Hautes Études de l'Armement, École Militaire, Paris. He has written extensively on international security issues, particularly with regard to France, Europe, NATO, and U.S. foreign and defense policy. His publications include *Soviet Ballistic Missile Defense and the Western Alliance* (Harvard University Press), and monographs such as *France's Deterrent Posture and Security in Europe* (International Institute for Strategic Studies) and *Alternative Structures of European Security* (Woodrow Wilson International Center for Scholars). Professor Yost conducted research for this book while serving as a senior fellow in the Jennings Randolph Program for International Peace at the United States Institute of Peace during 1996–97.

UNITED STATES INSTITUTE OF PEACE

The United States Institute of Peace is an independent, nonpartisan federal institution created by Congress to promote research, education, and training on the peaceful resolution of international conflicts. Established in 1984, the Institute meets its congressional mandate through an array of programs, including research grants, fellowships, professional training programs, conferences and workshops, library services, publications, and other educational activities. The Institute's Board of Directors is appointed by the President of the United States and confirmed by the Senate.

JENNINGS RANDOLPH PROGRAM FOR INTERNATIONAL PEACE

This book is a fine example of the work produced by senior fellows in the Jennings Randolph fellowship program of the United States Institute of Peace. As part of the statute establishing the Institute, Congress envisioned a program that would appoint "scholars and leaders of peace from the United States and abroad to pursue scholarly inquiry and other appropriate forms of communication on international peace and conflict resolution." The program was named after Senator Jennings Randolph of West Virginia, whose efforts over four decades helped to establish the Institute.

Since 1987, the Jennings Randolph Program has played a key role in the Institute's effort to build a national center of research, dialogue, and education on critical problems of conflict and peace. More than a hundred senior fellows from some thirty nations have carried out projects on the sources and nature of violent international conflict and the ways such conflict can be peacefully managed or resolved. Fellows come from a wide variety of academic and other professional backgrounds. They conduct research at the Institute and participate in the Institute's outreach activities to policymakers, the academic community, and the American public.

Each year approximately fifteen senior fellows are in residence at the Institute. Fellowship recipients are selected by the Institute's board of directors in a competitive process. For further information on the program, or to receive an application form, please contact the program staff at (202) 457-1700.

Joseph Klaits
Director

NATO Transformed
The Alliance's New Roles in International Security

This book is set in the typeface Garamond Light; the display type is Akzidenz Grotesk. Cover design by Marie Marr; interior design by Joan Engelhardt and Day Dosch. Page makeup by Helene Y. Redmond of HYR Graphics. Maps and figure designed by Kenneth P. Allen. Copyediting and indexing by EEI Communications, Inc.